Democracy and Exchange

Also by David Reisman

Adam Smith's Sociological Economics
Alfred Marshall: Progress and Politics
Alfred Marshall's Mission
Anthony Crosland: The Mixed Economy
Conservative Capitalism: The Social Economy
Crosland's Future: Opportunity and Outcome
The Economics of Alfred Marshall
Galbraith and Market Capitalism
The Institutional Economy: Demand and Supply
Market and Health
The Political Economy of Health Care
The Political Economy of James Buchanan
Richard Titmuss: Welfare and Society
Schumpeter's Market: Enterprise and Evolution
State and Welfare: Tawney, Galbraith and Adam Smith
Theories of Collective Action: Downs, Olson and Hirsch

Democracy and Exchange

Schumpeter, Galbraith, T.H. Marshall, Titmuss and Adam Smith

David Reisman

Edward Elgar
Cheltenham, UK • Northampton, MA, USA

Published by
Edward Elgar Publishing Limited
Glensanda House
Montpellier Parade
Cheltenham
Glos GL50 1UA
UK

Edward Elgar Publishing, Inc.
136 West Street
Suite 202
Northampton
Massachusetts 01060
USA

A catalogue record for this book
is available from the British Library

ISBN 1 84542 042 X

Typeset by Cambrian Typesetters, Camberley, Surrey
Printed and bound in Great Britain by MPG Books Ltd, Bodmin, Cornwall

Contents

Acknowledgments

The publishers wish to thank the following who have kindly given permission for the use of copyrighted material.

'Galbraith: Ideas and Events', reprinted from the *Journal of Economic Issues* by special permission of the copyright holder, the Association for Evolutionary Economics, David Reisman, vol. XXIV, no. 3, September 1990: 733–60.
Elsevier for 'Richard Titmuss: Welfare as Good Conduct', reprinted from the *European Journal of Political Economy*, David Reisman, vol. 20, 2004: 771–94.
Verlag JCB Mohr (Paul Siebeck) for 'Adam Smith on Market and State', *Journal of Institutional and Theoretical Economics*, David Reisman, vol. 154, no. 2, June 1998.
HarperCollins Publishers Inc and Taylor and Francis (for Routledge) for excerpts from *Capitalism, Socialism and Democracy* by Joseph A. Schumpeter, 1st edition, 1942.
Pluto Press for excerpts from *Citizenship and Social Class* by T.H. Marshall.

Every effort has been made to trace all the copyright holders but if any have been inadvertently overlooked the publishers will be pleased to make the necessary arrangements at the first opportunity.

1. Introduction: democracy and exchange

Democracy is the sovereignty of the ruled. Profoundly out of sympathy with the traditional aristocracy of birth or the new plutocracy that wants to buy its way into control, it is the commitment that the people alone can be the principal, that self-rule alone can put oughtness into authority.

Exchange is the quid pro quo. It is the self-interested negotiation of equivalence and the factored-down freedom of choice. It is the market mechanism that makes the contract between the buyer and the seller the sole test and measure of value.

Democracy and exchange are the two pillars of the liberal order. Each is an embodiment of individualism and equality. Each stands for tolerance, acceptance and pluralism. Democracy settles disputes through consultation and participation on the basis of one person, one vote. Exchange mediates and adjudicates through matching the revealed preference to the reservation price. Both democracy and exchange are about conflict resolution and collective choice. Each is a civilised way of saying that consent is superior to banditry, compromise to command.

The subject of this book is the politics and the economics of making ordinary people feel tolerably happy with the outcomes that define their lives. More specifically, its subject is how different thinkers have perceived the relationship between the State and the market in the real-world mix where both pillars are essential if the liberal order is to hold. Perceptions are not facts, eternal truths that must be swallowed whole. Rather they are alternatives, different windows on a world which reveals all too little about what it is and what it is becoming. This book concentrates on the insights of Schumpeter, Galbraith, T.H. Marshall, Titmuss and Adam Smith to show that the theories of political economy can be as stimulating as the subject-matter of political economy will always be an invitation to debate.

1.1 DEMOCRACY

Democracy means that the *demos* is in control: 'In democracies the people are sovereign, in oligarchies the few' (Aristotle, 1981: 187). In democracies the multitude has the last word, the final say, 'even over the laws':

'Whatever the majority decides is final and constitutes justice' (ibid.: 279, 362).

Democracy cannot be compared to a colony that is ruled from abroad: 'A government is democratic to the extent that it is responsible to its subjects' (Plamenatz, 1973: 110). Democracy, whether in a nation, a locality, a factory or a union, is government made legitimate by the consent of the governed. Without the consent of the followers there can be good governance or bad governance but not the power of the people over itself.

Locke, reasoning from the world of things that the empiricist can see and touch, reached the conclusion that 'all men by nature are equal' (Locke, 1689: 141). Tawney, starting from the revelation that God the Father had created all humankind in his image, said that 'the necessary corollary . . . of the Christian conception of man is a strong sense of equality' (Tawney, 1937: 182). Equality to Locke and Tawney was a non-negotiable constant. It is a bedrock absolute upon which political democrats have built in order to construct their principled defence of inclusiveness and involvement.

Democracy, direct or representative, presupposes universal adult suffrage. While children and madmen are logically excluded since they lack a rational understanding of the benefits and costs, no other citizens can equitably be denied the franchise on the grounds of politically non-relevant characteristics such as race, age, income, wealth, gender, tribe, religion or level of education. A man's a man for a' that. A woman is no different. Democracy is plebescitarianism. Democracy is equal rights.

Democracy is the process 'by which ordinary citizens exert a relatively high degree of control over leaders' (Dahl, 1956: 3). It is the imperative that each is to count as one, no one for more nor less. It is, as Aristotle explains it, an open and free order in which no individual has greater voting power than any other, in which every citizen has the right to hold office and rise to the top: 'A basic principle of the democratic constitution is liberty. . . . "Ruling and being ruled in turn" is one element in liberty, and the democratic idea of justice is in fact numerical equality, not equality based on merit' (Aristotle, 1981: 362). Democracy is dependable accountability to the popular base. Democracy is participation and power sharing, not dominance and the tyranny of autocracy. Democracy is the equal opportunity to mould and shape.

Locke argued strongly that 'the appointment and consent of the people' was the sole source of legitimacy but that the primary function of the polity was peace: 'The end of law is not to abolish or restrain, but to preserve and enlarge freedom . . . Where there is no law, there is no freedom' (Locke, 1689: 230, 142). The supporters of universal suffrage believe that the Lockean means of consent cannot be at variance with the Lockean end of social harmony. The opponents of universal suffrage are less confident. They say that innate equality need not point to an equal vote. They deny that an equal vote will necessarily ensure that personal security that attracted men out of the Lockean natural state. Ireton, in the Army debates at Putney, spoke for such sceptics when he made clear that he was no radical Leveller who would give a man a vote merely because he was born in England. Citizenship, Ireton said, carries with it no ipso facto right to deliberate upon the laws or to share in the choice of the representatives. Affiliation is necessary. It is not, however, sufficient.

Ireton took the view that no person should have a right to influence common affairs 'that hath not a permanent fixed interest in this Kingdom': 'All the main thing that I speak for, is because I would have an eye to property' (cited in Woodhouse, 1938: 54, 57). Ireton rejected the idea that a man cannot be bound by a law to which he has not given his consent: a resident foreigner is expected to conform to the local statutes or leave. A citizen without permanent property is, like the foreigner, a tourist without a stake. Since he has not made an investment in the nation, there is no reason for him to be given a vote.

Speaking against Ireton at Putney in the Commonwealth interregnum that had just put a hereditary monarch to death was Colonel Rainborough. Rainborough made a case for equality through democracy on the basis of his conviction, expressed as a Civil War soldier who was risking his life for the group, that person and birthright were every bit as valuable a property as was the possession of an estate: 'Really I think that the poorest he that is in England hath a life to live, as the richest he; and therefore truly . . . I think it is clear, that every man that is to live under a government ought first by his own consent to put himself under that government; and I do think that the poorest man in England is not at all bound in a strict sense to that government that he hath not had a voice to put himself under' (ibid.: 53).

No hewer of wood, no drawer of water, should be excluded from the assent-seeking process. To be so excluded would be to become the slave or instrument of another. That, Colonel Rainborough concluded, would have no moral basis at all: 'I do not find anything in the Law of God, that a Lord shall choose twenty burgesses, and a gentleman but two, or a poor man shall choose none: I find no such thing in the Law of Nature, nor in the Law of Nations' (ibid.: 56).

Rainborough may have spoken too soon. Equal citizens may or may not be equal in their stake. What is much less likely is that they will be equal in their database and their critical apprehension. Nature in that sense plays the unkind trick of making the birthright equals functionally unequal. Intelligence and capacity are a pyramid-shaped distribution. Madmen and children are all around.

Edmund Burke was the frightened Jeremiah who inveighed against the 'rabble' and the 'mob' at the time when the French Revolution was extending the right to vote even to the hairdressers and the tallow-chandlers: 'The State suffers oppression, if such as they, either individually or collectively, are permitted to rule. In this you think you are combating prejudice, but you are at war with nature' (Burke, 1790: 138). Adam Smith had no greater faith in the common sense of the common people, 'so jealous of their liberty' but 'never rightly understanding wherein it consists' (Smith, 1776: I, 157). Debased into 'drowsy stupidity' (Smith, 1776: II, 303) by the mind-numbing division of labour, the worker is the victim of nurture rather than nature but a fallen creature nonetheless: 'Of the great and extensive interests of his country he is altogether incapable of judging' (ibid.: II, 303). Democracy presupposes the responsible exercise of rights and functions. It falls into disrepute once the hairdressers and the tallow-chandlers make it an excuse for legalised looting and the settling of scores.

Marx, like Adam Smith, believed that, in Tocqueville's memorable phrase, 'the art advances, the artisan recedes' (Tocqueville, 1840: II, 159). The spiritual decline is the inevitable consequence of productivity-enhancing processes that leave the spindled operative '*mentally* and physically *dehumanized*' (Marx, 1844a: 121). Mutilated into a 'fragment of a man', shrunken into 'an appendage of a machine' (Marx, 1867: 645), the worker is not in a position to give his informed consent for the simple reason that there is no considered opinion that he can call his own.

The Marxian proletariat is 'dehumanisation which is conscious of its dehumanisation, and therefore self-abolishing' (Marx and Engels, 1845: 36). It is 'poverty *artificially produced*', a nothingness in its own eyes which 'can only redeem itself by a *total redemption of humanity*' (Marx, 1844b: 190). At least it has a clear enough insight into the causal link between private capital and its own 'misery, agony of toil, slavery, ignorance, brutality, mental degradation' (Marx, 1867: 645) to want to force through a revolution against the class-driven order that has for too long been the negation of its gravediggers: 'The emancipation of society from private property, etc., from servitude, is expressed in the *political* form of the *emancipation of the workers*' (Marx, 1844a: 118). The Marxian proletariat, 'annihilated in estrangement', wants to execute 'the sentence that private property pronounces on itself', to 'abolish itself and thereby its opposite, private property' (Marx and Engels, 1845: 36). The Leninist proletariat does not want even that: 'Slumbering, apathetic, bound by routine, inert, and dormant' (Lenin, 1920: 73), the Leninist masses must forever dwell on their privatisation shares and their summer holidays in the absence of a communist vanguard that knows it is futile to put real faith in the shallow consciousness of the man in the street.

Burke and Smith, Marx and Lenin, all inferred that egalitarian democracy could be frustrated by a stunted individualism that had nothing much to say. Tocqueville, predicting that the modern era will be the era of cultural conformity and regression to the mean, was able to trace back the erosion of self-confident independence to the tyranny of all over each that makes the democratic masses too frightened, too 'other-directed' (Riesman, 1950: 21), to want to stand out from the crowd: 'In the ages of equality, it may be foreseen that faith in public opinion will become for them a species of religion, and the majority its ministering prophet' (Tocqueville, 1840: II, 11). Democracy and individualism are supposed to allow each citizen to give voice to his convictions. Coercion by consensus causes each shaky ego to question whether the face in the crowd has any right to convictions at all: 'As men grow more alike, each man feels himself weaker in regard to all the rest; as he discerns nothing by which he is considerably raised above them or distinguished from them, he mistrusts himself as soon as they assail him' (Tocqueville, 1840: II, 261).

Individualism threatens individuation. The Americans are the proof: 'It seems at first sight as if all the minds of the Americans were formed upon one model, so accurately do they follow the same route' (Tocqueville, 1835: I, 267). If the division of labour did not undermine individual differentiation, Tocqueville believed, then equality and public opinion would do so. The result was likely to be a mass-produced society in which the will of the people would be the will of Mill's 'collective mediocrity'. Mill writes that 'at present individuals are lost in the crowd' (Mill, 1859: 131). Where the equal individual has disappeared into the group, political democracy cannot realistically be a meaningful forum for the intrinsic self.

Aristotle said that some people are too 'slave-like' to be able to think creatively, some so savage that they are 'hardly any better than wild animals' (Aristotle, 1981: 203, 204). Plato's hostility towards the *canaille* had evoked undoubted resonances in the Lyceum that was built upon his Academy.

Reservations about the downside of equality have caused nervous democrats to recommend selective discrimination in favour of the *hoi mesoi*, selective safeguards against the *hoi polloi*. Their proposals have embraced a literacy test, double votes for graduates, university-specific Members of Parliament, an electoral college, a presidential veto with the power to reverse a rogue result. Education – 'We must educate our masters' – and, indeed, occupational upgrading have the same effect in the sense that they strengthen the middle-class electorate that knows its camembert from its brie, its Richmond from its Putney. When all is said and done, however, democracy is individualism and the acceptance of equality. What the *hoi polloi* want, the *hoi polloi* must have. That is what give and take and respect for persons are all about: 'Democracy is not only or even primarily a means through which different groups can attain their ends or seek the good society; it is the good society itself' (Lipset, 1960: 403).

A strict moralist like Lipset believes that democracy is an absolute and not an economic tradable. A cautious instrumentalist like Dahl takes the less uncompromising position that rectitude has its costs as well as its benefits – and that, in the marketplace for institutions, 'most of us are marginalists': 'Political equality and popular sovereignty are not absolute goals; we must ask ourselves how much leisure, privacy, consensus, stability, income, security, progress, status, and probably many other goals we are prepared to forego for an additional increment of political equality' (Dahl, 1956: 51). Democracy in some cases will be the most cost-effective tool for the job. In other cases a different mechanism will deliver a more satisfactory result. There is, Dahl argues, no a priori reason to think that democracy will always score best on the pragmatic test of performance. Nor is it in keeping with common sense to treat democracy as an inviolable objective that must always come first. Dictatorship without crime and government unions that never go on strike have their selling points as well.

The discipline of the barracks succeeds where front-line polling booths would fail. So transparent is the up-and-doing image of the benevolent despot who gets things done that it is easy, as with the invisible hand of the economic market, to overlook the frequency with which decentralisation and not concentration will maximise the quality of collective choice. Aristotle was one of the first not to mistake the Great Man for the substance.

Democracy, Aristotle says, produces good results since large numbers cancel out self-regarding partialities: 'A crowd is, on numerous occasions, actually a better judge than one man, whoever he may be' (Aristotle, 1981: 222). Many heads will often be better than one. Even a philosopher–ruler in the sense of Plato will fall victim to intellectual constraints and information overload. The 'superiority of the many over the sound few' lies precisely in the fact that the few lack the knowledge and the perspicuity that a large pool is able to concentrate: 'An individual ruler, if he has been well educated by law, gives good decisions; but he has only one pair of eyes and ears, one pair of feet and hands. . . . It would be a paradox if he had better vision in judgement and action than many men with many pairs' (ibid.: 203, 228).

Sectional clashes are defused where conflicting interests are given a say. Consensus is reinforced where 'elections to office by all from among all' (ibid.: 363) net out the divisive irritants of clan, wealth, religion or locality. The 'rule of all over each and of each by turns over all' (ibid.: 363) rotates the chairmen and keeps coercion in tune with its roots. Democracy gives the people what they want. They buy the product because the product delivers the voice that they desire.

Specialisation is a problem: each citizen sees only a part of the bundle.

Democracy is the solution: the many together have a better overview than any single expert can in isolation command. The whole in that sense is logically superior to the sum of the parts: 'It is possible that the many, no one of whom taken singly is a sound man, may yet, taken all together, be better than the few, not individually but collectively, in the same way that a feast to which all contribute is better than one supplied at one's expense' (ibid.: 202). Galbraith, writing of the technostructure, praises the committee for its ability as a democracy to synthesise a heterogeneity of perspectives: 'Decision in the modern business enterprise is the product not of individuals but of groups' (Galbraith, 1967: 79). Aristotle, pioneering the insight that diverse beings can 'become one in regard to character and intelligence', makes the same point, that there is 'virtue and practical wisdom' (Aristotle, 1981: 202–3) in the magnifying lens of the whole.

Aristotle was able in the circumstances to extend a cautious welcome to the kind of society in which Rainborough's 'inferior persons' have 'sovereign control' – and Ireton's 'respectable sort' (ibid.: 205) do not. The masses at least are too numerous to be in a position to turn the State into a family firm: 'The many are less easily corrupted. As a larger amount of water is less easily polluted, so the multitude is less easily corrupted than the few' (ibid.: 222). Plato's wise oligarchs were wise enough to recognise where their fortune lay. History is the record of their avarice: 'The good men did not remain good: they began to make money out of that which was the common property of all' (ibid.: 223). Democracy at least provides a decision making structure within which the decision makers will be less likely to bend the law.

1.2   EXCHANGE

Life in the State-less state of nature was not sociable and harmonious. It was 'solitary, poor, nasty, brutish, and short' (Hobbes, 1651: 82). Anarchy was red in tooth and claw. Thus it is that rational man may be presumed to have signed away a small part of his liberty to the State in order to preserve the greater part of his freedom for himself: 'The end of civil society' is 'to avoid, and remedy those inconveniences of the state of nature, which necessarily follow from every man's being judge in his own case' (Locke, 1689: 159). The political order is a mutual-defence compact according to which the signatories agree to be bound by the enforcers because the protection-less depredation of the *bellum omnium contra omnes* is too dreadful a dystopia to bear: 'This is that, and that only, which did, or could give beginning to any lawful government in the world' (ibid.: 165). The restrictions are a bind. Absolute licence, however, is many times worse. The quid pro quo is the rational response.

Man, Locke argues, is unreservedly born free. He is born with 'a title to perfect freedom, and an uncontrolled enjoyment of all the rights and privileges of the law of nature, equally with any other man, or number of men' (ibid.: 157). The fact that not *one* man but *every* man is born with the same unquestionable title to 'his life, liberty and estate' (ibid.: 157) is precisely the reason why coercion is unacceptable save where it is coercion that is legitimated by consent: 'Men being . . . by nature, all free, equal and independent, no one can be put out of his estate, and subjected to the political power of another, without his own consent. The only way whereby anyone divests himself of his natural liberty, and puts on the bonds of civil society is by agreeing with other men to join and unite into a community' (ibid.: 163).

Consent may be expressed and formal (the case of the ab initio congress that drafts a greenfield constitution) or it may be tacit and implied (as where an existing code is passively perpetuated by a citizenry that is satisfied enough). Newly negotiated or merely pass-through, what is crucial is the compact that is the sine qua non. Free men sign the social contract because they are prepared to live under the laws that are validated by the majority: 'And thus the community may be said in this respect to be always the supreme power' (ibid.: 191). The power of the politicians is 'derived from the people by a positive voluntary grant and institution' (ibid.: 188). That power is not discretionary, arbitrary and *in perpetuo* but rather fiduciary, delegated and *pro tempore*. Pirates and robbers should not think that they can act as a Leviathan because of a mandate that in truth is only theirs on loan.

Free men hire a governor because they believe contracted constraint to be the optimal means to their consensual end. Their obedience is, however, forfeit when their servant, promising to protect them from 'polecats, or foxes', himself exercises unlimited prerogative and turns into an uncaged lion instead: 'In all states and conditions the true remedy of force without authority, is to oppose force to it' (ibid.: 161, 194). Such a revolt is absolutely in line with the spirit of the contract: 'It can never be supposed to be the will of the society, that the legislative should have a power to destroy that, which everyone designs to secure, by entering into society' (ibid.: 227). Stakeholders hire a governor because they are dissatisfied with the natural state. They feel deceived and cheated if a Hobbesian absolutist thereupon enters into a state of nature with them.

Salus populi suprema lex: 'the end of government' is 'the good of the community' (ibid.: 199). *Vox populi, vox dei*: the hired representative is only the conduit for 'the public will of the society' (ibid.: 192). The model is consumer sovereignty. The political exchange is market economics from start to finish.

Liberal democracy, historically speaking, evolved from an abstract ideal into an institutional expectation in the capitalist era that was ushered in by the Industrial, the French and the American Revolutions: 'Liberal-democracy and capitalism go together. Liberal-democracy is found only in countries whose economic system is wholly or predominantly that of capitalist enterprise' (Macpherson, 1966: 4). Political democracy and market exchange, historically speaking, have been closely correlated. To find one leads to the expectation that the other cannot be far away.

Association can be established. Causation, however, is far from clear. Decentralised enterprise may have made necessary a listening State. One person, one vote may have made possible a self-confident economy. The economy may have caused the polity. The superstructure may have shaped the basis. Both together, alternatively, may themselves be the dependent variables that were moulded by Calvin on individualism and Newton on observation because authority was challenged by predestination and belief undermined by experiment. What is clear is that democracy is seldom found without exchange and that exchange is usually the complement that makes democracy whole.

Choice is the intellectual link: 'Liberal-democracy is the politics of choice. Everything is up for choice, or may be up for choice at any time – everything, that is to say, except the liberal society and the democratic franchise themselves' (ibid.: 33). Exchange, like democracy, is goal-orientated and self-aware. Democracy, like exchange, acknowledges the sovereignty of the individual and the competitiveness of the entrepreneurs. In the one case as in the other, the citizen is seen as a purposive improvement-seeker who shops rationally so as not to waste scarce resources and reveals preferences that must be respected as uniquely his own.

We buy what we want with our money. 'We buy what we want with our votes' (ibid.). Democracy, like exchange, is only the procedure that tallies up the tastes. The irreducible locus of power remains the equal individuals with equal rights that are the highest court of appeal. Yet there is a difference between the two modes of command. In the political market the rule is one person, one vote: we 'treat each other in a democratic spirit, that is to say, on an equal footing' (Aristotle, 1981: 324). In the economic market the distribution of income is itself an *explicandum* and a *disputandum*: one man 'wears several men's clothes, eats several men's dinners, occupies several families' houses, and lives several men's lives' (Tawney, 1921: 39). The felt unfairness is a reason why good democrats sometimes vote to overturn effective demand. Even if it is efficient, they will say, still the market leaves equal citizens with unequal power and that does not seem right.

Individuals make choices but they do so within the framework of the two distributions. Culture imposes a further constraint. The market is a shared language where consumers buy symbols that are badges and trophies in a normative pattern. Political democracy is the common identity where citizens make choices in the light of their national loyalty. Togetherness and unity arguably play a secondary role where consumers swap apples for oranges in

an impersonal exchange. Statehood is different. A common past and a collective future are more prominent in the choice calculus of voters for whom cooperation and cohesion mean an affectual overlap that is less frequently found in
the economic market.

Ein Reich, ein Volk is not the Smithian 'higgling and bargaining' of disembodied dyadic exchange. Political choice is more than strangers assembling
periodically for an election and then going their own way. It is also patriotism
and conservatism, collective emotions and the consciousness of a common
task. Democracy is the individual because only the individual can make a
choice. Yet democracy is also groups of individuals because socialisation and
role will influence the mixed portfolio that the situated individual will select.

Democracy and exchange must not be confused with growth and affluence.
Yet there is a link. Lockean civil liberty is the precondition for the Smithian
invisible hand that sets the dynamic loose. Both democracy and exchange owe
much of their legitimacy to the fact that both are associated in the popular
mind with rising living standards and mass consumption. It is doubtful if either
would enjoy as much support if it were synonymous with stagnation and
poverty.

Entrepreneurship produces prosperity. Prosperity is conducive to democracy. Mass production standardises the consumer culture and reinforces the
consensus that one citizen is the equal of another. Material insecurity is the
historic breeding ground for the intolerance of xenophobic scapegoating.
Economic well-being, on the other hand, is associated with permissive accommodation and across-the-board self-determination: 'The affluence created by
industrialization will undermine totalitarian regimes, for a high mass
consumption society cannot support the extremist fervour and revolutionary
dedication such regimes require' (Lively, 1975: 64).

A rapidly progressing economy, moreover, will produce a range of intermediate associations which multiply the concentrations of power and make the
democracy more representative: 'Since industrialization depends on increasing division of labour and skills, it will add to the number of interest-groups
making demands within the political system and so encourage the social
pluralism in which democracy flourishes' (ibid.: 64). The sheer number of the
competing coalitions makes the government more aware of the heterogeneity
of opinion, more responsive to the variety of the groupings that add up to the
whole. 'Polyarchy' is the term Dahl uses to describe the system of not majority rule and 'not minority rule but *minorities* rule' (Dahl, 1956: 132, emphasis
added). The outcome is a set of policies that brings the nation closer to
unanimity of consent than would the either/or of elective despotism: 'The
making of governmental decisions is not a majestic march of great majorities
united upon certain matters of basic policy. It is the steady appeasement of

relatively small groups . . . The numerical majority is incapable of undertaking any co-ordinated action. It is the various components of the numerical majority that have the means for action' (ibid.: 146). Growth increases the number of intermediate affiliations and embeds the power equilibrium more deeply in the civil society. In that way it makes the democracy more representative still.

Growth is change, qualitative and quantitative both. That too is a reason why industrialisation, urbanisation and electrification must in the long run weaken the power of the tyrant to force matter into a momentum that he prescribes. It is hard to be a dictator in a dynamic economy, uncertain and innovative, forever on the move. Planners cannot plan for unknowledge. At some point they will have to choose between prosperity and control.

Exchange can reinforce democracy. Democracy can reinforce exchange. While the Lockean State might wish to confine itself to the law and order that is written down in the compact, it is also the case that an extended agenda might be demanded precisely because good democracy is also good business.

Thus the citizens might demand infrastructure such as cheap public transport because the market has no incentive to supply public goods. They might request laws to contain pollution because externalities lead to illness and cost days off work. They might insist on compulsory education because skills and attitudes are essential and on-the-job training is unlikely to be enough. It would be a mistake to think that citizens who believe in exchange will fail to use democracy to make the State more influential and more involved. If a cut in corporation tax grows the economy by creating new jobs, so, some will argue, does the nationalisation of the banks, because it distributes capital in accordance with social rather than private net return.

There are, moreover, further dimensions to felt well-being besides the commercial exchanges that feed through into exponential acquisitiveness. People demand inner-city parks and subsidised theatres because fresh air and heroic verse improve the quality of life. Statutes like child labour laws and minimum wage laws are desired because they come between the vulnerable and the abusive. Income maintenance when the individual is unemployed or incapacitated or simply too old confirms to the beneficiary and the community as a whole that citizenship is not contingent on being able to contribute to economic growth.

Aristotle took the view that a minimum guarantee of human decency is an affirmation of the whole even as it is an acknowledgment of the part. In calling for public support, he emphasised that the We has an interest in harmony and social stability that is not to be confused with the stake held by the I in a square meal and a hospital bed: 'The duty of the true democrat is to see that the population is not destitute; for destitution is a cause of a corrupt democracy' (Aristotle, 1981: 375). Exclusion being a threat to the organism and not just to the cell, 'every effort therefore must be made to perpetuate prosperity. And since that is to the advantage of the rich as well as the poor, all that accrues from the revenues should be collected into a single fund, and distributed in block grants to those in need' (ibid.).

Aristotle did not want to see a dependency culture. He was clear that cash and kind should be treated as seed corn that would empower the left-out to rejoin their fellows. That is why the grants, not mean but generous, should be paid 'if possible in lump sums large enough for the acquisition of a small piece of land, but if not, enough to start a business, or work in agriculture' (ibid.). The community should assist the destitute into an occupation by which they can earn their living. The destitute in return should make their proper contribution to political democracy and economic exchange. They should certainly not burn the shophouses down. Welfare has its rights as well as its duties. Welfare is a We. It is not just an I.

It might, of course, all go badly wrong. Democracy and exchange can subvert the planning and strengthen the decentralisation. They can also work against one another and blunt the sensitivity of the consultation.

The exchange economy in the prediction of Schumpeter and Galbraith must achieve progress at the expense of the small and medium enterprise that is crowded out by the giants. Competition becomes regimented as oligopolists and monopolists try to eliminate surprises from their scenarios. Profit seekers are marginalised by bureaucrats and technocrats who have no strong need to put the customer first. Corporate executives play golf with prime ministers and wrest disproportionate concessions that one man, one vote cannot secure. If economic progress means a stronger attachment to democracy, it can also mean a reduction in the influence of the man in the street relative to the grandees and the plutocrats who wield disproportionate power at the top.

Just as exchange might be a threat to democracy, so democracy might undermine the legitimacy of exchange. Since the majority are less well-off than the penthouse, democracy could discredit itself by oppressing decent meritocrats merely because they have done abnormally well. Courting popularity, politicians could impose punitive rates on high incomes and spend more than they can afford on transfers. Paper money might irresponsibly be created since conspicuous kindliness buys wavering votes. An intergenerational deficit might recklessly be passed on since the unborn future cannot swing a marginal constituency that needs a dam.

Incentives to save, to work, to take risks become less. Price signals become distorted by inflation. Unemployment balloons as the out-of-work refuse the going wage. Ultimately the liberal order, seen to have lost control, is replaced by a strong man and a non-democratic State which alone can keep active enterprise on the road.

1.3 THEORIES OF POLITICAL ECONOMY

This book is about explanations and models. It is about the way in which five important thinkers have sought to make sense of the two-way relationship between democracy and exchange, politics and economics. Chapters 2 to 5 deal with Joseph Schumpeter, Chapters 7 to 10 with T.H. Marshall. Chapter 6 is about J.K. Galbraith, Chapter 11 about Richard Titmuss and Chapter 12 about Adam Smith.

Chapters 2 and 3 are concerned with Joseph Schumpeter's two theories of democracy. Chapter 2, on the classical doctrine, considers the General Will and the imperative of consensus. Citing authorities like Pericles, Aristotle, Rousseau and Bosanquet, it suggests that politics is not problematic where the rulers passively rubber-stamp what the common man or woman already knows to be right. Chapter 2 shows that Schumpeter was profoundly dissatisfied with an approach that could not account for dissensus or for the tyranny of the majority. Schumpeter was particularly critical of the classicals because they ignored the constructive lead of imaginative champions who maximised the common good by delivering a product that Henry Dubb had not yet discovered that he liked.

Chapter 2 concludes by showing that Schumpeter did not support industrial democracy: he felt that the division of labour dictates that wise and thinking commanders should be allowed to get on with the job. Chapter 3 continues the discussion of leadership by arguing that Schumpeter believed democracy to be the rule, not of the people, but of the elected politician. Ill-informed, biased, easily manipulated, the masses are exposed to supplier-induced demand to such an extent that the reader half expects Schumpeter to jettison altogether any defence of voter-pleasing oligopoly. Schumpeter did not have a great deal in common with the calculative rationality of Downs. He had a great deal more in common with Pareto, Mosca and Michels, who wrote about the elite and treated the Shop of State as the den of fraud and prejudice. Yet Schumpeter remained a democrat. Good procedures produce tolerable outcomes. Even if they did not, a conviction liberal cannot convincingly speak for 'I am the State'.

Chapter 4 goes behind the voting mechanism to discover in what circumstances the system functions best. Schumpeter felt that the best democracy was one in which politicians and bureaucrats were internally motivated by a professional ethic, where the agenda was not too long to be manageable and where normative self-control provided the greater part of the checks and balances. Schumpeter was more interested in the consensual binding than he was in the codified constitution. A sociologist more than a political engineer, he shared his interest in values that circumscribed activities with his near contemporary, Max Weber.

Chapter 5, on economic systems, situates Schumpeter's preconditions for the success of democracy in the context first of market capitalism and then of planned socialism. Schumpeter believed that democracy stood as good a chance in the directed order as it did in free enterprise. He also believed that, irrespective of economics, the State would expand its influence into social policy and the relief of distress. The same central value system that protected political democracy from *one man, one vote, once* also insured the poor, the unemployed, the victims of geographical mobility, the social pathologies of entrepreneurial upheaval against the contingencies of cold and hunger, exile and embarrassment. The Schumpeterian community is just, altruistic and caring. Schumpeter believed that economic progress and social progress would inevitably go hand in hand.

Chapter 6 examines the welfare capitalism of J.K. Galbraith. Galbraith is an evolutionist who believes that matter is in motion and that thought only photographs what the economic world creates. Looking to the future, Galbraith anticipates public spending on roads and schools, State subsidies to small businesses, government safety nets for corporate risk takers, the protection of beauty spots because the environment is a public good. He is absolutely confident that democracy will automatically validate the policies that have to be. Voters have no choice. They will understand that ideas are powerless before the might of events and ratify what they must.

Chapter 7, turning to T.H. Marshall, shows that this strong supporter of Britain's Labour Party redefined socialism to mean, not principled nationalisation and economic regimentation, but social integration and complementary infrastructure. It emphasises his debt to Green and Hobhouse on social policy as the full unfolding of self. It demonstrates that the stunted rejects, like the detribalised successes, could not be called proper citizens since they were deficient in the common culture which injected comradeship into what would otherwise be a paper nationhood that had no heart.

Chapter 8, continuing the theme of citizenship as belonging, builds on the canonical names of Weber, Tönnies, Durkheim and the Alfred Marshall who wanted every man to be a gentleman to show that T.H. Marshall is a part of a tradition which embeds even narrow commerce in something social beyond exchange. Marshall as a historian traces the evolution of rights in Britain from the civil rights of the eighteenth century through the political democracy of the age of Empire to the welfare services of the final stage on the road to mix. The rights strengthen one another. The power of the three makes the modern synthesis both effective and popular.

Chapter 9, about social distance and social class, asks how a stratified society can also be a unified one. Marshall, closer to Weber than to Marx, does not see the capital–labour dialectic as an unacceptable architect of inequality. Status and opportunity are more disruptive. The dynamo of growth was already narrowing the perceived gap in self-presentation. Business was making the Englishmen more and more alike. Yet welfare was needed as well. Social policy would release blocked potential. It would also bring fellow citizens closer together through common experiences that unite.

Chapter 10 demonstrates that Marshall in his retirement years returned to his three sets of rights to model a 'hyphenated society' of political democracy, capitalist economics and the welfare support which corrected an interpersonal shortfall. It compares Marshall with Anthony Crosland to show that welfare plus affluence legitimated by democracy was not a combination which Marshall was alone in expecting and endorsing. Marshall's socialism is comprehensive schools and the National Health. It is social-ism that leaves the economy by and large to exchange. It is not Schumpeterian economics-ism that delegates the quantity and the quality to the Plan.

Chapter 11 revisits the idea of a citizenship-based Health Service as an exemplar of socialism as mutual aid, equal access and shared facilities. It explores the reasons why Richard Titmuss felt that the median citizen had an innate need to donate children, blood and money in order to ensure the survival of a multigenerational concern of which he was proud to be a part. The representative voter had a strong sense of collective responsibility. He had expressed the wish to redress the privatisation of satisfaction and to befriend the needy who could not pay. Democracy and capitalism had enjoyed a long and productive association. Titmuss was convinced that the typical democrat was increasingly insisting on the new freedom to give to his neighbours through the State.

Chapter 12 concludes the book with a discussion of Adam Smith on the greatest happiness of the greatest number. Smith wanted the invisible hand because gain-seeking enterprise alone would release the genie that would supply the wealth. Smith also wanted the visible hand because pragmatic management was essential if unguided interest rates were not to misprice scarce capital nor neglected education leave the masses vulnerable to a Savonarola and or a Jack Cade. Smith was not a democrat. An Ireton and not a Rainborough, he was, however, a believer in universal betterment, self-perceived. He expected the market and the State to work together to supply the well-being that the citizens would have demanded if they had had their statesman's superior knowledge and his ability to do what was best for all.

We today live on the middle ground. This book is about the middle ground. It does not say which insights are right and which are wrong. Different people like different dogs and that is the way it is. This book is not about scoring winners and spotting losers. It is something that in a sense is more in keeping with the tolerance both of democracy and of exchange. It is about discussion. It compares the contentions, comments on the evidence and, in the end, concludes that the exchange of views is what prevents the democracy from slipping back to the *bellum*.

C.B. Macpherson has this to say about the active and the passive stance: 'It is better to travel than to arrive. Man is not a bundle of appetites seeking satisfaction but a bundle of conscious energies seeking to be exerted' (Macpherson, 1973: 5). The study of stimulating theories is always a dialogue and a process. The reader takes in what the author has to say. The reader then adds his own intellectual potential to that of the author whose ideas are the catalyst that empower him to grow.

2. Schumpeter on democracy: the classical doctrine

Schumpeter said that democracy, like the market, is not an ideal but an instrument: 'Democracy is a political *method* . . . and hence incapable of being an end in itself' (Schumpeter, 1942: 242). Democracy is an 'institutional arrangement' (ibid.). It is chosen because it is the most expedient means to an end of which the method per se in no sense forms a part.

Democracy is not the highest value: 'There are ultimate ideals and interests which the most ardent democrat will put above democracy' (ibid.). It is precisely those 'hyper-rational values', indeed, which attract the practising democrat to the system: 'He feels convinced that democracy will guarantee those ideals and interests, such as freedom of conscience and speech, justice, decent government and so on' (ibid.: 243, 242). Democracy is believed to protect the *summum bonum* of human dignity and individual autonomy. Democracy is believed to embody the Christian equality of respect that is implied in the credo that 'the Redeemer died for all' (ibid.: 265). Democracy is believed to make each person the best judge of his own private interest and to treat each preference revealed as an ethical absolute in itself. Democracy, in short, is the material embodiment of moral values like freedom, equality and respect. If the method did not deliver the ethics, it would lose the function that more than anything else made it attractive and legitimate.

This chapter, like Chapters 3, 4 and 5, is concerned with Schumpeter's democracy in the interstices of the economic systems. Section 2.1, 'Schumpeter as a liberal democrat', explains why the natural elitist threw in his lot with the fickle masses that he tended to regard as weak-willed and underinformed. Section 2.2, 'Classical democracy', examines first Schumpeter's own reconstruction and then the insights of prominent classicals in order to understand what it was that Schumpeter was so eager to reject. Section 2.3, 'Internal contradictions', shows why Schumpeter was so dissatisfied with the classicals' concordance that he chose to abandon it altogether in favour of the competitive, market-modelled Machiavellianism that is the subject of Chapter 3.

2.1   SCHUMPETER AS A LIBERAL DEMOCRAT

America had struggled for its independence against a foreign aristocracy. It had grown rich on the rough equality of the rags-to-riches 'American Dream'. Its past had become embedded in a 'national ideology' (Schumpeter, 1942: 266) of 'No taxation without representation' and 'We, the people'. Schumpeter, as a naturalised American, knew about Jefferson and Hamilton, just as he understood what the Statue of Liberty had represented to so many new immigrants from tyrannical regimes. Even so, he was, culturally speaking, always a European. His political views reflect the ethical baggage of an Austrian who was 35 years of age when the abdication of the last emperor put an end to the only political order that he had ever loved.

Schumpeter had grown up with the landed, the conservative and the snobbish. His father, a small textile manufacturer in Moravia, died when he was four and his new stepfather was upper-class. One consequence was that he was educated at the Theresianum, an Austro-Hungarian Eton that trained many top administrators for the Empire. Not a blue blood by birth, Schumpeter must have known that he was and always would be a cuckoo in the nest. After that he studied law and economics at university. While the economics was Menger on search, sensation and unknowledge, law by its nature is a past-dominated discipline that emphasises cultural reproduction and social order.

As an academic in the First World War, Schumpeter while Professor of Economics at Graz wrote at least four confidential position papers on political economy. One such memorandum, on tariff agreement with Germany, shows just how much he then expected from the leaderly aristocrat, the nobleman–ruler, the 'grand seigneur' who had been bred to command: 'Only a man with a historical name and who has the active support of the whole top aristocracy will be able to end the present disorganisation of all political will' (cited in Swedberg, 1991: 51–2). Schumpeter before the old order fell was a royalist and a traditionalist. He put his faith not in democratic parliaments but in a strong leader – a political entrepreneur – whose ancestors had beaten back the Turks and who would be able to get things done.

England had set a good example. Schumpeter praised 'the technique of tory democracy' (ibid.: 32) because the Conservatives, astute paternalists, were sensitive to public opinion but still not the passive servants of the untutored will. He had spent a year (1906–7) in England – he had gone foxhunting and owned his own horse – and the first of his (three) wives was English. His admiration for the British compromise never faded. Thus, in 1936, he was writing that England had 'the very best political system' (Schumpeter, 1936: 304), while in the Lowell Lectures in 1941 he was still praising the lords and ladies who never went to the club or a ball before Henry Dubb had been properly fed and watered: 'An extremely able high aristocracy . . . has a sense of the technique of ruling, a sense of the great religion of national success and victory. Thus it keeps together, the masses following willingly' (Schumpeter, 1941: 393).

Before the First World War, Schumpeter had been attracted by the ideal of the Great Man and of *noblesse oblige*. After the Hapsburgs had gone the way of the Hohenzollerns and the Romanoffs, he saw that his Austria could never return to the protective guidance of the pre-democratic order: 'I realize that that world is dead and buried and there is no way back to it' (ibid.: 388). Before the War there had been norms, rules and self-restraint. After the War the dam had burst and the invisible hand had released a cacophony of 'anything goes': '*All* standards were lowered in *everything*, art – witness dadaism and the expressionist excesses – and sexual morals included, down to rules of civilized behavior in private life. A world had crashed. A Jazz civilization emerged. And this was so everywhere' (Schumpeter, unpublished manuscript [1941], cited in Swedberg, 1991: 146). The age of the aristocracy had been the age of good manners. The age of the commercial and the manual grades was boorish and uncouth.

Politics, clearly, was not the only area of life that had been affected by the collapse of the old ways. Yet it had been affected. In 1927, writing sadly about 'Social Classes', Schumpeter deplored the side-lining of the natural leader who hurls himself into politics as his ancestors hurled themselves into battle: 'The warlord was automatically the leader of his people in virtually every respect. The modern industrialist is anything but such a leader' (Schumpeter, 1927: 279). Society had changed. Charisma had given way to 'unemotional drabness' (Schumpeter, 1942: 123). Egalitarianism had levelled the people down. It had squeezed out the vision, the imagination and the courage that would make a great chieftain stand out from the crowd.

Schumpeter himself was active, however briefly, in politics. In 1919 he served (as had Böhm-Bawerk much earlier) as Finance Minister, in a socialist government. The appointment only lasted for seven months: he fought Cabinet disapproval to attract foreign capital and he opposed serious proposals for rapprochement (even unification) with Germany. It is striking that he should have agreed to serve at all with men like Kautsky, Bauer and Renner. As Swedberg writes: 'He always detested socialism' (Swedberg, 1991: 146). Nor was it his only collaboration with the advocates of phased nationalisation. In 1918–19 he had sat with socialists on the Socialisation Commission in Berlin. Its brief had been to identify the industries that were ripe for State ownership. It was not the sort of commission that an advocate of capitalist entrepreneurship would normally be expected to join. *The Theory of Economic Development* in 1912 was evidently not meant to be his last word on market and State.

Schumpeter's involvement with socialists was not quite as unexpected as it seemed to contemporaries who called him a two-faced opportunist. Schumpeter was already reading Marx on historical evolution. He was beginning to think that the long-term trend was towards statism even if the Russian Revolution had had to rely on repression because the time was not yet right. He had been impressed by Hilferding's interpretation of bank credit as the magnetic field that concentrates and centralises. He was critical of the classical economists for taking perfect competition to be their ideal. Schumpeter may have detested socialism but he also thought that the socialists would one day be whistling the winning tune.

Above all, however, Schumpeter became involved with socialists because he wanted to be at the centre of things. He was, in Swedberg's opinion, an intellectual who 'had little talent for practical realities' but who nonetheless saw himself as a man of action who could get things done: 'At heart he was a political animal. He loved to follow what was going on in the political world' (Swedberg, 1991: 47). After 1919 he never sought political office again. The interest, however, was always there. At heart he was a *political* economist. He had no abiding interest in pure economics that left no room for the State.

Schumpeter left Vienna for Bonn in 1925. He left Germany for America in 1932. He was naïve about the Nazis and surprisingly ignorant about their intentions. He underestimated Hitler's desire for *Anschluss* despite the fact that he himself favoured an independent Austria. In Bonn in the early 1930s he was advising Erich Schneider and others to join the Nazi Party (he himself did not) in order to further their careers. He seems not to have understood how dangerous the Nazis would be. He thought they were just another political party.

Later, in America, Schumpeter (and his new wife Elizabeth) continued to flirt with fascist language and concepts. This brought them to the attention of the FBI: no direct affiliation was ever found. Although he was not a real Nazi, one can see what for Schumpeter would have been the attraction. The Nazis offered him, a cultural romantic with reactionary tendencies, the thrill of spectacle and history. The bourgeoisie promised nothing but Marshallian supply and demand: 'Few things are so irritating to me as is the preaching of mid-Victorian morality, seasoned by Benthamism, the preaching from a schema of middle-class values that knows no glamour and no passion' (Schumpeter, 1952a: 104).

The Nazis stood for the old values of nation, family, saving and work. The Nazis were not afraid to do what was required to defend the *Volksgeist* against the cosmopolitans, the expressionists and other rootless subversives. The Nazis, most of all, called a leader a *Führer* and appreciated that the masses, as Medearis says, would do well to let themselves be led: 'Schumpeter's Nazi sympathies, though they never spurred him to practical action, should be understood, at least in part, in light of his continual search for some means of staving off what he considered the dangerous social tendencies linked to democratization' (Medearis, 2001: 22–3). Schumpeter was writing his great book, *Capitalism, Socialism and Democracy*, published in 1942, at the same time that the FBI was trying to ascertain in what sense he could be called an enemy of the American way.

Schumpeter in America was a mix of attitudes and convictions, contradiction and provocation. An aphorism in his diary gives a valuable insight into his state of mind: 'Have you ever seen a sign-post that walks the way in which it points?' (cited in Swedberg, 1991: 202). Nor is it always clear in which way the sign-post actually points. Schumpeter was a joker and a tease with a strong line in *épater les bourgeois*. It is not easy to know when he is exaggerating for effect.

Besides that, Schumpeter was a man whose politics 'merged very strongly . . . with his cultural likes and dislikes' (ibid.: 146). Schumpeter, as Allen writes, was never a joiner who went on marches or campaigned actively for a favourite team: 'Schumpeter had few political beliefs and did not embrace any particular political ideology' (Allen, 1991: I, 285). Perhaps in reaction to authors like Schmoller who, he felt, were using economics for party-political purposes, perhaps because he genuinely believed that matter was in motion and there was not very much that moral philosophy could do, Schumpeter hid his manifesto and let his ambivalence speak for itself. His cultural likes and dislikes are much less in dispute than is his political agenda. Yet he was a political animal and a *political* economist.

Schumpeter in his Harvard years had come to appreciate that he could not go home: 'Often, he referred to himself as a monarchist, professing his belief that the Austro-Hungarian monarchy was the best political system' (ibid.). In 1948, speaking for the Republicans in a debate with Seymour Harris, he said that he was doing so only because 'we don't have a monarchist party in the United States' (cited in Allen, ibid.: 192). The Republicans were not a close substitute. Schumpeter always admired the 'mystic glamor' of inherited authority, the 'lordly attitude' of benevolent despotism: 'The stock exchange is a poor substitute for the Holy Grail' (Schumpeter, 1942: 137). He was insistent that the commercial interest without the traditional nobility was incapable of taking a lead: 'Without protection by some non-bourgeois group, the bourgeoisie is politically helpless and unable not only to lead its nation but even to take care of its particular class interest. Which amounts to saying that it needs a master' (ibid.: 138). Schumpeter in his Harvard years was telling the Americans, rational, utilitarian and meritocratic, that their country was politically unstable because it had no time-hallowed aristocracy and no vestige of feudal authoritarianism. It was not the sort of message that the pro-business Republicans probably wanted to hear.

Schumpeter in his Harvard years must have felt that he was an intellectual outsider and a spiritual exile. What he says about Pareto may have been intended to refer to himself as well. Pareto's background and personality, Schumpeter writes, was patrician. His character was such that he never felt himself to be the 'brother in spirit' of the middle-class engineers and business people with whom he came into contact: 'It also prevented him from establishing *emotional* relations with the creations of the bourgeois mind, such as the twins that are called democracy and capitalism' (Schumpeter, 1952a: 115). What explains the estranged Pareto may also explain the time-remembered Schumpeter. Not all intellectuals wear red and drive on the left.

Schumpeter's relationship with capitalism is not too difficult to explain. As with Locke and Smith, he saw the market as a workable forum for accommodation and reconciliation in a world of self-ish motivation: 'His economic and sociological studies convinced him that man's rule for behavior was self-interest' (Allen, 1991: I, 285). Besides that, he was attracted by the initiative-taking alertness of competing entrepreneurs. Over and above the high living standards and the national wealth, market freedom gives the challenge-seeking a chance to excel while organisation and socialism crush the creativity out of the free spirit who does not fit in. Capitalism was in any case the natural next step along the historical trajectory. Like it or not, capitalism had to take the place of feudalism before being in its turn superseded by socialism because historical tendencies have a logic of their own.

In respect of democracy, the position is less clear. Schumpeter was an uncompromising elitist who always denied that the *demos* knew its own mind: 'The mass of people are not in a position to compare alternatives rationally and always accept what they are being told' (Schumpeter, 1942: 129). Medearis writes that Schumpeter was always afraid that government by the governed would degenerate into the anarchy of undisciplined egalitarianism, into the populist's pandering to the prejudiced, the emotional and the haven't-a-clue: 'Throughout his life he was concerned to thwart or contain what he saw as the dangerous implications and effects of spreading democratic practices and beliefs' (Medearis, 2001: 99). Schumpeter threw in his lot with the 'competitive struggle for the people's vote' (Schumpeter, 1942: 269). Seldom has a lot been thrown in more reluctantly by a political economist who wished he could have been voting for Franz-Josef instead.

Democracy was not the only political system capable of delivering good governance and reasonable outcomes. McCord Wright recognises that Schumpeter did not regard it as the only horse in the race: 'I believe that Schumpeter felt that the rule of a dynasty or an oligarchy, even of quite an absolutist nature, but with strong family traditions of kindness, tolerance, and public service would be likely to give just as good results as many political democracies' (Wright, 1951: 132). Democracy need not perform much better than rival models of collective coordination. It was at the same time at the mercy of the immature and the impulsive whose window on the world philosophers with fewer reservations had taken to be the ultimate social test. The real mystery is therefore why, in the light of his reservations, Schumpeter was in favour of liberal democracy at all.

One reason, as with Marx, would have to be its historical inevitability: 'Historically, the modern democracy rose along with capitalism and in causal connection with it' (Schumpeter, 1942: 296). To choose the economic basis, historically speaking, had been to choose the political superstructure. Second-best or first-best, it is what it is until it evolves into something else. Determinism and futurology are here to stay. They set limits to what the social scientist can realistically propose.

Living in Boston and not in Vienna or Bonn, Schumpeter knew that American democracy, like American capitalism, was a fait accompli. His implied constitution and intended readership were the stable Anglo-Saxondom of Britain and the United States where no one had any desire to revisit the great decisions of 1688 and 1776. Titular monarchs and extraparliamentary presidents were a detail. The crucial similarities were franchise and representation. *What is* ups and does even if *what ought to be* ifs and buts: the House was not a variable but a constant, Western democracy an unavoidable fact of life. The future might be different. The present, however, was quintessentially the dyad with which the Anglo-Saxons had become so familiar. Vienna or Bonn (or Moscow or Rome or Madrid) certainly did not suggest that Darkness at Noon was an especially serious competitor: 'The case for democracy stands to gain from a consideration of the alternatives' (ibid.: 289).

Schumpeter, moreover, was a disequilibrium pathbreaker and a marketeer. As a methodological individualist he knew that he had to begin with the unique unit actor because psychology and science dictated that he had to work his way up from one individual's one revealed preference. As an economist whose theories were built around decentralised search, he must also have recognised that his whole investment in supply and demand would vanish at a stroke if he did not subscribe to the core values of individualism, tolerance, interest, the freedom to say what one wants and an even-handed respect for Aristotle's 'Live as you like' (Aristotle, 1981: 362). Having subscribed to the ethical binding in his economics, even error, bias and manipulation might not have been enough to make him withdraw and recant in his theory of the State. It makes no sense to suppress the citizen if one wants also to *caveat* the *emptor*.

Schumpeter pretended to be a curmudgeon but in fact he was a pussycat. The shortcomings he identifies in democracy are cracks in the fabric. They are never intended as a real threat to the foundations. Schumpeter's political market is in any case no more than the periodic selection of the Great Clique that will take over the choices. It is not the demand for the policies but the demand for the decision makers who will demand the policies. In classical democracy the citizens are expected to know their general will. Things can clearly go wrong if Shakespeare's 'common race of curs' is not up to the task. In Schumpeter's democracy the moot is required only to select its agents. The knights will thereupon disempower the pawns and tell them what to do.

Democracy and exchange are genetically linked by a common intellectual code, a shared belief-system. Each parallel manifestation of revealed preference is 'an ideal or rather a part of an ideal schema of things' (Schumpeter, 1942: 266). It is this ethical schema most of all that forced Schumpeter to be a conviction democrat. Allen writes of Schumpeter that 'he had definite personal values and views, particularly about personal and civil liberties' (Allen, 1991: I, 285). Allen accepts that Schumpeter was in two minds about the liberal way: 'He was a democrat with severe reservations, especially of the majority-rule variety of democracy since he had little faith in the "common" man's ability to make sound decisions' (ibid.: 285). The fact that Schumpeter was in two minds is picked up by the fact that he had two theories. Direct democracy was for man as he *ought to be*. Ballot-box representation was for man as he *is*. Schumpeter had two theories. Both, however, were theories of democracy. Schumpeter was, as Tawney once said of Marx, 'as saturated with ethics as a Hebrew prophet' (Tawney, 1935: 160). It was his ethics that prevented him from expounding or endorsing any political system save that of legitimation through democracy.

Schumpeter said that coercion or terror would simply not be entertained by the social consensus even where autocracy might be capable of accelerating the economic throughput: 'We certainly do not want to be the objects of dictatorial efficiency' (Schumpeter, 1942: 288). The 'we' and the 'want' demonstrate that Schumpeter believed that liberal democracy could be used to validate liberal democracy. His appeal to ethics raises difficult questions about his complacent acceptance of the coming socialist plan. Schumpeter never explains why democracy, which evolved together with capitalism, can survive the loss of its ideational twin. Nor does he say what 'we' will 'want' when the planners at the centre take away our freedoms and state that the ethical heritage comes with no intertemporal guarantee.

Schumpeter accepted the liberal ethos of multiplicity backstopped by precommitment. Both in the economic and the political market, he situated the irreducible locus of sovereignty in the discrete individual who puts the I into identity by declaring that he will not be a slave. Schumpeter never said in so many words that he was a normative individualist. The character of his political economy shows, however, that he was. Things might have been different had the age of Schönbrunn and the Hofburg not come so decisively to an end.

Be that as it may, by the time he began to write about the political order Schumpeter had become a liberal democrat like all the rest.

2.2   CLASSICAL DEMOCRACY

Schumpeter felt that government by the governed could be modelled from two contrasting perspectives. The first concentrates on the continuous involvement of each citizen in the common cause. The second restricts democracy to the occasional election that votes in one monopoly of force and votes out its competitor. This section explains what Schumpeter understood by the former model, the 'classical' model. It also illustrates Schumpeter's ideal type with reference to representative thinkers (Pericles and Aristotle, Rousseau, Bosanquet) who proudly made political democracy a topic in teamwork, cooperation and consensus.

2.2.1   Schumpeter

Central to the classical doctrine, Schumpeter believed, is the idea of the common good. The common good, not ambiguous and not problematic, is 'the obvious beacon light of policy' (Schumpeter, 1942: 250). It is a salient value, 'always simple to define', which 'every normal person can be made to see by means of rational argument' (ibid.). Ignorant people can be made to see it and antisocial people will not wish to do so. For the rest, there will be a 'Common Will of the people', a 'will of all reasonable individuals', that is 'exactly coterminous with the common good or interest or welfare or happiness' (ibid.).

The goal is 'common to nearly all' (ibid.). It is no more nor less than 'what people really want' (ibid.: 254). Each rational member of the community is well-informed. He sees clearly the difference between welfare and illfare, between food and poison. Political orchestrators add nothing to the purpose: 'These specialists simply act in order to carry out the will of the people exactly as a doctor acts in order to carry out the will of the patient to get well' (ibid.: 250). It is economical of social resources for responsible officers, dividing labour, to carry out the day-to-day work of running the going concern. Even so, they are only the permissive delegates of a constituency that alone knows what it wants. The people rule. The commanders merely obey. The community of interest is 100 per cent. Government is only an executive that does what it is told.

Citizen sovereignty in the classical model is both a means and an end. It is a means most conspicuously in the Swiss town meeting or the referendum on a leading issue, but also in the appointment of politicians selflessly committed to the dictates of public opinion. It is an end in the sociological sense of convergence, concord and unanimity because We are We and We wish to remain a One. The essential element in the perspective is 'a uniquely determined common good discernible to all' (ibid.: 252). Words like 'uniquely', 'common' and 'all' leave little room for manoeuvre.

It is easy to say that the classical model never existed. Plamenatz in particular is critical of Schumpeter for making use of so simplistic, so primitive an Aunt Sally: 'In attacking it, he attacks, not a dead horse, but one that was never alive' (Plamenatz, 1973: 96). Referring to thinkers who are alleged to have held 'the absurd belief that in democracies governments give effect to the people's will', Plamenatz says: 'In fact very few of them ever did believe this' (ibid.: 120).

Yet the evidence is on Schumpeter's side. Realistic or misconceived as may well be, it would be unfair to write off the *volonté générale*, the inalienable Rights of Man, the German romantics' semi-mystical 'Soul of the People' merely because market economists do not know what to make of the diffuseness of the 'collective will' and innovative adventurers feel uncomfortable with the smothering wholeness of the holist's 'A polity is like a ship or a living organism' (Plato, 1961: 1491). The classical model is not a straw man chosen, as Keynes did with a different set of classicals, to highlight the uniqueness of an iconoclast's personal contribution. As the following sections will show, the common good is prominent enough in social thought for Schumpeter to have been rejecting a real, existing heresy when he singled it out as a false utopia that he wanted to expose.

Doubts abound. Since Schumpeter did not name a single author whom he believed to be classical, there is an ever-present risk that the democrats cited in this chapter will not be truly representative of the Schumpeterian black box. Besides that, no one author formulated his theory in precisely the manner that Schumpeter suggests: active participation in decision making is an integral part of Greek democracy but is not a central tenet in Schumpeter's ideal type. Schumpeter referenced no authorities and was selective in his generalisations. Even so, classical democracy was a fact and remains a choice. This section explores the assumptions of four thinkers who have looked to articulated agreement and not simply to the electoral mechanism for the confirmation that political democracy truly furthers the well-being of the community as a whole.

2.2.2 Pericles and Aristotle

The Athenian *polis* sought to educate and train good citizens with a commitment to the *res publica* that lay beyond the private self. The aim of the State in a world-view that puts involvement above interest and activities above wants is not the cost-benefiting of material outcomes. Rather it is the ethical end of voluntary cooperation because good character itself is the supreme *desideratum*: 'It is to provide a stage on which men can enact a public role. In a sense, the public performance is self-sufficient, with no need of justification in terms of government outputs' (Lively, 1975: 138). Because we are actively involved in the life of the group, the actor is fulfilled and the nation is at peace with itself.

The Athenian *polis* was rooted in the perception that all who belonged to the city should be able to share in shaping the collective fate. The Greeks, Lindsay writes, were sensitive to 'the visible isolated community with its own distinctive way of life' (Lindsay, 1943: 194). Autonomous, harmonious, ordered, stable, 'the city,' they believed, 'exists for the sake of the good life' (ibid.: 195). The city, Plato said, was a whole beyond its parts, a history and an expectation that transcended the short-term myopia of the here-and-now: 'Neither your own persons nor the estate are your own; both belong to your whole line, past and future, and still more absolutely do both lineage and estate belong to the community' (Plato, 1961: 1475). Administration could have no more lofty function than to act as an expression of brotherhood, fellowship and organic unity: 'The function of the state . . . is to serve the community and in that service to make it more of a community' (Lindsay, 1943: 245).

Platonist, philosopher, Master of Balliol, Labour Party peer, Lord Lindsay of Birker was not prepared to treat the State as an Other confronting Me when it was the British people as a unit that was challenging Hitler's Blackshirts in Europe, poverty and inequality at home: 'The task of democracy is to make the organized power which is government subservient and sensitive to the whole complex common life of society' (ibid.: 283). In saying this, Lindsay knew that he was standing on the shoulders of Greeks like Pericles and, especially, Aristotle, who more than anyone else had understood that a *polis* could only be its people: 'A citizen, he concludes, is one who shares in the activity of politics or citizenship. The peculiar activity of politics is direction or ruling of the common life. Politics means conscious control of common life' (ibid.: 55).

Pericles' Funeral Oration, delivered in 431 BC, demonstrates the emphasis placed by the classical Greeks on the common good. Athens was at war with Sparta. Pericles, Thucydides records, told his fellow citizens that civic virtue was a strong reason to fight to the death for a self-governed city-State in which the laws were consensually self-imposed: 'Our constitution is called a democracy because power is in the hands not of a minority but of the whole people . . . Here each individual is interested not only in his own affairs but in the affairs of the state as well: even those who are mostly occupied with their own business are extremely well-informed on general politics. . . . We do not say that a man who takes no interest in politics is a man who minds his own business; we say that he has no business here at all' (Thucydides, 1972: 145, 147).

Pericles saw democracy as active citizenship and uninhibited discussion. Recognising that there would have to be rulers, he made much of rotation in office and appointment based on merit in order to ensure that the condition of 'ruling and being ruled in turn' was met and no citizen could say that a caste at the top was permanently out of touch: 'When it is a question of settling private disputes, everyone is equal before the law; when it is a question of putting one person before another in positions of public responsibility, what counts is not membership of a particular class, but the actual ability which the man possesses' (ibid.: 145). In classical Athens all 6000 or so free male citizens were entitled to debate in the Assembly, meeting at least ten times a year. Even so, a sub-set had to be selected by lot (like jury service) to serve as delegates on the Council of Five Hundred. They were paid a salary so that even the poor could afford to hold office. Pericles told the Athenians that their reliance on non-professional representatives taken straight from the cross-section was one of the great strengths of their democratic State: 'No subject can complain of being governed by people unfit for their responsibilities' (ibid.: 148).

Thucydides, ostensibly only reporting what wise Pericles actually said, could himself be surprisingly ambivalent about participation and agreement. This is evident when he praises the prudent headship of an aristocrat such as Pericles himself: 'It was he who led them, rather than they who led him. . . . So, in what was nominally a democracy, power was really in the hands of the first citizen. . . . It was under him that Athens was at her greatest' (ibid.: 134–5). Plato wanted control to be retained by a minority made up of expert pilots, of omniscient guardians able to avoid the faction and the chaos of untutored opinion. Thucydides could see the argument for the rule of the intelligent and the virtuous. Pericles, however, was too committed an Athenian to do other than put participation and agreement first.

Because we agree on the big issues, we can afford to go our own way on the secondary ones. Respect for the law, Pericles says, leads directly to respect for our fellow citizens: 'We do not get into a state with our next-door neighbour if he enjoys himself in his own way. . . . We are free and tolerant in our private lives; but in public affairs we keep to the law. This is because it commands our deep respect' (ibid.: 145). It commands our respect because it is our own. Democracy makes even constraint into freedom precisely because we are all the proprietors and the captains of our common venture.

Aristotle is the ultimate theorist of the common life. It was he who laid the solid foundation for Schumpeter's 'common good' through his celebrated declaration that man is a social being in whose *nature* it is to live in a *polis*: 'Man is a political animal . . . The real difference between man and other animals is that humans alone have perception of good and evil, just and unjust, etc. It is the sharing of a common view in *these* matters that makes a household and a state' (Aristotle, 1981: 60). Man is a thinking animal, able to distinguish the useful from the harmful. Man is a communicating animal, able to speak and valuing interaction. Man, in short, is a community-building animal, only able to realise his essence as a part of the group.

We are all parts one of another. The organism is different from, greater than, the sum of its cells: 'The state has a natural priority over the household and over any individual among us. For the whole must be prior to the part. Separate hand or foot from the whole body, and they will no longer be hand or foot except in name' (ibid.). People, not cut off like the *idiotes* who has privatised himself into his own bounded ego, are aware that their 'full self-development' is a function of their union: 'Among all men, then, there is a natural impulse towards this kind of association' (ibid.: 61). They enjoy the life in common and want it to thrive: 'Men have a desire for life together, even when they have no need to seek each other's help.' (ibid.: 187). Instinctual sociability is the cement that holds them together. The pursuit of private advantage is not the primary reason why they love to dwell together in the *polis*.

Yet they do have a need to seek each other's help. Aristotle, emphasising natural gregariousness, immediately invokes the survival-standards of law and economics – Locke's 'necessity' and 'convenience' alongside Locke's God-given 'inclination' (Locke, 1689: 153) – to demonstrate that the life in common also delivers a material payoff: 'Nevertheless, common interest too is a factor in bringing them together, in so far as it contributes to the good life of each. The *good* life is indeed their chief aim, both communally and individually; but they form and continue to maintain a political association for the sake of life itself' (Aristotle, 1981: 187). Union and solidarity make men feel fulfilled and at one. *Life itself*, however, is the sine qua non.

Law protects the whole from the aggression of any or all of the parts: 'In the state, the good aimed at is justice; and that means what is for the benefit of the whole community' (ibid.: 207). Justice, like democracy, treats one as one. It must be impartial and can never be *ad hominem*. That is why the rulers as well as the ruled must be subject, equally, to the binding authority of general principles: 'Every human soul must have feelings, whereas a law has none' (ibid.: 221).

Aristotle uses the term 'deviated constitution' to refer to a political order in which one section, large or small, takes precedence over the common good. A democracy can itself be a locus of inequity where the majority unfairly uses its sovereignty to impose its private interest upon a minority that it wishes to regiment or rob. Justice means that no government should be allowed to 'look to the private advantage, be it of the one or the few or the mass' (ibid.: 189). Justice means that Rousseau's General Will is put in the place of Hobbes's zero-sum game: 'Those constitutions which aim at the common good are right, as being in accord with absolute justice; while those which aim only at the good of the rulers are wrong. They are all deviations from the right constitutions. They are like the rule of master over slave, whereas the state is an association of free men' (ibid.).

The life in common can deliver the tangible benefit of equality before the law. It can also deliver the associated benefit of adequate sustenance. The State should not be too small since 'if it has too few people it cannot be self-sufficient': 'It must have the largest population consistent with catering for the needs of a self-sufficient life' (ibid.: 404, 405). The State by the same token must not be 'so large that it cannot be easily surveyed': 'A great state and a populous one are not the same. . . . It is difficult, if not impossible, for a populous state to be run by good laws' (ibid.: 405, 403). Plato in *The Laws* had suggested that the ideal size of his imagined 'Magnesia' might be 5040 citizen farmers (plus their families and slaves, and resident aliens): 'The territory should be large enough for the adequate maintenance of a certain number of men of modest ambitions, and no larger' (Plato, 1961: 1323). Aristotle in *The Politics* does not give a figure. He says only that his middle-ground community should be neither too large nor too small for the two related functions of protection and of sustenance to be properly ensured. In this mix it would be a serious error to overlook the economy: 'It is reciprocal equivalence that keeps a state in being' (Aristotle, 1981: 104). Cohesion is important. Square meals are important too.

2.2.3 Rousseau

Rousseau in *The Social Contract* made individual autonomy the irrefragable condition and the ultimate test: 'To renounce liberty is to renounce being a man, to surrender the rights of humanity and even its duties. . . . To remove all liberty from his will is to remove all morality from his acts' (Rousseau, 1762: 8). Self-determination is implicit in the very concept of the human being. It is also the foundation for an ethically informed common good.

Initially there was the state of nature. Finding it unsatisfactory, rational optimisers made a conscious choice to seal a social compact: 'Were there no point of agreement between them all, no society could exist. It is solely on the basis of this common interest that every society should be governed.' (ibid.: 20). The legitimacy of the contract lies in the consensus that called it into being. That consensus in turn is no more than the general recognition that it is in the private interest of each part of the whole to live harmoniously in a network of rights and duties: 'The undertakings which bind us to the social body are obligatory only because they are mutual. . . . Their nature is such that in fulfilling them we cannot work for others without working for ourselves' (ibid.: 24).

The self alone legitimates the constitution. It is also at the root of the in-period rules: 'The people, being subject to the laws, ought to be their author: the conditions of the society ought to be regulated solely by those who come together to form it' (ibid.: 31). It is absolutely in line with the primacy of individual freedom for the actor to feel himself bound by a convention which has been validated by consent: 'The mere impulse of appetite is slavery, while obedience to a law which we prescribe to ourselves is liberty' (ibid.: 16). If each is forced to obey a code to which he has freely given his assent, 'this means nothing less than that he will be forced to be free' (ibid.: 15).

Purposive men hire the protective State: they 'set up chiefs to protect their liberty, not to enslave them' (Rousseau, 1755: 208). The contract is a straight-forward exchange of equivalents like any other. It is an agreement 'by which both parties bind themselves to observe the laws therein expressed, which form the ties of their union' (ibid.: 212). The governed retain their independence and their initiative. The governors, 'mere officials of the Sovereign' (Rousseau, 1762: 47), exercise power exclusively because they have been made the servants of rational masters who rank the political order above the solitude of nature.

The original compact presupposes unanimity of consent: no man can make another his subject without his permission. Even in-period, if the questions are 'grave and important', then the agreement should 'approach unanimity' (ibid.: 89). Where the interest is not vital, however, or where a decision must be reached without delay, there 'the vote of the majority always binds all the rest' (ibid.: 88). A majority of only 51 per cent will be large enough. So long as the 49 per cent gave their full consent to the rule-making rules, they cannot reasonably complain that they have later fallen victim to the despotism of the greater headcount.

The ideal democracy is the direct democracy of classical Athens: 'All that the people had to do, it did for itself; it was constantly assembled in the public square' (ibid.: 79). Representation introduces an unnatural breach between the State and civil society that reduces the sensitivity of the law-making process: 'The moment a people allows itself to be represented, it is no longer free: it no longer exists' (ibid.: 80). Democracy means that the people governs itself: 'Every law the people has not ratified in person is null and void – is, in fact, not a law' (ibid.: 78). Ideally, if representatives are required, the deputies will be no more than passive stewards who do no more than their constituents would intend. In practice, 'a real democracy is only an ideal' (ibid.: 90). Once active and continuous participation has been pushed aside by the division of labour, the fact is that the servants will all too frequently do what they like: 'The people of England regards itself as free; but it is grossly mistaken; it is free only during the election of members of parliament. As soon as they are elected, slavery overtakes it, and it is nothing' (ibid.: 78).

Because the citizens should validate the rules, it follows that a small State will be better placed for democracy than will a large one: 'The larger the State, the less the liberty' (ibid.: 48). Long distances and dispersed populations make for administrative slippage. Standard edicts need not suit heterogeneous circumstances. In a small State there is face-to-face contact such that one citizen can monitor all the rest: 'The individuals being well known to one another, neither the secret machinations of vice, nor the modesty of virtue, should be able to escape the notice and judgement of the public' (Rousseau, 1755: 144). In a small State the strength of personal ties makes patriotism a topic in lasting friendships and the brotherhood of blood: 'The pleasant custom of seeing and knowing one another should make the love of country rather a love of the citizens than of the soil' (ibid.). Rousseau's politics is familiar representatives, frequently seen, and self-governing neighbours who gather together in one place to discuss. It is very different from the liberal economics of market anonymity, geographical mobility and cosmopolitan trade that has so often meant the transformation of stable affiliations into interchangeable parts.

Rousseau was making worthy Geneva his ideal, just as Pericles and Aristotle had modelled their college on congenial Athens. The message is clear enough, that devolution and decentralisation ought to be ranked above the monolithic and the top-heavy: 'It is better to count on the vigour which comes of good government than on the resources a great territory furnishes' (Rousseau, 1762: 39). Small is beautiful. Grassroots collaboration is difficult or impossible once the polity has grown too large.

Population and territory can become a threat to active democracy. So can social stratification and social distance. Rousseau was not a primitive communist, committed to the unqualified equality of possessions and of purchasing power. What he did believe was that political freedom would be problematic in an economic order where one equal citizen was a supplicant, another equal citizen the big boss upon whose whim his livelihood depended.

Plato had said that the good society was incompatible with extreme values of absolute deprivation and absolute privilege: 'There must be no place for penury in any section of the population, nor yet for opulence' (Plato, 1961: 1328). He also recommended that the law should confine the dispersion of economic relativities to no more than the proportion of four to one: 'If a man acquires further possessions . . . he may retain his good name and escape all proceedings by consigning the surplus to the state and its gods' (ibid.: 1329). Tawney, convinced like Plato that democracy 'is unstable as a political system, so long as it remains a political system and nothing more', wanted to mobilise the levelling down of progressive taxation, the levelling up of welfare services, in order to achieve the same great objective of eliminating the 'violent contrasts of wealth and power' that made fellow citizens such strangers one to another: 'The extremes both of riches and poverty are degrading and anti-social' (Tawney, 1931: 196, 81, 40). Aristotle, agreeing that conspicuous ostentation can be the cause of resentment and discord, was less inclined to rely on the confiscations and the transfers of the Procrustean State: 'It is more necessary to equalize appetites than possessions, and that can only be done by adequate education under the laws' (Aristotle, 1981: 129). Aristotle said that men should use self-control to moderate their greed and contain their gluttony. Rousseau was less convinced that ideas and ideals would by themselves be powerful enough to negate the negation of the acquisitive economy.

Rousseau, writing in advance of Smith, Marx and the Industrial Revolution, expressed the view in *The Social Contract* that the real danger was the employment contract that separated the hired hand from the full fruits of his labour: 'No citizen shall ever be wealthy enough to buy another, and none poor enough to be forced to sell himself' (Rousseau, 1762: 42). Seven years before, in 1755, he had been even more outspoken about the gap between rich and poor and about the inheritance of property that perpetuated the domination. In his 'Discourse on the Origin of Inequality', Rousseau had situated the Hobbesian state of war not in the original state of nature where, to Rousseau, free man is innately good, but in the alienated state of possessiveness where the human essence has been corrupted by covetousness and appropriation: 'The first man who, having enclosed a piece of ground, bethought himself of saying "This is mine", and found people simple enough to believe him, was the real founder of civil society. From how many crimes, wars, and murders, from how many horrors and misfortunes might not any one have saved mankind, by pulling up the stakes, or filling up the ditch' (Rousseau, 1755: 192).

Man is born peaceable and sociable because bounteous nature provides adequately for material security and because visible disparities are so modest that vanity and rank are successfully kept in check. Competition, private property, concentration of ownership, and with them the 'universal desire for reputation, honours, and advancement' (ibid.: 217), have released the demons. They have inflamed the passions and set free the enmities that make one *amour propre* a wolf to every other.

Rousseau, trying to understand the market economy, explained fear and insecurity in terms not of material self-preservation but of an obsession with status and prestige which the more uniform, less emulative culture of the self-reliant existence had mercifully been spared: 'Insatiable ambition, the thirst of raising their respective fortunes, not so much from real want as from the desire to surpass others, inspired all men with a vile propensity to injure one another, and with a secret jealousy, which is the more dangerous. . . . In a word, there arose rivalry and competition on the one hand, and conflicting interests on the other, together with a secret desire on both of profit at the expense of others. All these evils were the first effects of property, and the inseparable attendants of growing inequality' (ibid.: 203). Man's nature is not changed but his self-development is nonetheless thwarted. Uninterrupted gain-seeking builds barriers where previously there had been open and democratic acceptance: 'Usurpations by the rich, robbery by the poor, and the unbridled passions of both, suppressed the cries of natural compassion and the still feeble voice of justice, and filled man with avarice, ambition, and vice' (ibid.). It is commercial go-getting and not pre-industrial poverty that corrupts the fair-minded equality of respect. Without that unprejudiced tolerance the listen-and-learn of meaningful democracy will inevitably be crushed down by deference and knee-jerk subordination.

Schumpeter's own theory of democracy as elected representation is not out of line with Rousseau on the self, the contract, the size of the State, the economic distance that is compatible with cultural approximation. What marks Rousseau out as a 'classical' in a sense that Schumpeter could not share is the 'general will'. Rousseau stated explicitly that revealed preference and the common good need not always be the same: 'The general will is always right and tends to the public advantage; but it does not follow that the deliberations of the people are always equally correct. Our will is always for our own good, but we do not always see what that is; the people is never corrupted, but is often deceived' (Rousseau, 1762: 22–3). The collective interest and the 'will of all' need not always be the same. In making a distinction between the *moi* and the *moi commun*, Rousseau was showing that he could be an intellectual totalitarian even as he believed himself to be a liberal and a democrat.

The 'general will,' Rousseau writes, is all-encompassing: 'It must both come from all and apply to all' (ibid.: 25). The 'general will' is the vision and the values of the All. It is a thing apart from the particular will, from the expressed opinion that is no more than one individual's interpretation of his own private interest. The particular will cannot bind the whole, neither as an ego nor as an aggregation. The 'general will' alone is orientated towards the good of the whole and not the narrow advantage of a specific selfish part: 'As long as several men in assembly regard themselves as a single body, they have only a single will which is concerned with their common preservation and general well-being. . . . The common will is everywhere clearly apparent, and only good sense is needed to perceive it' (ibid.: 85). Purified of partiality and cleansed of intrigue, 'the whole people decrees for the whole people' (ibid.: 30). Imbued with the 'general will', citizens converge on a common standard and express themselves with a single voice. Justice is then ensured precisely because there is no minority that stands out from the crowd: 'No one is unjust to himself' (ibid.).

Schumpeter makes the particular will the fulcrum of his electoral contest. Rousseau, less sanguine about where the invisible hand would lead, says that the real will cannot be entrusted with a job that the 'general will' alone can do: 'Nothing is more dangerous than the influence of private interests in public affairs' (ibid.: 55). His theory of a goal-function that is free from immoral bias recalls Kant on the universality of normative standards, Durkheim on the *conscience collective* of a *sui generis* that is more than the sum of its parts, Rawls on a veil of ignorance so thick that no traveller can recognise his separate stake. The will is a *general* one. What each believes to be right for himself will also be perceived to be right by his peers.

Yet there is a problem. The 'blind multitude' might not grasp what can best serve the collective purposes of the group: 'Of itself the people wills always the good, but of itself it by no means always sees it' (ibid.: 31). The real will is always the 'general will' provided that the people are equally and adequately enlightened. A fall from grace occurs, however, whenever the people do not see things as they are; or when momentary impulse blots out their better judgment.

That is the logic of relying upon the 'elective aristocracy' of shrewd legislators who have 'superior intelligence' and the wish to govern for the profit of the people, 'not for their own' (ibid.: 32, 57). What Rousseau is saying is that direct democracy is the ideal but that it also makes sense to decide that 'the wisest should govern the many' (ibid.: 57). So long as the rulers serve the 'general will' and not their own particular purpose, it is fully in keeping with the plebiscitarian licence of the social compact for mere officials to make themselves the mouthpiece for a robust vision that the unenlightened and the overheated might not be in a position to see.

The totality alone has access to truth. The truth in turn is the ultimate locus of legitimation: 'As nature gives each man absolute power over all his members, the social compact gives the body politic absolute power over all its members also; and it is this power which, under the direction of the general will, bears . . . the name of Sovereignty' (ibid.: 24). Democracy need not mean consent. A number of unexpected inferences would seem to follow from Rousseau's insistence that sometimes absolute power will be the people's friend. One is that it might be appropriate to bend particular preference to the 'general will' in order to transform smoking, spitting, gum-chewing men and women into the fulfilled and community-minded creatures that they ought to be. A second is that intermediate bodies like unions, classes, regions and guilds must be harmful since the nation-State alone can be the corporate representation of the whole. A third is that a minority as small as one party or even one man can see what the commonwealth requires and finesse constituents into a common good of which all or most are completely unaware.

Nisbet recognises that there is an ambiguity in Rousseau's theory of the 'general will'. On the one hand there is the social compact that makes it Athenian democracy pure and simple: 'Legitimacy is given only by the mass of people who participate in it and who, by the very fact of participating, cannot therefore be said to be enslaved by it, no matter what its intensity' (Nisbet, 1967: 109). On the other hand there is the all-wise leadership that Robespierre in the French Revolution called 'the despotism of freedom against tyranny': 'If five hundred persons could express the will of the people, why not fifty? If fifty, why not three? And from this it was but a short step to the fateful idea that in one man might lie possibility of fulfilment of popular will . . . that ordinary representative government could never equal' (ibid.: 110). The doctor knows best what the patient needs. So does the vanguard Jacobin who looks to centralised government and not the discrete shopper to distinguish the 'general will' from the particular will that can all too easily be a licence for appetite and indulgence.

Rousseau himself sensed that totalitarian democracy could be closer to the Bolshevik People's Republic than to the chattering *polis* of Pericles and Aristotle: 'Peoples once accustomed to masters are not in a condition to do without them.' (Rousseau, 1755: 145). Lenin's *What Is To Be Done?* of 1902 is just round the corner. The dominance of a *Führer* might, however, be a step in the direction of empowerment. The 'general will' is not protected by electoral majority where citizens vote on the basis of their own narrow bias and do not put the good of their community first. In such circumstances the leaderly elite, omniscient and beneficent, might be the best way of insulating rationality, tolerance and integration against the great corrosives of superstition, stereotype and, of course, self-maximising economics.

2.2.4   Bosanquet

Bernard Bosanquet was an English Idealist whose point of departure was the mind: 'Every institution is a belief, every activity is a want or desire' (Bosanquet, 1899: 44). Spirit alone is the truth. Bosanquet was also a sociological holist who believed that even the ego's subjectivity can be the common baggage that he shares with his fellow citizens: 'Ideas do not spring from nowhere; they are the inside which reflects the material action and real conditions that form the outside . . . The common life shared by the members of a community involves a common element in their ideas' (Bosanquet, 1895: 134). As *we* interact, so *I* perceive.

Ideas are embedded in a matrix that both complements and magnifies: 'Every social group is the external aspect of a set of corresponding mental states in individual minds' (Bosanquet, 1899: 170). Among his most influential writings are 'The Reality of the General Will' (1895), *Psychology of the Moral Self* (1897) and *The Philosophical Theory of the State* (1899). In works such as these Bosanquet emphasised that existence is overlapping and that images are mass-produced: 'Each individual mind . . . is an expression or reflection of society as a whole' (Bosanquet, 1899: 174). That 'unity of the social mind', that 'totality of minds in a given community' which can 'only be complete in a plurality of individuals' (ibid.: 177, 170, 176) is, Bosanquet argued, a fact of social life. It is also a necessity for continuity and reproduction: 'Life simply cannot go on unless the organising ideas in different people's minds . . . correspond definitely to one another' (Bosanquet, 1895: 134). As *I* perceive, so *we* interact.

Society is structured relationships and salient interpretations. What Bosanquet calls the 'general will', like Durkheim's *représentations collectives*, Pareto's derivations, the historicists' Spirit, is another name for the common mind: 'We may identify the general will of any community with the whole working system of dominant ideas which determines the places and functions of its members' (ibid.: 135). Without that consensus, that 'working system', the component atoms would find it difficult to think and act as one: 'If it were extinct, human life would have ceased' (Bosanquet, 1899: 109). *Human life would have ceased*: the state of nature is nasty, brutish and short not because other people invade our integrity but, worse still, because other people leave us alone.

Thus it is that Bosanquet distanced himself from the normative individualism of the classical libertarians. Whereas the market economists preached consumer sovereignty and the political democrats praised the purposive vote, Bosanquet, like Hegel, had some difficulty in focusing on the private self of the detached and isolated monad. The problem that he identified is that the private self is well and truly stamped with the same die that shaped and formed its fellows. A given individual, while not a clone, contains in his mind much that is a social constraint: 'His reality may lie largely outside him. His will is not a whole, but implies and rests upon a whole, which is therefore the true nature of his will' (ibid.: 177). The dichotomy between the individual and society is an artificial one. To discuss the part is to discuss the whole. To discuss the whole is to discuss the part.

Socialisation is belonging. Belonging is self-actualisation: 'The General Will seems to be, in the last resort, the ineradicable impulse of an intelligent being to a good extending beyond itself' (ibid.: 109). Liberty to so other-oriented a creature is self-evidently not licence. Society has a common will. Man has the opportunity to fit in and play by the rules: 'By subservience to social law, he attains the civil liberty through which alone he becomes truly man' (ibid.: 100).

It is civil society and not unfenced open space that emancipates moral
liberty from the fetters of loneliness, appetite and short-horizoned impulse:
'The negative relation of the self to law and government begins to disappear
in the idea of a law which expresses our real will, as opposed to our trivial
and rebellious moods' (ibid.: 101). Like Rousseau, Bosanquet could see no
reason why the fallen self should not be forced to be free in order that the
fuller self might escape the imperfection of bias. Like Durkheim, Bosanquet
saw liberty not as negative freedom *from* but as an affirmation of solidarity
and 'a transition from the private self into the great communion of reality':
'We only feel ourselves real in proportion as we identify ourselves with it'
(ibid.: 126). Freedom is other people. It is not running away but running
towards.

Freedom *to* in the sense of Bosanquet is the freedom to live the common life:
'It is in the difference which contributes to the whole that the self feels itself
at home and possesses its individuality' (ibid.). Freedom *to* is also 'the development of human nature' that Bosanquet took to be 'the ultimate standard of
life' (ibid.: 174). True liberty consists in 'being able to be yourself' (ibid.:
128). Not static but dynamic, it may be identified with 'the condition and
guarantee of our becoming the best that we have it in us to be, that is, of
becoming ourselves' (ibid.: 127).

Bosanquet's freedom is growth, maturity and personal evolution. A man is
not truly free, he reasons, who is prevented by ignorance or poverty from
moving on from what he *is* to what he *wants to be*: 'It is not merely what we
are born *as* . . . but what we are born *for*, our true, or real, or complete nature'
(ibid.: 30). Freedom is not merely the deliverance of the slave but also the
chance to develop one's potential to the full. It is not just non-constraint but
positive empowerment as well. It is the triumph of unfolding promise over the
'alien and partial will', the 'foreign influence' (ibid.: 142) that is blocking its
path.

Macpherson is insistent that democracy is nothing if it is not the realisation
of 'a society in which all men could enjoy and develop their human capacities'
(Macpherson, 1973: 79). Just as Bosanquet did, he refuses to limit politics to
the electoral mechanism alone: 'As soon as democracy is seen as a kind of
society, not merely a mechanism of choosing and authorizing governments,
the egalitarian principle inherent in democracy requires not only "one man,
one vote" but also "one man, one equal effective right to live as fully humanly
as he may wish" ' (ibid.: 51). Man is by nature a 'doer', an 'exerter', a 'devel-
oper', an 'enjoyer of his human capacities' (ibid.). Politics is about enabling
man to make the most of himself: 'That is now an essential principle of any
democratic theory' (ibid.). Macpherson, just as Bosanquet did, refuses to limit
democracy to consumption and utility alone.

Liberty in the sense of Bosanquet is belonging and becoming. It is also the State: 'The State is, as Plato told us, the individual writ large' (Bosanquet, 1899: 153–4). The State is not a criminal breaking in but another name for 'Society as a unit': 'Sovereignty is the exercise of the General Will' (ibid.: 184, 232). The State is the shared purposiveness of a common consciousness: 'What makes and maintains States as States is will and not force' (ibid.: 295). To speak as Spencer did of man *versus* the State is to split an 'inviolable unity' (ibid.: 183) into a misleading and fictive antithesis that in a democracy will sensitively have been transcended by the We: 'The end of the State, then, is the end of Society and of the Individual – the best life, as determined by the fundamental logic of the will' (ibid.: 186).

The starting point is home, fatherland, nationality, 'friends and neighbours', 'sensuous contact' (ibid.: 310, 308), kith and kin: 'Each of us . . . must belong to a State, and can belong to one only. For an ultimate authority must be single' (ibid.: 188). What this means is not the spiritless legalism of paper citizenship but rather an ethical unity that is an emanation from, the embodiment of, the national mind. The district or locality, a microcosm of the whole, is too small to exhaust the possibilities for normative bonds and cultural imperatives. Broad humankind, on the other hand, is too dispersed and too heterogeneous to enjoy the mutual affirmation of a value pool: 'We cannot effectively share the general will of any community with which we have no common life and experience' (Bosanquet, 1895: 139). Thence the conclusion that the borders on the map are also the frontiers of rules and connections: 'The Nation-State . . . is the widest organisation which has the common experience necessary to found a common life' (Bosanquet, 1899: 320).

Nationhood is culture. Statehood is authority. Bosanquet was insistent that the polity is effectively the society with a gun: 'The State . . . cannot be understood apart from the nation' (ibid.: 322). The suggestion that the State and the people are one flesh and one hope sharply differentiates the theorist of 'a single pervading life' (ibid.: 169) from the faceless internationalism of the free traders whose maximand was satisfaction through exchange, not language, race or territory. Hegel comes closer: the nation being One Will, Hegel argued, it is only natural that the spokesman for one nation-ness should be given absolute power in order that he might be in a position to do absolute good.

Adolf Hitler shared in the emotionalism of a self-congratulatory one-ness that goes beyond reasoned debate: 'He sometimes claims to be a democrat because National Socialism is concerned equally with all Germans: in regarding their *Deutschtum* as something they have in common which outweighs all their other differences' (Lindsay, 1943: 166). Lindsay did not share Hitler's opinion that democracy was the creature of the Will more than of the vote. He has this to say about his fellow Englishman who believed that 'the State . . . can have no ends but public ends' (Bosanquet, 1899: 322): 'Much of

Bosanquet's argument about the general will is compatible with Hitler's speeches' (Lindsay, 1943: 250).

The Will comes first. The government only does what it has been commanded to do: 'All State action is at bottom the exercise of a Will; the real Will, or the Will as logically implied in intelligences as such, and more or less recognised as imperative upon them' (Bosanquet, 1899: 233). The State is not above and beyond. The State is one of us.

There is no Locke-like list of natural rights and no sign of Montesquieu on the separation of powers. What there is instead is Schumpeter's classical common good: 'Rights . . . are claims recognised by the State, i.e. by Society acting as ultimate authority, to the maintenance of conditions favourable to the best life' (ibid.: 202). Rights have the function of keeping in good repair the fabric of the community. That is why they are never more than conditional: 'No rights are absolute, or detached from the whole . . . All have their warrant in the aim of the whole' (ibid.: 233).

As with the rights, so with the duties: 'My own position and function as a man and a citizen . . . makes reasonable care for my life imperative upon me' (ibid.: 208). The individual has the right to expect a decent Health Service from the State. The State, reciprocally, has the right to expect a balanced diet and reasonable aerobics from the individual. In the one case as in the other, the obligations are socially-conditioned claims. They are embedded conventions which 'derive their imperative authority from their relation to an end which enters into the better life' (ibid.: 209).

Ought-ness is conferred by the 'single expression of a common good or will' (ibid.: 203). It is a collective and not a private possession. Bosanquet, like Rousseau, warns against 'false particularisation' that detaches the member from the group: 'No right can be founded on my mere desire to do what I like' (ibid.: 203, 213). Real people, 'misled in their knowledge and judgement of details' (ibid.: 109), might not know what they want or what is in their own best interest. Real people, the weak-willed slaves of tobacco or alcohol, might need to break free and yet not have the strength of purpose to quit. Real people, narrow maximisers even as they are committed citizens, might vote on the basis of interest when the 'better life' requires a broader vision. The 'will of all' leaves much to be desired. The 'general will', fortunately, is never wrong. Politicians are a selfless estate whose strength lies in the fact that they can identify the common good even when it is not supported by consensus: 'The statesman's function is to be wise for the community' (ibid.: 314).

In touch with the 'general will', the statesman must use the powers at his disposal to promote felt membership, enable each to perform his function, ensure 'the realisation of capacities for good' (ibid.: 213). This is clearly not the minimal charter of the laissez-faire State. It is Bosanquet's intention that the government should be proactive and leaderly, unafraid to hinder hindrances that come between the community and the 'best life or common good' to which it aspires: 'In hindering such hindrances it will indeed do positive acts' (ibid.: 191).

T.H. Green had already seen the need for a new Liberalism of social assistance as personal transcendence: 'We do not mean merely freedom from restraint or compulsion. We do not mean merely freedom to do as we like irrespective of what it is that we like. We mean the greater power on the part of the citizens as a body to make the most and best of themselves' (cited in Richter, 1964: 204). John Stuart Mill had recommended that the State should be up-and-doing in order to bring about the amelioration of character: 'The most important point of excellence which any form of government can possess is to promote the virtue and intelligence of the people themselves' (Mill, 1861: 193). Much later, A.D. Lindsay was to reiterate that inclusion and not merely protection had to be regarded as the prime duty of the State: 'That the end of all state activity is the development of human personality can never be sufficiently emphasised. This is to assert the moral basis of the state. ... Personality develops in a fellowship or a common life, and if men are to be treated as persons they must be enabled to share the common life' (Lindsay, 1943: 92). The evangelical Christian, the utilitarian engineer, the theorist of freedom *to* on the threshold of the welfare State – all of these democrats were at one with Bosanquet on the need for the government to liberate the untapped 'resources of character and intelligence' (Bosanquet, 1899: 193) that were going to waste because of the preventable evils of overcrowding, unemployment, underskilling, illiteracy and insecurity.

Bosanquet looked to the government to assist the negated ego to become itself: 'The State as such is a necessary factor in civilised life' (ibid.: 184). The state is the agent of the 'general will' and the ally of the 'common conscience' (ibid.: 226). It encroaches on automatism only in order to open up 'new possibilities to self-conscious development' (ibid.: 193). The State should be welcomed in as a friend. It is not to be feared.

2.3   INTERNAL CONTRADICTIONS

In some countries the concurrence is so strong and the variance so limited that, there at least, 'the classical doctrine will actually fit facts with a sufficient degree of approximation' (Schumpeter, 1942: 267). This would be the case in small farming communities such as indeed 'served as a prototype to the authors of that doctrine' (ibid.). Even larger nations can cluster around the median, 'provided they are not too differentiated and do not harbor any serious problems': 'Switzerland is the best example. There is so little to quarrel about in a world of peasants' (ibid.). There is not much capitalism and not much industry. The main issues in public policy are 'so simple and so stable that an overwhelming majority can be expected to understand them and to agree about them' (ibid.). In the land that invented the cuckoo clock the classical theory may be a reasonable description of reality, 'but only because there are no great decisions to be made' (ibid.). Most nations, however, will live in a tougher world than that of the sleepy Swiss canton, Plato's Magnesia or the Athenian *polis*.

2.3.1   The Common Good

Classical democracy in Schumpeter's sense is founded upon the expectation of consensus. That, however, is just the problem: 'There is . . . no such thing as a uniquely determined common good that all people could agree on or be made to agree on by the force of rational argument' (Schumpeter, 1942: 251). The difficulty is not just that antisocial deviants put private interest above the general welfare, not just that the uneducated and the unenlightened lack the exposure to scientific evidence that would return them to the single right path. The difficulty, more fundamental, is that 'to different individuals and groups the common good is bound to mean different things' (ibid.). One man's meat is another man's poison. *De gustibus* makes their society a babel of conflicting choices and non-rational aspirations.

The dispersion is the consequence of normative pluralism. Ultimate values – 'Our conceptions of what life and what society should be' (ibid.) – lie, in contrast to the instrumentality of tools and techniques, beyond the ambit of logico-experimental refutation. Agreement might be impossible where different people define their 'best-ness' to mean a radically different route. Nor can it be expected that democratic give-and-take will necessarily grind out a satisfactory compromise between the implacable and the rigid. Where there are 'irreducible differences of ultimate values' it was the wisdom of Solomon that an enforced convergence can only 'maim and degrade' (ibid.).

Besides that, even where citizens are in accord on the principles and the objectives, their unanimity might not translate into a single-valued consensus on the specifics or the means. People whose maximand is economic growth might still differ on investment versus consumption, present versus future, socialism versus capitalism. People whose maximand is good health might 'still disagree on vaccination and vasectomy' (ibid.: 252), prevention and cure, abortion and euthanasia. The utilitarians had too much of the shopkeeper mentality to perceive that philosophies and morals could drive a wedge: 'They saw little beyond the world of an eighteenth-century ironmonger' (ibid.). Schumpeter's vision of multiplicity and differentiation is a less comfortable one.

　　Classical theory suggests that public opinion will be broadly in line with the common good. Schumpeter, examining the advanced democracies, is less confident about the meeting of minds. The real world, Schumpeter writes, is an 'infinitely complex jumble of individual and group-wise situations, volitions, influences, actions and reactions' – a mish-mash, in short, which 'lacks not only rational unity but also rational sanction' (ibid.: 253). The word is 'chaotic', the end state unconnected with 'the realization of any definite end or ideal' (ibid.). Whatever the common binding may be, it is not the classicals' 'good' that is too nebulous, too ambiguous, to unite.

The recognition of dissensus is a reminder of repression. Schumpeter is critical of the classical democrats for failing to see what less than 100 per cent concord must mean: 'The will of the majority is the will of the majority and not the will of "the people". The latter is a mosaic that the former completely fails to "represent" ' (ibid.: 272). A percentage that 'completely fails' is not much good as a metric. Each individual voter is invited to let his own private cat out of his own personal bag. As many as 49 per cent of those voters are then told that their tastes have been crossed off the menu by a simple majority that prefers dogs to cats and will wear only blue.

　　Democracy is the rule of the people. The will of the majority is, however, a way of telling the marginalised that they have bought no claim with their vote. The bigger group gets what it wants: 'The moral power of the majority is founded upon [the principle] that the interests of the many are to be preferred to those of the few' (Tocqueville, 1835: I, 256). The smaller group finds itself whispering down a well: ' "The tyranny of the majority" is now included among the evils against which society requires to be on its guard' (Mill, 1859: 62). Arblaster is sensitive to the feelings of the periphery whose preferences have been netted out of the general good by an all-or-nothing centre that offers no consolation prize to the voted down: 'I can see nothing in democratic thinking which allows us to think of "the people" as anything other than the whole body of citizens, minorities as well as majorities, those who oppose and dissent as well as those who belong to the dominant majority' (Arblaster, 1994: 66). The smokers have to burn their cigarettes. The Christians have to burn their Bibles. The rich have to surtax their wealth. The Sikhs have to lose their turbans. The family-centred have to give up their honour killings. The majority imposes a negative externality upon a minority in its jurisdiction. The minority is required to live according to norms with which it does not agree.

　　The minority problem is a welfare conundrum in the democratic State. Schumpeter, distancing himself from the classical Will, acknowledged a contradiction within liberal democracy between the tolerance of liberalism and the yours/mine of the majority vote. Tails do not wag dogs. Yet it did not seem

right to him to deny equality of respect to the idiosyncratic and the entrepreneurial merely because they did not want to conform.

It is not possible to say what 'the' people 'really' want if different segments,
well-informed or less rational, have different priorities. Politics at least can
diversify the portfolio. Parties can offer a mixed manifesto sweetened by
extensive side-payments in order to capture support from the overshadowed.
A majority of 66 per cent or 75 per cent instead of the minimum 51 per cent
will presumably reduce the extent to which minority viewpoints can be called
a lifestyle pollutant to which an offended majority can refuse the courtesy of
'live and let live'. Proportional representation is often said to be a way of
ensuring that there will something even for the single-issue clusters. The
student of Schumpeter on the voting rule that 'completely fails' ought ideally
to ask himself if political solutions such as these can be found that will satisfactorily bring the niche back into the mainstream.

Democracy might prove too blunt. If it does, then exchange might be the
more sensitive tool. Competitive capitalism can be a vote for diversity and
coexistence: 'An impersonal market separates economic activities from political views and protects men from being discriminated against in their
economic activities for reasons that are irrelevant to their productivity –
whether these reasons are associated with their views or their color'
(Friedman, 1962: 21). One size need not fit all where people are willing to put
their money where their mouth is.

Friedman is insistent that the supply-and-demand swap is the most reliable form of proportional representation. Schumpeter anticipates Friedman's
later contention when he asserts that economic liberalism has the advantage
over politicised allocation that both parties to an exchange gain in utility as
a result: 'There exists no more democratic institution than a market'
(Schumpeter, 1942: 184). Free markets maximise felt satisfactions. Majority
rule deprives and disenfranchises. It is hard to know what policy-mix can
meaningfully be called the *common* good when the non-standard size is all
around.

Friedman favours the paid-for alternative since surplus centralisation
exposes the one-off to the tyranny of the crowd. The rich can pay for non-
generic drugs and the privacy of exclusive suburbs. Religious groups can pay
for headscarves and single-sex schools. Music lovers can pay for their concert
tickets even if their fellow citizens want only sport. Friedman is eager to
protect minorities through the willingness to pay and the slimmed-down State.
The reader expects Schumpeter to say the same. Since he criticises the classicals for ignoring the ordinals of the train spotters and the cardinals of the
teapot collectors, the reader expects him to say that exchange at least can do
what democracy cannot. Instead he predicts socialism and more of the State
than ever before.

Harassment, expropriation, expulsion, even extermination can all be consequences of the majority vote: 'The earlier persecutions of the Christians were
certainly approved by Roman public opinion' (ibid.: 241). The suppression of
dissent, legitimated by the vast majority of the Romans, enjoyed the full
ought-ness of a democratic consensus that saw no reason to extend human
rights to self-appointed trouble makers who did not want to live by the
Romans' rules. Majoritarian democracy in such a case is clearly at variance
with the liberal ideals of equality and respect that breathe life into the democratic mechanism.

Schumpeter, referring to the persecutions, says that they were 'repulsive':
'We should certainly not approve of these practices' (ibid.: 241, 242). In
putting the protection of a small minority above the sincere convictions of
everyone else, he is clearly ranking liberal ethics above the democratic validation. He is appealing to 'ultimate ideals and interests' (ibid.: 242) for the
right to reject the intolerance and unfreedom of the *vox populi*. When in Rome,
do *not* do as the Romans do.

Liberal values are more powerful than the in-period consensus. Presumably
the reason is that, without the antecedent values, there would be no *raison
d'être* for the democratic mechanism itself. Minorities discriminated out of
universal suffrage by the mean – women, Jews, 'Orientals', 'Negroes', the
propertyless (ibid.: 243, 244) – clearly have a strong case to make for the
extension of full citizenship to the fringe. The triumph of moral constants over
the current consensus, of Locke over Durkheim, is not, however, as unequivocal as it seems. Schumpeter does not make clear which fringe should be
koshered as *hallal* and which should be put in prison because it is cannibalis-
ing its neighbours. It is never easy to tell a serial killer from a freedom fighter
or to say who is a bank robber and who is merely a Christian. Bird watchers
are likely to get their licence. Serial smokers are more likely to be victimised
as if Hitler's Jews to whom Heinrich Dubb did not really warm.

Schumpeter associates the common good with the popular consensus; but he
also knows that classicals like Rousseau had said that the 'general will' could
not be reduced to revealed preference alone. Schumpeter is aware that, in classical democracy, the 'Common Good ... exists' and remains the single
'beacon light' even if real-world individuals are so blinkered by 'ignorance',
'stupidity' and 'anti-social interest' that they 'do not see it' (ibid.: 250). He
describes the free-standing will, knowledgeable, rational and impartial, as a
'semi-mystic entity' (ibid.: 252). Enshrouded in amorphous metaphysics, it is
not nearly as tractable as public opinion, polled through the surveys and quantified by the votes. Schumpeter clearly felt more comfortable with the man in
the street than with a benchmark judge who was notoriously difficult to interview.

Schumpeter underestimates the significance of the 'general will' in the world-view of the classical democrats. One consequence is that he fails to grasp the way in which the classicals imposed consistency upon social choices that Schumpeter himself found incompatible with their 'common good'. Consider Napoleon's Concordat with the Church. Ex post it met a real if unarticulated need. Ex ante there had been no popular demand at all. Schumpeter uses this illustration to argue that even a top-notch dictator will not pass the strict classical test: 'If results that prove in the long run satisfactory to the people at large are made the test of government *for* the people, then government *by* the people, as conceived by the classical doctrine of democracy, would often fail to meet it' (ibid.: 256).

Schumpeter's assessment of failure is here directed at the conscious-choice classicals who felt that the people in council had to reach their consensus in advance. It is not, however, a fair interpretation of the more totalitarian, more all-encompassing vision that refused to make the *volonté de tous* a simple synonym for the *volonté générale*. In the case of the Concordat, the popular will was indifferent but the 'general will' was engaged. It follows that the Concordat was not a violation but a confirmation of the democratic theory of classicals who believed that a whole could have a mind of its own.

Just as Schumpeter underestimates the significance of the 'general will', so he shows little interest in the evolutionary and dynamic dimension that is so central to classical collective choice. He says that politicians can manufacture voters' preferences using their own desired mould. What he does not recognise is that democratic institutions can have precisely the same causative impact on perceived interaction and personal growth. Medearis describes the missing link in the following words: 'It is not too difficult to see where Schumpeter's argument went wrong with respect to the problem of the common good. For developmental democratic theorists, the common good and the pursuit of it through democratic institutions could not be separated from the educational and developmental benefits of democratization. The common good aimed for was in this sense not distinct from the democratic means of attaining it' (Medearis, 2001: 132).

The point is an important one. Nationalists would say that a war breeds patriotism and inculcates the we're-all-in-it-togetherness of a cohesive team. Welfarists would say that the National Health promotes good fellowship and strengthens the common culture that will lead to more intervention in its turn. Institutions, in other words, can be the active ingredient and not merely a leaf blown about in the wind. Democracy is not just a mechanism for adding up the votes.

Man needs the protective State because without law and order he could not acquire capital or patent his discoveries. Man needs the welfare State because without the transfers and the schooling he would lack the health and the skills that he needs to realise his potential. Man needs the democratic State because without the consultation and the collaboration he would be an isolated gain-seeker and not a social animal who becomes himself through the tribe: 'Democracy is a theory of society as well as a theory of government. If the end of the state is to serve the community and to make it more of a community, that will mean in a democracy making it more of a democratic community' (Lindsay, 1943: 249). Schumpeter does not incorporate the knock-ons and the momentum that meant so much to the classical democrats. He does not ask how political democracy is likely to transform either the partial or the general will. He does not say what the feedback will be for political democracy itself of the release of dammed-up *becoming*. An evolutionist in his economics, his settled democracy seems not to be on the move.

Macpherson writes that 'Human society is the medium through which human capacities are developed' (Macpherson, 1973: 57). He is critical of Schumpeter-type democracy for its focus on man the consumer to the exclusion of man the creator who stamps his image on the institutions he invents: 'It is counter-democratic . . . Democracy is reduced from a humanist aspiration to a market equilibrium system' (ibid.: 78–9). Classical democracy had much nobler aims.

Probably the most important reason why Schumpeter could not accept the classicals' common good was the classicals' misplaced concreteness. Whether the reference is to the Jacobins' totality or the Leninists' vanguard, to Bosanquet's 'fundamental logic of the will' (Bosanquet, 1899: 186) or Bergson's social welfare function (Bergson, 1938), the truth is the whole and the ego but a face in the mob: 'Solitary men could not produce the effects we observe in society' (Asch, 1952: 163). The classical theory imputed a single mind to a collectivity of minds and pooled a hypothetical aggregate from discrete men and women who had no wish to be summed. The Austrian approach, diametrically opposed, factors down and proceeds bottom-up: 'Society is nothing but the combination of individuals for cooperative effort' (Mises, 1949: 143). Schumpeter was an Austrian who never turned his back on the psychologism of his youth.

Bentham expresses the reductionist 'I believe' in the following words: 'The community is a fictitious *body*, composed of the individual persons who are considered as constituting as it were its *members*. The interest of the community then is . . . the sum of the interests of the several members who compose it' (Bentham, 1789: 12). Schumpeter as a microeconomic subjectivist knew that the one-off alone was capable of feeling and sensation: 'Value is a psychological phenomenon' (Schumpcter, 1906: 532). Schumpeter as a methodological individualist appreciated that reifications and constructions were 'mere

clotheslines on which to hang propositions' (Schumpeter, 1954: 886): 'The
starting point of our system must therefore be the economics of the individual'
(Schumpeter, 1906: 533). The classicals' common good simply does not exist.
An individual can have a single will. A mixed bag of individuals cannot.

2.3.2   Democracy as Participation

Schumpeter's democracy is the election of the ruling elite. It is not the active
involvement of equal citizens in the day-to-day decisions that shape and form
their lives. Pericles and Aristotle had looked to the *demos* for the continuous
lead. Rousseau had made ideal Geneva a city of glass and of debate.
Schumpeter, on the other hand, rejected classical democracy expressly
because so many of its proponents had wanted politics to be the rule of the
people and not of the politicians. In national and international affairs,
Schumpeter wrote, 'individual volition, command of facts and methods of
inference soon cease to fulfil the requirements of the classical doctrine'
(Schumpeter, 1942: 261). Politics is a job for the professionals. Madmen, children and ordinary citizens will inevitably be out of their depth.

Schumpeter was convinced that the ordinary voter lacked the intellect and
the maturity to collect data, to interpret evidence, to draw the reasoned conclusions that the Greeks and the Enlightenment alike had expected: 'The ideology of democracy as reflected by the classical doctrine rests on a rationalist
scheme of human action and of the values of life' (ibid.: 296). That was just
the problem. The ordinary voter, experiencing a 'reduced sense of responsibility', a 'lower level of energy of thought', a 'greater sensitiveness to non-
logical inferences' (ibid.: 257), does not match up to the classicals' high
standards. Rule of the people would not churn out either the common good or
the 'general will' or the developmental freedom *to*. Instead it would mean
confusion and anarchy and in the end the 'whiff of grapeshot' and the
Leviathan *ex machina* who gets things done.

The mass of people will never rule, will always be ruled: 'The mass of
people never develops definite opinions on its own initiative. Still less is it
able to articulate them and to turn them into consistent attitudes and actions.
All it can do is to follow or to refuse to follow such group leadership as may
offer itself' (ibid.: 145). The popular will is manipulated by the elected
servants. Declared policies are the verbalisations of partial interest. Equality is
'the most stupid of all credos', 'the ideal of the sub-normal' (cited in Allen,
1991: II, 190, 191). Democracy is the 'govt. of fools for the fools by the fools',
'for mediocrities' even if not 'of mediocrities' (ibid.: II, 189, 191). Classical
theory, Schumpeter said, was wrong to lionise the common man while under-
valuing the contribution of the parliamentary entrepreneur. It 'attributed to the
electorate an altogether unrealistic degree of initiative which practically

amounted to ignoring leadership' (Schumpeter, 1942: 270). Schumpeter was a liberal democrat whose liberal democracy extended exclusively to the selection of the chiefs. The officers once selected, the voters must then 'respect the division of labor between themselves and the politicians they elect': 'Political action is his business and not theirs' (ibid.: 295).

Schumpeter criticised classical democracy because it expected ordinary citizens to do more than vote. At least he believed that the politicians should be appointed by the constituents. Managers and business executives were a different matter: 'No responsible person can view with equanimity the consequences of extending the democratic method, that is to say the sphere of "politics", to all economic affairs' (ibid.: 299). No responsible person can want the capitalists to be accountable to the production line or the MBAs to be subject to the union representatives. The reason is 'the consequences': 'There is an obvious relation between the efficiency of the economic engine and the authority over employees. . . . This is not simply a privilege conferred upon Haves in order to enable them to exploit Have-nots. Behind the private interest immediately concerned there is the social interest in the smooth running of the productive apparatus' (ibid.: 210). Top-down command is the precondition for economy and innovation. Industrial democracy is noise on the line.

Tawney had a different view of what it takes to make the wheels of trade spin round: 'It is idle to expect that men will give their best to any system which they do not trust, or that they will trust any system in the control of which they do not share' (Tawney, 1921: 149). Tawney believed that economic justice had an economic payoff. Cooperative self-management under hands-off State ownership would, he was convinced, act as an investment in morale and commitment that would improve performance and feed through to growth. Schumpeter, in contrast, argued strongly against interference from politicians, from 'fussing citizens' committees' (Schumpeter, 1942: 299), from the workmen themselves who should do as they are told. Management must have autonomy if the enterprise is to be productive. Direct democracy would put the wealth of nations at risk.

The future meant socialism. Socialism meant planning. That to Schumpeter showed beyond any doubt that the egalitarians' power-sharing would be pushed aside by events: 'Industrial or Economic Democracy is a phrase that figures in so many quasi-utopias that it has retained very little precise meaning. . . . Much of this economic democracy will vanish into thin air in a socialist regime' (ibid.: 300n). Schumpeter as early as his essay on 'Sozialistische Möglichkeiten', published in 1920–21, when so many on the left were fiercely anti-authoritarian, made clear that he saw the alternative order not as Bauer's consultation, Sorel's syndicalism or Cole's guilds but rather as Galbraith's technostructure in eternal symbiosis with Weber's bureaucracy: 'A central organ controls all means of production, works out an economic plan, and regulates the distribution of final goods as between the individual citizens' (Schumpeter, 1920/21: 458). The shop floor in Schumpeter's socialism does not go to meetings and the trade unions do not sit on boards. What happens instead is that hierarchy is unbending, discipline enforced, obedience expected: 'Effective management of the socialist economy means dictatorship not *of* but *over* the proletariat in the factory' (Schumpeter, 1942: 302). In politics the people vote at agreed-upon intervals for the officers who will order them around. In economics they have no choice at all.

Schumpeter saw the firm as a *productive* unit, not as a home away from home. Efficiency and effectiveness being the only meta-objectives that he entertained, he saw no need to consider how the firm could maximise utility at the active level of input rather than exclusively at the output end stage of passive consumption. Predicting socialism (which in his view meant the Olympian plan), defending performance (which in his view precluded muddle-making decentralisation), he may have felt that he had no choice but to confine the universal franchise to the democratic polity alone. Others, unable to share his economics of statism and cost, more willing to recognise that economics is not the only test, will be less convinced about the inevitability of the put up/shut up that excludes.

Robert Dahl is one such democrat. Dahl has expressed the view that 'one person, one vote' is badly impoverished where it is no more than one-sided, selective and asymmetrical: 'If democracy is justified in governing the state, then it is also justified in governing economic enterprises. What is more, if it cannot be justified in governing economic enterprises, we do not quite see how it can be justified in governing the state. Members of any association for whom the assumptions of the democratic process are valid have a *right* to govern themselves by means of the democratic process' (Dahl, 1985: 134–5). Schumpeter, apparently putting his economics above his liberal democracy, identifies no such 'right' either in capitalist or in socialist society. Dahl, on the other hand, believes it to be both fair and sensible for the workers who invest their quality time, who exert and exhaust themselves, who take real risks with their skills and health, not to be blocked out from representation by the moneyed profit-recipients who supply the funds or the executive-intrapreneurs who administer a property that they do not own: 'In this perspective, the ideal of the polis is transferred to the workplace, and the enterprise becomes a site for fulfilling Rousseau's vision of political society' (ibid.: 94).

Workplace democracy, Lively writes, is itself the civic experience, extensive and diffuse: 'If the experience is to be meaningful, individual citizens must be personally involved in some demanding and rewarding social functions. . . . Only a few can be more than marginally involved in the management of a large modern state' (Lively, 1975: 144). Participation in *economic* affairs satisfies a psychological need that politics since the classicals has tended to ignore. It makes a useful contribution to personal development and personal growth – to *becoming* in the sense of Green, Bosanquet or Maslow about which Schumpeter has so little to say. It also generates a valuable spillover for *political* democracy to the extent that, produces good collaborators, less self-seeking and more public-spirited. Civic virtues are a public good. Schumpeter was arguably too quick to write off the role of economic democracy as the learning-by-doing that produces the social capital.

Schumpeter's refusal to treat the firm as a democratic State is indicative of a broader resistance to intermediate associations that stand between the atom and the monolith. Schumpeter assigns little importance to local government or civil society in his theory of the elite and the mass. Making the choice to separate the control bunker from the trenches, he seems to be saying that personal liberty and political equality cannot fully be made compatible even in the liberal democracy.

Rousseau, like the Greeks, had been attracted by small polities where integrated citizens gather round the orator's voice. They anchor their rule-making in the Burkean conservatism of microsocial solidarity, face-to-face. Tocqueville regarded the myriad affiliations of the hands-on culture as an education in belonging and a bulwark against repression: 'If men are to remain civilized or to become so, the art of associating together must grow and improve in the same ratio in which the equality of conditions is increased' (Tocqueville, 1840: II, 110). John Stuart Mill in *On Liberty* reiterated the need for 'voice' in preference to 'exit', partly because activity is morally superior to apathy and partly because 'a State which dwarfs its men, in order that they may be more docile instruments in its hands . . . will find that with small men no great thing can really be accomplished': 'The management of purely local business by the localities . . . is further recommended by all the advantages which have been set forth in this essay as belonging to individuality of development and diversity of modes of action' (Mill, 1859: 187, 181). Schumpeter shared none of this enthusiasm for regionalism, devolution, voluntarism, trade unionism, self-help collectives, non-governmental organisations, the extra-parliamentary opposition. Nor did he share the Hayekians' fear of a centrally planned serfdom that concentrates dominance in an oppressive monopoly. Seeing no reason to believe that central control would be wasteful or dictatorial, he saw no need to slim the State or to pluralise the loci of power.

At the end of his life he might have changed his mind. In his late paper of 1946 on 'The Future of Private Enterprise in the Face of Modern Socialistic Tendencies', he showed that he had become concerned about the status of the common good under the onslaught of the invisible hand: 'Our society is in the process of falling apart' (Schumpeter, 1946: 403). Schumpeter in that paper suggested that the antidote to social dislocation might be not so much improved law and order as the vocational associations and participative values of the Papal Encyclicals (Reisman, 2004: 168–76).

As Durkheim had done, Schumpeter sought to buttress his creative destruction with professional corporations like the guilds of the Middle Ages that would cut across the class conflicts and ensure a consensus on standards. He also accepted that socialism need not after all stop short at the Plan: 'Some form of guild socialism is not entirely off the cards' (Schumpeter, 1950b: 422). Schumpeter in the last five years of his life seems to have been uncharacteristically responsive to the conciliatory opinion-seeking of the classical democrats. If he did change his mind, then he did so too late to change his model. Catephores concludes that Schumpeter by the end had become 'the most internally defeated bourgeois of them all. He ended up falling for the siren-song of medievalism' (Catephores, 1994: 9).

3. Schumpeter on democracy: the economic approach

The classical theory posits that the people hold a definite and rational view which a passive State obediently translates into law: 'Government is nothing more than a national association acting on the principles of society' (Paine, 1792: 169). Classical democracy is a system in which the issues are debated and decided upon by the citizens. It is a *tâtonnement* in which public opinion converges on solutions and social consensus dictates the road.

Schumpeter alters the stance. Democracy, he says, should be defined not in terms of endstates but of procedures, not of soups but of cooks, not of policy options but of elected office holders. Democracy means that the people vote in the governors who will thereupon take over the collective choices: 'The principle of democracy . . . merely means that the reins of government should be handed to those who command more support than do any of the competing individuals or teams' (Schumpeter, 1942: 273). Democracy does not mean that the grassroots actually settles the issues: 'Democracy is the rule of the politician' (ibid.: 285). It means only 'that the people have the opportunity of accepting or refusing the men who are to rule them' (ibid.).

Democracy means not that the people rule but that the people delegate. Schumpeter's interpretation of democratic politics as the selection and reappointment of a trusted nanny will be considered in 'The political market', the first section of this chapter. The second section, ' "Policy is politics": Downs and Pareto', travels from public choice to irrationality and dominance to emphasise that there is more to Schumpeter than prudent shopping alone. The third section, 'Political failure?', asks in what circumstances the sheep will declare themselves tolerably satisfied with the shepherd and in what circumstances discontented Ulysses will want to contract anew.

3.1 THE POLITICAL MARKET

Competition for office resembles competition for customers 'with which it may be usefully compared' (Schumpeter, 1942: 271). Democracy is 'free competition among would-be leaders for the vote of the electorate' (ibid.: 285). Democracy is supply and demand.

3.1.1 Supply

Adam Smith, arguing that narrow egoism can be the cause of good service, said that no one should criticise the merchant or manufacturer for doing what the profit motive would suggest (Smith, 1776: I, 18). Smith was making the point that even self-regarding intent can deliver a socially beneficial outcome, as if guided by an unseen Architect working to a grand design. Schumpeter took the view that the political market is more of the same: 'It does not follow that the social meaning of a type of activity will necessarily provide the motive power' (Schumpeter, 1942: 282).

Pro bono publico does not protect the public good. Private self-seeking corrects the imbalance in supply. Unintended outcome is the link that proves that greed is good: 'The social function is fulfilled, as it were, incidentally – in the same sense as production is incidental to the making of profits' (ibid.). Consumers are fed and clothed not because of authenticated need but because of *turpe lucrum*. Citizens are guaranteed the government they desire by the same logic, that rival power-seekers are in competition for the vote: 'The democratic method produces legislation and administration as by-products of the struggle for political office' (ibid.: 286). There is no social welfare function and no common good copyrighted as such in Heaven. What there is instead is the elementary truism that the next election is just round the corner.

The politician deals in votes as a businessman deals in oil (ibid.: 285). Because politics is oligopoly, no policy proposal can have any greater value in itself than 'the brands of goods a department store sells' (ibid.: 283). In a war, the choice of a hill or field is determined exclusively by strategy and tactics and not at all by philosophy or aesthetics. As with the military campaign, so with the electoral manifesto. The choice of terrain is determined exclusively by the expected vote-value and the will to win: 'The first and foremost aim of each political party is to prevail over the others in order to get into power or to stay in it' (ibid.: 279). The nature of the product is of little or no significance to the shopkeeper who wants to sell: 'The decision of the political issues is, from the standpoint of the politician, not the end but only the material of parliamentary activity' (ibid.). Victory over the opponent is the sole objective. Clergymen trade in ideas and ideals. Politicians sell policies for votes.

The theory seems harsh, even 'cynical' (ibid.: 285n). What it teaches is that checkmate is all. Schumpeter believed that politicians were an estate that put power above ideology, a 'set of people for whom ruling is more important than the purposes and interests to be served by ruling' (Schumpeter, 1939: II, 728). Imbued with 'the political hack's craving for office' (Schumpeter, 1942: 365), they supply a vote-winning product through a firm called a party that wants to maximise its market share: 'A party is a group whose members propose to act in concert in the competitive struggle for political power' (ibid.: 283). Parties that define public welfare too rigidly in the principled sense of unbending conviction face early defeat at the hands of an established opposition. Should, moreover, a settled duopoly prove insufficiently responsive to the vote-spenders' demand, an entrepreneurial new entrant has the freedom to market a better-adapted brand: 'Everyone is free to compete for political leadership by presenting himself to the electorate . . . in the same sense in which everyone is free to start another textile mill' (ibid.: 272, 272n). Firms compete for votes. Shoppers pay fees and buy elites. Cynical it may be, but both the buyers and the sellers have a fair chance of getting what they want.

3.1.2   Demand I: Error

In the ideal political market the voter makes a rational choice of the most pleasing manifesto. So focused an exercise of citizen sovereignty presupposes that the independent individual has a definite, determinate and unambiguous ranking that he wishes to reveal: 'If we are to argue that the will of the citizens *per se* is a political factor entitled to respect, it must first exist. That is to say, it must be something more than an indeterminate bundle of vague impulses loosely playing about given slogans and mistaken impressions' (Schumpeter, 1942: 253). The assumption underlying the ideal democratic market is that the modal citizen has a shrewd idea of what he wants and of the costs that would means-ends him his benefit. The real world may be less charitable to the well-specified utility function and the impartial inference from fact. Schumpeter is a theorist of democracy who is all too eager to say that the majority in the street really hasn't a clue. Scoring goal after goal for the opponents' side, the liberal wonders if he knows which jersey he has made his own.

Bottom-feeding in the mud there are the 'fools', the genetically 'subnormal', the permanently confused. Unable to impose order on the data set or to sustain consistent transitivities for long, these fully enfranchised non-rationals are 'the great problem and the great enemy of humanity' (ibid.: 213). Schumpeter estimates that they make up 25 per cent of the population. Since few elections are decided with a clear lead of at least 25 per cent, what Schumpeter seems to be implying is that the absolutely stupid have the power to swing the results.

Less stupid than the absolutely stupid but worryingly stupid nonetheless are the relatively stupid. These are the mediocrities and second-raters who pyramid saloon-bar inanities upon a 'reduced sense of reality', a 'reduced sense of responsibility', an 'absence of effective volition' (ibid.: 261). Schumpeter rejected popular involvement in the specification of the common good in part because he felt that the common man had no real understanding of the issues.

Simultaneously, however, he was prepared to entrust the selection of the governors to broad sections of the population who were barely able to name the Shadow Home Secretary or find the Spanish Costas on the map. Liberals never call for the hurdle of an educational qualification or an intelligence test. Elitists are less generous to judges who are obviously not the equal of their evidence.

Non-rationality leads to the choice of the less-than-economical path. So too does gut-reaction irrationality that leaps before it looks. Schumpeter believed that there was a tendency on the part of the ordinary citizen to 'yield to extra-rational or irrational prejudice and impulse' (ibid.: 262). Emotive spontaneity is an asset in the poet or the painter. Politics is different. Schumpeter argued that the voter is doing little for the common interest where he lets his non-calculative subconscious crowd out his problem-solving reason: 'This will make it still more difficult for him to see things in their correct proportions or even to see more than one aspect of one thing at a time' (ibid.). Acting on the dictates of his heart, the voter who puts instinctual self-expression first is substituting vague impressions for the solid probabilities upon which optimising science must depend. The result is a diswelfare that can also be a threat: 'At certain junctures, this may prove fatal to his nation' (ibid.).

In the smiling file there is the 'burst of generous indignation' (ibid.). As well-intentioned as Titmuss's gift of blood, a Schumpeter would remind the soft-hearted that altruism can also be dysfunctional and sometimes even counter-productive. Income replacement can create unemployment. The suppression of the user charge can lead to overuse. In the scowling file there are the Roman persecutions and the pogroms of genocidal cleansing. These eruptions of death-wish negativity Schumpeter regarded not as *obiter dicta* but rather as the *memento mori* that guide the ordinary citizen in his journey down the non-thinking road: 'He will relax his usual moral standards . . . and occasionally give in to dark urges which the conditions of private life help him to repress' (ibid.). Logic and information-gathering are presumed by the cultured Schumpeter to cut back on that. Schumpeter was writing of 'dark urges' in the Second World War. He had also been a contemporary of Freud in Vienna at a time when positivism versus instinct, Akademie versus Sezession, were hotly debated in the coffee houses on the Ring.

Schumpeter had read Freud on Eros and Thanatos, Suetonius on Nero, Le Bon on the crowd, Pareto on *Mind and Society*, Wallas on *Human Nature in Politics*. What he had found was something that 'dealt a serious blow to the picture of man's nature which underlies the classical doctrine of democracy' – 'the sudden disappearance, in a state of excitement, of moral restraints and civilized modes of thinking and feeling' (ibid.: 257). Durkheim's sociology is built around the magnifier and the multiplier of the 'group incarnated and personified': 'We see the most mediocre or harmless bourgeois transformed by the general exaltation into a hero or an executioner' (Durkheim, 1912: 212, 213). Schumpeter knew enough of the world to understand the echo chamber properties of social agglomeration. What all will do, one will not. It is adding up and not just Original Sin that makes vandals and football hooligans even of honest citizens who on their own would almost certainly have carried a lost puppy across the road.

Voters, not always the dispassionate calculators of the neoclassical text, become a 'rabble' in a 'state of frenzy' when they become blurred faces in a 'psychological crowd' (Schumpeter, 1942: 257). The intellectuals and the media direct their appeal at precisely those 'animal spirits', 'infantilisms', 'primitive impulses', 'criminal propensities' (ibid.) that mass irrationality can explain and *homo economicus* cannot. Politicians themselves display 'a lower level of energy of thought and greater sensitiveness to non-logical influences' (ibid.) once they have become enmeshed in the interpersonal team-building of parliaments and committees.

The ordinary citizen, undereducated, 'unintelligent' and 'irresponsible' (ibid.: 262), votes not like a prudent businessman but like a pig in a pastry shop. Crossing the border from economics to politics, he becomes 'infantile', 'associative', 'affective', 'a primitive again' (ibid.). Marx's theory of class conflict itself owes much to the way in which 'a hotbed of prejudice' (ibid.: 14) will bring out the worst in mob solidarity. Schumpeter, although a *methodological* individualist, accepted, like Marx, that the part absorbs its paradigm through the second skin of the group. One consequence of the sociologisation of the psyche was that error creeps into the choice.

3.1.3 Demand II: Bias

National issues are remote. Even if the butcher, the brewer and the baker are fully rational in their swaps, the citizen as a voter is less likely to search out the cost-effective choice: 'In politics he lacks all the alertness and the judgement he may display in his profession' (Schumpeter, 1942: 261n). In his business he makes a personal gain or incurs a private loss. In politics there is not the same incentive to collect information or to become involved.

Local politics, arguably, engages the citizen more directly than national: 'Local patriotism may be a very important factor in "making democracy work" ' (ibid.: 260). Only within limits, however: 'Even there we find a reduced power of discerning facts, a reduced preparedness to act upon them, a reduced sense of responsibility' (ibid.). Even at the level of the Athenian city-State, even after allowance has been made for network contacts and informal learning, the fact is that voter after voter 'does not feel responsible for what the local politicians do' (ibid.). The detachment at the national and international level are greater still. Business is business and time is money. It is nothing less than rational to be indifferent and ill-informed where the dividend to critical competence is low, speculative, diffuse and unreliable.

The outcome is democracy in a darkness for which sensible citizens made manifest their demand: 'Information is plentiful and readily available. But this does not seem to make any difference' (ibid.: 261). The professional has a financial incentive to keep abreast in his own narrow field. In unrelated areas, however, he has no need or will to invest in a public good from which he personally is unlikely to derive much benefit: 'Without the initiative that comes from immediate responsibility, ignorance will persist in the face of masses of information however complete and correct' (ibid.: 262). The typical citizen 'drops down to a lower level of mental performance as soon as he enters the political field' (ibid.). The typical citizen becomes an economical democrat. He decides to dwell in the darkness because costly intelligence does not pay him a competitive return.

Classical democracy is general equilibrium: all citizens, conscious, conscientious and enlightened, are active in the specification of the common good. Schumpeter's democracy is partial equilibrium: a local maximum emerges as a reflection of a disproportionate and non-negligible stake. A presses for a subsidy. B demands a protective tariff. Each is striving to move himself to his best attainable partial equilibrium, self-perceived. Neither, however, shows any real interest in the general well-being of the society as a whole. One of the reasons why Schumpeter laid so much stress on the wisdom of the leadership is precisely because of the prevalence of this asymmetry and this bias. The consensus model implies that the issues are the property of all. The selective stake means, however, that the popular will cannot be measured for the simple reason that it does not exist.

At the periphery there is the great majority for whom 'the sense of reality is ... completely lost' (ibid.: 261). Aware of the issues only if politics is a leisure-time hobby, prone to act on intuitions and daydreams because facts and inferences cost time and money, the intellectually semi-detached articulate vaguely defined preferences which hardly add up to 'what we call a will – the psychic counterpart of purposeful responsible action' (ibid.). The question is too remote, too lacking in personal relevance, to warrant careful study. Where the expected betterment is small, it is rational even for the well-educated to economise on economics.

At the centre, in sharp contrast, there is a small minority for whom a given policy is a recognisable asset. Where the debate is concerned with 'issues involving immediate and personal pecuniary profit to individual voters and groups of voters', there the passionate will react 'promptly and rationally' (ibid.: 260) since they will be the most sensitive to the pinching shoe. Farmers will press for a grant. Manufacturers will lobby for a quota. The private interest will be defended well: 'Pressure groups are just as powerful as parties and much less responsible, hence more effective battering rams' (ibid.: 382). The social interest, forever exposed to distributional coalitions with 'an axe to grind' (ibid.: 263), is more vulnerable. Highly apposite is Mancur Olson's warning that a global balance will be inconceivable so long as the higgledy piggledies fight out a Hobbesian *bellum* over the rents and the spoils that biased democracy puts within their grasp: 'There will be no countries that attain symmetrical organization of all groups with a common interest and thereby attain optimal outcomes through comprehensive bargaining' (Olson, 1982: 74).

Bias is all around. Olson and Schumpeter, proceeding issue by issue from the parts to the whole, say that much if not most of statute law reflects not the will of 'all of the people' but rather the special pleading of 'some of the people' with a direct and intimate interest. The government will be swayed and swayed again by a sequence of single-issue minorities able to impose their will because the single-issue majorities do not really care. It is an unusual form of tyranny since the victims are in the dark as to the abuse, and since it was their own rational choice not to lay in precautionary stocks of what they believed to be low-return information. Unseen and unfelt, the revolving door is tyranny nonetheless. Partiality after partiality is given privileges. Yet no global decision is ever taken on an equitable mix.

In classical democracy the citizens make public policy on the basis of a common good that is purified of selfish interest-seeking. In Schumpeter's democracy the voters never decide collectively on the basis of all interests taken together, but only severally, in the light of the de facto bribes that each gang of bullies wants to squeeze out of public expenditure. What is rational for the part is evidently not rational for the whole. Even so, there is little that electoral reform can do to promote a general equilibrium. The majority has made up its mind that knowledge is for fools. Liberal values would suggest that even the wish to be ignorant should be treated with respect.

The time discount makes worse the multiple distortion. Not only are the blinkered and indeed the mercenary 'bad and indeed corrupt judges' (Schumpeter, 1942: 260), they are also singularly indifferent to the future spinoffs and their own long-run prospects: 'It is only the short-run promise that tells politically and only short-run rationality that asserts itself effectively' (ibid.: 261). The short run gets the meat. The long run is left with the bones. The result is that evolution is shaped not just by narrow-minded pressure groups but by the path dependence that is the material embodiment of their short-horizoned gain-seeking: 'History . . . consists of a succession of short-run situations that may alter the course of events for good' (ibid.: 264). The tyranny of small decisions alters the parameters of history-to-come, unplanned and unanticipated. Bosanquet's *polis* would never have regarded so rudderless and chartless a craft as an acceptable vehicle for the common good.

The electoral process itself abridges the aspirations. Politicians do not need to 'fool all of the people all of the time' since they do not market themselves in an infinite number of rounds. What they do need to do is to maximise immediate vote-value even if investment in infrastructure must be scrapped in favour of quick-fix public consumption. Politicians plunging public money in the formation of brand loyalty are apprised of nothing so much as the truism that the here-and-now has a vote and the future does not: 'Any party which makes a sacrifice in the national interest will suffer for it in the short run' (ibid.: 369).

The prime minister in a democracy is like a horseman on a maverick. He is 'so fully engrossed in trying to keep in the saddle that he cannot plan his ride' (ibid.: 287). The interest of the party is here at variance with the welfare of the nation. The principals do not receive from their agents the service they would have demanded had they been perfectly informed. Nor will they receive the package they would have put first had they been altruistic enough to love the future as they loved themselves.

3.1.4   Demand III: Manipulation

The political entrepreneurs get the bright new ideas: 'Latent' volitions 'are called to life by some political leader who turns them into political factors' (Schumpeter, 1942: 270). Consumers largely rubber-stamp what the suppliers want to sell: 'The will of the people is the product and not the motive power of the political process' (ibid.: 263). The classical democrats had derived their legitimacy from the popular will and the market individualists had made the sovereign consumer their supreme court of appeal. Schumpeter alters the sequence. Propagandists and persuaders, he writes, are 'able to fashion and, within very wide limits, even to create the will of the people. What we are confronted with in the analysis of political processes is largely not a genuine but a manufactured will' (ibid.).

A genuine will is a body of imperatives that emerges spontaneously from undirected interaction. A manufactured will is a set of tastes imposed *ex cathedra* by leaders who have information and experience and insist they know best. Schumpeter is convinced that a clear distinction can be made between the authentic and the artificial in the theory of demand. Others will be less confident about the watershed he believes he has seen.

Schumpeter does not explain in what way a non-ego preference acquired from a political paternalist is qualitatively different from a non-ego preference learned and honed through uncoordinated socialisation. He does not distinguish between the delegated manufacturing that is the contractual duty of the tried-and-trusted filter and the exploitative manufacturing that is the predatory impost of the trickster and the knave. Schumpeter does not acknowledge how much of the political agenda is set at the base by popular attitudes to great issues like poverty, education and crime: not all policies are distant and remote and not all citizens are unable to reason logically from cause to effect. Nor does he integrate his theory of want creation with his theory of market competition: where there are at least two parties, there are at least two options from which the pre-manufactured can select. Candidates propose alternatives because they appeal to differences of opinion. When all is said and done, however, it is the voter who picks one manifesto and discards its rival coteries.

Schumpeter's distinction between the 'genuine' and the 'manufactured' is hedged about on all sides with ambiguities such as these. The author's own reservations are captured by his 'wide limits' and his 'largely' which serve as a reminder to the reader that it would be a mistake to exaggerate a good case. Even so, there is no doubt that Schumpeter assigned the highest importance to the phenomenon of supplier-led demand. The choice of the electorate, Schumpeter stated, 'does not flow from its initiative but is being shaped, and the shaping of it is an essential part of the democratic process' (ibid.: 282). Whatever the choice may be, it is unmistakably dependent and not the independent emanation of an inborn innateness. That means, using the liberal model of the economic market, that the revealed preferences, supplier induced, do not 'qualify for ultimate data of the democratic process' (ibid.: 254). The politicians stride out in front. The common good shambles along behind.

Imagery and salesmanship are an intrinsic part of the package: 'The psycho-technics of party management and party advertising, slogans and marching tunes, are not accessories. They are of the essence of politics' (ibid.: 283). The franchise of command is traded in an oligopolistic market. To ensure consumer loyalty the producer must invest heavily in perceived differentiation.

The business corporation has shown what can be done. Conviction liberals like Adam Smith modelled the market as if guided by individual choice, rational rankings, ego-guided aspirations. Advanced capitalism stands the textbook rhetoric on its head. For one thing, consumers are often confused and tentative: 'Their wants are nothing like as definite and their actions upon those wants nothing like as rational and prompt' (ibid.: 257). For another thing, buyers are suggestible and easily swayed: 'They are so amenable to the influence of advertising and other methods of persuasion that producers often seem to dictate to them instead of being directed by them' (ibid.). In early capitalism the consumer was king. In later capitalism the producer takes the lead: ' "Needs", whatever they may be, are never more than conditioning factors, and in many cases mere products of entrepreneurial action' (Schumpeter, 1939: II, 1035).

Salesmanship in business is insidious, and it works: 'Mere assertion, often repeated, counts more than rational argument and so does the direct attack upon the subconscious which takes the form of attempts to evoke and crystallize pleasant associations of an entirely extra-rational, very frequently of a sexual nature' (Schumpeter, 1942: 257–8). The appeal is to emotion and prejudice, not to logic and reason. The fact that it has been so spectacular a success suggests to Galbraith, as it did to Schumpeter, that the neoclassical sequence of demand-led supply has effectively been left behind by events: 'The mature corporation has readily at hand the means for controlling the prices at which it sells as well as those at which it buys. . . . The revised sequence sends to the museum of obsolete ideas the notion of an equilibrium in consumer outlays which reflects the maximum of consumer satisfaction' (Galbraith, 1967: 216–17, 218).

Consumer sovereignty, Schumpeter was convinced, had been seriously weakened by the evolving dominance of supply. Citizen sovereignty too had become a target for the wiles and the snares. Politicians were making use of 'evasions' and 'reticences' to bypass the demand for argument and proof: 'Effective information is almost always adulterated or selective' (Schumpeter, 1942: 263, 264). Politicians were falling back on 'reiterated assertion' to foster the feel-good familiarity of the anchored reference: 'Public opinion in England and the United States will swallow anything provided it is served up in the garb of familiar slogans' (ibid.: 263, 360). Politicians, in short, were becoming the masters of selective disclosure and of spin in precisely the same way that their counterparts in business were seizing upon the media campaign and the celebrity endorsement in order to sell soap.

Politicians were using the same techniques. Not only that, they were reaping the greater returns: 'The picture of the prettiest girl that ever lived will in the long run prove powerless to maintain the sales of a bad cigarette. There is no equally effective safeguard in the case of political decisions' (ibid.: 263). Consumer sovereignty or citizen sovereignty, this much at least is clear. It is in the shop of State and not the shop of shop that the individual is most at risk and most alone.

Political choice, for one thing, is less likely to be repeat business. Changing circumstances and changing personalities make it difficult to extrapolate from performance, while an electoral package does not by definition lend itself to tasting and sampling at a moderate cost. Shoes are more amenable to rational choice. The desire for footwear is a 'genuine want' which 'prolonged experimenting clears of much of the irrationalities that may originally have surrounded it' (ibid.: 258). Buying regularly, consumers become experts who can rely on learning and memory to avoid the errors that lie in wait for the uninitiated: 'It is simply not true that housewives are easily fooled in the matter of foods, *familiar* household articles, wearing apparel' (ibid.). The core consumable is a family friend. Politics, in contrast, is a maze and a vortex in which the one-off is unlikely to strike twice.

Political choice, moreover, has the character of a public good. The purchaser of an orange who plans to eat the orange has a private incentive to choose his orange well. Not so the powerless isolate buried in the anonymity of the Olson-type 'very large' or 'latent' group (Olson, 1965: 50): 'He is a member of an unworkable committee, the committee of the whole nation, and this is why he expends less disciplined effort on mastering a political problem than he expends on a game of bridge' (Schumpeter, 1942: 261). Where the group is large and the member insignificant, it makes better sense to be a free rider on the knowledge of others than to volunteer a stranger gift that is unlikely to affect the outcome of the race.

Political choice, finally, has an agency dimension. An orange is a final utility. A governor, however, is an advisor and a facilitator. Schumpeter, precisely because he believed that elections were more for leaders than for policies, was bound to conclude that voters required less background than did consumers. It was, after all, the essence of the political contract that the trustees should take over the thinking once the proprietors had offered them their mandate. The voter, seldom sure what he wants, tends always to rely on candidates to take the initiative in proposing a competitive mix: 'Voters confine themselves to accepting this bid in preference to others or refusing to accept it' (ibid.: 282).

No self-interested office-seeker, clearly, can afford to neglect the 'genuine group-wise volitions' (ibid.: 270) of the ordinary citizens upon whose support he must rely. He knows that he can most easily win elections 'by organizing these volitions, by working them up and by including eventually appropriate items in his competitive offering' (ibid.). Yet he also knows that the agency relationship is a discretionary nexus that enables him to suggest new departures where an obedient postman would merely pass other people's messages on. Demand-side choices can be influenced and moulded by supply-side creativity: 'Effective political argument almost inevitably implies the attempt to twist existing volitional premises into a particular shape and not merely the attempt to implement them or to help the citizen to make up his mind' (ibid.: 264). Manipulation channels the desires and mobilises the will. That, however, is the very essence of the fiduciary contract. No one buys a donkey and then walks stubbornly to work.

3.2 'POLICY IS POLITICS': DOWNS AND PARETO

The State is not the 'public good' and not the Hegelian whole. The State is the butcher, the brewer and the baker and the 'social power relations' which enable them to maximise their own private hoard: 'One should never really say "the State does this or that". It is always important to recognize who or whose interest it is that sets the machine of the State in motion and speaks through it. Such a view must be repulsive to anyone for whom the State is the highest good of the people, the acme of its achievement, the sum of its ideals and forces. However, only this view is realistic' (Schumpeter, 1919: 138n). The State is people. People have their own agenda.

Not the 'good' and not the *Geist* but rather alliances such as parties are 'the real agents in the social process' (Schumpeter, 1950a: 440). Each team pretends that it is no more than the delivery man and the spokesman for the absolute will: 'Every group exalts the policies that suit it into eternal principles of a "common good" that is to be safeguarded by an imaginary kind of state' (ibid.: 441). Each team exaggerates the extent to which its half-truths and its blood-curdling rhetoric are unashamedly 'the servants of political intent' (Schumpeter, 1942: 264): 'In general, declared policies are nothing but verbalizations of group interests and attitudes that assert themselves in the struggle of parties and for points in the political game' (Schumpeter, 1950a: 441). Politics is not veracity but weasel-words that persuade vote-holders to spend. *Der Sieger hat immer Recht*: 'Nobody has attained political maturity who does not understand that policy is politics' (ibid.).

The State is people. The State is weasel-words. In denying that the government subserves the 'common good', in insisting that 'policy is politics' and not the *vox ex machina*, Schumpeter may be said to have situated himself in a reductionist tradition which embraces calculative democrats like Downs but also treacherous oligarchs like Pareto. Teleological individualism is a broad church. This section examines the very different contributions of Downs and Pareto. It concludes that Schumpeter, too clever to be consistent, managed simultaneously to stand at the window that looked out over Jefferson and at the window that revealed the truth about the Brownshirts, the Blackshirts and the march on Rome.

3.2.1 Downs

The Calculus of Consent (1962) mentions Schumpeter only once. *Social Choice and Individual Values* (1951) does not mention him at all. Mueller is speaking for many when he expresses his surprise that so few works on the economics of politics cite Schumpeter or refer explicitly to his theories: 'One of the curiosities of the public choice literature is the slight *direct* influence that Schumpeter's work appears to have had' (Mueller, 2003: 2n). Public choice, Bruno Frey writes, seems to have developed '*independently* of Schumpeter': '*Nobody* seems to have been aware that Schumpeter developed many of the most central ideas in modern political economy' (Frey, 1982: 129, 130).

The exception might be Anthony Downs. Downs in his *Economic Theory of Democracy* (1957) speaks of his 'debt and gratitude' to Schumpeter for the 'brilliant insight' that the competitive struggle for office could rightly be modelled as an economic-man market: 'Schumpeter's profound analysis of democracy forms the inspiration and foundation for our whole thesis' (Downs, 1957: 29, 29n). Schumpeter, admittedly, is mentioned only twice in Downs's book (the major endorsement being relegated to a brief footnote). The sole quotation (on unintended outcomes) is trotted out in both instances as if there were nothing else in Schumpeter but the philosophy of the invisible hand. A careful reading of Downs confirms, however, that his public choice is close in a number of its most telling predictions to Schumpeter's self-interested economic model of the State.

Downs shares with Schumpeter the vision that politics is a market in which rival oligopolists vie for votes: 'Our main thesis is that parties in democratic politics are analogous to entrepreneurs in a profit-seeking economy. So as to attain their private ends, they formulate whatever policies they believe will gain the most votes, just as entrepreneurs produce whatever products they believe will gain the most profits for the same reason' (ibid.: 295). Politicians, not the depersonalised automatons of classical democracy but the conscious maximisers of power, income and prestige, carry little ideological baggage and take little interest in the national good. What motivates the politicians and drives them on is not ideas and not altruism but almost exclusively the trappings of victory for which they contend: 'In our model, the government does not care whether the utility incomes of its citizens are affected by its behavior; it is interested only in their votes' (ibid.: 248).

Politicians, precisely because 'their only goal is to reap the rewards of holding office *per se*' (ibid.: 28), resemble the butcher, the brewer and the baker in that they aim at the product for which the identified client is most likely to pay. Non-prescriptive and non-normative, they supply not 'the creation of a better society' (ibid.: 111) but 'what the people want' (ibid.: 91). The citizens for their part understand well the nature of the game. They know that they will get less felt value from their vote if they spend at random than if they are sensible and efficient in squeezing marginal party-differential from their limited marginal cost.

One implication is that they will not waste time and money on information that will not be worth its keep: 'In an uncertain world, rational decision-makers acquire only a limited amount of information before making choices' (ibid.: 207). That is why, in an economical democracy, economic policies tend to be 'biased against consumers and in favor of producers' (ibid.: 239). People earn in one market but spend in many. The payoff being asymmetrical, it is rational for them to concentrate their fact finding and their lobbying in the areas where their resources will secure them the maximum return. Policy makers, aware of the skewness, have no choice but 'to regard some voters as more important than others' (ibid.: 95). Reason and equality were among the great *desiderata* of the age of Enlightenment. In this case, however, instrumental rationality undeniably 'modifies the equality of influence which universal suffrage was designed to insure' (ibid.).

In modelling politics as if it were a market, Downs is making use of the deductive, subjectivist, marginalist, purposive tool-kit that he had acquired through his dialogue with political *economists* like Schumpeter. Yet there is a difference. Downs like most liberals takes it on trust that the individual is a competent judge of the utilities and the prices: 'We have . . . assumed that citizens behave rationally in politics' (ibid.: 295–6). Schumpeter, on the other hand, takes men as they are. Emotion, image, intuition, instinct, interpersonal sanctions, the tyranny of the crowd all come between *homo sapiens* and the best road to his self-appointed goal. Choosing policies in the sense of Downs or leaders in the sense of Schumpeter, the market theology breaks down where non-rational men do not know what they want.

Because the consumer is so often dithering and malleable, the producer has an opportunity to 'sex up' *de gustibus* in order to lure more spenders to his brand. Downs rules out the endogenous transformation of tastes: 'No citizen can possibly influence another's vote' (ibid.: 83). Schumpeter, on the other hand, makes preference-creation and not just the disclosure of information an essential part of the trader's competitive strategy. A Schumpeter would in the circumstances accuse a Downs of sleeping too soundly at night.

Downs says that he is writing comparative statics and 'general equilibrium' (ibid.: 3). Schumpeter, creative destroyer, would reply that there can be no such thing as restful inertia so long as it is in the nature of the political innovator to convert an uncertain future into an internally generated dynamic. The politician cannot wait for democratic demand to dictate what the parties should supply. A merchant who is supine rather than imaginative will lose out to vote-chasers more willing to huckster, to embellish and even to deceive. What the politician must do instead is to intervene proactively to influence demand and even to manufacture it. Down's democracy might be the beneficent optimisation of the invisible hand. Schumpeter's democracy is more like Sir telling the rest of us that we will get no ice-cream until we eat up our greens.

It does not have the feel of the liberal market maximum. As Mitchell writes, clearly approaching the end of his tether: 'I find it difficult to believe that Schumpeter would have found *The Calculus of Consent* or *An Economic*

Theory of Democracy very convincing methodological statements. . . . Schumpeter would have us believe that while man is selfish in both the market and politics he is a good deal less rational if not irrational and unethical . . . in the polity. Because of this near-bifurcation in the choice of basic axioms Schumpeter has not influenced Public Choice' (Mitchell, 1984a: 149).

Frey agrees that the gulf is there: 'Schumpeter advances some ideas which according to public choice are *mistaken*' (Frey, 1982: 129). What he adds, however, is that even public choice is not as yet perfect: 'Once we leave the straightjacket of today's public choice theorizing, Schumpeter's ideas have indeed a great deal to contribute' (ibid.: 133). Economists like to assume rational choice, an information reflux and an error-correction mechanism. When stumps are drawn, what matters is the *what is*. If irrationality and incorrect perception do influence the real-world vote, then there is no point in demanding that facts that are incompatible with the a prioris will have to be rejected since they are obviously wrong.

3.2.2 Pareto

Schumpeter's political economy shares much with the public choice politics of enthusiastic shoppers like Downs. No less, however, is it in tune with the controlling exclusivity of new Iagos like the old and disillusioned Pareto who declared that the common man can never, must never rule: 'Ochlocracy has never resulted in anything save disaster' (Pareto, 1966: 135). Pareto in his *Cours d'Economie Politique* (1896), his *Systèmes Socialistes* (1902), his *Manuale di Economia Politica* (1906), most of all in his *Trattato di Sociologia Generale* (*The Mind and Society*) (1916), conveyed the message that the liberal democracy of 1848 had proved effete and corrupt and that the strong Mussolini who made him an honorary senator might be the only way out of the politics of grab.

By the late 1890s the former engineer, economist, positivist and free trader had decided that means/ends reasoning and empirical verification were only able to explain a small part of social interaction: 'The diffusion of a doctrine depends hardly at all on its logical value. Quite the contrary. . . . Faith alone strongly moves men to act' (Pareto, 1966: 126, 150). Whereas the logico-experimental method that underlies public choice would highlight observation, detachment and goal-oriented economising, Pareto said that non-logical emotion and non-rational belief had the greater explanatory power: 'Human beings follow their sentiments and their interests, but they like to think they follow reason' (ibid.: 151). Human beings are profoundly self-deceived.

Perceptions and realities are not necessarily two sides of the same coin. Just as a straight stick thrust into water appears bent, so distortions and misapprehensions, 'indeterminate words and defective reasonings', are the order of the day: 'We are like a man who sees objects in a curved mirror' (ibid.: 208, 124). People use rationalisations and generalisations to create a link where no link exists. It is the task of the psychologist and the sociologist to look beneath the masks of verbalisation in order to gain a purchase both on the 'residues' (the visible manifestations of invisible psychic states) and on the 'derivations' (the interpretations and ideologies which mediate subsequent action). Illusions built upon instincts, pseudo-scientific justifications need not be an accurate explanation of non-ego reality: 'They define the unknown by the unknown' (ibid.: 208). What matters is not their accuracy but only their existence. The mind is as the mind does. An elite wishing to win over the masses must appeal to the residues and remember that only a derivation can face down an opinion.

An elite, in power or aspiring to power, must know how to market its product. Rational choice would suggest that it should concentrate on the objective selling-points. Pareto, on the other hand, says that images and fictions will attract more customers to part with their effective demand: 'The art of government lies in finding ways to take advantage of . . . sentiments.' (ibid.: 244). Like Plato's 'noble lie' and Sorel's 'myth', governing means persuading in such a way that the select few in the end get what they want: 'It is always an oligarchy which rules and finds ways of expressing such "will of the people" as the (ruling) few wish to see expressed' (ibid.: 44). Henry Dubb does not issue the commands, even in a democracy: 'The worthy Demos thinks he is following his own wishes, whereas in fact he is following the behests of his rulers' (ibid.: 268). He thinks he is in charge. He could not be more mistaken. Cunning and artifice are being used to pull the wool over his eyes.

The cream rises to the top. The dregs mind their own business. The exclusion of the non-elite is a law of nature which 'rests on an indisputable fact: human beings are not equal physically, intellectually or morally' (ibid.: 110). Even if the playing-field is level, the law of nature is that the players are not: 'The assertion that men are objectively equal is so patently absurd that it is not worth refuting' (ibid.: 155). Democracy is about oligarchy. Democracy is about dominance: 'A community is always governed by a small number of men, by an *elite*, even when it seems to have an absolutely democratic character' (ibid.: 159).

One Eleven goes up and another Eleven goes out: 'Aristocracies do not last. . . . History is a graveyard of aristocracies' (ibid.: 158, 249). What is as striking as the rise and fall of the elements is the continuity of the structure. There will always be concentrated authority at the apex: 'The sole appreciable result of most revolutions has been the replacement of one set of politicians by another set' (ibid.: 110). A new entrant, seeking to make himself the patron of another's passive client, will use rhetoric equal to that of the demogogues of ancient Athens in order to convince the hesitant that he is the people's friend: 'A new aristocracy which seeks to take the place of an older one as a rule declares war, not in its own name, but in the name of the greatest number. A rising aristocracy always wears the mask of democracy' (ibid.: 163). The powerful secure their mandate from the powerless. Once in the saddle, they put in place a new feudalism which is a world away from the consumer sovereignty of the economic approach.

Pareto was an elitist who did not think that democracy was especially democratic. His critique is echoed almost point by point in Schumpeter's theory of error, bias and manipulation. The will of the people is indeterminate and vague. The crowd is excitable, impulsive and irrational. Slogans and catch phrases speak louder than facts. Elections are about governors and only tangentially about issues. Manufacturers mould demand in the chosen image of supply. The bull always leads. The herd always follows.

Downs was a liberal who used economic analysis to explain the market for the State. Here again Schumpeter seems to sign off on a significant number of the hypotheses. Party-political competition means that the power-seeker must supply a vote-winning product. Ignorance is rational where peripheral information has no more than entertainment value. Bias is economic where a pressure group pursues its industrial interest through a tariff or a subsidy. Small groups are more focused since free riding means flab. Public consumption is put first since public investment takes too much time.

Schumpeter's democracy clearly draws elements from more than a single tradition. What this means is that anyone who sees his theory only as trickery or only as shopping is failing to understand the uniqueness of his vision. Schumpeter was a natural Junker who was also an instinctual Yank. The duality in his personality is matched by the duality in his model. Schumpeter's democracy is both active citizenship and passive acceptance. Looking forward to Downs but also backward to Pareto, the reader wonders if the eclectic mix might not lead in the end to underperformance and disappointment.

3.3   POLITICAL FAILURE?

Voters are ill-informed, prejudiced and suggestible: 'The electoral mass is incapable of action other than a stampede' (Schumpeter, 1942: 283). Politicians thrive on ' "unfair" or "fraudulent" competition or restraint of competition' (ibid.: 271). They have no principled commitment to the truth: 'The first thing man will do for his ideal or interest is to lie' (ibid.: 264). The 'rabble' at the bottom is Scylla, always out to lunch: one must 'fight its criminality or stupidity by all the means at one's command' (ibid.: 242). The 'moron' at the top is Charybdis, always on the make: the 'windbag' sells his personality package through smiles and handshakes which, the self-publicist once in office, are 'often inimical to performance' (ibid.: 289). Demand or supply, democracy has the feel of an unstable system that is bound to fall short.

Business markets function satisfactorily. Political markets are perverted by error, bias and manipulation to such an extent that democracy itself may be a hidden cause of capitalism's inevitable demise. Mitchell, studying the propositions, the *obiter dicta*, the 'footnote asides', is struck by the distance between the two pillars of the liberal compromise: 'While Schumpeter took a romantic view of capitalism and the entrepreneur, his views of the politician, democracy and politics, more generally were anything but romantic' (Mitchell, 1984b: 162, 163). The shills are gullible. The hustlers are devious. Parliament is the floating crap game which is the focus of their contract.

Held, like Mitchell, is deeply troubled by Schumpeter's asymmetry. His assessment – 'strikes at the very idea of individual human agency' – strikes at the very idea that Schumpeter could have been a believer in democracy at all: 'Schumpeter acknowledged that individuals can be "active" in the realms of consumption and private life, but he came very close to denying that such a capacity existed in the sphere of politics. His emphasis both on the degree to which the "popular will" is "manufactured", and on the vulnerability of individuals to "extra-rational" forces strikes at the very idea of individual human agency by striking at the idea that humans can exert power by making choices' (Held, 1996: 193). Athenian democracy is democracy: politicians submissively execute a clearly specified consensual will. Downsian democracy is democracy: voters calculate their marginal utilities and competitors supply the paying policies. Schumpeter's democracy is less obviously democracy. Democracy is not just popular sovereignty but a non-random choice. In Schumpeter's democracy, however, the *demos* is thoroughly confused.

Schumpeter knew just how easy it was to list the shortcomings of political democracy. What he also says is that it is 'just as easy' (Schumpeter, 1942: 289) to cite its impressive successes. In ancient Rome the politician-generals held office by election: 'On the whole, these politician-soldiers did remarkably well' (ibid.). At least in ancient Rome, it would appear, elections could deliver a satisfactory product. Schumpeter's advice is therefore not to jump to a prioris but to rely instead on pragmatism and a neutral stance: 'Exactly as there is no case for or against socialism at all times and in all places, so there is no absolutely general case for or against the democratic method' (ibid.: 290). Sometimes democracy succeeds and sometimes democracy fails. Agnosticism and eclecticism have cornered the market. There is no choice but to have an open mind.

Schumpeter does not explain what he understands by political success and political failure. Approaching democracy as a liberal and an economist, however, one would have to say that his sole test must have been that of the butcher, the brewer and the baker who through their private and personal subjectivity move their circular flow to what they themselves would take to be their highest attainable level of felicity. In such circumstances the test of performance reinforces the absolutes of ethics in explaining why it was that Schumpeter, despite being Schumpeter, could have been a liberal democrat as well.

The one-stage interpretation is that principals spend votes in order to purchase policies. Schumpeter expresses reservations about collective choice as a mix-and-match: 'Voters do not decide issues' (ibid.: 282). His declaration is curious in view of his references to lobbies and pressure groups, single-issue coalitions and special-interest legislation. What he seems to be suggesting is that a *minority* of citizens might influence policies through non-electoral channels but that the *majority* of citizens do not influence policies through the ballot box. His contention is debatable: not all preferences being manufactured, strongly-held opinions on key issues such as unemployment, a foreign war or the restructuring of the health service can and do sway the attribution of the mandate. His point, however, is clear enough. Democracy should not be conceptualised as a town meeting or a referendum. Democracy, instead, should be seen as the citizens' selection of the wise dentists to whom they entrust their teeth. The 'acceptance of leadership is the true function of the electorate's vote' (ibid.: 273).

The two-stage interpretation is therefore that the populace spends votes in order to buy in representatives. 'The role of the people is to produce a government' (ibid.: 269). Schumpeter's democracy clearly has much in common with an electoral college set up not to capture voiced preferences but to construct a risk-averter's firewall against the excesses of the half-cocked and the half-baked. Representation enhances well-being since it limits the spillovers that the out-of-control can snowball: even if foolish Dubb believes that the earth is flat, his judicious guardians will ensure that he does not smash Ulysses' craft on to the false-perceived Sirens' rock. Simultaneously, however, the suffrage provides a check on the delegate's abuse: the voters, as Matthews puts it rather well, 'have a choice as to *who* is to wash their brains' (Matthews, 1985: 6) and can hire new brainwashers after an agreed-upon four or five years. Democracy is a contract. The contract made, the voters leave the issues to the father-figures they have hired to rule and guide: 'Collectivities act almost exclusively by accepting leadership' (Schumpeter, 1942: 270).

In market economics the butcher buys beer from the brewer. In Schumpeter's democracy the citizen buys drink selection from a decision maker who knows best. Political success in such a scenario must mean that the voter, the benighted victim of error, bias and manipulation, nonetheless manages to identify the surrogate who best satisfies the latent desires that ego himself would have articulated had he possessed the true leader's clarity of vision. Political success in that sense is issues politics, but issues politics at one remove. The leader ex ante is given a free spirit's discretion within the law. The leader ex post brings back crowd-pleasing outcomes that repay the confidence: 'In the best instances, the people are presented with results they never thought of and would not have approved of in advance' (ibid.: 278). Issues are not an irrelevance in Schumpeter's political economics. Simply, it is expected competence and not focused minutiae that is the essence of the competition for appointment.

Political success is consumer satisfaction. It is a reasonable choice made by a non-rational electorate. Political failure is the opposite. It is the visit to a dentist who cannot manage his drill.

Success is utility. Failure is disappointment. The invitation to trust the people is pure market economy. Error, bias and manipulation, however, are not. Bureaucrats controlling bottleneck information could slant the flow in order to empire-build their bureaus: Henry Dubb, fed filtered intelligence, would then put demand-side money into a supply-side need. Politicians able to manufacture public opinion could use want-creation in order to power their private ambitions: 'The esteem of the leaders for the masses is,' Mosca writes, 'not as a rule very profound' (Mosca, 1896: 151). Success is utility. Yet the patient's utility might only be another name for the dentist's persuasiveness.

Success is satisfaction. Schumpeter knew that the economist's definition was fraught with ambiguities when applied to the pooled purchases of public policy. An illustration would be the 'inflationary financing of government expenditure' (Schumpeter, 1939: I, 261). Taxes are unpopular but spending wins votes. The destabilising opportunism of a permanent deficit is the fall from grace that is imposed by short-termism, the vote motive and the need to win over the ambivalent. Prices rise but the paper is not at fault. The blame must lie with the politicians who recognise that hyperinflation will ruin their prospects but that moderate inflation will not harm them at the polls.

Rising prices, Schumpeter says, are 'unavoidable in the present political pattern' (Schumpeter, 1942: 374). Inflation could be contained by cutting the government overspend, raising taxes and interest rates, striking at the heart of union cost-push. In the long run prices would return to being microeconomic signals and would no longer be a macroeconomic headache. In the short run, however, there would be a veil of tears: 'Nobody can counteract threatening inflation without also interfering with production.' (ibid.: 392). In the short run at least, 'all really effective measures are unpopular' (Schumpeter, 1948: 242). Political success is consumer satisfaction. Voters feel profoundly dissatisfied when growth slows and they lose their jobs.

Short-run political success is long-run political failure. Yet there is no inbuilt corrective that can save the system from itself. The historical record speaks with a single voice, that rising prices 'were not stopped because the people who counted politically did not *want* to stop them': 'Each cabinet felt that this task might be more fitly undertaken by its successors who were welcome to spoil their electoral chances by doing so' (ibid.: 241, 242). Democracy lets the prices rise. Sooner or later there will be no alternative to a strong leader who, throwing early popularity to the winds, terminates the paper-powered euphoria and does what the long run demands.

The strong leader satisfies needs, not wants, and does so at the cost of bound Ulysses' in-period will. In the short run his action does not meet the economist's standard of political success. Ulysses complains bitterly that he will never hire so bossy a nanny again. In the long run, however, the democracy is on the other foot. Ulysses expresses his sincerest thanks because his health improved when his hired servant made him eat up all his greens.

4. Schumpeter: the preconditions for politics

Schumpeter's democracy is an institutional arrangement within which the people influence the issues through the decision makers that they elect. The procedure is most likely to be a success where four social conditions can be met. First, there must be an adequate number of adequate politicians. Second, the agenda must be in line with the capacity of the State to deliver. Third, there must be dependable back-up from a skilled and self-policing bureaucracy. Fourth, the charter must be such that the leaders are bound by internalised obligation and the masses amenable to democratic self-control.

Schumpeter's four preconditions will be considered in the first four sections of this chapter. The fifth section shows that Schumpeter's constitution of the mind was more powerful to him than the legislative correctives of less sociological economists. The sixth section invokes the magisterial name of Max Weber. Convinced like Schumpeter that democracy is a method, Weber like Schumpeter made much of the moral precommitment that keeps the self-interest-seeking within manageable limits. Schumpeter preferred the economic interpretation of democracy to the classical model of Aristotle and Rousseau. Even so, he, like Weber, saw that the exchange in the second approach was crucially dependent upon the value consensus of the first. Schumpeter did not have two theories of democracy at all. What he did have was an economic theory that was buttressed on all sides by the ethical judgments of the group.

4.1 THE POLITICIAN

The first condition is that politicians 'of adequate ability and moral character must exist in sufficient numbers' (Schumpeter, 1942: 290). Candidates should score well in the 'competitive struggle for power and office' (ibid.: 282), have the skills of a diplomat in 'the handling of men' (ibid.: 289), be in a position to outmanoeuvre cunning opponents and possess the intellectual strengths necessary to address the underlying trade-offs. Lacking the full portfolio, electoral successes alone 'may well be failures for the nation' (ibid.: 288). Not everyone in the population will have the vocation that is required. Nor will they necessarily have the interest. So exhausting is the dual challenge of competition plus administration that it can easily 'repel most of the men who can make a success at anything else' (ibid.: 290). Those who can, do. Those who cannot, stand for Grimestead South.

Schumpeter did not warm to the image of the politician as a man of the people who dips in late and bows out early. As far as he was concerned, professionals like dentists acquire a last and then stick to it. The same should be true of specialists like politicians whose job it is to make Parliament or Congress into a well-oiled machine: 'In modern democracies . . . politics will unavoidably be a career' (ibid.: 285). Politics being a function and not a hobby, it is crucial to establish in what circumstances the requisite standard of skill and talent can be expected. Schumpeter's answer is stock and flow, tradition and penetration, past and present. On the one hand there are the tramlines of blood. On the other hand there is the gradualism of merit. The expectation is a dual one, old in collaboration with new. It is not a requirement which *ab initio* democracies will find very easy to meet. Only a society can make a social contract. States of nature should take up whist instead. And buy a gun.

The baseline is birth and breeding: 'Experience seems to suggest that the only effective guarantee is in the existence of a social stratum, itself a product of a severely selective process, that takes to politics as a matter of course' (ibid.: 291). Easy entry and bygones forever bygone are the recipe for success in the liberal market. Restricted entry and time-out-of-mind are the functional buffers in the liberal State. Seldom has an open society been made less open by design.

The political stratum should not be so exclusive that it cannot assimilate new talent. An elite that logrolls favours and speculates in election-year giveaways will find it a positive advantage to enlist aptitude salesmen who have spent their formative years squeezing cash out of bonds. Innate endowments are unevenly distributed. Equality of opportunity has the obvious advantage that it opens the door to fresh potential with a comparative advantage.

Schumpeter in his essay on 'Social Classes in an Ethnically Homogeneous Environment' had written of 'movement across class lines', the 'rise and fall of families within a class', the 'rise and fall of whole classes' (Schumpeter, 1927: 247, 238, 254). His emphasis on slow circulation and not absolute rigidity is carried over from the genus of sociology to the sub-set species of politics. In the case of the State, he expected the successful to succeed and the redundant to drop out. The mechanisms can be debated: Schumpeter says little about the links between inherited wealth, privileged schooling, social networks and political power which impede deserved entry into the aristocracy of talent. Not in dispute, however, is the ideal of access. Schumpeter cannot be accused of pulling up the drawbridge in order to keep the outsiders out.

Schumpeter wanted contestability. Yet he also wanted continuity. It is this mixed polity of the stock with the flow, the past with the present, that is picked up by his statement that room at the top should be 'neither too exclusive nor too easily accessible' (Schumpeter, 1942: 291). Schumpeter believed that, while new people should be allowed in, they should not be admitted before old people had had a hand in their indoctrination into the organisational memory of a going concern. Institutions and culture will in that way 'increase their fitness by endowing them with traditions that embody experience, with a professional code and with a common fund of views' (ibid.).

Convention marches alongside change in an old country in which settled patterns persist: 'Social structures, types and attitudes are coins that do not readily melt' (ibid.: 12). One of the greatest strengths of British democracy has been the ability of its Conservative Party to bring in the ambitious young Disraelis but at the same time to draw upon the disciplined ethic of the pre-commercial landowners who had honed their service reflex when feudalism and not capitalism was still the economic base. England is 'the only country to fulfil our condition completely' (ibid.: 291). Motivated by money and not by power, the business class had no strong interest in taking a lead: 'Without protection by some non-bourgeois group, the bourgeoisie is politically helpless' (ibid.: 138). History confirms the conjecture that most businessmen have preferred profits to high office: 'The bourgeoisie ... did not produce a successful political stratum of its own' (ibid.: 298). The children of Hastings and Agincourt, luckily enough, were on hand to correct a management failure that had been the direct consequence of Arkwright and Watt.

Tory democracy was the template fusion of the interloper with the incumbent. Weimar Germany, precisely the opposite, shows what can happen when politics is unable to rely on either the dazzling new meteors or the long-established known stars. In Germany in the 1920s, 'ability and energy spurned the political career. And there was no class or group whose members looked upon politics as their predestined career' (ibid.: 291). The merchants were not looking beyond their stalls. The Kaiser and the Adelstand had been defeated and discredited. The leadership vacuum was a real one – and below-par potential paved the way for something even worse. The 'lack of inspiring democratic leadership' (ibid.) smoothed the passage for the anti-democratic politics of Hitler and the Nazis that ultimately pushed Weimar aside.

Schumpeter saw social evolution as the unceasing cycle of assimilation and elimination embedded within the stable confines of a relatively constant structure. His emphasis on restlessness in alliance with rest recalls Marshall's comparison of new businesses to the new trees of a self-renewing old forest: these grow to maturity and thereafter decline and decay to 'make room for other and more vigorous life' (Marshall, 1890: 269). It also recalls Pareto's defence of continuous, slow transformation because caste without mobility can only lead to ossification and stagnation: 'The governing class is renovated not only in number but also – and this is more important – in quality, by recruiting to it families rising from the lower classes, bringing with them the energy and proportions of the residues necessary for maintaining them in power. It is renovated also by the loss of its more degenerate elements' (Pareto, 1966: 249).

The role that rules is a relatively constant constant: 'Everywhere there exists a governing class, even in a despotism' (ibid.: 268). The membership of the club and the clique is, however, susceptible to the circulation of elites which renews and rejects. The moving staircase up and down is central to Pareto's sociology of power. It has a double significance. Circulation, first of all, means the *carrière ouverte aux talents*: energetic individuals come in and uninspiring individuals seek less leaderly jobs. Circulation, secondly, means the merry-go-round of coalitions: military lions are succeeded by plutocratic foxes until such a time as shrewdness and intelligence (class I residues, Pareto's 'instinct of combinations') give way to confrontation and force (class II residues, Pareto's 'persistence of aggregates') and the soldiers and the rentiers replace the quick-witted and the entrepreneurial once again. Individuals circulate. Coalitions circulate. The box at the top, however, goes on and on.

Pareto's vision of the box that is constant, the composition that is variable, is echoed in the *Elementi di Scienza Politica* (translated as *The Ruling Class*) of his near contemporary, Gaetano Mosca. Writing in 1896, Mosca expressed the view that human societies are always governed by a politically dominant oligarchy, by an 'organized minority' that inevitably 'imposes its will on the disorganized majority': 'In all societies ... two classes of people appear – a class that rules and a class that is ruled ... What Aristotle called a democracy was simply an aristocracy of fairly broad membership' (Mosca, 1896: 154, 50, 52).

Subordination is inevitable. The danger, Mosca said, is that the team that controls the State will become incestuous and self-perpetuating: 'All ruling classes tend to become hereditary in fact if not in law' (ibid.: 61). Competence is not encoded in the genes: 'The children of men of highest mentality often have very mediocre talents' (ibid.: 63). A polity that wants its representatives to be both progressive and accountable would evidently do well not to resist 'the democratic tendency ... to replenish ruling classes from below' (ibid.: 413).

Democracy has been more successful than pre-modernism in respect of renewal, restocking and recruitment from outside. An additional benefit has been the upward circulation of new social groupings, 'antagonistic to the class that holds possession of the legitimate government' (ibid.: 116). Individuals circulate. Groupings circulate. As in the case of Pareto, however, the zenith that crowns the structure emerges intact from the struggle: 'In elections, as in all other manifestations of social life, those who have ... the moral, intellectual and material *means* to force their will upon others take the lead over the others and command them' (ibid.: 154). Mosca writes that the masses may choose but they will never rule: 'The great majority of voters are passive' (ibid.: 155). What he also maintains is that an open elite will do a better job than a closed one will.

Robert Michels, like Pareto and Mosca, was a theorist of minority rule – 'No undertaking can succeed without leaders' (Michels, 1911: 89) – who believed that the rank and file, suffering from 'apathy' and in need of 'guidance' (ibid.: 205), were no better able to look after themselves than is a patient without his medical specialist: 'The incompetence of the masses is almost universal throughout the domains of political life, and this constitutes the most solid foundation of the power of the leaders' (ibid.: 86). Michels, in *Political Parties* (1911), formulated an iron law of oligarchy which postulated that 'in every organization ... the aristocratic tendency manifests itself very clearly': 'Society cannot exist without a "dominant" or "political" class' (ibid.: 32, 390).

Michels was convinced that the role that rules is a fact of social life. As with Mosca, Pareto and Schumpeter, however, he was reassured by the fact that the predictably durable summit was, in modern times, 'subject to a frequent partial renewal' (ibid.: 390). Even if the majority is 'permanently incapable of self-government' (ibid.), nonetheless the minority that gives the orders is in the liberal meritocracy being recruited from a broad cross-section of high achievers whose legitimacy is derived from their value added.

The political stratum should not be so exclusive that it cannot assimilate new talent. Schumpeter's rotating elitism of entry and exit stands on the shoulders of thinkers like Michels, Mosca and Pareto who recognised that even an individual born into Plato's race of silver ought to be given reasonable access into Plato's race of gold. Nor, however, should the political stratum be so inclusive that unmentored transients could find their way too quickly into what ought to be a *non facit saltum*. Pareto, Mosca and Michels expected a stable core with a fluctuating entry. The constant script, the rotating players, was the essence of their marriage of past and present. Schumpeter wanted their mix but he wanted one thing more: the pre-commercial nobility, because without the fourteenth earl and his dedication to community service the new boys would lack a role model and a standard of excellence that could never be bought and sold.

4.2   THE AGENDA

The second condition is that 'the effective range of political decision should not be extended too far' (Schumpeter, 1942: 291). Politics becomes discred-

ited where the politicians lose their grip. The leaders should in the circumstances promise no more than they can realistically perform.

Schumpeter is too much the proceduralist to define the proper scope in terms
of normative functions. He does not provide a hard-and-fast list of duties such
as relief of poverty or control of the money supply. Instead, he says, the agenda
should be determined, 'at any given time and place', by 'the particular circumstances of each individual case' (ibid.). The proper mix of the mixed economy
will be influenced by factors such as the technical competence of the government, 'the quality of the men who form that government' (ibid.), the calibre of
the bureaucratic back-up, the thrust of public opinion, the degree of consensus,
the pressure from rivals. Circumstances and situations will have the final say:
'Policy is politics; and politics is a very realistic matter' (Schumpeter, 1949:
300). There is not much a priori that can be treated as a natural law.

The size of the State cannot be prescribed for all time. Schumpeter insists
that it is not his recommendation for the agenda to be the bare minimum and
nothing more: 'It would be a serious misunderstanding if the reader thought
that such a limitation is necessarily implied' (Schumpeter, 1942: 292). Warren
Samuels, reading Schumpeter's *Capitalism*, is content to take him at his word.
The book highlights the 'inseparability of economy and politics' (Samuels,
1985: 67). It does not, however, come off the fence in favour of any single
point on the interventionist's compass: 'Although Schumpeter was personally
attracted by the idea of a limited state . . . the book as a whole comprises an
exercise in political economy, not economics' (ibid.).

Held takes a different view. Accepting that Schumpeter never said precisely
what the State ought to do, Held inputs the error, the bias and the manipulation and concludes that Schumpeter could not have expected the State to do
very much: 'Schumpeter's case for democracy can support, at best, only minimum political involvement: that involvement which could be considered sufficient to legitimate the right of competing political elites to rule' (Held, 1996:
182). Democracy is a limited mechanism. A limited mechanism cannot
produce more than a limited state.

Galbraith concentrates on matter much more than mind. A political evolutionist who believes that circumstances prescribe their single-valued cure, he is
better placed than Schumpeter to specify the 'correct' role of the State in terms
of objective criteria such as natural monopolies, public goods, merit goods,
infrastructural deficit and wage control. Schumpeter, in contrast, explains State
intervention in the language of popular preferences and not of structural imperatives. Pigovian externalities are as tangential to his democracy, as are the
exploited Marxian proletariat and the socialisation of surplus value.
Schumpeter explains the functions of the State in the language of attitudes and
choices of tastes and preferences, in other words, which the political elite can
demand-manage at will to 'create the conditions of its own legitimacy' (ibid.:

196). As far as Held is concerned, only the minimal State can make sense in a Schumpeterian world where the people are not intelligent enough to articulate a ranking that is fully their own.

Schumpeter was aware that an overexpanded agenda could put dispropor- tionate power in the hands of insensitive paternalists. His rediscovery of Catholic corporatism in the last years of his life (Schumpeter, 1946) demon- strates that he could see some role for across-the-board participation as a complement to the national plan. His asymmetrical socialism, politicising the quantity but leaving the price to demand (Reisman, 2004: 151–8), shows that even his statism could operate in tandem with the decentralised market. State intervention per se might not be a threat to democracy. What is just as telling is the kind of intervention and the concentration of control.

Consider the government-linked organisation. Schumpeter as early as the Socialisation Commission in 1919 had been attracted by the parastatal struc- ture, fully owned by the State but granted operational independence nonethe- less. Illustrations of arm's-length depoliticisation in line with the parastatal model are provided by the law courts, the regulatory commissions, the public sector universities and the Bank of England after 1946. Quasi-separation and insulation from the party-political power struggle make it possible in cases such as these for nationalised enterprise to function satisfactorily. Continuous guidance would have led to multiplied inefficiencies and in the end to a demand for divestiture.

Parastatals pluralise the magnetic field. What they cannot do is solve the problem of people: 'The politician's power to appoint the personnel of non- political public agencies, if remorselessly used, will often suffice in itself to corrupt them' (Schumpeter, 1942: 293). Schumpeter tried hard to Pollyanna the Hobbesians who see the *homini lupus* in every such mention of remorse- less corruption: 'That does not affect the principle in question' (ibid.). The Hobbesians being an anxious bunch, they are likely to reply that Schumpeter should have pluralised less and privatised more if he had really wanted to keep the democracy sensitive and alert.

4.3   THE BUREAUCRACY

The third condition is that there should be reliable support from 'a well-trained bureaucracy of good standing and tradition, endowed with a strong sense of duty and a no less strong *esprit de corps*' (Schumpeter, 1942: 293). Parliamentarians do not have the time or background to acquire the specialist expertise that the issues demand. The civil service corrects the political fail- ure: 'Bureaucracy is not an obstacle to democracy but an inevitable comple- ment to it' (ibid.: 206).

Skilled administrators have the technical competence that revolving-door ministers so conspicuously lack: 'Bureaucracy is the main answer to the argument about government by amateurs' (ibid.: 293). Rational and efficient, the bureaucracy must at the same time have the personal skills that allow it to exercise hidden leadership where the elected policy makers do not know their spanner from their wrench: 'It must also be strong enough to guide and, if need be, to instruct the politicians who head the ministries . . . It must be a power in its own right' (ibid.). Independent-minded administrators seem almost to be telling the political professionals what to do. The vote motive is that much less the jug-and-mug of statute where appointed office holders, protected from inter-party competition, have so great an impact on the allocation of public resources.

The power of the technocracy tends to take the *what is* out of party-political debate. Factual matters such as the cost of agricultural protection or the employment profile of the small firm 'cease to be political questions to be settled by the relative weights of pressure groups': they 'become technical questions to which technicians would be able to give unemotional and unequivocal answers' (ibid.: 302). Just as the manager in corporate capitalism is inheriting the routines if not the initiative of the old-style owner–entrepreneur, so the technocrat in the sophisticated civil service is able to execute many procedures that would before the separation of challenges have been a deadweight burden on the vote-seeking generalists. The *what is* hived off to the fact-finders, the politicians are in a stronger position to concentrate on the *what ought to be* in which they have a comparative advantage.

Technical training and virtuosity are important. They are, however, only 'secondary' (ibid.: 294), by themselves not enough. Primary is the salience of the ethos and the strength of the 'traditional code' (ibid.) that keeps the bureaucrat on message. An ingrained commitment to selfless duty is essential. A strong and pervasive *esprit de corps* is essential. Schumpeter's penpushers are *wertrational* at least as much as they are *zweckrational*. Human calculating-machines though they may well be, they must also be missionaries and preachers with a moralist's belief in the time-honoured lines that it would be a violation of the unwritten constitution for a gentleman to cross.

Schumpeter makes much of internalised obligation as an absolute end and of 'corporate opinion' (ibid.: 293) as an education from the past. He expects appointment and tenure to be a reflection of common standards and a perpetuator of institutional memory. That is why he counsels patience when, writing as a cultural conservative, he recommends that the civil service be given the time it needs to mature. Spencer says that 'society is a growth and not a manufacture' (Spencer, 1860: 269). His view that constitutions are not made but develop is echoed in Schumpeter's assertion that a bureaucracy, an organic thing, 'cannot be created in a hurry. It cannot be "hired" with money' (Schumpeter, 1942: 294). Effectiveness presupposes continuity. Without a few grey hairs, a bureaucracy is unlikely to be very good.

Because stability is so important, Schumpeter once more looks to birth and breeding for supply: 'An official class of this kind can be most easily secured if there is a social stratum of adequate quality and corresponding prestige that can be drawn upon for recruits – not too rich, not too poor, not too exclusive, not too accessible' (ibid.). Needed, it would appear, is an educated middle class that feeds the hierarchy with merit and capacity but also with discipline and solidarity. Rough diamonds can pass the competitive examinations. Only a long-lived societal affiliation, however, is able to inculcate the affectual tribalism that makes the bureaucrat a *civil* servant and not a butcher or a brewer in search of cash.

Schumpeter treats societal origins as the intertemporal bulwark against evanescent interest: American bosses hire by psychometrics and intelligence tests but British employers know how to extrapolate productivity from school tie and house. He seeks to countervail the impatient immediacy of the vote motive with the conventional wisdom of lasting institutions: American top mandarins arrive and depart with their political masters but British permanent secretaries remain Sir Henry throughout blue and red. As old as the *Burschenschaften* and as high-minded as the Church, Schumpeter's value-driven bureaucracy is closer, clearly, to the European model than it is to the more instrumental bang-bang of Schumpeter's own United States.

Daniel Bell, recognising the mixed mentality, is right to say that Schumpeter was a stranger and not the mirror of his new home: 'Schumpeter was too much of a European to believe that government could ever be an auxiliary or mediating body. For him, the State would be an autonomous force taking over the direction of society for its own bureaucratic impulses' (Bell, 1965: 85). Schumpeter admired America's dynamic entrepreneurs. He also admired Europe's settled traditionalists. He never managed to reconcile the creative destroyers with the family dynasties that had thrown up the bureaucracies in the country of his birth.

Schumpeter's vision is of a self-monitoring, self-denying bureaucracy that never abuses its strategic position in order to score a monopoly rent. However much his interpretation of interest-seeking politicians will have shared with the world-view of Downs and Pareto, his assessment of the civil servant adds up to training plus ethos and little more. Schumpeter's Grade 3, Scale 4, leaves his ego behind when he clocks on for the job.

Schumpeter is curiously indifferent, even oblivious, to the partialities that can distort the general. He shows no awareness of the extent to which office holders' goals like prestige, expansion, promotion, a quiet life or an exciting challenge could redirect the puppets' performance away from the outcomes that the puppeteers (the voters, like the shareholders) would have preferred. He seems not to appreciate that the conservative filter of learned schemata can itself lead well-drilled replicators to err on the side of inertia by selecting information that confirms a handed-on prejudice while concealing new surprises that would pension off a comfortable old heuristic. Schumpeter, indeed, is remarkably complacent about cold science in the age of kaleidoscopic uncertainty. The voters and the politicians may be underinformed but the bureaucrats are in possession of *all* the relevant facts. Given a good filing system and the correct amount of knee-jerk professionalism, there is not a lot the human factor can do that would put snakes and apples into a well-tended Eden.

Schumpeter is confident that the obedient servants will leave initiative taking to their elected chiefs. Others are less optimistic. Good Hegelians are hard to find. The unprincipled and the slippery, on the other hand, have all but secured a stranglehold on the debate.

Thus Michels, grounding his pessimism in 'psychological determinism', observes that all office holders suffer from a 'natural greed for power': 'The desire to dominate, for good or for evil, is universal. These are elementary psychological facts' (Michels, 1911: 205, 206). A self-made achiever without the back-up of a family fortune is bound to be interested in financial reward: that far can his purpose be warped by cash. What Michels is saying is that the *Wille zur Macht* in the sense of Nietzsche is even more powerful than limitless accumulation in the sense of Marx in explaining why it is that an otherwise decent human being will set out with determination to get his own way.

Mosca encapsulates the top-dog motive in the following words: 'In a society that has attained any degree of civilization at all, the struggle between individuals is not a struggle for existence but a struggle for preeminence' (Mosca, 1896: 121). People who have power like it so much that they want to consolidate it, defend it, extend it. Michels said that the influence on their 'moral character' was 'essentially pernicious' (Michels, 1911: 205). Even an organisation ostensibly as democratic as Germany's Social Democratic Party had, he wrote, developed an *internal* oligarchy which was standing between the leaders and the followers on whose support the politicians were so conspicuously dependent: 'In a party, it is far from obvious that the interests of the masses which have combined to form the party will coincide with the interests of the bureaucracy in which the party becomes personified' (ibid.: 389). The card-carrying want representation because the cadre is always right. Their salaried officers demand the last word because the road to God can never, must never, bypass the priest. Schumpeter brushed aside the possibility that the brooms might take over the brainwork from the sorcerer who was supposed to be in charge. Michels was far more concerned about what could happen when discretion was passed down from the barking dog to its wagging tail: 'For democracy . . . the first appearance of professional leadership marks the beginning of the end' (ibid.: 36).

Michels sees the bureaucracy as a self-serving entity, an independent estate 'with aims and interests of its own' (ibid.: 389). Anthony Downs, reasoning outward from the individual cog, is in no doubt that the bureaucracy must indeed be modelled on the economist's assumption of personal and private ends: 'The fundamental premise of the theory is that bureaucratic officials, like all other agents in society, are significantly though not solely motivated by their own self-interests. Therefore, this theory follows the tradition of economic thought from Adam Smith forward' (Downs, 1967: 2). Be it bribes or be it promotions, be it Michels' lust for power or Veblen's instinct of workmanship, what Downs is saying is that Herbert Simon is right to find it implausible that the man in a hierarchy 'turns off the switch of his own desires from nine to five' (Simon, 1957: 167). People are people and wants are goals. Robots are means that harbour no objectives. Bureaucrats in the liberal democracy are more likely to stand on their dignity and declare 'I am I'.

Niskanen, modelling up from the objectives of the part to the evolution of the whole, deduces the hypothesis that 'bureaucrats act so as to maximize their bureau's budget': 'Among the several variables that may enter into the bureaucrat's utility-function are the following: salary, perquisites of the office, public reputation, power, patronage, output of the bureau, ease of making changes, and ease of managing the bureau. All of these variables except the last two, I contend, are a positive monotonic function of the total *budget* of the bureau during the bureaucrat's tenure in office' (Niskanen, 1971: 38, 41). Niskanen's prediction is at variance with Schumpeter's complacency. Niskanen is saying that the bureaucrat takes the initiative and does what he thinks is right. Schumpeter, on the other hand, assumes that the 'public interest' is some noncontroversial maximand that somehow exists 'out there'.

As far as Downs is concerned, it most certainly is not: 'The "public interest" is here defined as what each official believes the bureau ought to do' (Downs, 1967: 84). The 'national good', Downs contends, is as problematic as filtered intelligence, as self-protective as organisational stasis. Schumpeter's official is more likely to keep his mouth shut and rubber-stamp what he is told.

4.4 THE CHARTER

The fourth condition is that there should be an adequate supply of the moral capital that Schumpeter terms 'Democratic Self-control' (Schumpeter, 1942:

294). Impatient opportunism and adventurous experimentation, the preconditions for the mould-breaking market, must be contained within the long-honoured limits that mark out the consensual State. The market presupposes voluntary subordination. Willing acceptance presupposes the agreed-upon rules. Lacking that consent, the future would be grim indeed: 'We require rules for living together,' Buchanan warns, for 'without them we would surely fight' (Brennan and Buchanan, 1985: 3).

Schumpeter is sympathetic to the British view of the constitution. He does not call for written codes to spell out working democracy's pre-existent yeas and nays. What he says instead is that the multi-period standards are as diffuse as the central value system, as specific as the *Volksgeist* that makes each polity unique. Integrated voters and responsive politicians must be expected to have internalised those public-good rules of the game before they can launch themselves successfully in any but a rudderless ship of State.

Remembered, unquestioned, self-enforced, non-calculative, the ethical constraint seems closer to feudal statics than it does to liberal capitalism. Schumpeter is aware that he is calling for an unfamiliar compound of the constant and the variable: he makes clear that he is grounding rational democracy not just in proven effectiveness but in a 'super-empirical sanction', an 'inherited sense of duty' (Schumpeter, 1942: 127). His appeal to stable social values seems closer to the high-minded Rousseaus and Bosanquets of classical democracy than it does to the one-period competition for votes that Schumpeter finds to be the more realistic explanation. The duality is not a contradiction but two sides of a coin. It would perhaps be most in keeping with the spirit of Schumpeter's law for the economic model to be seen as the logic of short-period choice, the classical model as the precondition that supplies the indispensable complement of democratic self-control.

Democratic self-control on the part of the voters must mean that the great majority who are not Plato's Guardians will respect the conventional division of labour. They must let their elected representative get on with his job: 'They must understand that, once they have elected an individual, political action is his business and not theirs' (ibid.: 295). At the next election the privates can vote their generals out. Before the next election, abstaining from back-seat driving in forms such as letters, telegrams, marches, criticism, the sovereign, however ill-informed, however stupid, must know enough of the world not to 'attempt to rush the shop' (ibid.: 294).

The unwashed select the chancellors. The leaders decide the issues. Schumpeter's interpretation of the contract as accountability *to* but not interference *from* is clearly in the tradition of Burke's great manifesto to his constituents in Bristol: '*Authoritative* instructions, *mandates* issued, which the member is bound blindly and implicitly to obey, to vote, and to argue for,

though contrary to the clearest conviction of his judgement and conscience –
these are things utterly unknown to the laws of this land' (Burke, 1774: 156).
Wisdom resides in Parliament. Beauty is *not* in the eye of the beholder. The
people do *not* know best.

Elected representatives are not bound, like ambassadors, to serve the
narrow interests of their constituents. Nor are they duty-bound to follow public
opinion (even if quantified and dignified through a referendum) where the
general good forces them down a different road: 'Not local purposes, not local
prejudices, ought to guide, but the general good, resulting from the general
reason of the whole' (ibid.). As in Rousseau's theory of the General Will, it is
Burke's injunction that popular control not be allowed to degenerate into
narrow selfishness. Contracted governance once in place, the voters must
grant their assemblymen the independence and the discretion they require in
order to be the servants of '*one* nation, with *one* interest, that of the whole'
(ibid.). The constituents select the officers. The delegates decide the issues. On
that crucial locus of opinion and authority, Schumpeter was in every sense a
Burkean lest the untutored masses foolishly tear the good democratic fabric to
shreds.

Democratic self-control on the part of the citizens must be complemented by
democratic self-control on the part of their representatives. Decent men and
women are led by their self-image not to abuse the fluid clauses of an underspecified employment contract. Scoundrels have no such compunctions about
doing what they themselves know to be wrong. Scoundrels 'discredit democracy and undermine allegiance to it' (Schumpeter, 1942: 294). Decent men and
women, on the other hand, are the walking guarantee that the voters' trust will
not be hijacked by 'the crook and the crank' (ibid.) who respect no aspirations
but their own.

The temptation is ever-present in politics to give in to bribery and corruption, to amass a personal fortune in numbered bank accounts, to seize short-
term gains at the expense of an unconsulted future. While some would seek the
antidote in careful auditing and a cast-iron constitution, investigative journal-
ism and a fault-spotting opposition, Schumpeter believes that the best-possi-
ble bulwark is to be found in internalised norms and beliefs. The democratic
system presupposes 'just the right amount – not too much, not too little – of
traditionalism' (ibid.: 294–5). A society that gets the proportions right has
nothing to fear from vote buying, vote rigging, sequestration of property,
imprisonment of judges or a spectacular *coup d'état* that seals in a monopolist's power.

The democratic system requires the checks and balances of a deep traditional rut. Debate is governed by parliamentary procedures and gentlemanly
etiquette. Members support their party and do not embarrass it. Free spirits are

not hounded nor school books rewritten to glamorise the incumbent. The reason is not so much external preventatives as it is the democratic ethos that dwells within the mind. Professional politicians are constrained by 'the wide adherence to the creed that exists throughout the community' (Dahl, 1961: 325). A few will break free. The majority will fit in.

Politicians in a liberal democracy are imbued with 'a large measure of tolerance for difference of opinion' (Schumpeter, 1942: 295). It is this tolerance which legitimates the freedom of speech and the multi-party panorama. Each competitor for office should have the chance to 'present his case without producing disorder' (ibid.). He in turn must listen respectfully to his opponents when his own ideals are under attack. A 'genuine respect for the opinions of one's fellow citizens' (ibid.) is an integral part of the self-control without which democracy must fail. As much as he was angered by left-wing intellectuals and self-appointed opinion-formers, it is interesting that Schumpeter never fell back on censorship, propaganda, terror and the one-party State. That way lies Stalinism. Schumpeter was a liberal democrat through and through.

4.5   THE CHARTER AS A CONSTITUTION

There must be an adequate supply of reliable politicians and self-denying bureaucrats. The political agenda must not be overextended or unmanageable. Above all, there must be general agreement on the charter and the purpose: 'Democracy cannot be expected to function satisfactorily unless the vast majority of the people in all classes are resolved to abide by the rules of the democratic game' (Schumpeter, 1942: 301). The preconditions for politics all hinge on the strength of 'Democratic Self-control'. Without a high degree of consensus on the decision-making framework, the hostile camps would surely fight.

Machinery alone is not enough. Central to the democratic system is the 'democratic creed', the 'democratic beliefs' (Dahl, 1961: 316) that give thinking citizens their *whys* and *wherefors*. The heart pumps blood without having to decide if the game is worth the candle. Thinking citizens, on the other hand, find it difficult to go through the motions without a workable image of their polity and of where they fit in: 'Democratic politics is a system of behaviour which cannot be defined apart from the intentions of the persons whose behaviour it is and the rules they consciously observe' (Plamenatz, 1973: 28). Deliberate and self-aware, people in a democracy have subjective predispositions that lead them to produce the sounds and the gestures that are required. This section, coming after Schumpeter on the charter and before Max Weber on *Verstehen*, shows that Schumpeter's fourth precondition situates him in a tradition of constitutional political economy which argues that it is values and not mechanisms that keep the system on course. Absent the attitudinal capital, even the most conducive architecture would not be enough to make the citizens appreciative of rituals which for them would have no meaning or function.

Democracy, Tocqueville says, is in the mind. Its strengths and weaknesses derive from 'the whole moral and intellectual condition of a people', its '*customs*' and '*mores*', its 'notions and political habits' (Tocqueville, 1835: I, 299; 1840: II, 310). Democratic institutions are subordinate to the manners of the people. They are the emanation of its cultural attitudes and the footprint of its 'practical experience' (Tocqueville, 1835: I, 322). Given the democratic outlook, the society will gravitate effortlessly into the democratic groove. Without the democratic compass, the ship will founder and sink.

Democracy presupposes, first and foremost, the general conviction that democracy itself is somehow right and good: 'The democratic process is unlikely to be preserved unless the people of a country preponderantly believe that it is desirable, and unless the belief comes to be embedded in the habits, practices, and culture of that people' (Dahl, 1985: 30). The people of a country must have an internalised commitment to the reconciliation of interest through the *demos* and the delegates that it appoints.

Lindsay traces the viability of the system to the respect for the constitutional order: 'The fundamental fact is the acceptance of the principles of parliamentary democracy' (Lindsay, 1943: 233). Schumpeter's politicians found a new party but do not funnel their factious dissent into a violent revolution. Schumpeter's bureaucrats act *pro bono publico* despite the specialist's discretion to conceal inconvenient permutations. Schumpeter's citizens freely donate their vote despite the low probability that one chad will ever swing an outcome. Value-driven even more than maximising, what these people are saying is that democracy to them seems somehow right and good. Their attachment to democracy forms part of the unwritten constitution. The commitment to the letter and the spirit of the rule-making rules ensures that both the governors and the governed will make a determined effort not to overstep the handed-on bounds.

Just as there must be the *demos*, so there must be the *nomos*. Schumpeter exaggerated the influence of rootless intellectuals. Far more politicians have been lawyers than poets. This is entirely to be expected. As well as an attachment to the system per se, democracy presupposes the internalised conviction that the good citizen is one who lives by the rules. A responsible democrat does not cross when the lights are red. A responsible democrat buys a television licence and road-taxes his car. Citizens in a democracy must be prepared to make normative codes their alarm clock and to put regular habits in the place of impetuous spontaneity. Socially disciplined and socially controlled, they inhibit their passions and do what the laws prescribe. *Nomos* for them is a part of a sanctioned way of life.

Irrespective of specific regulations, a law-abiding society must be in broad agreement on the constitutional procedures. There must be a general conviction that the social contract broadly defends the common interest and that the legislative compromise, given time, will offer most alliances a decent piece of cake. Yet the specific content of the twigs in the bundle is of relevance as well. Operational rules have to be broadly in line with commonly held ideals: 'The conduct they demand cannot go above the average moral standard of most members of the community. Rules are not rules if they are not kept' (ibid.: 93). A law that most citizens believe to be a trespass and an insult is next to impossible to enforce. A law that only codifies a pre-existent tradition is, however, a law that ratifies itself. Manipulation is evidently not without its limits.

Lindsay, attracted by the democracy of the 'General Will', sees the consensus as a dual one. First, as with Schumpeter, he believes that there must be unanimity of concord on the rule-making framework. Second, in contrast to Schumpeter, he feels that the laws themselves should only be your views and my views written down: 'The rules which can be enforced in any society depend largely on how far they represent what people are prepared to do. For the state's compulsion . . . can only help to make all men always do what most men are prepared usually to do' (ibid.: 92). Spencer makes the same point about the need for antecedent opinion to bear a family resemblance to the contours of the laws: 'When they are out of harmony with the national character, they are practically abrogated. The failure of Cromwell permanently to establish a new social condition . . . shows how powerless is a monarch to change the type of society he governs' (Spencer, 1860: 268). As soon as the Wall came down, the Russians quickly scuttled the Leninism. They returned to the Russianism that they knew and understood.

Schumpeter would agree that the content of the laws cannot be dramatically at variance with the median mind. He would probably regard it as a truism that there are some things that people simply will not wear. Rather than deriving legitimacy from the consensual component in the operational rules, he, however, prefers to focus his attention on the broad acceptability of the decision-making framework which grinds out the laws. The adherents of Schumpeter's first democracy are prepared to say that 'all the people' have a preference for welfare or to defend the progressive income tax with the phrase 'What greater pleasure can a millionaire have?' Schumpeter, inclined to his second democracy, states only that the laws produced by the system must be believed to be deserving of general respect.

The anomic contractarian proceeds *ab ovo* from the private interests of the unanchored particle. Conservatives and functionalists like Lindsay, Spencer and Schumpeter prefer to start mid-river in a continuing flow. The difference is the content. The similarity is the *nomos*. Rule following in the perspective of Lindsay, Spencer and Schumpeter is not so much a quid pro quo as an expression of identity. It is the personal affirmation of the historically-situated who refuse to be called independent or discrete when in truth it is only in their established community that they feel fully at home.

Equality of respect is a third value that is a hidden assumption in Schumpeter's 'Democratic Self-control'. No one calls for regular elections if he thinks that *rege divino non est disputandum*. If blue blood is enough, then one person, one vote is not required. If, on the other hand, citizens are imbued with the idea of equal rights and equal moral worth, then they will not be satisfied with the *ancien régime* of hereditary distinction. They will demand democracy. No order less inclusive will satisfy their non-rational stipulation that each citizen should be treated as the equivalent of any other.

Equality is a state of mind. That is its great strength but also its Achilles' heel. Lipset stresses that 'acceptance of the norms of democracy requires a high level of sophistication and ego security' (Lipset, 1960: 115). He is by no means convinced that all citizens will have the intellectual self-confidence to think that they have an opinion which ought to be listened to, to believe in their own intrinsic merit, to think that a lad from a log cabin has a moral right to go to the top. Legal rights are not enough where the submissive and the suggestible, suffering from low self-esteem, are convinced that blind obedience to the articulate and the thrusting is the most the nation can expect from the rightly eclipsed who failed everything but football at school.

Lipset infers from the evidence that perspective and assertiveness, compliance and deference, are closely correlated with the social structure. The professional and executive classes are more likely to vote, to join voluntary associations, to indulge in the rhetoric of citizenship rights. The manual and the poorly educated are more likely to put their faith in authority figures because the successful and the intelligent are more likely to know what to do. The lower income groups are less likely to generalise from observed recurrences or to challenge a person of superior status. They are more likely to have been brought up by parents who seldom asked *why* questions or explained punishments in the language of the rules. They are more likely to smoke since health horizons are abridged. They are less likely to save since deferred gratification is lah-de-dah. More authoritarian, less intrepid, the lower-paid and the less conspicuous will not always be able to convince themselves that they are the political equals of the natural frontrunners who were born to lead. Democracy tells them that they are. In their heart, however, they know that they are not.

The self-stigmatised are wrong, of course, to confuse Brideshead self-presentation and university book-speak with the non-judgmental humanity that is sensitive democracy's cause and effect. That they are wrong is, however, beside the point. What they *think* is where they *are*. Tawney accused the silent and the obsequious of contributing to their own disenfranchisement through their docile acceptance of the 'Mumbo Jumbo' that the Empire learned on the playing-fields of Eton: 'To kick over an idol, you must first get off your knees' (Tawney, 1934: 67). Schumpeter, like Tawney, saw that new entry into the political and the bureaucratic estate presupposed the perceived self-ness of aspiring meritocrats; while democratic validation would have no meaning if the masses simply refused to question the judgment of the *virtuosi* who knew best. Tawney wanted the State to intervene in order to cleanse society of corrosives such as independent schooling. Schumpeter preferred to leave it to economic growth to upgrade the sense of self. Where both were in full agreement, however, was that true democracy was impossible so long as the attitudinal muscles had not properly been built up. Democracy is a seminar and a debate: 'The key to democracy is the potency of discussion' (Lindsay, 1943: 281). Democracy cannot function so long as apathetic citizens feel that they have nothing to contribute to the exchange of ideas that makes politics into active production and not passive consumption that leaves it to others to see us through.

Legislators and office-holders must be subject to multi-period constraints that they cannot refashion to suit their own immediate convenience: 'The law ought to rule over all ... Then we can decide we have a constitution' (Aristotle, 1981: 251). There is no point in proclaiming that self-serving 'government by one's own law' (autonomy) has been transcended by fair-minded 'equality before the law' (isonomy) if the leadership retains unlimited discretion to rethink the rules of the game. The democratic system requires a constitutional code in order to ensure that no opportunistic cabal can resume the predatory confiscation of the lawless void.

Schumpeter was a constitutionalist who knew that 'malice is contagious' (Brennan and Buchanan, 1985: 61) and that an underspecified contract turns bullying Thanatos loose: 'Each person seeks mastery over a world of slaves' (Buchanan, 1975: 92). What distinguishes him from the majority of constitutionalists is his almost total lack of interest in dragon-worded checks and balances. Written rights can be abrogated. Clauses 'under God' can be statuted in and statuted out. Paper constitutions can be torn up. Memories and conventions are more difficult to expunge. Old habits are hard to break. Schumpeter believed that the unwritten constitution of conservative consensus was the real and insurmountable barrier against the 'polecats, or foxes' who always seek their solution in the man on horseback and the barrel of a gun.

Schumpeter held that democracy had to be a cultural value. It would not survive so long as its charter was not the property of all. It is the moral and not the written constitution that stays the hand of an ambitious majority when it is tempted to suppress future elections; that causes military leaders to disobey their president when he orders them to imprison the opposition and stage a *putsch*; that prevents self-respecting statesmen from censoring the press and making the schools into indoctrination centres. Absolute power corrupts absolutely. Indeed it does; and that is why Schumpeter appealed to social values to ensure that even intrigue and interest would force itself to abide by the rules.

In putting the charter first, Schumpeter was playing down the need for formal mechanisms that would protect the constituent from the abuses of 'might is right'. Montesquieu was more open to the need for safeguards such as the rigorous separation of the legislative, executive and judiciary branches: 'All would be lost if the same man or the same body of principal men, either of nobles, or of the people, exercise these three powers; that of making the laws, that of executing public resolutions, and that of judging the crimes or the disputes of individuals' (Montesquieu, 1748: 157). Montesquieu had studied the English constitution on the spot. Although it was unwritten, he felt that it was robust. The triangle of forces, the bicameral legislature, the royal assent itself, all seemed to him to be constitutional formalities that kept the hyper-active State within the limits of its remit.

Further safeguards can be encoded in access to office and steady rotation at the top. Aristotle says that the democratic right to vote brings with it the demo-cratic desire to stand for election: 'Whatever authority in the *state* is consti-tuted on a basis of equality and similarity between citizens, they expect to take turns in exercising it' (Aristotle, 1981: 188). Yet popularity can mean populism, demagoguery a tenure for life. In order to prevent megalomaniacs and sociopaths from making themselves into emperors and despots, Aristotle put forward two proposals: 'short terms for all offices' and 'the same man not to hold the same office twice' (ibid.: 363). The logic is solidly minimax: good rulers are to be pushed out lest bad rulers ride roughshod over the precedent. The appeal is nonetheless vintage Acton: good rulers will become bad rulers in time once they learn how heady is the drink that is brewed from *fiat*, *diktat* and a generous use of the sword.

The American Constitution, amended in response to Roosevelt's four wins, had to be changed to limit the number of presidential terms to two. Americans in addition enjoy the protection of a written Bill of Rights to enshrine their civil liberties and a Freedom of Information Act to expose selective miscalcu-lation. Devolution and decentralisation pluralise the scope for 'voice' (Hirschman, 1970). States' rights open the door to fiscal federalism as a citi-zen's verdict on local government (Tiebout, 1956). The Senate is made up of two representatives from each state in order to prevent California or Texas from outvoting all the rest. The president is directly elected by the people rather than being the leader of the ruling party in the legislature. A British prime minister who scores well in elections is better placed to fix his own agenda without the unsolicited advice of his Cabinet colleagues or his parliamentary back-bench: 'The House of Commons does not rule, it only elects the rulers' (Bagehot, 1867: 157). It is concealed authoritarianism, concentrated dominance. The American Constitution makes impossible such a merger of the executive with the legislative branch on the grounds that it is incompatible with the checks and balances of the democratic process.

Schumpeter does not discuss built-in barriers in forms such as those protected in the American Constitution. Nor does he discuss a range of other constitutional settlements that could defend Locke's 'life, liberty and estate' against the intolerable infringement of accountability and transparency. A qualified majority could be required where major issues such as the death penalty, abortion or euthanasia have to be decided. The written constitution could have a clause prescribing a money supply rule and proscribing an unbalanced budget. An upper house to check the jockeying and scheming of the Commons could be made up of traditional noblemen, or of eminent statesmen, or of experienced elders aged over 45, or of representatives from the universities, or of delegates from minority tribes. There are a variety of institutional arrangements that would impose a parental curfew on short-term enthusiasms. They are intended to ensure that equal voting rights do not mean the equal right to be pushed about by arrogant tyrants who say they know best.

Schumpeter's answer to all of these legalisms would be that there is nothing wrong with good laws but that the rules by themselves are not enough. Behind the rules there must be the commitment to the rules, the belief in the rules, the conviction that the democratic system is a good system that ought to be preserved. The real checks and balances are those not of the political constitution but of the social constitution that makes the political constitution possible. Schumpeter's emphasis on the charter and on 'Democratic Self-control' is a strong reminder of his belief that democracy as a political system is unworkable and impracticable so long as it is not situated in a lasting matrix of belief. The best liberals to Schumpeter were always cultural conservatives as well.

4.6   SCHUMPETER AND WEBER

Max Weber (1864–1920) was 20 years Schumpeter's senior. Trained under Knies as a historical economist before he became an economic and a political sociologist, the product of a generation that had debated determinism with Marx and culture with Adam Müller, he shared with Schumpeter an overriding interest in capitalism, class, power, mobility and State. Schumpeter, more

an economist, had more to say about monopoly, credit, consumption, investment and the periodicity of trade. Weber, more a sociologist, wrote more fully
about the origins of individualism, about Catholics, Protestants and Hindus as
profit-seeking entrepreneurs, about ascetic assiduity as a value-function in
itself. The emphasis was different. The similarities, on the other hand, were
striking.

Both Schumpeter and Weber were interdisciplinary social scientists, prone
to espouse *Verstehen* and methodological individualism but socially sensitive
enough to know that even a thinking fragment shares its paradigm with its
peers. Both used ideal types, formulated tendency-laws and acknowledged the
prevalence of unintended outcomes: Weber on the Calvinism that unleashed
the commercialism has its counterpart in Schumpeter on the socialism-struc-
tured corporation that ends free-market capitalism's stage-specific hegemony.
Both were conviction academics who kept their distance from the infighting
of the political parties: they criticised the *Kathedersozialisten* for putting
ideology and prejudice above value-free investigation. Both were cultural
conservatives, in touch with the continuity of habit, memory and custom: they
saw even rational bureaucracy as the time-warped creature of its lenses and its
pigeonholes. Both were reluctant democrats, aware that the Emperor and the
Kaiser were gone for good and that the sun was rising on the man-of-the-
people representation that each had seen for himself in no-nonsense America.
Both, crucially, were *political* economists. Each went out of his way to make
the preconditions for politics a central part of his far-reaching synthesis.

Weber returned frequently to the prerequisites for democracy. Of particular
importance are his essay on 'Politics as a Vocation' (1918) and the two
sections on 'Bureaucracy' and 'The Sociology of Charismatic Authority' in his
Economy and Society (1922). These late writings appeared at a time when the
young Schumpeter was still exploring subjects like methodology, innovation
and cycles. A decade and more later, adding human nature in politics to his
syllabus, the older Schumpeter is likely to have been glad that he had studied
Weber's *political* economy before he had had to think through the economics
of politics for himself.

In 'Politics as a Vocation', Weber defines leadership in terms of 'monopoly',
'legitimate use' and ' physical force': 'A state is a human community that
(successfully) claims the *monopoly of the legitimate use of physical force*
within a given territory' (Weber, 1918: 78). The State alone has that right. It
has that right in a democracy because it has confirmed its popularity through
free and fair elections held at regular intervals.

Weber, like Schumpeter, saw that power was an axiom. It is the elected and
not the rejected who get things done: 'He who is active in politics strives for
power either as a means in serving other aims, ideal or egoistic, or as "power

for power's sake", that is, in order to enjoy the prestige-feeling that power gives' (ibid.). The money-motivated want the portfolio because they want the kickbacks, the insecure because they want the standing, the psychopathic because they want the executions, the mission-minded because they have convinced themselves that their 'life has *meaning* in the service of a "cause" ' (ibid.: 84). Weber, like Schumpeter, makes no strong distinction between the absolutes and the instrumentalities that shelter together under the umbrella-name of office. *De gustibus non est disputandum.* The nub of the matter is simply that the end presupposes the means. A politician without office does not have the opportunities and the possibilities that an electoral win would confer.

Weber suggests three reasons why the masses might be willing to legitimate their chief. The first is tradition, 'the authority of the "eternal yesterday" ', the unthinking respect for blood and patriarchy, the sanctification of command 'through the unimaginably ancient recognition and habitual orientation to conform' (ibid.: 78, 79). The second is charisma, the leaderliness of a prophet, a visionary, an orator whose product image and personal magnetism are enough to attract to him converts and disciples eager to share his non-rational new revelation. The third is legal, instrumental, calculative, the cost–benefit persuasiveness that enlists followers because it is committed to impartial rules and dehumanised procedures trusted to deliver a reasonably acceptable state of affairs.

Of the three alternatives, only the third provides a plausible explanation of obedience and consent in the liberal democracy. Unquestioning loyalty to inherited position is in conflict with the principle that all deserve equal access subject to the demonstration of performance; while the person-specific following is a short-run impermanence, unlikely to outlast the great dislocator's capacity for origination. In the modern era, in the long run, only instrumental rationality is likely to appeal to the 'plebescitarian dictator' (ibid.: 107), the *demos*, who alone appoints the parliamentarians. Weber's *demos* knows that it is the problem solvers who spread the butter most thickly on the common people's bread.

The *demos* wants problem solving, but it is not certain what else it wants: 'One may call the existing state of affairs a "dictatorship resting on the exploitation of mass emotionality" ' (ibid.). As Schumpeter does, Weber treats the electorate as ill-informed and inconsistent, unable to grasp the complexities of the issues, competent at best to select the political trendsetters who will make up the people's mind: 'The *demos* itself, in the sense of an inarticulate mass, never "governs larger associations"; rather, it is governed' (Weber, 1922a: 225). Legitimation does not imply participation and accountability does not mean consultation. The governed have equal rights on paper. The votes once counted, however, it is the winning candidates who legitimately dominate and rightly control.

The politicians rule. Not, however, all of them equally: 'Nowadays the members of Parliament, with the exception of the few cabinet members (and a few insurgents), are normally nothing better than well-disciplined "yes" men' (Weber, 1918: 106). Even their speeches are 'thoroughly censored' (ibid.: 112) by the new-style guilds called parties and the 'respective party leaders of the *demos*' (Weber, 1922a: 226) who have taken over the labour of policy-making from the voter and the backbencher alike. The net result is that power is concentrated in the hands of the few and that the prime minister is de facto a dictator for the duration of the mandate: 'The efficiency of "Caesarism", which often grows out of democracy, rests in general upon the position of the "Caesar" as a free trustee of the masses' (ibid.: 202). It is Paretian intrigue and not Marxian class that accounts for the profit and loss. In the end it is Nietzsche's Superman who comes out on top.

In *Economy and Society*, Weber turned from the elected leaders to their appointed staffs. Bureaucracy is rational, precise and impersonal. Bureaucracy filters documents through unambiguous precedents and stores new minutes in established files. Bureaucracy practises functional specialisation in order to focus the expertise on a narrow brief, rule-defined. Officials achieve status through qualifications and productivity. Seniority is used as a proxy for on-the-job learning. Positions, accessible in principle to all, are not inherited and not dependent on ownership. The officer normally holds his tenure for life. His disciplined attitude is an indicator of his professional ethic and his belief that his career is a calling.

Bureaucracy has a *wertrational* as well as a *zweckrational* dimension. The done thing dignifies pattern-maintenance into an old friend who no longer needs to cry his wares. Bureaucracy is internalised expectations and *sine ira ac studio*: ethics made a fence against scorn and bias, the functionary on autopilot has no option but to act out his 'trained orientation of obedient compliance to the rules' (ibid.: 229). All of this adds up to efficiency: 'The decisive reason for the advance of bureaucratic organization has always been its purely technical superiority over any other form of organization' (ibid.: 214). Bureaucracy maximises the throughput. Bureaucracy minimises the downtime and the waste.

Weber in 1922, like Schumpeter in his *Capitalism*, was emphasising the extent to which efficient structure can keep the unit costs down: 'The fully developed bureaucratic mechanism compares with other organizations exactly as does the machine with the non-mechanical modes of production' (ibid.). Large private corporations, 'unequalled models of strict bureaucratic organization' (ibid.: 215), are able to reap their production-line economies precisely because their brain is their internal hierarchy, tried-and-tested and true: 'More and more the material fate of the masses depends upon the steady and correct

functioning of the increasingly bureaucratic organizations of private capitalism' (ibid.: 229). Bureaucracy is not another name for the lethargy, arrogance
and indolence of socialist statism to which market privatisation is said by the
Smithian de-organisationalists to be the bracing cold alternative. Instead it is
the steel frame around which big business is built when it does its best for
Moneybags and his coupon clippers.

Socialist or capitalist, the sturdy steel is the same: 'It does not matter for the
character of bureaucracy whether its authority is called "private" or "public" '
(ibid.: 197). The older Schumpeter predicted that planned statism was all but
inevitable. Sharing with Weber the confidence that the bureaucracy will be
structurally undisturbed, he was prepared to say that the economy will remain
safe in its hands: 'The kind of responsibility that exists in the large-scale
corporation could no doubt be reproduced in a socialist society' (Schumpeter,
1942: 206). Neither Weber nor Schumpeter had any liking for socialised
control. Nor, however, did either think that it would necessarily mean slippage,
confusion and the stationary state. The reason was that reliable bureaucracy
was here to stay: 'It is an inevitable complement to modern economic development . . . It will be more than ever essential in a socialist commonwealth'
(ibid.).

The older Schumpeter felt that the Smithian competitor had no intrinsic
superiority over the man on a salary who knew what to do: 'Socialist management may conceivably prove as superior to big-business capitalism as big-
business capitalism has proved to be to the kind of competitive capitalism of
which the English industry of a hundred years ago was the prototype' (ibid.:
196). The young Schumpeter had been less willing to follow Weber in treating
the top executive as 'just another office worker – and one who is not always
difficult to replace' (ibid.: 133): 'The means of production are replaceable, but
not the leader' (Schumpeter, 1912b: 143). The Schumpeter of 1912 was
imbued with Nietzsche's Dionysian values: he was searching for 'genius of the
first order' (Schumpeter, 1942: 402n) since determined non-conformity alone
would have the strength to pull the sword from the stone. The Schumpeter of
1942 was more in sympathy with Nietzsche's Appolonian mindset. Not
ecstasy but order was needed to ensure the cost-effective administration of a
going concern.

A shift in emphasis is not a repudiation or a switch. Schumpeter even in his
later years could find Dionysian elements in the corporation that is run by its
staff: ' "Giant" concerns . . . often are but shells within which an ever-changing personnel may go from innovation to innovation' (Schumpeter, 1939: I,
96). Schumpeter never said that with the growth of bureaucracy the spark of
creative destruction would inevitably go out. For all that, an irreversible shift
was taking its course. There was no doubt in Schumpeter's mind that the
enchantment of surprise and the thrill of novelty would be subject to severe

practical impediments in the Weberian new world of the organisational chart. Schumpeter in his later years saw rationality wherever he looked – not just in capitalism and democracy but even in the modern lounge suit (Schumpeter, 1942: 126). It was a development that made him feel very sad about the greyness all around: 'I share the rejection of my own times of the rationalisation of life and thought' (Schumpeter, 1932: 602).

Schumpeter felt sad that 'repulsive rationality' (ibid.) was marginalising the spontaneous impulse, that the organisational speck was leaving no room for the Strutts and the Fords. Max Weber expressed a similar pessimism about the 'specialists without spirit, sensualists without heart' who were inexorably making what used to be an adventure of discovery into the 'nullity' (Weber, 1904–5: 182) of a flat and boring plain. That 'nullity', Weber reflected stoically, was at once the prize and the price of progress. On the one hand impartial calculations and unbending frames of reference empower the large organisation to respond swiftly in an age when modern means of communication make essential the quick adaptation: 'The optimum of such reaction time is normally attained only by a strictly bureaucratic organization' (Weber, 1922a: 215). On the other hand it is in the nature of the non-arbitrary and the drilled that it has no way of incorporating the entrepreneurial free spirit who finds no home in the methodical and the repetitive: 'In general, charisma rejects all rational economic conduct' (Weber, 1922b: 247). The iconoclast is a magician. The bureaucrat is a foot-soldier. The future is a flat and boring plain because that is what organisational tidiness is all about.

Democracy itself is losing its bite. Weber noted that democracy means the equal rights of the governed but that the new despotism tends to build high the wall: 'Democracy inevitably comes into conflict with the bureaucratic tendencies which, by its fight against notable rule, democracy has produced' (Weber, 1922a: 226). If the party bosses do not neutralise discretionary whims, there is every chance that the administrators will grind the will of the people into insipid cost-effectiveness. Public opinion has no box at all in the well constructed organisational chart.

5. Schumpeter: States and systems

Schumpeter anticipated that capitalism would give way to socialism once bureaucratic corporations had crowded out the independent entrepreneur. What he refused to say was that political democracy would simultaneously be eclipsed by the office holders and the commands. The three sections of this chapter explore the status of the vote motive when economic systems evolve.

Section 5.1, 'Capitalism and democracy', situates the politician, the agenda, the bureaucrat and the charter in the context of the decentralised order. Section 5.2, 'Socialism and democracy', traces the same four preconditions through the centrally planned economy where most of the big decisions are made at the top. Section 5.3, 'Democracy and welfare', asks if the social-services State was seen by Schumpeter as a credible halfway-house between the two polar systems.

Schumpeter believed that democratic procedures were system-neutral. Democracy, he said, is a function of its own inner logic and not, capitalist or socialist, of economic ownership and coordination. This chapter assesses his contention that neither production nor leadership is nowadays the powerful locomotive, neither market nor State the passive carriage that is drawn forward from without.

5.1   CAPITALISM AND DEMOCRACY

Democracy, historically speaking, has had a close and dependent association with exchange: 'Historically, the modern democracy rose along with capitalism, and in causal connection with it' (Schumpeter, 1942: 296). The push and the power went from economic basis to political superstructure: 'Modern democracy is a product of the capitalist process' (ibid.: 297). Friedman on the right, like Marx on the left, would be in no doubt that Schumpeter had got the rankings right: 'I know of no example in time or place of a society that has been marked by a large measure of political freedom, and that has not also used something comparable to a free market to organize the bulk of economic activity ... History suggests ... that capitalism is a necessary condition for political freedom' (Friedman, 1962: 9, 10). Freedom of speech presupposes competing newspapers and radio stations. Freedom of assembly presupposes multiple landlords willing to rent out meeting rooms. All things considered, if there had been no liberalism in the eighteenth century, there would have been no liberal democracy later on.

Economy made democracy an achievable aspiration. Democracy, created, more than repaid its debt: 'Democracy in the sense of our theory of competitive leadership presided over the process of political and institutional change by which the bourgeoisie reshaped . . . the social and political structure that preceded its ascendancy' (Schumpeter, 1942: 297). The bourgeois order produced institutions even as it produced goods and services: 'The democratic method was the political tool of that reconstruction' (ibid.). The bourgeois order employed political democracy to make it possible for the capitalist economy to stand out above the feudalism that went before and the socialism that no one thought would ever come.

Schumpeter deliberately limits his theory of democracy to 'the great industrial nations of the modern type' (ibid.: 290). Like T.H. Marshall, he is writing history and not guessing at hypothetical might-have-beens. Yet he also tries to anticipate the future; and he knows that there at least he is on his own.

Early capitalism was the small firm run by its independent owner–entrepreneur. Later capitalism is the large corporation staffed by its salaried bureaucrats. An obvious question must be whether later capitalism is able to nurture the democratic mechanism that early capitalism had called into being. The organisation expects obedience. Concentration narrows the choices. Specialised education mutilates the mind. Democracy if it is to be rational choice must be something more than a duopoly of personality packages competing through product image because the issues are too tough. While later democracy might still favour the bourgeois interest, the real question is how far the later political market is really Schumpeter's second *democracy* at all.

Evolution does not stop at the corporation. Schumpeter looks beyond capitalism to socialism. He does not think that the change in the mode of production need bring about a change in the State. Rationed foreign exchange limits personal exposure to alternative institutions abroad. A single employer means that dissidents will find it hard to find jobs. Publications and broadcasts screen out information that would threaten the Plan. Above all else, there is contentment. People do not hunger for opposition parties so long as the trains run on time. Schumpeter does not consider the danger that his socialist economics might be all but completely incompatible with his democratic liberalism. It is a curious position for an evolutionary economist to adopt. Modern democracy is a product of the capitalist process. Once in place, however, it has a good chance of surviving even when its historic hinterland has become something else. Like the fourteenth earl, it is an anachronism that still has a function to fulfil.

Democracy under socialism is a product that can be bought or left behind.

Attlee in the morning, Hitler at night – rejecting Hayek's road to serfdom because voting still leaves the common man in control, Schumpeter's confidence in the triumph of choice even at late capitalism's last gasp recalls nothing so much as Tawney on the ability of reliable old Henry Dubb to separate the faithful from the shady when he selects the representatives whom he wants to run his State: 'Fools will use it, when they can, for foolish ends, criminals for criminal ends. Sensible and decent men will use it for ends which are sensible and decent . . . Why, in heaven's name, should we be afraid of it?' (Tawney, 1949: 172).

Friedman, pointing to capitalism without democracy under the Tsar and under Franco, stresses that capitalism is the necessary but not the sufficient condition. Tawney and Schumpeter, reversing the order, say that democracy may still survive even after the historic capitalist conditions are no more. Friedman would reply simply that 'such a view is a delusion': 'There is an intimate connection between economics and politics . . . A society which is socialist cannot also be democratic' (Friedman, 1962: 8).

5.1.1   The Politician

The first condition stipulates that there must be a reasonable pool of politicians 'of sufficiently high quality' (Schumpeter, 1942: 290). The problem is that the bourgeoisie is far too busy with business to have the time or the interest to rule. In early capitalism the bourgeois is an adventurer who is driven by his competitors to live full-time for the family firm. In later capitalism the bourgeois is an executive who knows that earned wealth and status presuppose a single-minded commitment to the job. Small business or big business, Schumpeter concluded, the bourgeoisie is an eternal abstention that sends its apologies to the agora and never stands for the House.

The industrial and commercial estate can field an exceptional outlier. What it cannot do is to assemble an entire team, self-renewing and intergenerational: 'The bourgeoisie produced individuals who made a success at political leadership . . . but it did not produce a successful political stratum of its own' (ibid.: 298). The hegemons of today have left their contemporaries in the lurch. The landed aristocracy, fortunately, still has enough of its knightly chivalry to be able to plug patrician Wykhamists into what otherwise would be a political void. Atavism and vestigialism have produced a governing class imbued with 'traditions that embody experience, with a professional code and with a common fund of views' (ibid.: 291). The middle classes have produced bolts of calico and double-entered their invoices. It is a miracle, using Schumpeter's logic, that the Corn Laws were ever abolished or the Opium Wars ever fought. Where were Cobden and Bright when the fourteenth earl was sending in his gunboat to make sure that the trade routes remained free?

The landed aristocracy is a ruler without a rival. The bourgeoisie builds its identity around private gain. That is why it prefers the jam and the jute to the nebulous conglomerate of the State. Intellectuals and idealists, alienated and frustrated, preach division and exploitation. They would like the masses to catapult them into power but they are too selfish to render disinterested service for the common good. The proletariat is too passionate, too ignorant, too malleable to moderate the extremes of its untutored first impressions. Working men do not have the code and coal-face representatives cannot follow the debates. Seats in Parliament, it would appear, are not easy to fill. Only the date-stamped aristocracy can keep the ship of State afloat. Ex regiment and ex public school, it is the Pall Mall clubs and the hunts with dogs that stand between the capitalist democracy and the *bellum* that is brutish and short.

Yet the indispensable social resources, like Britain's irreplaceable fossil fuels, are inexorably being exhausted. The economy is growing – and it is growing middle class. Even the lord of the manor is discouraging his second son from Classics in favour of accountancy with a pension at Shell. Politics will have to move with the times. Schumpeter said repeatedly that the institutions that sustain market capitalism are also the institutions most susceptible to the corrosives of the new: 'The capitalist order not only rests on props made of extra-capitalist material but also derives its energy from extra-capitalist patterns of behavior which at the same time it is bound to destroy.' (ibid.: 162). The protective strata once used up, it must be a matter of doubt if political democracy thereafter can function very well.

Good leadership is an unintended outcome. Vestigial organs alone can keep the body politick alive. It is an unusual approach to rational choice in the liberal democracy. Bismarck and Lord Salisbury would no doubt applaud the ranking of the silver spoon above the sterling qualities. A common bourgeois like Margaret Thatcher or Tony Blair would on the other hand maintain that Schumpeter's politicians are frozen in the transitional mould of the early capitalist mix. When modern democracy was still in its pram, the lords, arguably, had to make up for the vacuum in command. That, however, was a long time ago. It is the view of the democratic liberal that politics today has matured into a professional specialisation for which the blue blood of the country gentleman is simply no longer enough.

The liberals have reservations about the cultural conservatism. The Marxists are even more sceptical about the capitalist's default. Schumpeter said that the business class was a buying-and-selling class, politically indifferent and politically uninvolved: 'The attitudes of capitalist groups toward the polity of their nations are predominantly adaptive rather than causative, today more than ever' (ibid.: 55). Marx and Engels, profoundly unconvinced that the money-seeking businessman never looks beyond his ledger, argued precisely the opposite: 'The executive of the modern state is but a committee for managing the common affairs of the whole bourgeoisie' (Marx and Engels, 1848: 82).

Marx and Engels wrote that 'political power, properly so called, is merely the organized power of one class for oppressing another' (ibid.: 105). They saw the post-feudal State as a stage-specific mode of repressive tolerance and tension management. Believing as they did that modern democracy is merely the cause and effect of machine-owners making money out of legitimated theft, they would have dismissed with contempt Schumpeter's untested hypothesis that elected delegates will so often 'fail to serve the interest of their class' (Schumpeter, 1942: 285). Marxists will say that they can make no sense of Schumpeter's expectation that a money-seeking class will deliberately neuter itself into the Hegelian totality. Even a sympathetic non-Marxist like Warren Samuels has expressed the view that Schumpeter was politically naïve in assuming away the special power of strategically placed *economic* advantage: 'Schumpeter may have failed consistently to recognize or make explicit deeply and thoroughly enough that in capitalist society dominance is institutionalized by capitalist control of government' (Samuels, 1985: 71).

Samuels goes back to Locke and Smith for his logic: 'Private property is what it is, in most if not all particulars, because the state protects certain interests as property and not others' (ibid.: 73). Samuels seeks the locus of parliament and statute in the societal hierarchy and in the economic forces which shock it into flux. Political economists do wrong, Samuels says, to speak of intervention per se when the truth goes beyond the Pigovian *what* to bring in the causative *by whom* and *for whom* as well. In feudal times it was the landed interest that was rewarded with the primogeniture and the entailing. In the age of the entrepreneur and the company it is the claims of manufacturing, trade and finance that are the best protected. Samuels is critical of Schumpeter for neglecting the partiality of the laws, and for underestimating the political power of a dominant sub-set that was disproportionately dictating to the whole.

Samuels sought to uncover the dominant sub-set. So, in *The Power Elite*, did C. Wright Mills. Referring specifically to the United States, where Schumpeter wrote his *Capitalism*, Mills contended that the oligarchy was able to 'occupy the command posts' (Mills, 1956: 23) quite specifically because power grows out of the Manhattan freeholds, a monopoly pipeline and the vault cash of a bank: 'The phrase "ruling class" thus contains the theory that an economic class rules politically' (ibid.: 277n). Competition between coalitions, each speaking for a single cause, each determined to 'impose the dictates of its class interest upon the management of the political affairs of the community', indicated clearly to a Marxist like Mills that, in Schumpeter's vivid paraphrase, 'mere political democracy is of necessity a sham' (Schumpeter, 1942: 235).

Mills said that some institutions make history jump and that other institutions get swept along by the tide. He was in no doubt that it was the triangle of Congressmen, guns and butter that in present-day conditions was ticking all the ballots Treasure: 'Families and churches and schools adapt to modern life; governments and armies and corporations shape it' (Mills, 1956: 6). Pareto had shown that lions are dependent on foxes for public finance, that the business interest gets defence and contracts in return. Weber had warned that party donors were investing their campaign contributions because they were expecting tariffs and progress payments in exchange: 'Frequently a crypto-plutocratic distribution of power has been the result' (Weber, 1922a: 230). Mills, convinced that one hand washes the other and that both hands launder the cash, shared the fears of Pareto and Weber. Interlocking elites have a stranglehold. Fat bank-accounts are shutting the *vox populi* out.

Schumpeter shows little interest in the Establishment linkages that make known faces of finance, church, small entrepreneurs, giant corporations and the military brass. There are no networks of high-return contacts mushrooming out from school, university, first job, second job, marriage, cronyism, nepotism or patronage. There is no Theresianum in his sociology and no Harvard University. What there is in Schumpeter's economics of politics is the individual, the vote motive and the ruling-class aristocracy that makes the capitalist democracy tick.

For a scholar who liked to trace out the systemic and the far-reaching, Schumpeter's account of voter-pleasing cut off from labour and capital is surprisingly one-dimensional. Yet Schumpeter's political economy is not always what it seems. Just as it is possible to show that the neutral statesman in the sense of Schumpeter is not the class-blinkered twister in the sense of Marx, so it is possible to show that Samuels and perhaps even C. Wright Mills can be superimposed upon Schumpeter's political supermarket and his neo-'Austrian' decomposition. No one since Alfred Marshall has concealed more in his *obiter dicta* than he revealed in his core.

Thus Schumpeter in one place complains that economic power talks louder than votes: 'There cannot be democracy so long as that power exists' (Schumpeter, 1942: 235). The rich seem able to buy better policies than the poor. Although Schumpeter does not spell out the mechanism, bribes and favours, media manipulation and the manufactured will are likely to have been on his list. The press baron demands hefty subsidies for the aircraft majors in which he has invested through his bank and attacks the single parents because they are scrounging off the State. The multinational conglomerate threatens to relocate abroad if the blackmailer's ultimatum is not answered through a tax holiday, a grant or a Draconian prohibition that shuts the unions up. The working stiff on minimum wage has less clout when it comes to restrictive practices or the growing inequality of wealth. If Schumpeter had written more fully about the power imbalance that shadowed the income distribution, he might have recommended solutions like public funding for political parties or gratuitous access to television time. As it is, all he did was to dig up a *dictum* only to bury it again as an *obiter*. Then he said that capitalist politicians do not speak for the capitalist class.

Ideology reinforces the dominance of the hegemon. A world-view is a powerful weapon in the struggle for legitimacy. Schumpeter defines the 'capitalist order' as 'a scheme of values, an attitude toward life, a civilization' (Schumpeter, 1950b: 425). It is an intellectual perspective that makes the capitalist economy function with tolerable efficiency. Internalised and absorbed, the 'order' makes acquisitive individualism and the drive to succeed an intrinsic part of the self. Matter in motion will see to that: 'The capitalist process . . . reshapes not only our methods of attaining our ends but also these ultimate ends themselves' (Schumpeter, 1942: 127). The class that pays the piper is the class that moulds the mindset. Totalitarians use education and indoctrination. Democrats rely upon self-validating economics. Either way, the election will be a walkover. Even a second-rate benchwarmer can get in so long as he parrots the values that his constituents have been conditioned to respect as the norm.

Hell hath no conviction like a median ethos ensconced. That may be an important reason why Schumpeter has little or nothing to say about working-class consciousness and working-class aspirations. There will be neither conflict nor frustration in an open society where each individual carries about in his head the same mental picture of an unobstructed road. The ideological contribution made by the expectation of ebb and flow cannot be underestimated. Unemployment, low wages, strike ballots or easy dismissals do not make the capitalist democracy into a battlefield of solidarities. The reason is simple. Cloth cap believes that he has a fair chance to join the bosses if he is good.

Influence bought in through opulence is an *obiter dictum*. The middle-class mind is an *obiter dictum*. The resulting inference, that the bourgeois class has developed into 'the leading class' (ibid.: 126), is an *obiter dictum* as well. Schumpeter refers to the power of 'the upper strata of capitalist society' (ibid.: 134). In his late *Capitalism* he stated that the sword was already unsheathed: 'The capitalist order entrusts the long-run interests of the society to the upper strata of the bourgeoisie' (ibid.: 160). In his early *Development* he asserted that the victorious entrepreneur had become a 'political and a social power', an economic luminary whose 'voice makes itself heard in politics': 'His economic success, as with success in general, ensures his influence on other areas of life' (Schumpeter, 1912a: 526). If his voice is already being heard, there is no point in pretending that it is not. Politics under capitalism might already mean the fat cats from the Exchange. It might not mean the fourteenth earl after all.

All the ingredients are there. Yet there is no stew. The Schumpeter of the *obiter dicta* could easily have become the Pareto of the *Manuale* who saw hard cash in every right and every exemption: 'There is no record anywhere of the existence of a situation, over any appreciable length of time, in which the government remains neutral and gives no help either to the upper classes' spoliation of the poor or to the poorer classes' spoliation of the rich.' (Pareto, 1966: 163). Instead of that he set his *obiter dicta* to one side and played down the causal impact of economic power upon law. The reason is possibly this. Schumpeter lacked both a compass and a watch. Schumpeter was never certain where he was or when.

Schumpeter was a conservative European living in open-society America. He admired the pre-War aristocracy but he knew that it was past its peak. He was in favour of active competition but he predicted the concentration of capital. Most of all, he conflated the bourgeoisie and the entrepreneuriat as if Arkwright and Watt still walked the earth. It was a choice which allowed him to predict that the money makers would be too preoccupied with buying and selling to waste time on elected office.

Schumpeter in *Capitalism* says that, 'economically and sociologically, directly and indirectly, the bourgeoisie . . . depends on the entrepreneur and, as a class, lives and will die with him' (Schumpeter, 1942: 134). The whole is pyramided upon the part. The part, however, has no class consensus and no strong perception of a journey shared: 'Because being an entrepreneur is not a profession and as a rule not a lasting condition, entrepreneurs do not form a social class' (Schumpeter, 1912b: 78). Aristocrats with stately homes have handed-on memories of the thirteenth earl and role-specific expectations for his line. Entrepreneurs who live out of suitcases, looking only for a room for the night, need neither friends nor allies who might steal their big idea. The bourgeoisie, it would appear, takes after the innovators and not the ermine. Evanescent, changing, moving in, moving on, the trees of the forest do not last long enough to learn that the isolates in truth live out a common fate. Perceived continuity would have the opposite effect. Class-bound politics would then become more attractive in order to secure good rules for a socially stratified game.

If the lifestyle was Schumpeter's reason, then 'the perfectly bureaucratized giant industrial unit' (Schumpeter, 1942: 134) was evolution's antidote. Schumpeter explicitly denies that the capitalist class will long survive once the owner–operator has been pushed into the history books by the modern corporation: 'In the end it also ousts the entrepreneur and expropriates the bourgeoisie as a class' (ibid.). The talk is of radical elimination. The reality, however, is a simple change of state. Industrial capitalists do not disappear into hard hat and sweat. Instead they retain a distinctive identity as corporate executives and capital-owning shareholders with a stake in profits and dividends. Captains of industry, captains of captains of industry, they are not evanescent but here to stay. Performance to them means not 'the common good' but 'making and losing money' (ibid.: 73). They expect the politicians to keep under constant review the needs and wants of the capitalist class.

5.1.2 The Agenda

The second precondition specifies that the political agenda should remain within manageable links. Crowded in-trays mean overload and inefficiency. Excessive demands paralyse the machinery of State.

Early capitalism expects only the magistrate and the constable. The small-business bourgeoisie is a free-market flux, a set of self-selected maximisers 'whose interests are best served by being left alone' (Schumpeter, 1942: 297). Self-reliant and parsimonious, the nascent bourgeoisie rapidly decided that it needed no more than law and order, freedom of trade, essential infrastructure, the minimal State to get on with getting rich. Wanting not help but freedom *from*, it wanted the State to be no more than a climbing frame that facilitated private advance.

In present-day capitalism the bourgeoisie is more demanding. The laissez-faire State has 'ceased to appeal to us' (ibid.). Its standards are 'no longer ours' (ibid.). What modern business wants is not just to be tolerated but to be supported. In microeconomics the business community treats hand-outs and exclusions as a citizenship right. In macroeconomics it looks to discretionary intervention to even out the cycle. Coincident with the transition to corporate capitalism there has been a swing towards the tinkering State. Action has become the norm. The agenda is no longer as manageable as it was.

At least a military–industrial complex is not to be expected: 'The industrial and commercial bourgeoisie is fundamentally pacifist' (ibid.: 128). Capitalism to Schumpeter was rationality and exchange, not militarism and imperialism. Business is business. Fighting is a waste: 'The more completely capitalist the structure and attitude of a nation, the more pacifist – and the more prone to count the costs of war – we observe it to be' (ibid.: 128–9).

The visceral aggressiveness, the latent viciousness, that culminated in German nationalism and the First World War cannot, clearly, be blamed on the moneyed classes who in classical Marxism are believed to be ruling the roost: 'Very little influence on foreign policy has been exerted by big business' (ibid.: 55). Casual references to 'war profits' and 'advantages to trade accruing from conquest' (ibid.: 128), weakening his generalisations, suggest resemblances to Galbraith and not just to Herbert Spencer. They are the exception and not the rule. Schumpeter tended to explain zero-sum conflicts not in terms of current imperatives but in terms of post-feudal anachronisms for whom 'life and vocation are fully realized *only* in war' (Schumpeter, 1918/19: 158). Jingoism is outdated. Capitalism is compromise: 'The bourgeois is unwarlike' (ibid.: 212). It is not clear where this leaves the fourteenth earl for whom the old habits were the major selling-point.

5.1.3 The Bureaucracy

The third precondition is a reliable bureaucracy, well-trained and dutiful. Schumpeter takes it for granted that capitalism can produce the skilled administrators that it requires. Economic growth itself generates a national dividend that can pay for education. The example of the state-of-the-art corporation demonstrates that a salaried hierarchy can be at the cutting edge of progress. There is every reason to think that the civil service will be every bit as effective in trying out new things while ensuring that old things work well.

Intrinsic motivation is more of a question mark. Whereas Schumpeter's entrepreneur is thrusting and advantage-maximising, Schumpeter's organisational cog is the uncomplaining Tommy who only does what he is told. Extracommercial self-denial is the rock upon which the modern civil service is built. Schumpeter often appealed to pre-capitalist survivals such as custom, loyalty, discipline and conscience to countervail the remorseless egotism of the age of interest. His civil service is able to hack its way through the I–me of the present since it is well padded with the ethos of the past. That is just the problem. Intellectual rootedness does not last forever. The market mentality is notoriously unkind.

5.1.4 The Charter

The fourth precondition is that subjects are broadly in sympathy with the rules and with the rule-making procedures: 'This in turn implies that they are substantially agreed on the fundamentals of their institutional structure' (Schumpeter, 1942: 301). Capitalism presupposes a threshold minimum of normative convergence. Notorious and unkind, however, it might not be entirely successful in protecting the acceptance upon which its future depends.

Early capitalism was able to ensure the requisite concord. Later capitalism is better endowed in its branches than in its trunk. In later capitalism, the fourth precondition for democracy often 'fails to be fulfilled': 'So many people have renounced, and so many more are going to renounce, allegiance to the standards of capitalist society that on this ground alone democracy is bound to work with increasing friction' (ibid.). Creative destruction and cycles mean that capitalist times are 'troubled times' (ibid.: 296). The corporate revolution proves that bureaucracy can speed up the process of change. Freedom of speech allows divisive intellectuals to puff the merits of their post-capitalist cause. One way or another, it all adds up to dissatisfaction and a challenge to the rules.

Capitalism, Schumpeter said, was beset by an internal contradiction. On the one hand it had shown itself to be a radical source of cultural change and technological betterment: 'All the features and achievements of modern civilization are, directly or indirectly, the products of the capitalist process' (ibid.: 125). On the other hand it was an ungrateful order that rooted out the lagged adaptation which had made possible the renewal: its 'very success undermines the social institutions which protect it, and "inevitably" creates conditions in which it will not be able to live' (ibid.: 61). Dislocation comes in. Legitimacy goes out. The threat to later capitalism's past-protected institutions is at once a threat to political democracy's important fourth precondition.

5.1.5 Schumpeter and Fukuyama

Schumpeter, like Marx, anticipated an evolution into socialism. Francis Fukuyama, writing just after the collapse of the old Soviet Union, saw the law of development as pointing to quite a different destination: 'The twin crises of authoritarianism and socialist central planning have left only one competitor standing in the ring as an ideology of potential universal validity: liberal democracy, the doctrine of individual freedom and popular sovereignty' (Fukuyama, 1992: 42). Fukuyama, like Schumpeter, was looking for a 'fundamental process', a 'Universal History of mankind', a 'common evolutionary pattern for *all* human societies' (ibid.: 48). He, however, found Hegel's 'final form of human government' (ibid.: 3) not in Schumpeter's State plan but in the Western liberal order. The descendants of Smith and Locke had unified 'the productivity of market-oriented economics' with 'the freedom of democratic politics' (ibid.: 31). Their synthesis would stand the test of time. It would put an end to history's search.

Market capitalism and citizenship accountability – liberty and equality – are the twin pillars of the historicist's final stage. Both are the products of the human need for self-worth, self-determination, personal dignity and social esteem that has a high income elasticity once *homo sapiens* has satisfied his threshold bodily wants: 'As standards of living increase, as populations become more cosmopolitan and better educated, and as society as a whole achieves a greater equality of condition, people begin to demand not simply more wealth but recognition of their status . . . This leads them to demand democratic governments that treat them like adults rather than children' (ibid.: xviii, xix).

Fukuyama is not denying that coordination through competition gives ordinary consumers a larger pool of goods and services than would a rigid and directive central plan. There he parts company with Schumpeter, who said that ministry and bureaucracy would prove the more efficient, the more rational choice. What he is doing, amplifying the economics with psychology, is to contend that the animal appetites will at some point cede their pride of place to the drives that Maslow calls the 'highest aspirations' – 'growth, self-actualization, the striving toward health, the quest for identity and autonomy, the yearning for excellence' (Maslow, 1954: xii–xiii). Human beings, Fukuyama believes, have a fundamental need to speak, to be listened to, to be accepted. Both market and democracy provide a channel for the dammed-up sense of self. Taken together, the end of history is also the guarantor of tolerance, pluralism and self-validating freedom *to*.

Fukuyama is unwilling to cut corners on the economic market: it satisfies both the material and the moral aspirations. He is, however, unconvinced that civil liberties, freedom of speech, the protection of minorities and the active involvement of citizens in their own political order will deliver the same double benefit: 'There is . . . no *economic* rationale for democracy: if anything, democratic politics is a drag on economic efficiency' (Fukuyama, 1992: 205). Political democracy is chosen because of a felt need for acknowledgment and participation. It is not chosen for the sake of the higher standard of living that it might or might not be able to produce.

Fukuyama invokes the vision of 'Lee Kwan Yew of Singapore, who has argued that democracy would be an obstacle to Singapore's spectacular economic success' (ibid.: 134). He does so to show that accelerating prosperity, at least in East Asia, might actually be better served by 'paternalistic authoritarianism' than it would by active consultation: 'If a country's goal is economic growth above all other considerations, the truly winning combination would appear to be neither liberal democracy nor socialism of either a Leninist or democratic variety, but the combination of liberal economics and authoritarian politics that some observers have labelled the "bureaucratic–authoritarian state", or what we might term a "market-oriented authoritarianism" ' (ibid.: 241, 123).

Schumpeter's *Capitalism*, Fukuyama writes, is broadly in sympathy with the mixed utopia of free market initiative responsibly superintended by a wise and thinking State. The people vote. The leaders guide. The market allocates. The nation grows. It is all in Schumpeter. No doubt it is – but so too is the inevitability of planned socialism that alone, and not Fukuyama's collapse of the old Berlin Wall, would be able to bring Hegel's 'Universal History' into the equilibrium of a close.

5.2   SOCIALISM AND DEMOCRACY

It is not mind but matter, Schumpeter wrote, that 'shapes things and souls for socialism' (Schumpeter, 1942: 220). Central planning, 'independently of anyone's volition' (ibid.), is on the way. Corporate capitalism is already a matrix of private bureaucracies, a patchwork of unaccountable fiefdoms ruled over by their managers and their technocrats. The next step will be for the Ministry of Production to centralise and concentrate the control. Whether the State should simultaneously nationalise the commanding heights is not made explicit. Probably the new way will mean that as well. It does not really matter. Capital ownership and surplus value are as tangential to Schumpeter's transition as is mental debasement at the place of toil, the age-old utopia of parity and brotherhood, or that stagnation in living standards and technology which the Marxians had incorrectly predicted because they had failed to grasp the scale economies of change. What is central to Schumpeter's transition is not property but power. Socialism is politics. Socialism is the right to decide.

Socialism is command. The question is whether that governance will follow the liberal–democratic route or whether the nationalisation of dominance will automatically produce a self-perpetuating pool. Schumpeter's answer is that there is nothing to debate. He says that competitive elections 'may be compatible' (ibid.: 417) with the Central Board, but that votes and parties are not the necessary precondition for the Plan: 'Non-democratic socialism is perfectly possible' (ibid.: 299). They may go together. They need not be combined. Schumpeter, in contrast to virtually every political economist from Marx to Friedman, insisted that the modern democracy arose along with capitalism but that the transcendence of capitalism had no predictable consequences for the State: 'The defining feature of socialism does not imply anything about political procedure' (ibid.: 238).

Socialism, Schumpeter always maintained, was culturally indeterminate. Anticipating separateness just as he could also imagine correlation, Schumpeter was extending his prediction of indeterminacy to the decision-making framework itself: 'Between socialism as we defined it and democracy as we defined it there is no necessary relation: the one can exist without the other. At the same time there is no incompatibility: in appropriate states of the social environment the socialist engine can be run on democratic principles' (ibid.: 284). Agnosticism is everywhere. Jointness is not assured. Yet there are grounds for hope. So long as 'appropriate states' can be brought into being, inevitable socialism need not inevitably be *1984*.

5.2.1   The Politician

The first precondition relates to the supply of socialist democrats able to get things done. In the Soviet Union there was 'one man who was strong enough to keep that population in abject poverty and submission' (Schumpeter, 1942: 399). Stalin was a Great Man, a maker of traditions; but that was because of himself and not because of socialism. Schumpeter, prone to hero worship, said that Stalin could do what he did because he was head and shoulders above the crowd: 'Stalin never encountered a man of comparable ability' (ibid.). Tyrant or despot, no social philosophy can be built upon so unusual, so unrepresentative, a man of steel: 'Abilities such as those of Russia's leader occur extremely rarely in any population' (ibid.: 402n).

Outstanding leaders are always in limited supply. In early capitalism, however, at least the economic cutting edge was able to ride free on the service ethic of the hunting and shooting class that in most other respects had lost its role. The owner-entrepreneurs of the forest produce no new dynasty to refresh the old: there will be the prominent one-off but never a self-renewing pool. Going red will not correct the management vacuum. Socialist society, like capitalist society, is dangerously exposed to the randomness of comets without a family name to uphold. Socialism lacks a 'political class of stable traditions' (ibid.: 302) that has living roots in conservative practices. Unable to rely on repeat business, it must always be the creature of passing trade.

The socialist plan takes over from the capitalist market. Socialist politicians are as empty-handed as their capitalist predecessors. That is Schumpeter's story – but his politics is missing out a step. In his economics he is saying that the perfect competitor gives way to the powerful corporation. In his politics, however, he jumps directly from early capitalism to the controlling State. Samuels, never convinced by the logic of the transition, suggests that the big-business stage could reasonably live on forever: 'On Schumpeter's own terms, what succeeds (individualist entrepreneurial) capitalism is not historic socialism but corporate capitalism' (Samuels, 1985: 61). He sees no reason why the private-sector bureaucracy should ever disappear into the State. Be that as it may, the final capitalist in Schumpeter's own economics is not the small man but the corporate executive. Schumpeter's politics, to be consistent, ought then to have followed suit.

In the late-capitalist stage top management will have more influence than the forgotten petty bourgeois. The executives might even address the State on behalf of the bourgeoisie as a whole. In early socialism the organisational elite will consolidate its power and move steadily closer to the State. Business joins the *Apparat*. The *Apparat* produces the politicians. Socialism, building on the corporations, generates a hunting and shooting class all its own. The captains of industry in that way earn the chance to make themselves the strong Stalins of the future.

Stalin was a great leader but he was not a great democrat. That to Schumpeter was less of a concern. Socialists, like all merchants, must adapt to their market. Most socialists in the course of history have 'lived in environments that would have strongly resented undemocratic talk' (Schumpeter, 1942: 238). The expectations of the public forced them to be democrats in order to retain their credibility. Socialists espouse democracy 'if, as, and when it serves their ideals and interests' (ibid.: 240). Stalin and Lenin would have behaved quite differently had their self-interest in power had to be reconciled with a consensus that valued consultation. A world-historical earth-shaker in England or Sweden could bring about great changes. His socialism would not be incompatible with a democratic State.

5.2.2 The Agenda

The second precondition specifies that the agenda should not be out of control. Early capitalism, making the invisible hand its guiding light, had been favourable to business automaticity and sharply critical of rent-seeking mercantilism: 'It is easier for a class whose interests are best served by being left alone to practice democratic self-restraint than it is for classes that naturally try to live on the state' (Schumpeter, 1942: 297–8). Corporate capitalism had seen that there were non-productive transfers to be reaped through special pleading and selective intervention: Pareto terms this 'bourgeois socialism, which operates by means of customs protection, export subsidies and devaluation of the currency' (Pareto, 1966: 117). State socialism, coming on the scene when it did, inherited the regulations and the directives, the dependency and the lobbying, that the votaries of Adam Smith had criticised as a hand up to the haves.

Socialism inherits the client–patron relationships of the up-and-doing State. It amplifies the demand-led concessions of the voter-pleasing democracy with a top-down plan that specifies the targets and prescribes the quantities. State socialism does not renounce its commitment to industry and trade: the Keynesianism and the regional exemptions remain firmly in place. To the old claims are, however, added the new directions in redistribution and reinvestment that meet the needs of social groupings previously relegated to the servants' entrance. Socialism means the politicisation of equity even as it means the promotion of affluence. Socialism leads to more government. It is unlikely to wind up with less.

As the agenda becomes longer, so, however, does the people's voice become more and more of an inconvenience. Professional regulators object that they are not in a position to forecast and shape so long as personal freedom converts their policies into guesses. Schumpeter acknowledges the 'tremendous power over the people inherent in the socialist organization' (Schumpeter, 1942: 302). He is in no doubt as to the politics to which the road can lead: 'The task of keeping the democratic course may prove to be extremely delicate' (ibid.).

On the one hand there is Stalin's Russia. On the other hand there is Attlee's Britain. Schumpeter, Mitchell writes, was extraordinarily complacent about the destination to which the political economy points: 'Schumpeter was much too sanguine about the compatibility of socialism and democracy' (Mitchell, 1984b: 162).

Becker infers growing vulnerability from the lengthening agenda itself: 'Contrary to Schumpeter, I believe that selfish pressure groups of workers, managers, intellectuals, etc., have an incentive to be more rather than less active under socialism ... because a much larger fraction of resources is controlled by the state under socialism than under capitalism' (Becker, 1985: 121). Influence-seeking is a function of the spoils. Where the size of the pot is seen continuously to expand, there the free-for-all for the politician's ear is likely to be an ever greater threat to the balance of democracy.

Schumpeter concedes that the Ministry of Production need not be removed from the partialities of faction. The planner-in-chief being a member of the cabinet, it must be his task to 'assert the influence of the political element' (Schumpeter, 1942: 301) even at the cost of the technology and the maximisation. Economic power becomes politicised. Political power becomes concentrated. The result is not 'fascist' in the strict sense that fascism to Schumpeter presupposes the substitution of 'monopolistic' autocracy for competitive elections (ibid.: 404n). Even so, Schumpeter writes, the socialism of the future is very likely to 'present fascist features' (ibid.: 375). Command is redistributed to the top. A strike becomes a 'mutiny' (ibid.: 215). Intellectuals manipulate legitimacy or else rethink their careers. Where the newspapers are nationalised and television is State-controlled, it is hard to see why he thinks the opposition will be given equal access – or any access at all.

Because the agenda can become unmanageable, there is an understandable temptation to say that 'democratic socialism must fail' (ibid.: 299). Schumpeter never denies that a Gosplan in the United States could 'violate the spirit as well as the organic structure of the commonwealth' (ibid.: 288). His point is simply that, while democracy clearly *can* be pushed out by socialism, yet this illiberal endstate 'does not necessarily follow': 'Extension of the range of public management does not imply corresponding extension of the range of political management.' (ibid.: 299). The public agenda is not the same as the political agenda. So long as the nationalised industries and the statutory boards retain their operational autonomy, the public corporations will be no more the servants of the politicians than are the structurally-similar hierarchies of profit-seeking private enterprise.

As in corporate capitalism, incentives and penalties, bonuses and promotions, can be used to 'prevent managers from losing capitalist vitality and sinking into bureaucratic ruts' (ibid.: 300). In that sense, 'socialist managers would not have differed very much from their capitalist predecessors' (ibid.). Searching out their surplus, maximising their gain, hands-off managers in the devolved public order would at once make the economy more cost-aware and the polity less controlling. Decentralisation would be a socialist vote for plurality and experimentation. It would confirm what late capitalism has already demonstrated, that property rights are less important than the power to decree.

Yet a plan is a plan. Schumpeter's vision of self-determination within a ministerial matrix is not easy to understand. He says that the planners select the commodities and fix the quantity supplied: demand may price the stock but it is authority that regulates the flow. He also says that the one-off under central planning might have more influence than he does under dividend-seeking: 'The freedom of consumer's choice, in a socialist community working under normal conditions, could be much greater than it is now' (ibid.: 417). Schumpeter does not explain how individual freedom can be 'much greater' in a business plan embedded within a national plan than it would be in a corporate plan embedded within an oligopolistic market. What he does say is that nationalisation is a useful weapon for an invading army that wants to keep the natives down: 'A nationalized industry is easier to manage and to exploit for a conqueror and cannot become a center of opposition' (ibid.: 405). While the natives are only foreigners whereas the locals are voting citizens, the reader wonders about the hidden logic that made Schumpeter so confident that the planners would honour the preferences of the unseen.

The grass is greener – that is the bottom line. Schumpeter made clear that, in economics at least, socialism performs better than the stage before: 'There is a strong case for believing in its superior economic efficiency' (ibid.: 188).

The nature of Schumpeter's case was never really that strong. Socialism puts up the tax rates: this disincentive causes 'injury to the productive process' and leads inevitably to 'unsatisfactory economic performance' (ibid.: 198). Socialism uses market values until the leaders discover that disequilibrium is a quicker fix: 'The business organism cannot function according to design when its most important "parameters of action" – wages, prices, interest – are transferred to the political sphere and there dealt with according to the requirements of the political game' (ibid.: 386). Suppliers are discouraged. Markets are confused. Schumpeter's strong case *for* socialism seems remarkably close to Hayek's strong case *against*. The consensus then follows the ambiguity. Individuals willing to exchange some democracy for some prosperity might decide in the end that the old grass is at least as green as the new.

The long agenda need not deliver the goods. Even if it does, moreover, it might be doing so in a way that conviction democrats will reject as illiberal. Conviction democrats might feel that 'a lower level of governmental efficiency may be exactly what we want. We certainly do not want to be the objects of dictatorial efficiency, mere material for deep games' (ibid.: 288). Some people will prefer to trade some prosperity for some democracy rather than to sell their politics in order to enrich their economics. They will resist the long socialist agenda because too much interference is not to their taste.

5.2.3   The Bureaucracy

The third precondition is that effective administrators can be persuaded to staff the expanding ministries. Arriving late, the new socialist State will be in a good position to attract and retain. In early capitalism the social ideal is the family business: where drive and initiative are drawn into owner-entrepreneurship, the State will have to make do with the lethargic and the unambitious. In corporate capitalism the best careers are in the state-of-the-art companies: especially if tax revenues are inelastic and wage rates lag behind, the public sector will be left with the second-raters whom the private sector did not wish to employ. In planned socialism, however, the pendulum finally swings toward the State. Arriving late, replacing the large who had driven out the small, Schumpeter's bureaucracy has a stage-specific opportunity to recruit good-quality office holders who want to play for the winning side.

Schumpeter's bureaucracy, public or private, is a hierarchy that takes pride in its ethic. Schumpeter's socialism, like Schumpeter's capitalism, is crucially dependent on the commitment value of disinterested service. The moment that selfless penpushers become self-conscious maximisers who exaggerate and conceal, the efficiency that is planning's selling-point may be called publicly into question. The machinery of State will not retain the people's confidence where military intelligence is asleep on the job and corrupt inspectors sell driving licences to the highest bidder. Schumpeter expects his bureaucrats to live by a self-checking code. Where they do not, they can discredit planned socialism to such an extent that the voters call for free enterprise instead.

5.2.4   The Charter

The fourth precondition is normative consensus. It is a criterion often articulated by the socialists themselves when they say that privately-controlled property is unable to supply the unifying legitimacy. Capitalism, the socialists say, splits the classes apart – but socialism, they add, 'may remove the rift': 'It may reestablish agreement as to the tectonic principles of the social fabric' (ibid.: 301). If it does so, then the evolution into socialism is an evolution into concord as well.

Socialists argue that there will be less conflict between large-scale and small-scale operation, between agriculture and manufacturing, between labour and capital, between economic power and political power. Pressure groups will become less influential since subjective preferences will be overtaken by 'technical questions': 'A good case may be made out for expecting that the sum total of controversial matter would be decreased . . . Political life would be purified' (ibid.: 302). Less division means less disagreement. More agreement means more democracy. Prisons and policemen would deliver the same endstate of social peace. Neither is as attractive as norms and harmonious accord.

Schumpeter had no quarrel with democratic socialism. Rejecting the Marxian economics of exploitation, antagonism and class, he could see the point of reforms that were made necessary by a paradigm shared. What he could not accept was the totalitarian darkness of Gulag abuse. The KGB and the police State are a shabby way of making the world safe for social justice. Stalin's Russia is a shabby country which neither seeks nor enjoys the support of its people.

Stalin's Russia, Schumpeter writes, does not stand for 'socialism in any of the more usual senses of the word': 'The Stalinist regime is essentially a military autocracy which, because it rules by means of a single and strictly disciplined party and does not admit freedom of the press, partakes of one of the defining characteristics of Fascism and exploits the masses in the Marxian sense' (ibid.: 405, 404). National character and the historical memory of the Tsars explain much of what is happening: 'The trouble with Russia is not that she is socialist but that she is Russia' (ibid.: 404). The economic system contributes little to the explanation.

Just as Schumpeter never wrote a political sociology of Continental Fascism, so he never explored in depth the underlying causes of *un*democratic socialism. What is, however, striking in his account of the Soviet Union (in 1942, the only existing socialist State) is how much he still believed, as he had said in his 'Imperialisms' just after the Kaiser's War, that the military is an instrument with a will of its own. The Bolsheviks were building up a military machine that was 'a pinnacle of imperialist success' (ibid.: 403). The reason why that machine had sought to control other countries such as Finland against their will was the momentum of militarism first and foremost, the proletarian ideology exclusively as an impoverished also-ran. Schumpeter criticised the United States for its isolationism and appeasement at the end of long and costly Hitler's War: 'A job half done is worse than nothing' (ibid.: 401). The Soviet Union had a powerful military estate. It was the responsibility of the Western allies to halt its otherwise unstoppable advance.

Schumpeter knew that in order to express moral condemnation of the Soviet tyranny he had first to find his Archimedean point. This absolute he took to be the philosophy of liberal democracy as it was embodied in his fellow

Americans' moral sense. Consider his appeal to the American 'we' to justify his rejection of 'cruelty and lawlessness': 'This country cannot tolerate a situation in which a great part of humanity is deprived of what we consider to be elementary human rights' (ibid.: 400). Consider his invocation of the American 'large majority' to support his revulsion towards 'the most powerful of all dictators': 'Tremendous power and prestige is concentrated in the hands of a government that embodies the negation of principles that mean something to the large majority of the people of the United States' (ibid.: 401). Schumpeter was a liberal democrat like all the rest. Had he not been a liberal democrat he would not have known how to distance himself from the communist experiment.

Socialist planning was well-informed and cost-effective. It could secure more output from the economic machine than would have been delivered by post-Smithian imperfect exchange. Destinations and endstates were, however, on a different plane. Where the choices were ideal and not technocratic in their thrust, there it was the conviction of the liberal democrat that citizenship involvement was likely to produce the more representative picture: 'General elections, parties, parliaments, cabinets and prime ministers may still prove to be the most convenient instruments for dealing with the agenda that the socialist order may reserve for political decision' (ibid.: 301). The democratic State can be a good complement to the economic plan. The two together can produce what Schumpeter probably believed to be the best attainable mix.

History shows that democracy has been 'the outgrowth of the structure and the issues of the bourgeois world' (ibid.: 300–301). Political liberalism has been the 'outgrowth' of economic liberalism. There is no reason why that democratic vestige should not survive and prosper in the new economic world of the central plan. The road to serfdom is not inevitable – but only if public opinion is resolutely on the side of electoral legitimation. Normative consensus is the last of the four preconditions that must be met. In a sense it is the most important. Without a belief in democracy it is most unlikely that there will be any viable democracy at all.

5.2.5 Pathways and Choices

On the one hand there is capitalism, owner-operated or mature. On the other hand there is socialism, State-planned from above. Schumpeter's evolutionary schema extends from the decentralised to the directed. There is no other way.

Schumpeter in *Capitalism* was not inclined to explore the alternative scenarios: 'Centralist Socialism seems to me to hold the field so clearly that it would be a waste of space to consider other forms' (Schumpeter, 1942: 168). By 'The March into Socialism' he had softened his line: 'I speak of centralist socialism only because it holds a place of honor in the discussion. But other possibilities should not be neglected' (Schumpeter, 1950b: 422). Schumpeter in 1949 was prepared to concede that central control was not the only point on the map, that historical tendencies 'may be compatible with more than one outcome': 'Existing tendencies, battling with resistances, may fail to work themselves out completely and may even "stick" at some halfway house' (ibid.). Schumpeter's middle ground is hedged about with reservations. The 'gratis services' paid for by 'the vast productive possibilities of the capitalist engine' are not socialism at all but merely *laborist capitalism*' (ibid.: 425). The halfway house will not be a permanent arrangement but only a stopgap makeshift 'for the next half century or so' (Schumpeter, 1942: 398). Reservations though there undoubtedly were, the older Schumpeter was still able to suggest that the middle-aged Schumpeter had been too quick to smooth away the permutations.

Schumpeter's sunset capitalism is octopus organisations crowding out obsolete competitors. A less apocalyptic vision would see modern capitalism not as an either/or but as a spectrum. The small and medium enterprise coexists alongside the giant private corporation. Family business and shareholder business are in their turn complemented by management buyouts, worker cooperatives, arm's-length government companies and politically-accountable statutory boards. The market is regulated by laws, taxes and subsidies even in the absence of a quantitative matrix. Unions bargain on behalf of workers. Industrial democracy generalises the assent. It all adds up to a range of possibilities. Modern capitalism is a thoroughly mixed economy. It is not just the business economics of size.

Sunrise socialism is no less a buffet. Schumpeter in 1942 said that his definition 'excludes guild socialism, syndicalism and other types' (Schumpeter, 1942: 168). In 1946 he was acknowledging Papal corporatism (Schumpeter, 1946) as a Catholic third way that 'would avoid the "omnipotent state" ' (Schumpeter, 1950b: 422). In 1949 he was concluding that 'some form of guild socialism is not entirely off the cards' (ibid.). The pluralistic Schumpeter of 1949 was clearly not the single-valued Schumpeter of 1942. The growing scepticism does, however, put a question mark after the prediction. As Fourier and Owen come in, so the transition to the Ministry becomes only one choice among many.

Choice is the operative word. Socialism, Schumpeter states, will come into being 'independent of our love or hate', independent of 'human volition or of desirability': 'Mankind is not free to choose' (Schumpeter, 1942: 3, 56, 129). Yet he also recognises that morals and ideals are what make the intellectuals so inspiring and the masses so committed: 'Much of the propelling force of socialism comes, even today, from those irrational longings of the hungry *soul* – not belly' (ibid.: 308). Ideas as well as events evidently play an active part in his vision.

It is, of course, possible to argue that consciousness is only the still photo-graph, passive and dependent, of the momentum inherent in matter. Schumpeter expressly makes this connection in reference to the sea change of bureaucratised business that was collectivising the intellectual capital: 'The scheme of values of capitalist society, though causally related to its economic success, is losing its hold . . . upon the public mind' (Schumpeter, 1950b: 424). Yet ideals are troublesome things. Belonging and not efficiency can make people flee into communes, cooperatives and intermediate technology. One Nation can lead to the welfare State. Christianity can interpret equality as God's will on earth. The inviolability of self can make political democracy a demand-led absolute. One way or another, values can be the trigger for events. They need not lag behind.

Since a value consensus is a community of belief, Schumpeter is right to say that desiderata travel badly: 'Every country has its own socialism' (Schumpeter, 1942: 325). Writing in 1946, he showed great interest in just-elected Labour's compromise of selective nationalisation, pragmatic regula-tion and the social-services State. He reached the conclusion that sociology alone could explain the *kind* of socialism that the tolerant British had built: 'Fabian socialism requires English political society' (ibid.: 336). The French were divided by their sub-groupings and disillusioned with their State. The Americans were the acquisitive individualists of the open frontier. The Russians were Russians and that says it all. The British were better placed to travel in the middle lane. Willing to listen, resistant to revolution, able to rely on an enlightened aristocracy, possessed of politicians and bureaucrats of acumen and integrity, the British could develop their own moderate form of democratic welfare socialism because it embodied the national character that was uniquely their own.

5.3   DEMOCRACY AND WELFARE

Socialism, Schumpeter says, 'turns on an exclusively economic point' (Schumpeter, 1942: 169). Its instrument is the central plan. Its attraction is its 'superior economic efficiency' (ibid.: 188). Neither democracy nor welfare is a part of the definition. Not included, not excluded, both disappear into the 'cultural indeterminateness' (ibid.: 170) that seals the irrelevances in a void. Things and souls are being transformed in such a way as to make inevitable the 'public management of economic affairs and public control of all means of production' (Schumpeter, 1941: 343). Things and souls show only a casual interest in old-age pensions or the National Health. These can be voted in or voted out without much affecting the evolution of events.

The social-services State was always a secondary concern for a theorist of production who had learned his socialism from Marx and Barone. Secondary though the complementarity may have been, the steady growth of the social in support of the economic was always a theme in Schumpeter's conjectural history. His 'Crisis of the Tax State' was a reference to the duality that was on its way: 'The hour will come. By and by private enterprise will lose its social meaning through the development of the economy and the consequent expansion of the sphere of social sympathy.' (Schumpeter, 1918: 131). Schumpeter says 'and': two spheres are socialised and not only one. Schumpeter says 'consequent': social sympathy is the predetermined superstructure that crowns the economic transformation. Schumpeter in 1918 said that efficiency *and* compassion would evolve together into the State-socialist stage. It was a prediction of mix from which Schumpeter the economist never subsequently withdrew.

5.3.1 Social Failure

As societies become more affluent, so public goods and public services are carried upward on the steady growth in demand: 'With increasing wealth certain lines of expenditure are likely to gain ground which do not naturally enter any cost–profit calculation, such as expenditure on the beautification of cities, on public health and so on' (Schumpeter, 1942: 120). The private sector has no incentive to supply clean streets and eradicate cholera, to take responsibility for 'education and hygiene and so on' (ibid.: 71). The State sector does have a reason to correct the market failure. Fresh air and good schools win votes and seats. Disappointing inaction means the back benches, the dole queues and so on.

Enterprise neglects the spillovers. Yet the private sector fails in other ways as well. The decay of infra-family welfare well illustrates the growth-sensitive shortfall. Once altruism shown towards blood kinsfolk was a major cause of assiduity and savings. Individualism has meant that filial commitments such as care for the elderly have had to be hived off to anonymous professionals: 'The modern child doesn't give a damn what happens to his parents. They think it is just as well to leave them to public charity' (Schumpeter, 1941: 379). Schumpeter, noting 'the contribution made by parenthood to physical and moral health' (Schumpeter, 1942: 158), was sad to see the gift relationship decline. Without children there would be more aches and pains and more neuroses. A dependent is in that sense a social investment in a good supply of healthy citizens.

Slower growth is a direct consequence of birth control and selfish myopia. Childless capitalists, as was shown by the pro-statist pass-through of Roosevelt's America, have no strong incentive to fight back against intrusive regulations and burdensome taxes: 'There was no real resistance anywhere against the imposition of crushing financial burdens during the last decade or against labor legislation incompatible with the effective management of industry' (ibid.: 161). The New Deal meant a less effective economy. The childless capitalist, however, 'does not really care' (ibid.).

Corporate scale has put the Malthusianism into reverse. Slower growth is the social failure that childless prosperity has had a tendency to breed. One-generation capitalists are pushovers and not tigers when it comes to the depletion and the deficits for which future generations will have to pay. The separation of ownership from control only accentuates the climate of passive acceptance. Decisions are more and more being made by salary earners and not by owner-entrepreneurs. Such bureaucrats are less likely to oppose the wealth-destroying distortions of the State. It is certainly profits but still not *their* profits that the waste and the lethargy are putting under threat.

Anti-capitalist attitudes flourish in an atmosphere where the State by default is getting the upper hand. Rootless intellectuals, overeducated and underemployed, take advantage of the weak opposition to drive home their message that profit maximising violates the organic compact: 'Private wealth is under a moral ban' (Schumpeter, 1943: 183). The masses lose their faith in a system which left-leaning journalists tell them scores its victory at the expense of the poor. Meanwhile the market itself is falling victim to chronic self-doubt. The business community is nowadays too ashamed to set a market-clearing price or to invade an understocked monopoly.

Function and preference are not marching in step. The failed connection is a threat to the whole. Modern capitalism needs the State to provide public goods like education and hygiene and to care for forgotten dependents like the incapable and the institutionalised. On the other hand modern capitalism gives birth to the family-less, the profit-less and the left-leaning who rank early intervention above the long upward road. It is a contradiction and a social failure. Late-capitalist society has a growing need for social welfare. Late-capitalist culture, however, makes it more difficult to secure the expansion without which the funding will never be enough.

5.3.2   Growth and Welfare

Economic growth is itself a topic in social welfare. Growth raises the living standards of all social classes, and not least the material threshold of the absolutely deprived: 'If capitalism repeated its past performance for another half century . . . this would do away with anything that according to present standards could be called poverty' (Schumpeter, 1942: 66). Except for the 'pathological cases' (ibid.), economic growth within less than a single human lifespan will 'eliminate anything that could possibly be described as suffering or want' (ibid.: 384). The Marxians had developed theories of labour displacement, unstoppable immiseration, the reserve army and the subsistence wage which made them conclude that the welfare services had 'been forced upon capitalist society by an ineluctable necessity to alleviate the ever-deepening misery of the poor' (ibid.: 127). Schumpeter could not have disagreed more strongly. What was most needed to help the poor was not handouts or pity but a fast-paced and vibrant economy.

Expansion creates jobs and productivity raises pay. Left behind are the 'pathological cases' such as 'the aged and sick' (ibid.: 71) who do not float upward on the tide of the growing product. Primary poverty, as Anthony Crosland argued so strongly, was something that capitalist evolution could eliminate for itself: 'If our present rate of economic growth continues, material want and poverty and deprivation of essential goods will gradually cease to be a problem' (Crosland, 1956: 155). It was not the poor in work who would forever need the help, Crosland said, but rather the last-refuge victims of 'natural misfortune, physical or mental illness, the decline in the size of the family, sudden fluctuations in income, and deficiencies in social capital' (ibid.: 113). Faced with the social challenge not of primary but of secondary poverty, there was no provider but the State.

Alfred Marshall had said as much in his *Principles* when he made it the centrepiece of his mission to address the vicious circle of the no-hopers and the dead-enders, of the abandoned and the lost who 'have not the strength, physical, mental and moral, required for working their way out of their miserable surroundings': 'The system of economic freedom is probably the best from both a moral and material point of view for those who are in fairly good health of mind and body. But the Residuum cannot turn it to good account' (Marshall, 1890: 29, 594). Schumpeter's welfare looked back to Marshall and forward to Crosland. The State had a duty to relieve residual deprivation in cash and kind even as it had a duty to go for growth in order to raise up the rest.

Growth creates employment that marginalises primary poverty. Simultaneously it creates new national income that can pay for public spending. Increasing affluence produces a plus-sum increment. It is that natural dividend that Schumpeter has in mind when he writes that statist welfare 'presupposes previous capitalist success' (Schumpeter, 1942: 69).

Kept within bounds, taxes do no harm to incentives or value added: 'Moderate taxation . . . may even act as a stimulus' (Schumpeter, 1939: II, 713n). The danger is excessive taxation which soaks up savings that might have become accumulation and discourages entrepreneurs from sinking energy and initiative in money-making creative destruction. Beyond some ceiling, indeed, higher rates would actually mean a fall in the take: 'There exists a level beyond which further tax increases mean not an increase but a decrease of yield' (Schumpeter, 1918: 112). Capitalism as a system cannot dispense with the premium on success. Welfare is the same since otherwise slower growth would badly hit the poor and the exposed: 'The real tragedy is not unemployment *per se*, but unemployment plus the impossibility of providing adequately for the unemployed *without impairing the conditions of further economic development*' (Schumpeter, 1942: 70). Where it does so, the poor will be worse off, not better off, as a result of the expansion stifled by the taxes levied to pay for the social commitment.

The problem is not the spending itself but the 'economically irrational methods of financing relief' (ibid.: 71). Nor is resourcing the only quandary. Welfare is vulnerable to 'rates that are high relatively to wages', to the 'loose administration of unemployment benefits', to 'that spirit of waste that delights in spending a billion where 100 million would do' (ibid.: 386, 385). The welfare services have to become more economical, just as the fiscal regime is obliged to remain realistic. First and foremost, however, there has got to be growth. Growth is the wonder-drug that makes welfare – 'ample' welfare – 'not only a tolerable but a light burden' (ibid.: 69).

5.3.3   Social Costs and Social Benefits

Welfare is a burden but it is also a duty. Implicit in the relationship between the cell and the organism is the notion of a multi-person, multi-period social contract which bulks large in the economic communitarianism of Brentano or Ashley and which is conspicuous by its absence from the determined commercialism of the American self-seekers. It was Schmoller and not Sumner who guided Schumpeter when he sought to situate personal deprivation in the context of the common condition and of the nationhood shared. Perhaps it was the Pope as well. Schumpeter was brought up a Catholic. Expressing his fear of 'social decomposition' and 'social disintegration' (Schumpeter, 1946: 403) in the years just after his *Capitalism* was published, he seemed to find in the Encyclicals a social economics of obligation that would restore the stranded to the group.

Capitalism is inseparable from involuntary unemployment precisely because the 'rejuvenation of the productive apparatus' (Schumpeter, 1942: 68) presupposes the 'complete destruction' of the 'hopelessly unadapted' (Schumpeter, 1912b: 253): benefiting as all of us do from the natural selection and the refreshing spring clean, it is incumbent upon the wider community to ensure that 'the suffering and degradation' (Schumpeter, 1942: 70) should not fall disproportionately on the front-line troops who lose their jobs. Capitalism is an innovative dynamic that charts its progress through a 'cyclical process' that is in truth 'not an incident but the whole of what is specifically capitalistic in economic life' (Schumpeter, 1939: I, 405n): wanting the weeding out of the Darwinian recession that makes possible a better harvest later on, it is the duty of the wider community to ensure that 'the destruction of human values' (Schumpeter, 1942: 70) should not be the tax upon the part that pays for the upgrade of the whole. Personal fault does not enter into the equation. If *we* demand the creative destruction, then *we* must do something to cushion the victims of our short-run ups and downs.

As a believer in Say's Law, Schumpeter did not expect an underemployment equilibrium or the Keynesian overhang of idle savings brought into being by growth. Because of the diminishing utility of marginal abstention, because of the moving frontier of new investment outlets, Schumpeter never regarded macroeconomic stagnation as an imminent threat: 'People with high incomes . . . save less intensively than people with low incomes, many of them not at all.' (Schumpeter, 1908: 308). Nor could he accept the Marxian prognosis that technological displacement meant a future of robots and computers that would inexorably make the joblessness worse: 'I also do not think that there is any tendency for the unemployment percentage to increase in the long run' (Schumpeter, 1942: 69). Schumpeter's unemployment was not a trend. It was, however, a perennial fluctuation, and that was bad enough.

Schumpeter's unemployment was a topic in the disequilibrium transition that always accompanies the collectivity's advance. Schumpeter knew what the retrenchments meant for the out-of-luck whom the escalator left behind. It was, he believed, fully in line with the social compact that the 'past social costs of capitalist achievement' should not be allowed to lie where they fall, that the 'private life of the unemployed' should not be 'seriously affected by their unemployment' (ibid.: 70). *We* gain. *They* should not lose.

Schumpeter's perception of unemployment as a social contract and not just a private contingency recalls Titmuss's defence of income maintenance in the language of a war or an epidemic. Benefits, Titmuss writes, 'represent partial compensations for disservices, for social costs and social insecurities which are the product of a rapidly changing industrial–urban society' (Titmuss, 1968: 133). Schumpeter is at one with Titmuss on the idea that a society that wants new production functions has a moral duty to look after the rejects of the old. He also notes that self-interest in itself is a good reason for the haves not to default on their debts.

Schumpeter argues that too much distress is a short-cut to collapse. Stability and democracy will not, he says, be secure where the unemployed are left to their own devices while the successes retain the whole of the usufruct for themselves: 'Secular improvement that is taken for granted and coupled with individual insecurity . . . is of course the best recipe for breeding social unrest' (Schumpeter, 1942: 145). Chapter 6 cites Galbraith to the effect that the excluded are not now in a position to mount a revolution but that they 'could make life uncomfortable for all' (Galbraith, 1980: 5). That being the case, a society would do well to ward off the negative externalities before anarchy and crime become the last resort of the malintegrated and the desperate.

State intervention can cause unemployment. Legal immunities granted to unions, perverse egalitarianism in violation of Pareto's constant, protective tariffs that reduce the flow of world trade, wage-fixing that prices willing workers out of jobs, premature pump-priming through public works that 'create the emergencies in which such expenditure imposes itself' (Schumpeter, 1942: 398) – Schumpeter had no doubts about the cost that bad government had imposed on the poor and the expendable: 'The unemployment figure has been increased by anti-capitalist policies beyond what it need have been' (ibid.: 71). Such regulation, creating rather than relieving unemployment, was always undesirable. The welfare State was different: 'Support to the unemployed is an all but inevitable element in our economic system' (Schumpeter, 1926/27: 160). As an economist, Schumpeter took the view that unemployment, frictional and structural, would never be eliminated by growth which was its cause. As a *political* economist, he was convinced that the community had a duty to pick up the pieces that collective betterment had left behind.

5.3.4 Altruism

Adam Smith predicted that empathy and generosity would enjoy a high income elasticity: 'If our misery pinches us very severely, we have no leisure to attend to that of our neighbour' (Smith, 1759: 205). Alfred Marshall found in on-the-job training, wages in excess of productivity and the democratic demand for progressive taxation 'a kind of deliberate unselfishness, that never existed before the modern age' (Marshall, 1890: 5). Schumpeter was building on the optimism of giants when he decided that a richer society would also be a more compassionate one. There has, Schumpeter wrote, never been 'so much active sympathy with real and faked sufferings, never so much readiness to accept burdens, as there is in modern capitalist society' (Schumpeter, 1942: 126). Richer societies are better able to pay. That is just as well, since they are also more likely to articulate the wish.

People in richer societies are 'alive to the duty in question' (ibid.: 71). Aware that the unemployed, the aged and the destitute cannot manage on their own, the community manifests 'genuine group-wise volitions' which are the proof of 'the will of other groups to help' (ibid.: 270). This caring consensus is the trigger for the 'political volition' (ibid.: 69) that complements private charity with the legislation that is required. The welfare State is not pure communism or a principled rejection of trade: 'Exclusive reliance on a purely altruistic sense of duty is as unrealistic as would be a wholesale denial of its importance and its possibilities' (ibid.: 207). It is nonetheless an admission that fellow citizens care.

Some thinkers have regarded the humanitarian externality as the institutional expression of citizenship, culture and integration. It was from belonging and not just from the Bible that Tawney derived his ideal of the socialist State as the social democracy's warm-hearted Samaritan: 'Social well-being does not only depend upon intelligent leadership; it also depends upon cohesion and solidarity . . . and a strong sense of common interests' (Tawney, 1931: 108). Schumpeter, whose economics was rooted in Mengerian enterprise and whose maturity was spent in the free-market United States, was never comfortable with the One Nation window on the world of instinctual collectivists who saw the *Volk* as loving and caring. Tawney was a good man. Hitler, however, was not. Schumpeter seems to have feared that any form of *national* socialism would be dangerously exposed to goose-stepping at Nuremberg, to *Blut und Boden*, to *Juden raus*, to I am We: 'To exalt national unity into a moral precept spells acceptance of one of the most important principles of fascism' (Schumpeter, 1942: 352n).

Nationhood could provide legitimation for totalitarian dictatorship. Equally, however, it could satisfy mankind's craving for identification and warmth. Schumpeter was a methodological individualist but he was also a historical sociologist, as committed to convention and memory as he was to atomistic reductionism. Customs and habits had for him the great attraction that they empowered the 'preceding state of affairs' (Schumpeter, 1912b: 9) to impose normative consistency upon a civil war of self-servers who might without the stability and the standardisation have lacked the common reference points that they required for decentralised interaction. A traditionalist, Schumpeter defined conservatism as 'the bringing about of transitions from your social structure to other social structures with a minimum loss of human values' (Schumpeter, 1941: 399). One Nation can smooth the path. While Hitler's conservatism might be nationhood gone wild, Tawney's welfarism might be a usefully Schumpetarian way of ensuring continuity while not stifling change.

A common fund of ideas derived from a common historical experience provides not only an intellectual public good but also an '*emotional* attachment to the social order' (Schumpeter, 1942: 145). Nothing could be more in the spirit of the welfare State than are internalised values and a felt commitment to a going concern. The business-like way of life is, however, a challenge to all the bulwarks: 'Capitalist civilization is a rationalist civilization. It tends to eliminate extra – or hyperrational sanctions and habits of mind without which no society can exist' (Schumpeter, 1943: 181). Rationality weakens attachment to culture and community. Moral authority, however, is undermined by unsettled mobility and a questioning scepticism.

Affect and allegiance seem not to pay their way. T.H. Marshall writes that 'in the twentieth century citizenship and the capitalist class system have been at war' (Marshall, 1950: 40). Should the cut-off quid pro quo triumph over the amicable integration of *Gemeinschaft*, democracy might flourish but welfare be crushed into residualism by the maximising economics of self.

6. Galbraith: ideas and events

John Kenneth Galbraith is an evolutionary economist. The principal themes in the influential works of this prolific author – and most of all in *American Capitalism* (1952), *The Affluent Society* (1958), *The New Industrial State* (1967) and *Economics and the Public Purpose* (1973) – are not marginal cost and marginal revenue, consumer's surplus and diminishing returns. Instead they are intellectual development, institutional progress and the constructive role of the State. Neoclassical economists wrestle with scarce endowments, alternative employments, equilibrium positions and allocative efficiencies. Galbraith addresses the big issues of corporate capitalism, political intervention, residual poverty and social trends. Neoclassicists sometimes say that Galbraithian economics is really economic sociology and that evolutionary institutionalism trespasses into non-scientific prescriptiveness. The Galbraithian is likely to reply, however, that it is the textbook orthodoxy itself that is limited and non-scientific, precisely because it treats as inert and invariant a systemic framework that is in truth organic and dynamic.

Organic, dynamic – and very, very constraining: 'Given the decision to have modern industry, much of what happens is inevitable and the same' (Galbraith, 1967: 388). Man's freedom to shape events in accordance with ideas is, evidently, severely circumscribed by the motion inherent in matter: 'The imperatives of technology and organization, not the images of ideology, are what determine the shape of economic society' (ibid.: 26). Keynes had concluded the *General Theory* with the ringing declaration that men are ruled by philosophy and 'by little else': 'Madmen in authority, who hear voices in the air, are distilling their frenzy from some academic scribbler of a few years back' (Keynes, 1936: 383). Keynes had said that 'it is ideas, not vested interests, which are dangerous for good or evil' (ibid.: 384). Galbraith, like Schumpeter, is more resigned to the reality that it is all an iron cage. *Die Weltgeschichte ist das Weltgericht.* You play the cards that you are dealt. Mankind is not after all very free to choose.

Galbraith is an economic determinist who insists that, 'for being right . . . it is better to have the support of events than of the higher scholarship' (Galbraith, 1973a: 11). Perhaps surprisingly, therefore, he is an active social reformer as well. Shocked by manipulative advertising and salesmanship, concerned about environmental pollution, alarmed at the disproportionate

growth of trivial consumables relative to essential services, fearful lest arse-
nals of sophisticated weaponry built up at the expense of slum clearance,
health and education should one day come to annihilate the persuaders and the
persuaded alike, Galbraith has consistently adopted the posture of a prophet
crying out to the wavering that they should abandon their errors and misapprehensions in order to return to the true road up: 'No one who believes in
ideas and their advocacy can ever persuade himself that they are uninfluential
... I have hopes that popular understanding will reverse some of the less
agreeable tendencies of the industrial system and invalidate, therewith, the
predictions that proceed from these tendencies' (Galbraith, 1967: 320).

Thence the paradox. Galbraith the social reformer is adamant that man can
and must make himself the master of his economic destiny: 'Knowledge of the
forces by which one is constrained is the first step towards freedom' (ibid.:
340). Galbraith the economic determinist, on the other hand, is equally
adamant that it is man's sad fate to dwell forever in that powerless realm where
even political proposals are thrown up 'not by parties and politicians but by
circumstance' (Galbraith, 1973b: 10). Galbraith the political philosopher is
convinced that ideas have consequences: 'If belief is the source of power, the
attack must be on belief' (Galbraith, 1973a: 247). Galbraith the social scientist
is, however, equally convinced that thought is afterthought: 'In social matters,
critics are an interim phenomenon. Given a little time, circumstances will
prove you either right or wrong' (Galbraith, 1958: 21). Galbraith the determinist strongly believes that events breed ideas. Galbraith the moralist is no
less persuaded that ideas shape events. It is not only the neoclassical economist who is bound to speculate on the extent to which Galbraith's intellectual
system is in fact overdetermined and perhaps even seriously flawed.

A horse divided against itself cannot stand. Much the same must be said of
an intellectual system of which the central supports are incompatible and
contradictory. It is the thesis of this chapter, however, that the Galbraithian
system is able without difficulty to reconcile the determinism with the morality, the evolutionary economics with the social reforms. The chapter proceeds
by way of two sections, the first headed 'Matter and mind', the second headed
'Mind and matter', to the conclusion that the vision is logically consistent and
internally coherent. The great attraction is the scope. As with Schumpeter, the
whole is greater than the sum of the parts.

Galbraith's conjectures are wide-ranging and complex. This chapter (fully
consistent in that sense with Galbraith's own practice) makes no attempt to test
his hypotheses. It is notoriously difficult at the best of times to prove the
factual accuracy of ambitious world-views. What this chapter suggests is not
that the predictions are correct but that Galbraith has identified the relevant
issues. Galbraith on ideas and events is well worth careful study. His intellectual system is not a horse divided that is bound to fall.

6.1   MATTER AND MIND

Economies are in motion, Galbraith argues. The capitalist system is no exception: 'We have a certain number of people who call themselves scholars of capitalism, who insist that it had a virgin birth in 1776 with Adam Smith, and it hasn't changed since. But I would urge that we must see capitalism, as we have seen socialism, as being in a constant process of transformation' (Galbraith, 1988: 77). The poorer countries would be ill-advised to emulate either the American or the Soviet model without assigning due weight to the constraints of historical process: 'The economic design appropriate to the later stages of development *cannot*, without waste and damage, be transferred to the early stages' (Galbraith, 1983a: 8). The richer countries would be no less ill-advised, themselves neglecting historical process, to treat today's design as some eternal blueprint: 'Economics is not durable truth; it requires continuous revision and accommodation. Nearly all its error is from those who cannot change' (Galbraith, 1981: 125). Economies are in motion. Mind that lags behind matter is doomed to radical misapprehension of the laws that govern development in the modern industrial state.

Economic systems have evolved significantly, Galbraith believes, since the time when Smith, Marx and later the young Schumpeter interpreted the capitalist system as predatory entrepreneurs scoring points in competitive markets. Some modern thinkers continue to espouse that now-outdated conceptual framework. Not the least of them is Friedrich von Hayek, theorist of markets as processes and 'one of the finest and most untouched of late-eighteenth-century minds' (Galbraith, 1975a: 404). Distinguished though such thinkers may be, Galbraith says, the truth is that history is not on their side. Events have moved on. The world has changed. The economist with an obsolete ideology should therefore update his ideas in line with the facts: 'Circumstances are the enemy of neoclassical economics, not Galbraith' (cited in *Challenge*, 1973: 76).

6.1.1   Large-scale Operation

Long production runs, long gestation periods, costly investment in sector-specific fixed capital, the premium on technological advance, the research and development overhead – all of this has led to the emergence of the Schumpeterian large corporation. Business is big both in absolute terms and in relation to a specific market. Large firms being in the vanguard of progress, Galbraith states, such size is more to be welcomed than to be feared: 'No important technical development of recent times – atomic energy and its applications, modern air transport, modern electronic development, computer development, major agricultural innovation – is the product of the individual inventor in the market system. Individuals still have ideas. But – with rare exceptions – only organizations can bring ideas into use' (Galbraith, 1973a: 62).

Size is not to be feared. What is to be expected, however, is that the advantages of scale will be bound up with the exercise of power. It cannot be otherwise in an uncertain world. The large firm is compelled by the very logic of its otherwise vulnerable position to 'plan' its market, to forecast the unforeseeable, to shape the inconvenient. So great is the financial commitment made many years in advance of the finished product finally being marketed (of the final consumer, indeed, even learning that the breakthrough commodity has actually been invented) that the corporation has no choice but to break free from the straitjacket of demand-led growth. It is obliged to utilise its muscle in its own interest. Time is on the horizontal axis, 'large tasks require large organizations' (Galbraith, 1977a: 277), and risk rises with duration and commitment. The large firm would simply not survive to confer its unquestionable benefits if it were not strong enough to be able to influence its environment: 'The modern large corporation and the modern apparatus of socialist planning are variant accommodations to the same need. It is open to every free-born man to dislike this accommodation. But he must direct his attack to the cause. He must not ask that jet aircraft, nuclear power plants or even the modern automobile in its modern volume be produced by firms that are subject to unfixed prices and unmanaged demand. He must ask instead that they not be produced' (Galbraith, 1967: 51). And that very few of us would actually wish to propose.

Economic evolution means large-scale operation. Large-scale operation in turn presupposes protection by means of 'plan'. The business 'plan' to Galbraith is not the same as the central plan in Schumpeter's socialist ministry. Galbraith's 'plan' is not a public-sector matrix but rather a corporate accommodation that tries to breed the unknowledge out of market freedom. Among its many forms, the 'plan' makes use of vertical integration (including multinational expansion) to secure guaranteed inputs and outlets; horizontal integration to ensure the suppression of an unpredictable competitor; inter-firm contracts to stabilise supplies and coordinate production targets; price-fixing in a tacit alliance with friendly rivals that promises to give each 'a reasonably reliable share of the market' (Galbraith, 1967: 211); expansion via retained earnings in an attempt to obviate dependence on outside lenders; cost-push inflation (accompanied by diminished dividends) as part of a policy of passing on to the consumer (or backwards to the shareholder) the burdensome overhead of buying off potential union disruption; automation of production, both because capital (being internally generated) is more secure than the supply of skilled labour and because machines, once in place, 'do not go on strike' (Galbraith, 1973a: 164); manipulation of microeconomic demand-levels via advertising and salesmanship in such a way as to obtain planned-for sales at planned-for prices; alliance between corporation and State such as produces tariffs, quotas, subsidies, contracts, complementary infrastructure and macroeconomic stabilisation. Large-scale operation is a characteristic of mature capitalism. So too is 'plan'. It is the indispensable antidote to the competitive uncertainties that would make technological advance in the large-firm sector all but impossible: 'The enemy of the market is not ideology but the engineer' (Galbraith, 1967: 51).

The failure of 'plan' would have serious consequences indeed for research and innovation. The reader who shares with Galbraith a positive attitude to creative destruction will therefore be pleased to learn from the evolutionary theorist that manipulation seldom fails, competitors seldom undercut, serendipitous discoveries seldom subvert predictable outcomes. Ordinary men and women might not be entirely pleased with a substitution of producer for consumer sovereignty that dependably tricks them into buying 'a lawn mower that can be guided by transcendental meditation' (Galbraith, 1978: 50) at some price that the corporation picks out of the air. They are unlikely to be very pleased with amicable competition among the few such as stops even the low-cost firm from cutting its price lest its friendly rivals then suspect it of seeking to invade their market share. Ordinary men and women might nonetheless be prepared to bear these social costs were they to be convinced that the corporations and the planning are linked, genuinely and inevitably, to technological advance.

Normally Galbraith is able to provide the reassurance. Sometimes, however, he is not. It is Galbraith and not Hayek who, drawing attention to 'the well-recognized tendency toward organizational stasis and senility in the modern great enterprise' (Galbraith, 1987: 279), goes so far as to cite the 'hardening of the arteries' brought about by corporate bureaucratisation as one of the causes of the decline of the steel industry in the United States: 'Until you had done business at length with top officers of the steel corporations, you didn't really appreciate the intellectual qualities of a billet of steel' (Galbraith, 1988: 92). Such organisations and corporations, it would appear, are just as likely to stigmatise novelty and eccentricity as they are to pioneer new products or to transform processes: 'In a great organization ... there is a strong tendency to measure superior intelligence by its resemblance to what is already being done' (ibid.: 45). Ordinary men and women are bound in the circumstances to ask if the innovativeness is really worth the centralised control. They will read with some concern Galbraith's concession that the ultimate scale economies of the giant organisation are more nearly those of dominance than of dynamism: 'For this planning – control of supply, control of demand, provision of capital, minimization of risk – there is no clear upper limit to the desirable size. It could be that the bigger the better' (Galbraith, 1967: 91). In such circumstances, ordinary men and women might suggest, perhaps there remains after all a germ of truth in the classical message that active competition is the constitution that keeps the scoundrels in their place.

Perhaps there does, but not in Galbraith's interpretation of the new industrial State. The modern economy, he believes, is a dual economy. He acknowledges the continuing existence alongside the 'planning system' of the small-firm sector and the textbook owner–entrepreneur. The two sectors of manufacturing are roughly equal in size: each system accounts for approximately half of private sector GDP (Galbraith, 1973a: 59). The market system is the world of the passive price taker and the perfect competitor. Technologically backward, lacking in the unit costs of size, prone to the self-exploitation of the small shopkeeper's seven-day week, crushed under the heel of their powerful trading partners, shown little mercy by the sovereign consumer who haggles callously for value for money, the participants in the market system are to Galbraith something of a footnote in the history of economic growth. They are yesterday's men. Matter is in motion. The fact is that events have gone beyond their reach or understanding.

6.1.2 The Technostructure

The archetypal scarce input at the stage of peasant agriculture is land. In early capitalism it is savings for investment. In the advanced economic system it is minds in groups. In the new industrial State the bottleneck input is skilled, trained manpower. It is highly-qualified specialists such as engineers, advertising experts, research scientists, accountants, lobbyists and lawyers. The premium being on the subdivision of labour, moreover, that manpower is only of value when it is situated in balanced teams making collective decisions in conferences and at committees. Each individual, however determined and idiosyncratic, will know a lot but only about a little. There is therefore no alternative to information sharing within teams and to the 'synthetic personality' (Galbraith, 1965: 88) that is nowadays the locus of decision making in the powerful planning system.

The planning system is powerful. It is also a worryingly small club. Galbraith writes that in the United States in 1971 'the 333 industrial corporations with assets of more than $500 million had a full 70 per cent of all assets employed in manufacturing' (Galbraith, 1973a: 59). The other rich countries provided not many more seats at the table: 'The concentration of economic activity has followed a similar course in the other industrial countries' (Galbraith, 1983b: 133). Given such power, and such *concentrated* power, it is clearly of the greatest social importance to identify the personal objectives of the powerful technocrats who dominate the top businesses. It is they, after all, who pipe the tune to which the whole nation dances: 'The goals of the mature corporation will be a reflection of the goals of the members of the technostructure. And the goals of the society will tend to be those of the corporation' (Galbraith, 1967: 170). As *they* decide, so *we* live: this Galbraith terms the 'Principle of Consistency'.

Technocrats make decisions. They do so in the interests of the salary earner who holds no property rights and receives no dividends. Given their economic position, business bureaucrats cannot be expected to put first the maximisation of profits that will be paid out to unknown strangers. Galbraith's views are closer to Downs and Pareto than they are to Weber and Schumpeter. Business decision makers, he argues, must be expected to develop maximands of their own. Those goals will be more closely in line with their own perceived interests than would be the pursuit of the textbook entrepreneur's return on capital.

One of these goals is likely to be job satisfaction. Graduates with trained minds welcome the challenge of the new. They are keen to put their hard-earned technical virtuosity to some use – even if the cost of incessant innovativeness and accelerated obsolescence happens to be a less-than-achievable coupon rate and slower capital appreciation for the firm. A second goal is security. The organisation man as an individual values continuity of employment. The technostructure as a whole cannot afford the loss of key specialists. Any committee, furthermore, that wishes to be effective must defend its autonomy against uninformed outsiders (politicians and property owners, managers and money lenders) who would seek through intervention to countervail its power. The third goal is growth. Expansion is a means for the consolidation of security. Yet it has an affirmative purpose as well. Expansion enhances the power, pay, prestige, perks and prospects of the organisational bureaucrats who bring it about. Promoting the business, they promote themselves as well. Three objectives – and not one of them the textbook case of maximum profit.

As firms grow large and ownership is dispersed, as language becomes specialised and 'exclusion by technical complexity' (Galbraith, 1983b: 167) becomes the order of the day, so events bring about the 'euthanasia of stockholder power' (Galbraith, 1967: 387). It is a development which ideologues committed, however passionately, to the profit-first motive will find totally impossible to reverse. Powerless, faceless and ill-informed, the modern shareholding capitalist is 'a passive and functionless figure' (ibid.: 386). His vote, being 'valueless' (ibid.: 94), is unable to influence the decision-making technocrats who are the modern corporation's meritocratic elite.

No fear of hostile takeovers, undervalued assets, founding families, institutional investors or shareholders' revolts clouds Galbraith's logic. This is why he is able to pass a judgment on capital that is likely to enrage the privatisers

and the nationalisers alike: 'The ultimate ownership of the very large industrial corporation, public or private, matters little' (Galbraith, 1981: 332).
Galbraith neglects the manifold techniques at the disposal of shareholders to
put pressure on managers to put pressure on technocrats to put profit-seeking
first. In spite of that, interestingly enough, the predictions of his model are not
radically different from those of the neoclassical school.

The Galbraithian firm is committed to growth with security. Determined to
retain its independence, it has no choice but to budget expansion out of its
retained earnings. Such a firm is driven purely by its organisational goals to
secure *considerable* profits even if not literally to *maximise* profits. Money is
money. The textbook capitalist is unlikely to be particularly disappointed with
the actual performance of the Galbraithian technostructure. Nor are the basic
predictions of the owner-centred economist likely to be called seriously into
question by the emergence of the new-style objectives. Profit as the means or
profit as the end, the economist will reason, theory predicated upon profit-
oriented motivation is not significantly less relevant in the one case than it is in
the other. Friedman's instrumentalism makes the test good results and not fancy
elaborations (Friedman, 1953). When God coughs he lights a cigarette.
Galbraith on bureaucracy explains the function of profits with precisely the same
high degree of success as the 'God-coughs' model of thunder and lightning.

Yet Galbraith regards the profit motive as having little explanatory power in
the world of the giant corporation and its sophisticated technostructure. It is in
no small measure because of the continuing obsession of the neoclassical
economist with maximum profits (not job satisfaction, not security, not
growth) that Galbraith dismisses the textbook economics as fundamentally out
of date. The textbook economics may, he concedes, provide a reasonable
account of what happens in the small-business sector. Sadly, he concludes, it
always mystifies and confuses by treating the planning system precisely as it
would the perfect competitor.

Profit is one instance of this propensity – since the non-evolutionary economist seems all but unaware of the organisational revolution. Power is a
further instance – since the theorist of discrete individuals (as opposed to
corporate blocs) in effect, and 'rather systematically, excludes speculation on
the way the large economic organizations shape social attitudes to their ends'
(Galbraith, 1967: 175). Plenty is a final instance – since the dismal scientist of
Ricardian scarcities has nothing to say about satiated societies in which the
overdeveloped consume too much rather than too little and where 'wants are
increasingly created by the process by which they are satisfied' (Galbraith,
1958: 152). Profit, power, and plenty – all three concepts are valuable illustrations of the important proposition that, there being few 'fixed and permanent
truths' in economics, economists must accept that the sheer mutability and

variance of their subject matter makes it all but impossible for their science to regard itself as the close relative of the timeless, static, eternal verities of theoretical physics: 'It is the paradox of the discipline that it is the wish so to see itself that commits economics to an obsolescence in a changing world that, by any scientific standard, is to be deplored' (Galbraith, 1987: 284).

It is to be deplored not merely because the escape from evidence about events into the spurious precision of mathematical logic imposes a high cost in the form of 'the removal of the subject several steps further from reality' (ibid.: 259). It is also to be deplored because too much abstraction communicates an unhealthy ideological message. A simplified textbook model of contemporary capitalism in which 'Exxon is held to be indistinguishable from the corner grocery or the village pharmacy in its exercise of power' (Galbraith, 1983b: 141) has the dangerous function de facto of hiding from view the market-suppressing propensities of the gigantic and the dominant: 'Marshall's world of competitive entrepreneurs, maximizing consumers and a suitably reticent state continues to serve the ends of comfortable orthodoxy today. It does not describe the world as it is' (Galbraith, 1981: 29). It does not describe the world as it is but neoclassical economists for all that continue to teach impressionable students as if the butcher, the brewer and the baker were still matching wits in the bazaar. Economists do not sell the services of obfuscation and indoctrination to the technostructure for cash. Those services are rendered, 'in the main, in innocence and in the name of scientific truth' (Galbraith, 1967: 175). Their commitment to ideas dramatically out of step with events nonetheless commits them just as effectively to the unintended status of high priests of distortion and disguise.

Economists unwittingly serve the goals of the technostructure when they fail to describe the world as it is. Civil servants, on the other hand, serve the goals of the technostructure not by concealing the revised aspirations but rather by sharing them. Civil servants perceptively grasp that the objectives of the person on a salary are not radically different whether he or she is in State employment or in a private hierarchy. They also know that the bureaucrat gets along by going along: 'The man or woman who fully accepts the policy and has belief therein is known as a good soldier . . . The administration of foreign policy thus comes very close to the enforcement of belief' (Galbraith, 1999: 160). Even if the officer sees that the nostrums are wrong, he will have no real incentive to challenge his superiors and a strong personal reluctance to throw away the crutch: 'Nothing better describes the making of American foreign policy since World War II than its controlling rigidity in the face of original error or needed adjustment' (ibid.: 161). It is not just the economists but the CIA and even the Ministry of Agriculture that becomes the prisoner of the past and unable to move on.

Because the private and public bureaucracies are so much alike, there develops a clearly defined 'bureaucratic symbiosis' between the two sets of organisation men. Each team is committed to job satisfaction, security and growth. Each is well placed to assist the other in the pursuit of the common objectives: 'Rarely does the private technostructure meet a public bureaucracy without discovering some area in which there can be co-operation to mutual advantage.' (Galbraith, 1973a: 176). Events to that extent have moved beyond the ideas of Marx on the monopoly State as well as beyond those of Smith on the largely self-regulating order: 'The modern state . . . is not the executive committee of the bourgeoisie, but it *is* more nearly the executive committee of the technostructure' (ibid.: 188).

Politicians, admittedly, can prove a problem to the civil service careerist. So can the free market ideology of the economic mind, which reinforces the taxpayer's not-unexpected reservations about an increase in public spending. Thus it is that American technocrats and American bureaucrats, aware of the superpower mystique of their nation and the paranoid anti-communism of so many of their fellow-citizens, selectively apply their pressures in precisely the area where they appreciate that resistance will be least. That area is national defence. Their calculation, Galbraith believes, has yielded them rich rewards: 'The ABM, the new generation manned bomber and the nuclear aircraft carriers serve not the balance of terror, but the organizations that build and operate them.' (Galbraith, 1970a: 77).

Soviet technocrats and Soviet bureaucrats, Galbraith adds, are presumably no less sensitive to organisational objectives subserved by military preparedness and Cold War mistrust. Not *Dienst*, not *Pflicht*, one goal-function is another goal-function's best friend. Reciprocal self-interest makes allies of the poacher and the gamekeeper. That is how salaried people get things done: 'The military establishment on the one side supports the military establishment on the other' (Galbraith, 1988: 115). The communist cogs join their voice to that of their American counterparts in exaggerating the dangers of multilateral disarmament and peaceful co-existence. Such de-escalation could, after all, cost them 'the occupation, prestige, promotions that go with active military operations' (Galbraith: 1970b: 144). Far better than de-escalation is re-escalation, the technocrats and the bureaucrats will say. What they will say is what they will do. The result is 'entrapment in an ever-increasing cycle of outlay': 'We force action on the Soviets, they on us. So it continues' (Galbraith, 1981: 532).

Morally speaking, Galbraith says, 'there is something uniquely obscene about competition to promote weapons of mass destruction for purposes of improving the stock-market position of a corporation' (Galbraith, 1969a: 174). There is also a more immediate concern. It is, Galbraith writes, not merely in the long-run that we shall all be dead if the arms race powered by organisational interest is not brought to a halt: 'In the aftermath of nuclear war, the difference between capitalism and communism is not going to be evident even to the most committed ideologist' (Galbraith, 1988: 5). Events have consequences. Those consequences, it is clear, need not have any appeal at all.

6.1.3 The Intellectual Revolution

The story so far is a dismal one. Large corporations with the capacity to 'plan' have disproportionate power relative to the insignificant competitors of the market system. Technocrats and bureaucrats have organisational goals that they impose on their society by means ranging from manipulative sales-strategies to militaristic propaganda and nationalistic fear-mongering. Free market economists conceal concentrated power by retreating into a fantasy-world of jargon and symbol. Interventionist politicians reinforce concentrated power by means of subsidies and contracts. The classical proletariat is pacified into acceptance through higher pay at the expense of consumers and capitalists. Matter is in motion and things are taking their course. No one but a technocrat or a bureaucrat could, however, be entirely satisfied with all aspects of the course that they are taking. Evolution, it would appear, has not always been beneficent. It has often turned malign.

Yet the story so far, however dismal, is not complete. Events produce the technostructure and in that way produce a problem. Events, fortunately, also produce a new class and in that way produce a locus of countervailing power. That new bloc in the world of groups is the intelligentsia, the writers and the thinkers, the educational and scientific estate. It is all very tidy. More educators are the sine qua non for an expanded technostructure. An expanded technostructure then leads inevitably to an expanded intelligentsia. Paper certification is the 'relevant class distinction in our time' (Galbraith, 1967: 249) Trained manpower presupposes academies and educators. Academies and educators are, however, by no means favourable to the kind of society that the manpower they train subsequently proceeds to breed and form. In other words: 'The economy for its success requires organized public bamboozlement. At the same time it nurtures a growing class which feels itself superior to such bamboozlement and deplores it as intellectually corrupt' (ibid.: 294). Thus do the negators beget their own negation.

All education, for one thing, is oriented towards the development of the critical intelligence. Most of all is this true at the higher levels, where a candidate doing original research is compelled by the logic of his loneliness to think for himself. Galbraith believes such independence of thought to be a transferable skill. As education spreads, he reasons, so therefore will the resistance to conditioning and persuasion. This evolutionary force is a guarantee 'that there will be systematic questioning of the beliefs impressed by the industrial system' (ibid.: 364). The manipulators will gnash their teeth at the increasing scepticism that will greet their claims. There is nothing they can do. The truth is that a more educated citizenry will also be a more evaluative one.

Education by its very nature is individualistic whereas the technostructure is collegial. In that way too the schools and colleges challenge the new corporate order. All education, after all, 'allows and encourages a self-assertion and a self-expression which are inconvenient for those who prefer the acquiescence inherent in accommodation' (Galbraith, 1983a: 19). The collectivity of specialists makes decisions cooperatively in teams. The new graduate, however, is used to intellectual entrepreneurship. There is also the point that the technostructure functions by means of *conditioned* power (power that operates through belief, commitment, identification, the common acceptance of a shared purpose). The new graduate, on the other hand, is more accustomed to thinking in terms of power that is *condign* (in the sense of being backed up by the threat of adverse consequences) or power that is *compensatory* (power buttressed, in other words, by rewards and privileges). (Galbraith, 1983b: 4–6). The new graduate, it would appear, is likely to be something of a misfit in the world of corporate capitalism. Perhaps with time he will adapt. Perhaps he will not – and perhaps an addiction to individualism, early acquired, will render him unwilling even to try.

Such tendencies, Galbraith reports, are already beginning to manifest themselves: 'Good students, when asked about business, are increasingly adverse. They hold it to be excessively disciplined, damaging to individuality, not worth the high pay, or dull' (Galbraith, 1967: 363). While some critics will object that Galbraith's evidence is always anecdotal and selective and other critics will suggest that tendencies detected on the campuses of the late 1960s have been more than reversed by unstoppable hedonism since then, the crucial point is that Galbraith's confidence in his own determinism is total and unshakable. The technostructure is condemned to negation. The individualism inherent in education is an important part of the process of change.

Then there are the educators themselves. Appreciative of good literature and the visual arts like all enlightened consumers who have been exposed at school and university to the finer things in life, tidily but sensibly dressed when commercialised fashion preaches conspicuous consumption, insistent that their work be non-pressurised and their research topics of their own choosing, prepared to put creativity and fulfilment above the remuneration package, the readers and writers of books and articles are the role-models for the post-acquisitive, post-competitive, post-materialistic society that is to come. The role-model will one day be the norm.

Yet the educational and scientific estate did not come into being for educational and scientific reasons: 'It is the vanity of educators that they shape the educational system to their preferred image. They may not be without influence but the decisive force is the economic system. What the educator believes is latitude is usually latitude to respond to economic need' (ibid.: 241). It was not an exogenous change in tastes and preferences or the high income-elasticity of demand for learning as a good thing in itself that stimulated the take-off in the field of education. Instead it was the rapidly rising demand for technocrats that was primarily responsible for the rapidly rising demand for educators as the economic system grew more sophisticated. Events changed first. Ideas changed later and as a result.

The numbers of educators initially expanded in order to train the scarce and prestigious technocrats. The academics at that early stage merely shared via reflected glory in the high social standing of the key economic input. Later, however, the nature of the status-hierarchy was altered as the reputation of the technocrat became tarnished by the excrescences of corporate planning and the prestige of the intellectual was heightened by the increasing concern of affluent societies with cultural uplift. Nowadays, Galbraith says, the signs of major change are clearly to be seen: 'The position of the intellectual is now far more secure than that of the businessman' (Galbraith, 1958: 163). The future, evidently, is almost upon us. Matter is in motion. Events create ideas. A new class is brought into being and prominence that is capable of revealing the truth.

6.2   MIND AND MATTER

Although it was events and not ideas that catapulted the intellectual into his newly found position of prestige and power, the man of ideas is by no means likely to be dissatisfied with the direction of change. Looking at the course of evolution from the perspective of his own self-interest, he will be deeply appreciative of the status-rent that an admiring history apparently defines to be his due. The intellectual, 'along with the public official and politician, is the natural competitor of the businessman for what may be called the solemn acclaim of the community' (Galbraith, 1958: 163). As the obfuscators wane, the emancipators wax. There is no other group that can fill the void: 'For the goals that are now important there are no other saviours. In a scientifically exacting world, scientists must assume responsibility for the consequences of science and technology. For custody of the aesthetic dimension of life there is no substitute for the artist' (Galbraith, 1967: 377).

Events have enhanced the prestige and power of the educational and scientific estate. Even so, they will always limit the mould shaper's freedom of initiative to an extent that radical individualists will neglect at their cost. Intellectuals trade in ideas. That much is clear. Yet to say that a person *trades* is not the same as to say that he or she *trades with success*. Just as a merchant is vulnerable to being left with a stock of goods for which no buyers can be found, so the intellectual is in grave danger of preaching to no one but himself should the ideas he advances happen to be manifestly inappropriate in the specific material conditions that economic evolution is bringing into being. It is the events that suggest the ideas. The persuader who wishes to persuade would therefore be well advised to go with the flow.

Thus it was that Adam Smith's great success in attacking the mercantilist system of intervention resulted from his times and not merely from his rhetoric: 'Unrestricted competition did not achieve its reputation as a major public good until the different circumstances of manufacturers following the Industrial Revolution made freedom from craft-guild and government restraint a preferable alternative. Then, as ever, the ideas – the social conditioning – were brought abreast of the need' (Galbraith, 1983b: 101). In the 1940s, similarly, the dissidents, the humanitarians and the revolutionaries who pressed for an end to the colonial system won independence so quickly because of 'the rather simple but persuasive fact that colonies had become no longer economically worthwhile': 'The colonial world having thus been marginalised, it was to the advantage of all to let it go' (Galbraith, 1994: 13, 159). Adam Smith in 1776, Gandhi and Nehru when the engine of growth was becoming global free trade, were successful as persuaders because they gave voice as intellectuals to the ideas that had already been selected and prescribed by the events. Several centuries before, the same ideas would have fallen upon stony ground and been lost.

This important lesson the present-day educational and scientific estate must take to heart in its incipient struggle with the technocrats and the bureaucrats. There is only one body of concepts that normally fits the facts. Nor are those ideas the property of the intellectual alone. The educational and scientific estate may be one step ahead of the social consensus but it is seldom two. Galbraith presents himself as 'a strong economic determinist' (cited in Pratson, 1978: 232). His primary contention would therefore be that it is events and not educators that are in the last analysis the true gravediggers of the planners and the manipulators.

Events produce ideas. There is one name only on the ballot. Democracy is a single yes. The car of any possible colour provided only that it be black may usefully be described according to three sets of perceptions.

6.2.1   Demystification

People in thrall to an out-of-date conventional wisdom must in the first instance question the intellectual status quo. An obsolete theory of demand is an obvious target. Nowadays, Galbraith says, there operates an extensive battery of instruments for contrivance and want-creation. There is the 'well-considered mendacity' (Galbraith, 1967: 323) and the 'ruthless psychological pressures' (Galbraith, 1958: 247) of persuasive commercialism lacking informational content: 'Only a gravely retarded citizen can need to be told that the American Tobacco Company has cigarettes for sale' (Galbraith, 1967: 208). There is the wasteful acceleration of product development that is more in the interests of the technocrat than of the consumer: 'To create the demand for new cars we must contrive elaborate and functionless changes each year' (Galbraith, 1958: 247). It was in order to draw attention to the naïveté of textbook consumer sovereignty in the era of 'medacity' and 'pressures' that Galbraith wrote his *Affluent Society*.

Doing so, he was also aware that he was not alone. A better educated and better informed populace was increasingly in a better position even without his guidance to see through the bamboozlement to the truth beneath. More and more frequently, Galbraith notes, 'the merest child watching television dismisses the health and status-giving claims of a breakfast cereal as "a commercial" ' (Galbraith, 1967: 324). Matter is in motion and events create ideas. The thinker arriving *post festum* has no choice but to accept that he codifies far more than he creates.

As with an obsolete theory of demand, so with a Cold War commitment to lethal weaponry. The problem is the organic interdependence of special pleaders in the form of munitions manufacturers and defence ministries. The solution is multilateral disarmament and peaceful coexistence. The catalyst is the educational and scientific estate: 'The nuclear test ban treaty of 1963 would not have been achieved except by the initiative of the scientific community. General public and political awareness of the dangers of nuclear conflict, the desirability of *détente* with the Soviet Union and the technical possibilities for disarmament owes a great deal to the scientific community. It owes very little to the military, diplomatic and industrial community' (ibid.: 374–5).

Intellectuals are intimately acquainted with the weapons of destruction. They have a universal distaste for further confrontation. Consider Dr Yevgeny Chazov who, with an American, Dr Bernard Lown, was instrumental in founding the International Physicians for the Prevention of Nuclear War, for which he and Dr Lown were awarded the Nobel Peace Prize in 1985: 'In recent years Dr Chazov has become widely known in American and world medical circles for his leadership in drawing attention to the medical consequences of nuclear war' (Galbraith, 1984a: 269). Consider Dr George Kistiakowsky, Harvard Professor of Chemistry, scientific adviser to President Eisenhower, the man who designed the detonating device for the first atomic bomb, the co-founder of the Council for a Liveable World, the committed 'keeper of the public conscience', whose expert knowledge gave him an insider's insight into the potential outcome of the arms race: 'George Kistiakowsy had a deep and

enduring sense of responsibility for his community and all who made it up'
(Galbraith, 1983c: 400). Consider Dr John Kenneth Galbraith, Harvard
Professor of Economics, political associate of progressive Democrats like
Stevenson, Kennedy, McGovern, McCarthy, co-founder of the Americans for
Democratic Action, co-chairman of the American Committee on East–West
Accord, moderate pragmatist and friend of moderate pragmatists – 'Arthur
Schlesinger, whose non-communist credentials were and have remained
adequate, was driven to express the thought that Laos was not a dagger pointed
at the heart of Kansas' (Galbraith, 1982: 47) – who repeatedly calls upon his
audiences and his readers to 'unite now in a crusade to get nuclear energy
under control' (Galbraith, 1980: 6), to ensure that 'no one is now elected,
Republican or Democrat, conservative or liberal, who thinks nuclear war an
option' (ibid.: 7).

Dr Chazov, Dr Kistiakowsky and Dr Galbraith – all three had this in
common, that they as responsible intellectuals took a principled and public
stand on the Cold War commitment to lethal weaponry. The contribution of
these thinkers and others like them in focusing the public awareness must not
be neglected, but nor should their autonomous influence, Galbraith warns, be
exaggerated. The intellectuals have only revealed the truth: 'To identify power
is to invite people to react against it' (cited in *Challenge*, 1973: 86). They did
not create it. Given enough time, the truths that he and his fellow intellectuals
revealed would have come to light in any case.

Events are stronger than ideas. That is why Galbraith was able at an early stage
to predict the implosion of communist imperative plans. Economic growth
makes productive activity more complicated and more diverse. The administrative impossibility of coordinating so multifaceted a productive order must
inevitably impose upon the Iron Curtain countries the need to decentralise, to
devolve, to experiment with market incentives: 'There is a popular cliché,
deeply beloved by conservatives, that socialism and communism are the cause
of a low standard of living. It is much more nearly accurate to say that a low
and simple standard of living makes socialism and communism feasible'
(Galbraith, 1952a: 187).

The East did not last because Plekhanov and even Derzhinsky were not
enough to buck the market: 'In the world as it exists, there is clearly no plausible alternative' (Galbraith, 1998: 17). People in the East wanted innovation
and novelty, rising living standards and state-of-the-art infrastructure. That
meant that they had to make their peace with individual freedom, wide-ranging choice and liberal democracy that makes the lift-off possible: 'Above a
certain level of economic achievement, human rights become not only a right
but an inevitability. They are the product, or at least extensively the product,
not of original virtue but of inescapable need. Nowhere does economic deter-

minism, the controlling role of economics in human affairs, work more relent-lessly and with so little recognition' (Galbraith, 1994: 224). Marx was right about economics. That is precisely why he was wrong about socialism. The Soviet Union tried to build its future around 'the comprehensive operation or control of industry by the state' (ibid.: 21). It was defeated not by NATO but by exchange.

The East went West. Yet the West too has had to bend. Government regu-lations save lives: 'The most committed ideologues are known to ride on airplanes, and they prefer on matters of safety to surrender authority to the state' (ibid.: 197). The nationalisation of the railways is the preferred alterna-tive to no railways at all: 'These are practical and not ideological questions. We're the only country that has tried having its railroads under private owner-ship and it hasn't worked' (cited in McClaughry, 1973: 103). State planning and big government had to come. There was no way that the 'traumatic power of events' (Galbraith, 1994: 10) could be addressed simply by appealing to ideas that had outlived their relevance: 'The one thing worse than trying to perfect the imperfectible is trying to resist the irresistible. I am absolutely convinced that government planning will increase in the future. The old reme-dies for economic ills don't work any more. Their cure will require a social contract on which only government can lead. We're not talking about an ideol-ogy, but about an absence of alternatives. We're subject, like it or not, to the tyranny of circumstance' (cited in Matthews, 1978: 114).

With evolution there comes convergence, with convergence acceptance: 'The age of presumed choice between alternative economic systems is over' (Galbraith, 1998: 17). The new era will be an age of middle-ground thinking and of unprejudiced trial and error to find out what works: 'The question of the private versus the public role should not be decided on abstract, theoreti-cal grounds; the decision depends rather on the merits of the particular case . . . Ideology can be a heavy blanket over thought. Our commitment must always be to thought' (ibid.: 20). With thought there comes tolerance. It is a globalisation of the intellectual frontiers for which it is events rather than ideas that must ultimately be assigned the primary causal role: 'To recognize that industrial systems are convergent . . . will, one imagines, help towards agree-ment on the common dangers in the weapons competition, on ending it or shifting it to more benign areas' (Galbraith, 1967: 384).

The well-publicised differences between the Eastern countries helped to erode the rabid anti-communism of more confrontational times. In the West, simul-taneously, the out-of-date stock of perceptions had been badly discredited by a variety of well-publicised disparities between bureaucratic self-deception and the real truth. One illustration of the credibility gap would be the abortive Bay of Pigs invasion in 1961: 'Organization needed to believe that Fidel

Castro was toppling on the edge' (Galbraith, 1969b: 17). Another illustration would be the inescapable *débâcle* in Southeast Asia a decade and more afterwards: 'Vietnam will be the graveyard of the old policy' (Galbraith, 1966a: 33). Vietnam was never central to America's strategic interests. Besides that, given enough time, Asian communism would succumb to the same pressures that were already destroying the Russians from within: 'The later history of Vietnam has shown that Communists can govern; it has also shown that they cannot sustain a Communist system' (Galbraith, 1999: 162).

The old ideas, rendered obsolete by the march of events, are increasingly *perceived* to be obsolete by a citizenry that increasingly substitutes nuclear-free conurbations for private fallout shelters, the nuclear freeze for the military incursion. They are being rejected by an electorate that increasingly puts pressure on its political leaders to supply that which is increasingly in demand: 'In the past there has been nothing more salutary in our governmental process than the speed with which we have discarded those public figures who have seemed to be casual about nuclear weapons and war' (Galbraith, 1980: 7). Thus it was that Galbraith in 1987 was able to write as follows about the military–industrial complex: 'I have a feeling that the people of the United States are very strongly aware of this problem. In the presidential election next year all of the candidates – the Democratic candidates, at least – will be talking about the need for arms control and for restraint on military spending. This will be in response to very clearly articulated public opinion' (Galbraith, 1988: 118).

That public opinion did not spring full-grown from nowhere. Nor, however, was it the manufacture of responsible teachers like Dr Chazov, Dr Kistiakowsky and Dr Galbraith. Men of ideas publicise and agitate. The perceptions for which they fight are unlikely for all that to enjoy any widespread currency unless they happen to be solid truths backed up by evolution and already gaining ground in their own right. Matter is in motion and people are not stupid. Critics who see Galbraith the persuader as a paternalist and a manipulator evidently see him both as less tolerant and as more influential than he would perhaps say that he saw himself.

6.2.2 Balance

Demystification done, the next task is to remix the mixed economy. The objective, quite specifically, must be to secure an expansion (both absolute and relative) in public expenditure. The change will not be too difficult to bring about. Matter is in motion and substance throws up the shadow. Evolution contains within itself the seeds of the balance that the bamboozlement will seek in vain to block.

Casual inspection reveals public poverty juxtaposed to private affluence.

There is on the one hand a visible scarcity of 'some of the most significant and civilizing services' (Galbraith, 1958: 133): the list includes roads, schools, parks, health insurance for the aged, medical care for the impoverished, law and order, low-cost housing. There is on the other hand a surfeit of trinkets and baubles of 'considerable, even extreme, frivolity and unimportance' (Galbraith, 1987: 290): they may be typified by the toaster that prints an inspirational message on each piece of toast (Galbraith, 1967: 82). The Fabian or the Democrat does not create the revulsion that ultimately leads to the transcendence of the 'obscene contrast' (Galbraith, 1966a: 30). All that the teacher or journalist can do is to ensure that no citizen is unaware of the great void in the cities and on the streets. Events themselves will create the revulsion once the extent of the imbalance is properly perceived. The sight and smell of decomposing rubbish will cause the sensitive to forgo the gold-plated mousetrap in favour of more frequent refuse collection. Race riots and crime waves will bring home the benefits both of better police services and detection units and of improved public libraries and inner-city swimming pools. The police deter. The swimming pools prevent. It is not a value judgment. It is a fact of life.

The dependency culture is a further reason for expanded public expenditure. Transfers cost money – and the drain can be stemmed. The best antidote to long-run benefits in cash is a major and immediate injection of pump-priming benefits in kind: 'Good health services increase the number of people who are physically and mentally able to take part in the economy. . . . Mostly this is what a good educational system accomplishes . . . We should help people to participate in the economy; we should help them to help themselves' (Galbraith, 1966b: 21). Market failure means that the State alone is in a position to offer training and retraining schemes, drug rehabilitation clinics and public housing estates that are healthful and safe: 'In no economically advanced country . . . does the market system build houses the poor can afford' (Galbraith, 1992: 44). The State, correcting the market failure, makes a self-liquidating investment in the take-off into self-sufficiency and self-reliance. Positive-sum economics leads to a popular demand for the 'significant and civilizing services' that would take the malintegrated and the marginal off the welfare rolls for good. Such a campaign is 'not ideological': it is 'compelled by circumstance' (Galbraith, 1973a: 295). Events producing ideas, it is bound to succeed.

In places, as in the following, Galbraith makes a direct and unashamed appeal to the enlightened self-interest of the prosperous middle class: 'Perhaps the disadvantaged are now too few to make a revolution. But they could make life uncomfortable for all' (Galbraith, 1980: 5). Even in the new industrial society, it would seem, the capitalist system still retains the two-way relationship with the welfare State that was so distinctive a characteristic of British and American economic history in the recent past: 'No one can suppose that capitalism would have survived without those attempts to remedy what was wrong ... This was an absolutely indispensable design for saving capitalism. Capitalism wouldn't have survived if it hadn't had the rough, harsh edges taken off by the welfare state' (Galbraith, 1988: 80–1). Market decentralisation is the only viable economic order. For it to succeed, however, there must be the complement of welfare that fills in the gaps: 'Capitalism in its original form was an insufferably cruel thing. Only with trade unions, the protection of workers and workers' rights, pensions for the old, compensation for the unemployed, public healthcare, lower-cost housing, a safety net, however imperfect, for the unfortunate and the deprived, and public action to mitigate capitalism's commitment to boom and slump did the market system become socially and politically acceptable' (Galbraith, 1998: 18–19).

Economic growth itself acts as a solvent of the social tensions once associated with inequality: 'Increased real income provides us with an admirable detour around the rancour anciently associated with efforts to redistribute wealth' (Galbraith, 1954: 195). Unaided and unsupported, however, the well-being that capitalism delivers is not enough to ensure a truce. The integrated go up. The underclass remain outside. In order to generalise the rise in living standards, there is no alternative to the State. Intervention, historically speaking, has 'saved classical capitalism from itself' (Galbraith, 1998: 18). The political right would in the circumstances be well advised to soften 'its opposition to what advances its own deeper, more durable interest' (ibid.: 19). Ideology makes it demand tax cuts. The longer view would make it demand food stamps instead. Those who oppose intervention 'are at odds with the great force of history ... We, not they, are in step' (ibid.: 32).

Enlightened self-interest plays an important role in Galbraith's account of mind, matter and balance. Not only are the discontented taken off the streets but the suburbs acquire their public universities and the affluent enjoy their motorways. Survival and subsidy certainly bulk large in Galbraith's theory of welfare. It would be wrong, however, to suggest that he attributes little significance to the social democrat's more idealistic constructs of compassion and citizenship. Galbraith states explicitly that economic evolution makes the caring externality the functional prerequisite for economic advance: 'In a complex and interdependent world, the sense of community must be strong and ever stronger' (Galbraith, 1980: 5). What *must* be, *will* be. The need for a social ethic must be expected over time to produce the social decency that the system requires: 'I am persuaded, as was Marx ... that economic development is itself an education in social cohesiveness and cooperation' (Galbraith, 1979: 95). Capitalism desiring survival came also to desire fraternity and to look after its own. There is no mention of Christianity or of Dunkirk. Events are enough to create the ideas that make the transition smooth.

As we grow more affluent, so we grow more altruistic, more integrated, more open to public and community initiative. Relying mainly on impressions and anecdotes, Galbraith reaches the conclusion that the supportive State is far less frequently in demand in earlier stages of economic evolution than it is in our own. Developed capitalism has come to reject the 'rigid adherence to individualist precept' of the self-help Victorians, to regard as too harsh 'the sacrifice of those who could not make it in a stern competitive struggle' (Galbraith, 1980: 5). Kindliness is in the air; and a not insignificant part of the explanation is 'a sense of community' (ibid.) that is not a simple rationalisation of enlightened self-interest. The sense of community is the product of events. It renders the citizens of an affluent society genuinely concerned about the incidence of suffering, alienation and failure within the broad church of a common humanity.

Galbraith makes no attempt to quantify the unquantifiable by providing any solid evidence that altruism has in fact advanced with prosperity rather than being eroded by the market ethos that has contributed so much to affluence. Nor does he provide any real answer to those of his fellow optimists who say that the flowering of an other-oriented culture points not to an interventionist welfare *State* but rather to a spontaneous and individualistic welfare *society*. There does not seem to be any blood donation or voluntary service in his theory of how the community might sustain its integrity without the *ex machina* of the suits. Omissions there may well be, and different thinkers will no doubt think different thoughts, but the logic of Galbraith's position remains clear nonetheless. Galbraith as a reformer believes he has uncovered the nature of the need: 'There are few problems in New York City which would not be solved by doubling the city budget' (Galbraith: 1971a: 33). Galbraith as an evolutionary economist is also convinced, events breeding ideas, that his fellow-citizens are not far behind him in demanding expanded public spending on the broadly-defined and open-ended fine-tuning of the social-services State.

Ordinary men and women are on the point of insisting that a welfare-conscious society should 'cease using sociology as a substitute for higher taxes' (ibid.). Ordinary men and women are also on the point of demanding more generous public funding for the arts. The historical truth is that, at some stage in the evolutionary process, 'as consumption expands, a transcending interest in beauty may be expected' (Galbraith, 1973a: 84): 'After things work well, people want them to look well, so the arts become important' (Galbraith, 1988: 99). More affluence and more education inevitably generate a demand for more beauty. The intellectual does not to any significant extent create that demand. He is likely, however, to share it and to approve of it. Some of the demand will, admittedly, be satisfied in the private sector (designer clothing, foreign travel, pay-per-view TV), and some of it even by small and non-bureaucratised service undertakings (the local gallery, the local boutique). Some of the demand, but not all. That is why, Galbraith maintains, if it is truly the case that 'beyond the age of the engineer and the scientist lies the age of the artist' (Galbraith, 1970c: 139), then a demand-led political system will have no choice but to supply the museums and sponsor the orchestras that a more cultivated citizenry will increasingly wish to consume.

Balance means support to welfare and to the arts. It also means support to industry, both large and small. Schumpeter says that the giant corporations are the cutting-edge of technology. Galbraith adds the rider that they are also loss-averting and afraid. Ordinary men and women are keen to consume the fruits. The problem is that private enterprise, without the government-guaranteed markets and the taxpayers' capital infusions, is simply not prepared to assume the risks: 'The old-fashioned subsonic jet passenger transport would not have existed except as a by-product of government-sponsored military development. The development of supersonic transport has had to wait on government initiative. One rewarding result of these necessities has been the discovery of how much government initiative is welcomed in a capitalist economy once it is discovered that capitalism cannot do the job' (Galbraith, 1965: 63).

The State should, once again because of a private-sector deficiency, subsidise research and development in central laboratories on behalf of the numerous small competitors in the market system. Consumers demand high-quality milk and grain but farmers are too weak and too isolated to bring about the requisite response. Intellectuals will in such a case call for State support in the interests of social balance. They will not be alone. Matter is in motion and history is in flux. A citizenry that wants the foodstuffs as it wants the flights will sooner or later see that it has no alternative but to join its voice to that of big business and small business alike in attacking the discredited dogma of laissez-faire. Thus do events breed ideas. They do as if guided by an invisible hand that never sees any reason to deviate from its line.

6.2.3 Regulation

Evolution produces demystification and promotes social balance. It is also a stimulus to moderate State regulation. *Moderate* regulation, however, cautious and selective regulation; for the fact is that the general consensus *non facit saltum*, and neither therefore should the intellectual or the politician.

One form of regulation that Galbraith both anticipates and recommends is regulation to protect the environment. The smog, the global warming and the traffic jams, in his perspective, are universally regarded as public bads. They are the product of events: 'The price of increasing production is unpleasant and even lethal surroundings. The air is less breathable, the water less potable, the countryside is invisible and the air waves unbelievable' (Galbraith, 1971a: 9). The intellectual sees correctly that something must be done, but so too do ordinary men and women. They come to develop reservations of their own about lead in petrol, acid rain, the siting of waste dumps, sprawling suburbs, intrusive advertising, blighted landscapes and unsightly bypasses. The intellectual's arguments evidently enjoy 'much persuasive assistance from pollution' (Galbraith, 1981: 338). Without that assistance it is unlikely that they would have had much influence. Ordinary people are normally cozened by Madison Avenue: 'We, quite literally, advertise our commitment to immaturity, mendacity and profound gullibility' (Galbraith, 1964: 19). They are occasionally cozened by the Elysée, the Istana and the White House: 'Mr Nixon was a premeditated assault on the public decency and interest committed in broad daylight' (Galbraith, 1974: 394). They are, however, seldom if ever cozened by the intelligent and articulate persuaders of Harvard Square.

Pollution does what the intellectuals cannot. Ordinary men and women come to see that something must be done. It is to their reactions, confronted with the ugliness and the risks, that the bans on highway advertising in Hawaii and Vermont (Galbraith, 1971b: 99), the controls on DDT, non-degradable detergents and supersonic aircraft (Galbraith, 1973a: 309–10) must be attributed. Environmental degradation is the event. Defence of amenity value is the idea produced by the event. The polluters are more effective than the persuaders in bringing about the laws that are needed.

Events produce the ideas that protect the environment. They are also to be credited with the discovery of the macroeconomic policies that pure thinkers mistakenly ascribe to the genius of Keynes: 'Here once again it was events, not economists, that took charge – events silent, without voice and, since unrecognized, unresisted' (Galbraith, 1987: 250). The simple fact is that monetary policy had demonstrably failed to bring about full employment and stability of total demand in the depressed conditions of the inter-war years. 'Harsh circumstance, that intractable force in economic policy, had already required what Keynes was to urge' (ibid.: 226): 'There remained one – just one – course. That was government intervention to raise the level of investment spending – government borrowing and spending for public purposes. A deliberate deficit. This alone would break the underemployment equilibrium by, in effect, spending – willfully spending – the unspent savings of the private sector' (ibid.: 234–5).

J.M. Keynes did indeed formulate an intellectual's case for precisely such fiscal regulation. His theoretical contribution cannot for all that be described as anything more than 'a powerful affirmation of the wisdom of what was already being done under the force of circumstance' (ibid.: 235): 'Keynes . . . made legitimate what governments of all the industrial countries, including the

United States, were already doing. Depression had reduced government revenues and forced increases in spending for welfare. The result was a deficit, and out of force of circumstance this was being covered by borrowing, exactly as Keynes urged' (Galbraith, 1981: 67–8).

Even Adolf Hitler had grasped the nature of the demand management that had become inevitable. He had done so in advance of what pure thinkers were later to call the Keynesian 'revolution': 'Not the least remarkable feature of this revolution was by how many it had been anticipated. There were Keynesians well before Keynes. One was Hitler, who, exempt from any restraining economic theory, launched a major program of public works construction upon taking office in 1933, the *Autobahnen* being the most visible effect. Civil works expenditure was followed only later by that for arms. The Nazis were also indifferent to the constraints of tax revenue; deficit financing was taken for granted. The German economy recovered from the devastating slump it had previously suffered. By 1936, the unemployment that had been so influential in bringing Hitler to power had been substantially eliminated' (Galbraith, 1987: 222–3).

Hitler in Germany, the New Deal in America, the Second World War in the offing – the young Galbraith and his fellow Harvard economists clearly had good grounds for their optimism when they launched their crusade for the Keynesian system in the 1930s: 'All of us were committed to a degree of evangelism I've never felt since. There was an enormous feeling we could change things. In some ways it was a very misleading experience, you had such a sense of what an intellectual could accomplish. From that time on we all believed that, if you had the right ideas, nothing stood in your way – it could be done' (cited in Halberstam, 1967: 51). It could indeed, given the fundamental premise that there was one and only one course of action that could rationally be adopted in the concrete material circumstances of an economy in slump: 'Not often in history do ideas and events combine so decisively to persuade' (Galbraith, 1994: 103). Events produce ideas. The Keynesian intellectuals only diffused those ideas that would ultimately have diffused themselves had there been no Keynes at all. It is no surprise that they had so great an influence in the depressed conditions of the 1930s. Obvious *must be*s are obvious *must be*s. It was in nothing more than obvious *must be*s that the Keynesian intellectuals of the Great Depression sensibly chose to trade.

The inflationary tendencies of the 1980s presented challenges somewhat different from those of the Great Depression. In the later period as in the earlier one, however, it remained the case that it was the circumstances and not the economists that defined the obvious *must be*s that would obviously solve the problems. Not all observers saw clearly what had to be done. Milton Friedman and Friedrich von Hayek did not. Margaret Thatcher and Ronald

Reagan did not. The outcome of the error was the temporary adoption of monetarist policies in Britain and America. These were 'aberrations', fortunately, 'which experience and good sense will reverse' (Galbraith, 1988: 110): 'I have been reluctant to attribute the word revolution to the changes that have occurred with Mr. Reagan. I think they are temporary in the history of capitalism; supply-side economics and monetarism are transitory steps and will disappear from sight' (ibid.: 109). The monetarist policies of Thatcher and Reagan were out of step with the march of events, 'immune to historical process' (Galbraith, 1983a: 73). They were doomed to failure. There was no way that the craft could fly.

Monetarism is 'one of the most grievously destructive policies of modern times' (cited in *Eastern Economic Journal*, 1988: 137). It brings with it cuts in investment, retrenchment of labour, even bankruptcies of businesses that would in time prove sound: 'Monetary policy controls inflation by drastically and even permanently damaging the industrial base of the countries pursuing it' (ibid.: 135) Monetarism, besides that, is analogous to a regressive tax. Redistributing towards the well-off and away from the deprived, it is palpably at variance with the welfarist consensus of advanced capitalism: 'Monetary policy has a strong tilt in favor of the financially favored . . . High interest rates reward those with money to lend. As a broad proposition, those who lend money are likely to have more money than those who do not!' (ibid.: 134).

Monetarism, finally, is politically unworkable save in the hands of truly iron-willed leadership. That strength of purpose was certainly not found in America under Reagan. Then, monetarism or no monetarism, 'high and stolidly defended Keynesian deficits' (Galbraith, 1984b: 320) were the order of the day, and 'on a scale', indeed, 'that Keynes himself could never have imagined' (Galbraith, 1975b: 403). That the shake-out could be short-run or the shake-up a boost to average productivity, that macroeconomic policy is not the only or even the primary arena for social policies that promote social justice, that weak administration is always and everywhere a problem but that strong Thatcherism converted a budget deficit into a budget surplus – these and similar monetarist arguments Galbraith puts to one side. His selectivity is highly beneficial; for it allows him to conclude that interest rates and money-supply policies are 'aberrations', 'temporary' and 'transitory'. All nations, like all persons, occasionally make mistakes. The withering away of New Deal interventionism in the run-up to the Second World War was evidently such a mistake: 'It was adversity that nurtured this programme; with prosperity social invention came promptly to an end' (Galbraith, 1952a: 25). The monetarist experiment in the inflationary conditions of the 1980s was no more nor less than another experiment. Historical evolution is tolerant of small steps backwards. So is Galbraith.

Monetarism does not provide the solution to the problem of inflation.

Neither, however, does Keynesianism. An increase in taxation (either progressive income tax or regressive duties on goods and services) is a traditional textbook remedy for an excess of demand over supply; but economic, social and political factors severely limit the extent of any feasible rise. A cut in public spending is an alternative. In the light of the growing popular enthusiasm for social balance it is clearly not an option that any sensitive democrat could safely contemplate. That leaves controls.

The private sector already plans its prices. It must do so. The loss in allocative efficiency is more than counterbalanced by the security that the planning permits: 'General Motors could not function without some assurance that its prices would be adequate. Price stability is necessary for its planning' (Galbraith, 1981: 103). The public sector is itself no stranger to the planning of nominal values. Controls were introduced in the United States in wartime (Galbraith himself was in charge) for the unassailable reason that 'circumstances appeared to offer no other course' (Galbraith, 1952b: 4). Later, in 1961, it was once again circumstances rather than preferences that led President Kennedy to promulgate his 'guideposts' (Galbraith, 1973a: 212). Austria, Germany, Switzerland and other European countries, Galbraith said in the late 1980s, continue to this day to secure stability without stagnation by means of the obvious expedient of wage and price controls. Given cost-push inflation, the obvious expedient was also the only expedient: 'Sooner or later, the English-speaking countries will be led to recognize this' (Galbraith, 1987: 297). They will do so because they will have to do so. They will have no choice: 'I see no alternative, no other way of reconciling high employment with price stability' (Galbraith, 1975b: 131).

It was one of the few issues on which Galbraith was ultimately to back down. In 1952, he had said that price controls presented few difficulties: 'It is relatively easy to fix prices that are already fixed' (Galbraith, 1952b: 17). By 1996, he was saying that controls were 'in conflict with the basic structural character of the market system and likewise with powerful economic and public attitudes and beliefs. The most that can now be urged is a sense of responsibility on wage-price negotiation that reflects the larger public interest' (Galbraith, 1996: 47). Controls were appropriate in the earlier period. They were not appropriate in the later one. That is just the point that Galbraith has always tried to make: 'In public affairs circumstance is far more influential and ideological preference far less important than is commonly supposed' (Galbraith, 1977b: 233). Matter is in motion and evolution is taking its course. While the intellectual is understandably tempted to 'try to advance the inevitable' (Galbraith, 1977a: 92), nonetheless it is events and not ideas that in the Galbraithian scheme of things must ultimately be given the last word.

7. T.H. Marshall: citizenship and social thought

Schumpeter's socialism is economic planning and post-competitive controls. Together with the Marxists who believe that market coordination will self-destruct and the Fabians who advocate the nationalisation of the commanding heights, the Schumpeterian vision is one which anticipates a transition into what T.H. Marshall calls 'Socialism A' (Marshall, 1963: 271). Socialism A, Marshall says, is full-bodied socialism. It is 'real socialism', the hard-line dogma that is the inspiration for 'all schools of thought which set out to transform the social and economic system by abolishing capitalism, whether by violence or by peaceful penetration' (ibid.: 271–2).

Marshall's 'Socialism A' looks forward to a future that has evolved beyond gain-driven enterprise. Marshall's 'Socialism B', social-ism and not preponderantly economics-ism, is 'milder and less alarming' (ibid.: 272). Socialism B raises no objection to the free market which it accepts will contribute much to allocative and dynamic efficiency. Its thesis is simply that there are high social values such as security and justice which the invisible hand, uncorrected, would leave in a state of intolerable neglect.

Marshall's 'Socialism B' is the material embodiment of the 'humanitarianism associated with the so-called Tory Socialists, combined with some emergent principles of social policy developed by the more advanced Liberals, and a readiness to rely on government action which had a definitely Socialist, or as Dicey would say, "collectivist" flavour' (ibid.: 272). Macmillan was a socialist since he did not believe that ignorance and destitution should lie where they fall. Asquith was a socialist since he was convinced that income maintenance filled a commercial void. Bevan was a socialist since he made subsidised healthcare the foundation for classless nationality. Nowadays, in fact, virtually everyone is a socialist: 'Socialist measures ... have been accepted by all political parties' (Marshall, 1950: 47). Unfettered exchange having met some but not all of society's reasonable expectations, Socialism B emerged as the democratic choice that alone could deliver the consensual mix: 'Our modern system is frankly a socialist system' (ibid.: 7). We like it that way.

Socialism B is public policy that had to be adopted in order to reunite the separated and reaffirm the fellowship: 'It recognized individual rights not created or measured by the market value of a man, but derived from his status as a citizen. It was in this sense that the principle of the Welfare State rejected the philosophy of the Affluent Society' (Marshall, 1963: 276). Socialism B is acceptance more than achievement, belonging more than independence, the gift more than the sale. It is ethical socialism, and T.H. Marshall was one of its most persuasive interpreters: 'With Tony Blair as the leader of the Labour Party in the 1990s,' Halsey writes, 'we have seen a return of Marshall's ideas to the centre of the political stage. Marshall was in one sense the outstanding sociological interpreter of British Butskellism, the subtle advocate of the British version of the welfare state' (Halsey, 1998: 81). The essence of Marshall's socialism is not macroeconomic stagnation or the choke-hold of finance. Instead it is positive attitudes, the hand of friendship and doing what is right: 'For Hobhouse, Tawney, Orwell and Marshall it is that distinctive if imprecise phrase from the British political lexicon – common decency' (ibid.: 95).

The subject of this chapter is British socialism as common decency. It is not about the inevitability of central planning in the sense of the sad-eyed Schumpeter but about 'the more complex conception of social justice' (Durbin, 1940: 32) in the sense of the hopeful Evan Durbin's *Politics of Democratic Socialism* that in 1940 had given young radicals an appealing glimpse of the ideal society that Labour could create. The chapter is divided into five sections. The first, 'Historian and sociologist', describes Marshall's evolution from Jethro Tull to social commitment. The second, 'Freedom *to*: Green and Hobhouse', is a reminder that Britain was the homeland not just of free trade and the workhouse test but of the upgrading, uplifting New Liberalism as well. The third, 'Sociology and social policy', explains Marshall's middle-ground methodology, eminently suitable for a social demo-crat in search of a compound. The fourth, 'Marshall's publications', considers his two-page list of books and papers and asks why he did not write more. The fifth, 'From Attlee to Thatcher', says that the Britain of the 1980s was not the Britain of the 1950s and that even great ideas can be left behind by events.

7.1   HISTORIAN AND SOCIOLOGIST

T.H. Marshall, born in 1893, was the child of Victorian prosperity and Edwardian high-mindedness. He died in 1981 when Mrs Thatcher as Prime Minister was showing that Britain was not after all stranded forever on the middle ground.

Marshall's grandfather had amassed a fortune in the Industrial Revolution. Marshall's father, William Cecil Marshall, was a successful London architect.

As a privileged youth, brought up in the cultured and affluent surroundings of a town house in Bedford Square, Bloomsbury, and a country place in Hindhead, Surrey, Thomas Humphrey was well acquainted with William Morris wallpaper and Adam ceilings. The man in the street was a different matter. Marshall later recalled that he 'knew nothing of working-class life, and the great industrial north was a nightmare land of smoke and grime through which one had to travel to get from London to the Lake District' (Marshall, 1973: 88). Marshall described his childhood as one-sided, 'limited' and 'naïvely unsociological' (ibid.). Only at university did he begin to mix with young people of working-class origin.

Marshall was educated at Rugby School and Trinity College, Cambridge. He obtained a first-class honours degree in history in 1914. By then he had lost his religious faith: he had been 'sincerely devout' (ibid.) at school and his mother was the daughter of a New Zealand archdeacon. Learning German in Weimar when the war broke out, he spent four years as a civilian prisoner of war in an internment camp at Ruhleben, near Berlin. He was to call it 'the most powerful formative experience of my early years' (ibid.: 89). Marshall observed how class divisions anchored in education and self-image survived unaltered in the closed community despite the fact that the inmates had no income, property or capital. He discovered how organised activity overtook initial spontaneity as structure emerged and binding conventions developed. The microcosm at Ruhleben, in short, aroused his 'sociological curiosity' (ibid.). It widened his horizons beyond his class.

No longer aiming at the Foreign Service, no longer considering a career as a professional violinist despite his acknowledged musical talent, Marshall returned to Cambridge in 1919 and secured a Fellowship at Trinity. Economic history was his main area of interest. Under the influence of Clapham, he made a study of the guilds in the early post-feudal period. The two-way relationship between law and economics was not a new thing for him. He had earlier been exposed to the insights of Vinogradoff, Maine and Maitland in a course on medieval history taught by Gaillard Lapsley: 'Marshall's later conception of capitalism, socialism and democracy was built on the foundations of the analytical construction of estate society fashioned by these historians' (Halsey, 1984: 3).

A quiet life as an upper middle-class historian in an upper middle-class university seemed on the cards. Nothing could be closer to the Establishment core than British history at Cambridge. Cambridge was a sub-culture where socialists were thin on the ground and sociology was not even taught until the 1960s. Events, however, were beginning to take a different course.

In 1922, Marshall stood as a Labour candidate for a safe Conservative seat in Surrey. Still under 30, he was already seeing himself as a Socialist B. Since the reforming Liberals shared the same emphasis on social services and equality of respect, it is not clear why he felt the need to join a party with its roots in the unions, the proletariat and the public ownership of capital. There were many in the Labour Party in 1922 who were strongly attracted by 'the belief that greater equality in the distribution of income and property can be combined with economic efficiency *only* in an industrial system that is centrally controlled' (Durbin, 1940: 32, emphasis added). It is hard to see what Marshall thought he had in common with people who believed that social betterment could not be expected so long as the economic market remained free.

In 1925, Marshall married Marjorie Tomson. She died in 1931. Marshall later, in 1934, was to marry Nadine Hambourg: Mrs T.H. Marshall, the mother of their son Mark, would be Durbin's research assistant when he wrote his *Politics* in the years just before the Second World War. In 1925, there came an even more radical step. Marshall left respectable Cambridge for the London School of Economics, widely regarded with suspicion as a hotbed of extremism. His audience at the LSE was made up of students of social work. It was a subject, he said later, about which he 'knew nothing' (Marshall, 1973: 90). He was not expected to know a great deal. As at Cambridge, his lectures were on economic and constitutional history.

When Hobhouse died in 1929, he was succeeded to the Martin White Chair of Sociology by Morris Ginsberg. Hobhouse had held the chair (the first Professorship in Sociology at a British university) since 1907. Ginsberg needed someone to take over Hobhouse's course on Comparative Social Institutions. Disciplinary boundaries were less rigid in 1929 and there was still a belief that a good man could turn his hand to anything. Ginsberg invited Marshall to make the move to Sociology.

Marshall in 1929 had not mastered the great classics of Durkheim, Weber and Marx: 'I was quite ignorant of sociology in the professional sense' (ibid.: 91). He never felt that he had entirely filled in the gaps. In his favour, however, there was the social commitment, the sociological curiosity, and the university of Ruhleben. There was also the grounding in history, itself 'the analysis of social systems and the interpretation of social change' (ibid.).

History *is* comparative social institutions. Marshall visited the past for his (admittedly not path-breaking) book on James Watt (1925) and his papers on Jethro Tull (1929) and on population expansion in the industrial revolution (1929). Travelling backward, he had learned to juxtapose the yesterdays to the todays and to explain to himself why ideas and events moved on. Marshall, like Parsons and Tawney, was acquainted with the evolutionism of the German organicists: 'Economic history and a knowledge of German scholarship often in the 1920s led to sociology' (MacRae, 1982: 4). He had also gained a purchase on social interdependence and the national purpose through the emphasis on facts at the service of policies in the work of the English historical economists. Economic history when Marshall was a student was not yet the neoclassical orthodoxy applied unquestioningly to underdeveloped backwardness that it was to become after the foundation of a separate Economic History Society in 1926. Instead it was a tolerant appreciation of social diversity and a way in to a restless reality, forever in flux.

7.2   FREEDOM *TO*: GREEN AND HOBHOUSE

Marshall took over Hobhouse's old course in Hobhouse's old Department. He also became the heir to Hobhouse's window on the world. Marshall believed that he became a sociologist 'very naturally, almost totally under the influence of Hobhouse, as interpreted by Ginsberg' (Marshall, 1973: 95). Works like *Democracy and Reaction* (1904), *Liberalism* (1911), *Social Evolution and Political Theory* (1911) and *The Metaphysical Theory of the State* (1918) deeply impressed the young historian with their vision of unity, integration, cooperation and intervention. Marshall in his later years described Hobhouse as 'the most famous and original of British sociologists since Spencer' (Marshall, 1965b: 159).

T.H. Green (1837–82) had formulated a theory of freedom *to* that was activist and developmental. In his *Lectures on the Principles of Political Obligation* (delivered in 1879) and in papers like 'Liberal Legislation and Freedom of Contract' (1881), the Balliol philosopher and teleologist of emancipation had invited the State to assist the individual in his journey of self-improvement and self-actualisation: 'It is the business of the state, not directly to promote moral goodness, for that, from the very nature of moral goodness, it cannot do, but to maintain the conditions without which a free exercise of the human faculties is impossible' (Green, 1881: 350). The end, Green wrote, is 'freedom in the positive sense: in other words, the liberation of the powers of all men equally for contributions to a common good' (ibid.: 347). The means is private responsibility supported through collective action. Public health, State schooling, the Factory Acts, the temperance rules – in ways such as these the State can release and empower that which the laissez-faire commercialism of Cobden, Bright and Gladstone would so regrettably stunt and bottle up.

Green was the most important political philosopher in Britain between 1880 and 1914. His emphasis on the removal of hindrances and the unlocking of potential had a great appeal to middle-class reformers whose religious faith had been shaken by Darwinism and science but who still hungered for the constructive purposiveness of community service and altruistic self-denial. Green, Richter says, proposed social commitment as a 'surrogate' for evangelical Christianity: 'Here is Green's strategy for reform. He asked the privileged to sacrifice their selfish advantages so that the poor and weak might be given the chance to realise their potentialities. In return, the privileged would gain the release from bad conscience and more: that moral development which comes from living in a moral society where all men are treated as agents, each of whom is an end equally to himself and to others' (Richter, 1964: 135).

It was a mix of Kant on respect for persons, Hegel on the world-spirit that must inevitably progress, Christianity on the perfection of Heaven made flesh through good works and transcendent citizenship on earth. Bosanquet, Gore and Asquith had studied with Green at Oxford, while the outreaching human-itarianism of Toynbee Hall was the practical incarnation of his ethos of phil-anthropy and fellowship. Beveridge was a regenerating Liberal who had learned from Green that freedom of trade was not enough to set free the genie of *becoming*. L.T. Hobhouse (1864–1929) was another.

Hobhouse saw liberalism as 'a movement of liberation, a clearance of obstruc-tions, an opening of channels for the flow of free spontaneous vital activity' (Hobhouse, 1911a: 22). Convinced that 'the function of State coercion is to override individual coercion' (ibid.: 71), he argued that freedom from restraint might presuppose not the minimal state but rather the political lead. Hobhouse followed Green closely in his contention that it is empowerment and unblock-ing that in the end make State intervention both expedient and just: 'The foun-dation of liberty is the idea of growth' (ibid.: 59). He knew that the negation of the negation could no longer stop at the repeal of misconceived directive: 'The further development of the state lies in such an extension of public control as makes for the fuller liberty of the life of the mind' (Hobhouse, 1911b: 203).

Hobhouse was a liberal who believed strongly in the virtues of thrift, sobri-ety, self-help, initiative and energy, in the value of 'individual right and personal independence, of which Socialism at times appears oblivious' (Hobhouse, 1911a: 101). He was less than sympathetic to Marshall's Socialism A which repressed economic alertness into a Schumpeterian plan: 'The State could never be the sole producer, for in production the personal factor is vital' (ibid.: 95–6). Hobhouse was a strict moralist who believed that it was up to the citizens to 'win by their own efforts all that is necessary to a full civic efficiency. It is not for the State to feed, house, or clothe them' (ibid.: 76). Hobhouse saw no role for a cosseting socialism that would undermine the sound market discipline.

It is not for the State to collectivise personal responsibility. What the State must do is to create the background infrastructure within which the normal man can look after himself and his family. Education builds up human capital. Medical inspection reduces industrial accidents. Health insurance shares the cost of care. Welfare in forms such as these only corrects a market shortfall. It does not take the place of the obligation to earn.

Sometimes, however, there is no work to be had. Overproduction in one industry – 'economic malorganization' (ibid.: 77) – can be the cause of retrenchments and a new process can displace an old skill. In such circumstances the defect lies in the system and not in the man himself: 'It is not his fault . . . He does not direct or regulate industry. He is not responsible for its ups and downs, but he has to pay for them. That is why it is not charity but justice for which he is asking' (ibid.). The collectivity has a duty to enforce the right to work. Where it cannot do so, it is bound by the social contract to compensate the victims of involuntary unemployment: 'We cease, in fact, to regard the public money as a dole, we treat it as a payment for a civic service' (ibid.: 87). Unemployment benefits are their right. It is the rest of us who have left them in the lurch.

The State must guarantee the right to work. It must also underwrite 'a civilized standard of life' (ibid.: 79). In the case of the chronically dependent this means old age pensions and poverty relief. In the case of the self-supporting it means the right to a living wage – and the right, therefore, to form trade unions precisely because a fair contract can never be a 'forced bargain' in which the stronger party simply dictates his terms: 'Full freedom of consent implies equality on the part of both parties to the bargain' (ibid.: 43). Freedom *to* is more nearly a reinforcement than a threat to balanced competition where it levels the playing field and reverses a market failure. Trade unions supply countervailing power. They purify the capitalist economy of unwarranted bullying. The State, in legalising the unions, has bent back the bent rod and raised up the overshadowed: 'It gave, upon the whole, far more freedom to the workman than it took away' (ibid.: 40). The State has made the business system more equal, more equitable, but it has not challenged its legitimacy, which is not in dispute.

The debt goes both ways: 'The individual cannot stand alone . . . Between him and the State there is a reciprocal obligation' (ibid: 79). Just as society must behave responsibly towards the citizen, so the part must make the customary contribution to the whole. Welfare dependency is not an option: 'Rights do not begin till duties begin' (Green, 1879: 124).

Green had argued that rights are created by consensus and that the *bono publico* always circumscribes their scope: 'A right is a power of which the exercise by the individual or by some body of men is recognised by a society, either as itself directly essential to a common good, or as conferred by an authority of which the maintenance is recognised as so essential' (ibid: 113). Green deduced rights not from nature but from function: 'If the common interest requires it, no right can be alleged against it . . . There is no such natural right to do as one likes irrespectively of society' (ibid: 110, 109–10). Criticising Rousseau's vision of an *ab initio* contract signed in the original state of void, Green, just as Durkheim was to do, makes the point that such a covenant is a contradiction in terms: 'If there was no morality prior to the pact there could not be rights' (ibid.: 124). Rights, Green says, are social roles and social facts. They are other people through and through. Without the voluntary acceptance of the common good, Green insists, there would be no rights and therefore no duties.

The common good to Green was the end that makes the empowerment an imperative: 'No one has a right to do what he will with his own in such a way as to contravene this end' (Green, 1881: 347). Hobhouse followed Green in making personal development a discretionary entitlement contingent upon the destiny of the whole. He had no problem in recommending repressive pattern-maintenance to the self-fulfilling monad whose greatest wish was to be free: 'The common good to which each man's rights are subordinate is a good in which each man has a share. This share consists in realizing his capacities of feeling, of loving, of mental and physical energy . . . In realizing these he plays his part in the social life, or, in Green's phrase, he finds his own good in the common good' (Hobhouse, 1911a: 61). Couched in so inviting a suggestion, perhaps the totality's vision of how the atom ought to live is not as menacing as Hayek's *Serfdom* would make it seem.

Hobhouse puts to one side the oppression of the fringe by the mainstream, the majority by an elite. There is no manipulation and no ambiguity in his conception of the public purpose as a commons and a pool: 'The liberty which is good is not the liberty of one gained at the expense of others, but the liberty which can be enjoyed by all who dwell together' (ibid.: 44). As Green had done, Hobhouse turned to the unbiased spectator for the confirmation that the consensus had defined the entitlement: 'A right is nothing but an expectation which will appeal to an impartial person' (Hobhouse, 1911b: 197). Society alone can indicate what the citizen may reasonably demand and what he is obliged by his affiliation to supply: 'The relation of the individual to the community is everything. His rights and his duties are alike defined by the common good' (Hobhouse, 1911a: 60–61).

The organs put in. The organs take out. The individual has the right to expect that his society will ensure him an equitable start and a civilised minimum. The society has the right to expect that the individual will work industriously for himself and his family. One hand washes the other and is made sparkling clean in its turn. The circular flow of rights and duties is the guarantee that no one will be forgotten or left out.

The primacy of the consensus presupposes the self-government of the people. Hobhouse had no doubt that political democracy was 'the necessary basis of the Liberal idea' (ibid.: 109). He praised the extension of the suffrage because it had already 'given to the mass of the male population the last word on public issues' (Hobhouse, 1911b: 183). He looked forward to a further extension of the vote, together with other consensus-capturing innovations such as proportional representation, the referendum, the reform of the upper house, devolution and regionalisation. The final result would be collective action inspired by 'a collective sense of responsibility' and in line with 'the combined will of individuals' (ibid.: 192, 191). The final result, in short, would be a 'social democracy', in the full sense of 'a democracy seeking, by the organized expression of the collective will, to remodel society in accordance with humanitarian sentiment' (ibid.: 183).

Green had said that paternalistic coercion could never be sufficient to make State constraint into social liberation. Hobhouse, like Bosanquet, shared Green's insistence that the 'sovereign power' had to serve as 'the agent of the general will' (Green, 1879: 103). Closer to Schumpeter's first theory of democracy than he was to Schumpeter's second, Hobhouse was critical of self-appointed seers like the Fabians because of their contempt for the average sensual man and their conviction that only philosopher rulers can know what is right: 'Some men are much better and wiser than others, but experience seems to show that hardly any man is so much better or wiser than others that he can permanently stand the test of irresponsible power over them' (Hobhouse, 1911a: 111).

Hobhouse's message is that collective intervention has moral value only 'in as far as it is expressing the will of its members' (Hobhouse, 1911b: 188). It loses its ethical legitimacy as soon as it is known to be 'imposing a law upon them which they do not freely and voluntarily accept' (ibid.). Hobhouse's 'will' is a unanimity which makes the excluded cringe. Fukuyama, writing in the shadow of superpower regime change and the genocide of ethnic cleansing, is less convinced that voting captures all: 'Democratic majorities can decide to do terrible things to other countries and can violate human rights and norms of decency on which their own democratic order is based' (Fukuyama, 2004: 114). Douglas said that slavery was justified so long as it reflected the will of the people. Lincoln by contrast refused to accept that the braying great majority had a moral right to have things all its own way: 'Lincoln . . . said that slavery in itself violated the higher principle of human equality on which the American regime was based. The legitimacy of the actions of a democracy are not in the end based on democratic procedural correctness but on the prior rights and norms that come from a moral realm higher than that of the legal order' (ibid.: 115). Schumpeter had made the same point when he rejected the verdict of Roman public opinion in favour of an absolute ethic: the persecution of the Christians, he said, was 'repulsive' (Schumpeter, 1942: 241) since the Romans had no right to violate a higher moral norm. The criticism that Fukuyama would make of the consensus model is that consensus is seldom 100 per cent and that there are things that even a great majority must not do.

The reply of Hobhouse and Marshall would be that democracy would not *be* democracy without equal respect for all. The democratic system in that sense is its own bulwark and constitution.

Democracy is respect. It is the way in which citizens, sometimes speaking, sometimes listening, leave childlike dependency behind. Believing as he did that true democracy can only be bottom-up and not the edict of a chief, Hobhouse insisted that men will only learn responsibility if they are permitted to practise responsibility: 'If men could be spoon-fed with happiness, a benevolent despotism would be the ideal system. If they are to take a part in working out their own salvation, they must be summoned to their share in the task of directing the common life' (Hobhouse, 1911a: 54). Democracy is 'share', and 'task' and 'directing'. It is production first and foremost, unthinking consumption a poor second.

Membership is the essence. People get involved because they feel involved. Intervention and democracy, fraternalism and participation – all derive their urgency and their imperative from the 'organic conception of the relation between the individual and society': 'We have come to look for the effect of liberty in the firmer establishment of social solidarity' (ibid.: 60). Freedom *to* is more than private and personal development. Freedom *to* is belonging. It is commitment and the awareness of the common bond.

Freedom *to* is an outward-looking freedom which integrates the self into a history and a culture shared. It is nationhood and community, the sociologist's manifesto that I am I because We are We: 'In as much as the true social harmony rests on feeling and makes use of all the natural ties of kinship, of neighbourliness, of congruity of character and belief, and of language and mode of life, the best, healthiest, and most vigorous political unit is that to which men are by their own feelings strongly drawn' (ibid.: 65). Territory and passport are also relevant. By themselves, however, they are not the social glue. A large country, indeed, where it is felt to be a tyranny of 'alien sentiments and laws, tends to mutilate – or, at lowest, to cramp – the spontaneous development of social life' (ibid.). Society is blood, kinship, memory. It is birds of a feather. Citizenship is another name for a way of life.

Hobhouse writes that the social bond is the cause and the effect of social evolution: 'Social progress may be regarded as development of the principle of union, order, cooperation, harmony among human beings' (Hobhouse, 1911b: 127). He also writes that market capitalism, beneficial as in so many ways it is, represents a threat to that benevolent concord to the extent that it distances and separates: 'Modern economic conditions engender inequalities of wealth and foster forms of industrial organization which constantly threaten to reduce political and civic equality to a meaningless form of words' (ibid.: 143). Evolution may be linear but it must also be managed. For society to trace out the single middle course in the unique direction of perceived good fellowship, there must clearly be collectivism as well as enterprise. Action as well as automaticity is essential if the comrades are to become aware that their lives after all are one.

7.3   SOCIOLOGY AND SOCIAL POLICY

The LSE in 1929 had one foot in the systematising generalisations of Green, Hobhouse and Ginsberg, and one foot in the pragmatic empiricism of Booth, Rowntree and the Webbs. When, aged 36, Marshall joined the Department of Sociology at the School, he knew that he was finding his way into a mixed world-view that looked two ways at once. The compromise, he recalled in Cambridge when that university was setting up its own Sociology degree, was very much to his taste: 'No scientific discipline worthy of the name ever advances along one road only, and on no route followed by the inquiring human mind, does one meet with crossroads only once' (Marshall, 1963: 26).

The speculative mindset favours 'the way to the stars': dazzled by its universal laws and its imagined abstractions, disembedded Grand Theory makes the social scientist into a social system-maker, little more than 'a slave to his concepts' (ibid.: 14, 16). The number-crunching orientation prefers the 'way into the sands' of mindless fact-gathering, 'with sometimes an inadequate sense of the purpose for which they are being collected': blinded by 'whirling facts which blow into the eyes and ears until nothing can be clearly seen or heard', the radical empiricist ends up 'a slave to his methods', no better placed than the detached analyst to attack 'the practical problems that face us' (ibid.: 14, 15, 16, 22). Marshall in his Inaugural Lecture of 1946 warned sociologists at the crossroads against the dangers of both extremes.

In contrast to the Parsonians and the statisticians, Marshall in 'Sociology at the Crossroads' recommended a 'middle way which runs over firm ground' (ibid.: 21). Neither telescopic nor microscopic, neither 'Gargantuan nor Lilliputian', such 'stepping-stones in the middle distance' would have the great attraction that they at least would enable the sociologist to shed some light on the current problems challenging the society in which he lives: 'Sociology need not be ashamed of wishing to be useful' (ibid.: 22). Robert Merton in the United States, in 1947 and 1949, was to advocate a 'middle-range functionalism' – neither 'minor but necessary working hypotheses' nor 'all-inclusive systematic efforts to develop a unified theory that will explain all the observed uniformities of social behavior' (Merton, 1968: 39) – that would have the similar objective of permitting theoretical propositions to be tested against observable evidence.

Marshall, so much in favour of the mixed methodology, had no doubt as to the source of his inspiration: 'Hobhouse's great work on social development and the evolution of morals was based on the careful and scientific comparison of institutions and processes' (Marshall, 1963: 34). Joining Sociology, already aged 36, Marshall believed that he took over from his predecessor not only the a priori expectation of statism, democracy, consensus, citizenship and freedom *to* but also the fact-finder's search for real-world evidence that would document the 'differences which distinguish one culture from another': 'Hobhouse grouped his empirical studies round the structure and functions of social institutions' (ibid.: 62, 22).

As a trained historian with a theoretician's interest in comparison, Marshall in some ways would have been well placed to combine the search for documentation with a structure of conjecture. He could have traced the growth of bureaucracy or the dynamic of stratification using fresh data on mobility and impediment. In the event he collected little evidence of his own and relied, as had Hobhouse before him, almost entirely on secondary sources. Marshall in his *Citizenship* stated clearly what he had seen as his niche: 'I have not tried to put before you new facts culled by laborious research' but rather to 'regroup familiar facts in a pattern which may make them appear to some of you in a new light' (Marshall, 1950: 27). Marshall at the crossroads was more intrigued by the insights than by the outturns. As Hobhouse had done, however, he recognised that both imagination and parochialism were important. Each complement had a useful role to play.

Marshall in 1930 became Reader in Sociology. He still had no publications in his chosen field. His first paper in sociology was 'Social Class – A Preliminary Analysis'. It appeared in the *Sociological Review* in 1934. Later, refusing to republish it, Marshall was to describe it as 'preliminary', 'naïve' and 'out of date' (Marshall, 1963: viii). A small number of other papers on class were to follow. It was not much to show for a whole decade's work.

From 1939 to 1944 Marshall was a member of the Foreign Office Research Department. He was awarded the CMG in 1947 for his wartime service, which included monitoring the German press and writing research papers on topics such as the proposed dismemberment of Germany. He returned to the LSE in 1944 to be Professor of Social Institutions, not in the Department of Sociology but in the Department of Social Science (later called the Department of Social Policy and Administration). This was the unit through which he had first joined the School. He was Head of Department from 1944 to 1949, recruiting Richard Titmuss to take over from him in 1950. Titmuss was given the first Chair of Social Administration in the United Kingdom and significantly raised the scholarly profile of the discipline.

In 1949–50 Marshall was Educational Advisor to the British High Commissioner in Germany. He was active in helping the German education system to recover from isolation and indoctrination under the Nazis. From 1951 to 1956 he was Head of the Department of Sociology at the LSE and, from 1954 to 1956, the third holder of the Martin White Chair. He was involved in the establishment of the new *British Journal of Sociology* that joined the older *Sociological Review* (earlier edited by Hobhouse) as an outlet for professional best practice.

From 1956 to 1960, Marshall was the Director, in Paris, of UNESCO's Department of Social Sciences. It was the task of his section to carry out cross-cultural studies and to conduct comparative research. The Department did not exclude economics. On the contrary: it regarded economics as pre-eminently a *social* science and as a valuable contributor to its multidisciplinary synthesis.

Marshall retired in 1962 to his home in Cambridge. The father figure and the gold standard, he was frequently asked for his advice on teaching and research. He was President of the International Sociological Association from 1959 to 1962 and the British Sociological Association from 1964 to 1969. He also received four honorary doctorates: Southampton (1969), Leicester (1970), York (1971) and Cambridge (1978). These honours came to him relatively late in his career.

Marshall's research in his final two decades was devoted exclusively to social policy in the mixed economy. Democracy and exchange were back on the agenda. Yet a sadness and a hesitancy may have crept into the world-view which were absent from the earlier papers of the late LSE years. Rees writes that there was in truth a 'bifurcated Marshall', a two-stage Marshall in which 'Marshall Mark Two' succeeded to 'Marshall Mark One' (Rees, 1995: 359, 354) once the English summer's cricket had been rained off by sober economics. Chapter 10, section 1 examines the publications from 1963 to 1981 in the light of this assertion. It reaches the conclusion that Marshall remained essentially Marshall even in an era that knew how hard it would be to squeeze top dollar from responsible decency wrapped up in the finest English wool.

7.4   MARSHALL'S PUBLICATIONS

Marshall's distinctions are more numerous than his publications. There is, however, one classic: 'It is a very short book, but its influence has deservedly been quite disproportionate to its size' (Giddens, 1982: 166). *Citizenship and Social Class* appeared in 1950. Marshall's first collection of essays, most of the text was made up of his (Alfred) Marshall Lectures, delivered at Cambridge in 1949.

All but one chapter of the 1950 book was reprinted as part of Marshall's *Sociology at the Crossroads* (1963). The title of the book is taken from its

author's 1946 Inaugural, although its chief contribution is arguably the fact
that it caused a significant revival of interest in the 1949 Lectures in a decade
in which sociology itself (to say nothing of Marxian sociology) was enjoying
a high public profile.

After his retirement Marshall wrote a short textbook, *Social Policy in the
Twentieth Century*, first published in 1965. His final revision was the fourth
edition of 1975, although there was a 1985 edition, updated by A.M. Rees.
Marshall in his later years also wrote the papers on democratic-welfare-
capitalism that Robert Pinker arranged for him to reprint, each accompanied
where appropriate by an 'Afterthought', in *The Right to Welfare* (1981). And
that is all.

Marshall was a quiet man who was uncomfortable with self-advertisement.
Halsey gives as one reason for his restricted output the likelihood that he
lacked confidence in the value of his mission: 'His awareness of his own limi-
tations tended to draw a modest veil over what we can now see as a genuinely
original sociological mind' (Halsey, 1984: 6). One consequence was that he
was reactive rather than proactive, prone to leave it to the invitations of others
to determine the thrust of his papers: 'As a professional sociologist, he somehow remained deceptively amateur, always amenable to the wishes of his
colleagues, and characteristically delivering his written work, even the excel-
lent best of it, as a *pièce d'occasion*' (ibid.: 8). Marshall was a gentleman. He
would possibly have written more had he been less self-effacing.

Marshall, besides that, was ill at ease with the confrontational dogmatism
of so much of social science debate. Pinker draws attention to 'the quality of
detachment that pervades Marshall's writings . . . He approaches questions of
value in a spirit of scholarship rather than partisanship' (Pinker, 1981: 8). He
might have written with greater passion had he not, like Anthony Crosland,
experienced the divided loyalties of a reforming Liberal determined to call
himself a socialist. Donald MacRae, his successor to the Martin White Chair,
rightly acknowledges this duality in Marshall's ideological loyalties when he
pays tribute to what he sees as the essence of Marshall's message – 'a kind of
benign, actively concerned, liberal virtue that far more than the bureaucratic
unction of Fabianism has been one of the splendours of English society'
(MacRae, 1982: iii).

Marshall saw sociology as a synthetic discipline at a time when subdivided
professionalism was less and less favourable to the cross-disciplinary cocktail
of economy, society, the State, the mind, the past which gave social disequilibrium its multidimensional context. Marshall was reluctant to use sociological jargon, cited few canonical authorities, relied on books and personal
experience for the confirmation that his theories were right. Increasingly, in
common with Green, Hobhouse and Ginsberg, he was read as a social philosopher and not as a sociologist who had his finger on the pulse.

Marshall made no attempt to fight his corner or to found a school. He attracted no disciples and energised no Titmice. His heavy administrative duties, both at the LSE and (for many years) outside, must have held him back. Even so, the fact that he wrote so little and was so casual about his public profile meant that his social theory was underappreciated. Built around citizenship and the two triads (civil rights, political rights, social rights in his early writings, capitalism, democracy and welfare later on) his intellectual system has a freshness and an internal consistency which marks it out as a major contribution.

7.5   FROM ATTLEE TO THATCHER

The *Zeitgeist* spills over into his work. Perhaps that is why it is possible to argue for a darker Marshall in 1981, a more hopeful Marshall in 1949.

The Britain of the Marshall Lectures was the Britain of Butler's Education Act, Beveridge's National Insurance, Bevan's National Health. The lesson was not lost on Marshall that a Conservative, a Liberal and a Socialist had fought shoulder to shoulder to level up the non-commanding depths irrespective of what might be happening in the controlling boardrooms of industry and trade. All the great factions in the British national family had made common cause successfully to show that 'security can be combined with freedom and enterprise and responsibility of the individual for his own life' (Beveridge, 1942: 170). The watershed 1940s had displayed to its best advantage the British genius for compromise and the tolerance of the mixed ethos. It had been the living proof of what Pinker describes as 'our national ability to reconcile the claims of self-interest and altruism' (Pinker, 1979: x). Marshall on the wartime coalition, the peacetime convergence, the patchwork quilt is a good illustration of the social-democratic credo that middle-ground policies follow naturally from a middle-ground consensus: 'It is not surprising to find that the Welfare State, when it eventually saw the light, was of mixed parentage' (Marshall, 1975: 86).

Marshall in 1949 was writing against the background of Labour's victory in 1945, the nationalisation of the basic industries, the general expectation that planning and management were essential for reconstruction. Hands-on macro-economics was popularly taken to be the guarantor of full employment whereas the free market was held responsible for the insecurity, poverty and long-term desperation of the hungry 1930s. Exchange controls were still in place. Postwar austerity had not ended. The last commodities were not de-rationed until 1954. Even so, revival was in the air. So, crucially, was the fact and the expectation of sustained economic growth.

Marshall, in the years of his LSE professorships, looked out of his window and saw with his own eyes the prosperity that would make good the bombed-out buildings. History teaches, of course, that the upswing would not last forever. As Pierson writes: 'In the long term, the welfare state is incompatible with a healthy market-based economy. Only the exceptionally favourable circumstances for economic growth of the post-war period allowed simultaneously for an expansion of the economy *and* the welfare state' (Pierson, 1998: 3). The Marshall of the 1940s, the 1950s and the 1960s was the product of the lull between the storms that, quite exceptionally, had been able to pay for its quid-less quo.

Most of all he was the graduate of Dunkirk and the Blitz. Marshall knew that the welfarism of the 1940s 'expressed a spirit that was definitely new': 'Its source was the common experience of the war, when the welfare needs that had to be met by government action had little or nothing to do with personal income or class distinctions, but sprang from the fortunes to which all the people were exposed' (Marshall, 1963: 279). *Citizenship and Social Class* was published in the same year as Titmuss's *Problems of Social Policy*. Agreeing strongly with Titmuss (whose *Problems* he cites), Marshall argued that the 'sense of national solidarity created by the war' had created a new and more inclusive culture in which the inquisition of a means test or the restriction of social services to an underclass of failures had effectively become unthinkable: 'It was so obvious that the mutual service society of the war should become the mutual benefit society of the peace' (ibid.: 282, 279). The Beveridge Report in 1942 'gave us something positive to fight for' (ibid.: 281). The relegation of the Five Giants was the symbol of the victory that would be won.

The 1970s were a colder winter. Stagnation and inflation showed that growth was not assured. The Cold War and Stalinist repression made people less comfortable with *dirigisme* and plan. Marxian class-incompatibility and New Right libertarianism polarised the discourse. Working-class self-help, once favourable to collectivism and mutual aid, was under threat from mobility and general prosperity. Disembodied economism was substituting dog-eat-dog individualism for the old-fashioned communalism of solidarity and street. Strikes discredited the unions. Red tape discredited the bureaucrats.

Besides that, Commonwealth immigration by the 1970s had introduced race into politics. The blacks looked black and the Indians talked funny. The influx of obvious newcomers undermined the 'happy breed' premise of cultural homogeneity in a way that Marshall, no longer young, found difficult to incorporate. *Social Policy* devotes only one page to race. What it concludes is, however, vintage Marshall. Even people who are 'culturally alien', Marshall writes, should enjoy the same rights and claims as everyone else: 'The needs of immigrants are not in essence different from those of the native population' (Marshall, 1975: 210). Social policy is about dependency and support. Dependency and support are colour-blind.

That is why positive discrimination based on ethnic background should wherever possible be avoided. Policies that singled out the minorities would 'almost certainly increase their detachment from, and impede their integration with, the rest of the community, which is exactly the opposite of what is desired' (ibid.: 211). Poor people need food and the homeless need housing. That is true irrespective of whether they have come in from abroad or grown up needy at home: 'The problem of race relations, and of immigrants in general, is basically one of participation and community development' (ibid.: 210).

Black or white, the need was to keep the community one. The mission was becoming more difficult. Britain by the 1970s was not what it was. Marshall in 1949 was swimming with the tide. Marshall in his later years must have known that the weather had taken a turn for the worse.

8. T.H. Marshall: citizenship and social rights

Citizenship is 'a status bestowed on those who are full members of a community' (Marshall, 1950: 18). It is integration and affiliation, belonging and entitlement. Citizenship is a 'basic human equality' in respect of rights and duties, a 'universal birthright', a 'single uniform status' a 'universal status' (ibid.: 6, 19, 21, 44). It is a common identity. It is a link with the past.

Citizenship is conservative and continuing. It is 'a claim to be admitted to a share in the social heritage' (ibid.: 6) and not just the *carpe diem* that nips in opportunistically and takes. Citizenship is 'a direct sense of community membership based on loyalty to a civilisation which is a common possession' (ibid.: 24). It is not just a legal document which allows its bearer to pass through Heathrow visa-free.

Citizenship does not presuppose blood kinship or putative parentage. There is no fiction that all Englishmen are descended from English, even if there is a myth that all Tiv are descended from Tiv. Subjective and sentimental, however, what citizenship does presuppose is a perceived stake in the 'national consciousness' and in the 'common heritage' (ibid.: 25). In the age of free enterprise and civil rights, Marshall observes, this felt commitment was all too often associated with the narrow exclusivity of 'jingo patriotism' (ibid.) and the aggressive national-ism of *Rule Britannia*. In the new age of welfare services and social rights, that same one-nationness must build upon the 'material enjoyment' (ibid.: 28) that integrates the masses with the classes in order to welcome the excluded and the needy into the fold.

Citizenship is the essence of Marshall on roles and rights. The first section of this chapter, 'Citizenship and nationhood', shows that citizenship to Marshall means *our* people and that nationhood is another name for the established way of life. Section 2, 'Civil rights', section 3, 'Political rights' and section 4, 'Social rights', explain Marshall's reconstruction of human history as a three-stage progression from status to contract to both. Section 5, 'The iron cage', asks to what extent the evolution from the old liberalism into the new may plausibly be regarded as a natural law that consumers and profits can never repeal.

8.1 CITIZENSHIP AND NATIONHOOD

Nationality is built upon membership, indivisible and inclusive. Entries and exits are logged scrupulously onto the Register of Citizens. Still, however, it is *mores* and not the passport per se that guards the gateway and says who is one of us.

8.1.1 Boundaries and Barriers

Marshall defines status as a latent capacity that has a future because it has a past: 'Status emphasizes the fact that expectations (of a normative kind) exist in the relevant social groups' (Marshall, 1963: 211). Status is affirmed by others. Without the confirmation no one would knew where he stood. That is why citizenship is a topic in sociological perceptions and not purely in formal legalisms that make no allowance for ego's own *Verstehen*.

Barbalet adopts Marshall's practice when he treats the term 'citizenship' as a synonym for 'settled human community': 'It defines those who are, and those who are not, members of a common society' (Barbalet, 1988: 1). Citizenship, Barbalet says, 'can readily be described as participation in or membership of a community' (ibid.: 2). Statutory identifiers are only a part of the status: 'It is also a matter of the non-political capacities of citizens which derive from the social resources they command' (ibid.: 1). Stewart makes a distinction between 'state citizenship' ('formal legal status', 'full formal membership of a nation-state') and 'democratic citizenship', the 'shared membership of a political community' (Stewart, 1995: 63). He, like Barbalet, recognises that it is sharing and community far more than passport classification that captures the meaning of Marshall on the warm glow of neighbourly allegiance.

Stewart, however, is not convinced: 'Marshall does not consider the possibility that there may be at the very least a tension between a welfare-rights version of (social) citizenship and a conception of citizenship focusing on emancipation and autonomy' (ibid.: 70). Stewart thinks that Marshall's perception of citizenship is too restrictive. While some people do want to live with their own kind, other people simply want to be left alone.

The distinction should not be exaggerated. Parents and pensioners want to be included (the welfare-rights concept) but they also want to be consulted (the element of autonomy and choice). In their case at least citizenship as belonging and citizenship as independence will be seen not as substitutes but as joint. But that is not to deny that there might be a rugged free enterpriser who reports that decent Marshall's togetherness feels to him unpleasantly regimented and oppressive.

The use of the word 'citizenship' is itself an invitation to misunderstanding.

While one can see that Marshall would wish to exclude tourists and transients, the word that he selects appears not to incorporate resident non-citizens who would say that they are not just changing planes and that they feel that they have put down roots. Permanent residents, workers on work permits, even illegal immigrants in underground sweatshops are adding value and pluralising the culture. They are doing this irrespective of whether or not they will one day become naturalised. Marshall's word 'citizen' cuts off the NHS nurse from the NHS patient she is trying to treat. It seems a bit harsh.

Perhaps it would be better to say 'normally resident' in order to capture the status of the demi-Briton who has bought a house and put his children in the local comprehensive. Such a phrase would bring in those non-citizens who have been participants long enough to have acquired a stake. The revision would only be a concession to the existing practice. Resident foreigners in most countries have access to welfare. In some countries (as with Commonwealth citizens) they even have the right to vote. Outsiders of all kinds can bring an action in the courts. Passport legality is not required to be a player with the rest.

Citizenship as a word is fraught with ambiguity. Passport legality cannot accommodate the cosmopolitan culture of dual nationals. It cannot account for felt attachment to a supranational polity such as the Holy Roman Empire, the United Nations, the Soviet Union or the European Union. It cannot explain the multiple affiliations, self-perceived, that are agglomerated willy-nilly within the multicultural State that mixes up the ways of life. Nor can it reconcile the cross-cutting loyalties of diaspora ethnicities like the Armenians, Jews, Arabs, Kurds and Chinese, some with a surviving homeland and some in perpetual exile. A British Bangladeshi might feel that he has more 'membership' in common with a Canadian Bangladeshi than he does with a fellow Briton who flashes the same *Honi Soit* at the Bahnhof or the Gare. Passport legality, important as it is, does nothing to reunite the subjective with the objective in cases such as this.

Marshall's citizenship relates to a nation State that is at once a culture and a polity. One does not have to invoke the Muslim schools and the headscarves to find instances, like Quebec, of two kittens warring in a single sack. While an American author in the 1950s and 1960s might have been more sensitive to melting-pot immigration or to the second-class citizenship of Negroes in Watts or Mississippi, it is interesting that Marshall showed little or no awareness of the harm that sectional strife between Ulster Catholics and Ulster Protestants was doing to the ideal of one people knitted seamlessly into a single skein.

Northern Ireland is not the only British illustration of conflicting identities despite the unifying passport. The Welsh, Cornish and Scots often complain that they lost their language, customs and political self-determination as a consequence of England's homogenising, centralising nation-building.

Internal colonisation, besides that, was accompanied by the denial of political rights abroad. Civil rights for British businessmen led not to inclusion but to exclusion in the colonies.

Jack will say that working men have no country and that his real nationality is the universal proletariat. Jill will say that her gender leaves her marginalised and that she wants equal opportunity as well as the right of abode. Marshall's reply is that Welshmen and women, Empire and exploitation, all will fall into place once the giant umbrella goes up. Citizenship is the giant forge that makes even a Scotsman the child of Bunyan and the Bard. We all eat fish 'n' chips. We all play cricket on the Green. We all drink cups of tea.

Yet Britishness itself is being attenuated by globalisation. In terms of culture, MTV and Hollywood make the world into a borderless village that cost-benefits the *Lowest Common Denominator* over the *Passport to Pimlico*. In terms of production, multinational businesses shift capital if not labour from country to country and have no clearly defined national base. In terms of defence, the United States is the military superpower and the engine of world Keynesianism without opening its elections to more than its own nationals. The ozone layer, terrorism, Third World deprivation and the relocation of jobs to low-wage economies are British concerns that extend beyond the remit of British democracy. If Marshall's citizenship does mean passport legality, perhaps it is a throwback to a unilateral response that is less and less the relevant choice in the open, the *inter*-national world.

Marshall's 'citizenship' is both culture and politics. The double universality conceals the fact that the politics is always a poor second to the sociology. Since full rights are normally restricted to true nationals, it is understandable that a theorist of enforceable entitlement should have been attracted by the precise language of passport legality. Even so, Marshall's nationality is primaeval clannishness and not the detached anonymity of the marriage of convenience. Paper citizenship may be the consequence but conservative community is always the cause.

Nisbet defines community as long-lasting interpenetration that transcends the calculative immediacy of interest, contract and expediency: 'Community . . . encompasses all forms of relationship which are characterized by a high degree of personal intimacy, emotional depth, moral commitment, social cohesion, and continuity in time. Community is founded on man conceived in his wholeness rather than in one or another of the roles, taken separately, that he may hold in a social order' (Nisbet, 1967: 47). Community is history and fraternity, integration and acceptance. It is the culture in common that makes Marshall's politics make sense.

Nisbet describes community as conservative acceptance, a 'fusion of feeling and thought' (ibid.: 48) that cannot be reduced to gain-maximising association. His description fits Marshall's 'membership' well. In the words of Donald MacRae: 'What Marshall had seen was that a welfare society returned social arrangements from being instrumental and contractual once again to status' (MacRae, 1982: v). Marshall would arguably have avoided much misunderstanding had he left the word 'citizenship' for the jurists and referred exclusively to 'community' that in his social thought is alone the effective cause of all the legal codes.

8.1.2 Influences and Resonances

It is impossible to know which books Marshall read, and at what stage in his career: he was largely self-tutored in sociology and in any case cites few references. The influences are not easy to document. The resonances are another matter. Marshall did not invent the idea of a national family, rooted and caring.

Thus the Greeks saw citizenship, while undoubtedly a legal title acquired through birth or naturalisation, as an invitation to active involvement in the rights and duties of a going concern: 'What effectively distinguishes the citizen proper from all others is his participation in giving judgement and in holding office' (Aristotle, 1981: 169). Citizenship is creation and not just absorption, doing things and not just enjoying the view: 'The association which is a state exists not for the purpose of living together but for the sake of noble actions' (ibid.: 198). Aristotle was in a good position to describe the feel of the barrier. A Macedonian, he himself was a foreigner and not a citizen at Athens. He could not own property or speak in the assembly.

Aristotle defines citizenship in the double sense of political democracy and the moral code: 'A citizen is in general one who has a share in ruling and in being ruled . . . So far as the best constitution is concerned, he is a man who is able and who chooses to rule and to be ruled with a view to a life that is in accordance with virtue' (ibid.: 213). Citizenship is unity and solidarity, both current and intertemporal. It is membership set in a value system that remains the same even as the population, like the water in Heraclitus's river, flows in and goes past: 'The main criterion of the continued identity of a state ought to be its constitution' (ibid.: 176).

Citizenship to Aristotle is the life in common of the small city-State. Physical needs must be met by the *polis*: that goes without saying. Yet something more is needed than simply the economist's *living well*. That something is the moral interconnectedness of 'marriage, brotherhoods, sacrifices to the gods, and the various civilized pursuits of a life lived together. All these activities are the product of affection, for it is our affection for others that causes us to choose to live together' (ibid.: 198). We live together because we belong together. The sense of identity is the essence of citizenship. The paper passport arrives *post festum*.

Marshall as a Rugby schoolboy will have learned all about the Greeks. Tawney, also at Rugby, is likely to have seen in the classics the same values of standards and obligations that he took to be the socialist message of Christianity as a gospel of loyalty to the whole (Tawney, 1931). So, certainly, did A.D. Lindsay, who had taken over from the Greeks the primacy of 'the framework of custom and habit upon which society usually depends so much' (Lindsay, 1943: 259).

Lindsay believed that fellowship and communication in the sense of Aristotle would not be possible without a reasonable equality of condition in the sense of Tawney: 'A modern democratic state is only possible if it can combine appreciation of skill, knowledge, and expertness with a reverence for the common humanity of everyday people. It is that conception of humanity which its institutions will have to express' (ibid.: 261). Marshall was a socialist who shared with Lindsay the Aristotelian's commitment to citizenship as something that goes beyond the cold instrumentality of effective laws. In Lindsay's memorable phrase: 'Gardens need walls or fences, but walls and fences are not flowers' (ibid.: 208). Citizenship is an end. It is not just the means.

Aristotle and Lindsay are resonances who might have been influences. The same must be said of the sociological giants who pioneered the idea that social bonds, territorial, religious, occupational, linguistic, ideational, should be seen as the non-rational multipliers of unthinking attachment.

Max Weber is a case in point. Weber, trying to establish what it is that builds four walls around the nation, seized upon empathetic identification as the power that overcomes the divisiveness of amorphous heterogeneity: 'A nation is a community of sentiment . . . which normally tends to produce a state of its own' (Weber, 1922c: 176). The sentiment comes first. The State-building follows on. Politics is the unintended outcome of mutual recognition.

The nation once built, the momentum of collective conventions seals precedent and permanency, expectation and perpetuation into the organic whole: 'National solidarity may be linked to memories of a common political destiny' (ibid.: 173). A nation is not a simple summation of the names trawled up in a census: the Spanish Basques are Spanish citizens but they often see themselves as a fringe or fragment apart. A nation cannot be reduced to a common language (consider Switzerland) or to a single race (national spokesmen have often been ethnic outsiders such as Jews) or to a shared religion (the Catholics have a Pope and a catechism but they are not a nation). Nationhood, Weber believed, is built up not from *Blut* and not from *Boden* but quintessentially from *Geist*. Spirit precedes felt citizenship in time. Spirit shapes the individual in the image of the group.

Ferdinand Tönnies too sought to explore the hidden origins of community and association. Community is non-calculative, non-commercial communalism that is supported by the 'three pillars' of 'blood, soil and spirit', of 'kinship, neighbourhood and friendship' (Tönnies, 1887: 204). Association is the competitive confrontationalism, the egotistical achievement-seeking that is the antithesis of the closely-knit and the nemesis of the non-scientific. In *Gemeinschaft* the social actors 'stay together in spite of everything that separates them'; in *Gesellschaft* they 'remain separate in spite of everything that unites them' (ibid.: 52). The *Gemeinschaft* is Max Weber's nationhood and ascription. The *Gesellschaft* is Invisible Hand's modernity and cosmopolitanism.

Tönnies is making a bipolar distinction between what some would see as the male and the female, others as the Catholic and the Protestant. In *Gesellschaft*, very different from *Gemeinschaft*, 'there are no activities taking place which are derived from an a priori and pre-determined unity and which therefore express the will and spirit of this unity through any individual who performs them. Nothing happens in *Gesellschaft* that is more important for the individual's wider group than it is for himself. On the contrary, everyone is out for himself alone and living in a state of tension against everyone else' (ibid.). In settled tradition there was reverence. In the open society there is indifference. Capitalism is not the cause but the effect of the new atomisation. Capitalism is made possible by the transition from the state of reverence to the state of Hobbes.

Hostility is coming back. Tönnies is not much impressed by what he sees: 'The entire culture has been overturned by a civilisation dominated by market and civil Society, and in this transformation civilisation itself is coming to an end' (ibid.: 257). The future looks nasty, brutish and short – unless, that is, some of the scattered seeds remain alive, 'so that the essential concepts of Community may be encouraged once again and a new civilisation can develop secretly within the one that is dying' (ibid.). The revival of *Gemeinschaft*, Tönnies writes, is not a luxury but rather a 'moral necessity' (ibid.: 210). Industrial cooperatives, he suggests, will help to arrest the deterioration into anonymity. Bismarck's social insurance could arguably have the same resocialising effect. The discrete are reunited by means of welfare rights. They are repositioned in a community that cares.

Strongest and clearest are the parallels with Durkheim on social cohesion and the normative consensus. Durkheim made internalised obligation the cause and consequence of peaceable interaction. Morality, he argued, was a collective possession. It was the product of group pressures *sui generis*. Moral standards are social facts, 'realities external to the individual' (Durkheim, 1897: 37–8) that are also duties towards the whole: 'Moral goals . . . are those the object of which is *society*. To act morally is to act in terms of the collective interest' (Durkheim, 1925: 59). Morality is never met with except in society. It can never be bought and sold through the reductionist utilitarianism of the market economist.

Oughtness is not interest, private and particular. Rather, it is the *conscience collective* of a marked-off set of persons who echo each other's voice: 'Society . . . is not a mere juxtaposition of individuals who, upon entering into it, bring with them an intrinsic morality. Man is a moral being because he lives in society, since morality consists in solidarity with the group, and varies according to that solidarity. Cause all social life to vanish, and moral life would vanish at the same time, having no object to cling to' (Durkheim, 1893: 331). Right and wrong are nothing but grand-sounding names for thee and me and he and she. Other people are our compass and our map. Collective representations hold us to the straight and narrow course.

Morality 'consists in the individual's attachment to those social groups of which he is a member' (Durkheim, 1925: 80). Rootlessness, estrangement and isolation are the best that the cheerless and the friendless can expect where the iron-willed eccentric breaks free from the constraint of reference. Where group attachment is weak, malintegration and normlessness leave the unbounded without the non-ego regulation that stands between the atom and the abyss: 'Man is the more vulnerable to self-destruction the more he is detached from any collectivity, that is to say, the more self-centred his life' (ibid.: 68). Bachelors, especially in urban agglomerations, are disproportionately suicidogenic. The same may be said of never-satisfied consumers, suffering from the morbidity of infinite aspirations, condemned forever to the pursuit of 'a terminal point that is non-existent, since it recedes in the same measure that one advances' (ibid.: 40). *Anomie* is not freedom. It cannot be liberty to live without limits.

Durkheim emphasised that cohesion and loyalty empower socialised man to glory in his function within the whole. Membership in the sense of T.H. Marshall gives meaning to what the melancholic pessimist would otherwise take to be a Midas-like emptiness: 'He must feel himself more solidary with a collective existence which precedes him in time, which survives him, and which encompasses him at all points. If this occurs, he will no longer find the only aim of his conduct in himself . . . Understanding that he is the instrument of a purpose greater than himself, he will see that he is not without significance' (ibid.: 373–4).

Collective sentiments, mutually magnified and regularly reaffirmed, are the cause of the strong emotions that are released through the ritual, ceremony, dogma and liturgy of worship: 'Religious beliefs proper are always shared by a definite group . . . They also belong to the group and unify it . . . In history we do not find religion without Church' (Durkheim, 1912: 41). Religious beliefs to Durkheim are shared ideas which come from and strengthen the personality of the group: 'Indeed it is invariably the fact that when a somewhat strong conviction is shared by a single community of people it inevitably assumes a religious character' (Durkheim, 1893: 119). Reciprocal reassurance is the reification of concord. It serves as a non-rational bulwark that stands against doubt and instability.

As with faith, so with rights; for there too it is the unifying symbolism that provides the normative force. Durkheim, like T.H. Marshall, saw no reason to treat human rights as a natural endowment that was inviolable and inalienable: 'Rights and liberties are not things inherent in man as such. If you analyse man's constitution you will find no trace of this sacredness with which he is invested and which confers upon him these rights. This character has been added to him by society' (Durkheim, 1924: 72). Human rights are social facts. The seeming sacredness is only the halo produced by strong convictions held in common by a group.

Even Kant's Categorical Imperative, Spencer's freedom of contract, T.H. Marshall's civil rights are the direct consequence of man's liberation through his voluntary submission to 'the great and intelligent force which is society, under whose protection he shelters' (ibid.): 'The individual becomes the object of a sort of religion. We carry on the worship of the dignity of the human person' (Durkheim, 1893: 122). The part is eulogised but still it is Marshall's membership, Marshall's citizenship, that supplies the binding legitimation. Morals are made and unmade by the *conscience collective*, enshrined par excellence in 'the political society, i.e., the nation' (Durkheim, 1925: 80). Civil rights, political rights, social rights – it is the community of all with each that, to Durkheim and to T.H. Marshall, must be relied upon to put backbone into belief.

8.1.3   Alfred Marshall

Citizenship as membership and memory is a concept that is firmly entrenched in the British vision of society as an organism and not a random heap. It is found in William Morris's dream of John Ball who smote the masters because they split the communion: 'Fellowship is heaven, and lack of fellowship is hell . . . The deeds that ye do upon the earth, it is for fellowship's sake that ye do them.' (Morris, 1886/7: 51). It is found in George Orwell's image of all England as 'a family', even if, still, 'a family with the wrong members in control': 'It has its private language and its common memories, and at the approach of an enemy it closes its ranks . . . It is *your* civilization, it is *you*' (Orwell, 1941: 35, 12). Tawney insisted on the past as the future of the 'common culture' (Tawney, 1931: 43). Titmuss made welfare a topic in duty, respect and recognition. Citizenship is an intrinsic part of the great chain of

British thought. One of the many places where citizenship can be found is in Alfred Marshall's early essay of 1873 on 'The Future of the Working Classes'.

In his early essay the great Cambridge economist, studying supply and demand because he wanted to do good, had confidently predicted that market capitalism, through lifestyle approximation, would make tolerant citizens less aware of stratum and class. Marshall argued that debasing, brutalising toil produces a proletariat of labouring animals, socially as far removed from their employers as was coarse Eliza from refined Professor Higgins. Economic evolution puts paid to that. Efficiency necessitates the mechanisation of exhausting toil. Productivity sets a premium on education and skill. Prosperity means rising incomes that upgrade the lower classes from the self-advertised stigma of the rock-bottom barrow into a one-class High Street in which every teenager looks the same.

Economic growth, tantamount to qualitative amelioration, integrates all of us into civilised production and recognisable self-presentation. Material affluence, Marshall writes, means that the 'official distinction between working man and gentleman' will inexorably pass away, 'till, by occupation at least, every man is a gentleman': 'I hold that it may, and that it will' (Marshall, 1873: 102). We *grow* into citizenship, reasoned the fallen evangelical in the shadow of Darwin's *Origin*. The economist's shopping spree and not the Marxist's red revolution will make brothers of us all.

T.H. Marshall, invited to give the Alfred Marshall Lectures at Cambridge in 1949, was able to find in Alfred's 'Future' and Alfred's one-nationness the same emphasis on citizenship that he himself was making the centrepiece of his rights. Alfred was a theorist of becoming and unfolding: 'Man himself is in a great measure a creature of circumstances and changes with them' (Marshall, 1885: 133). Alfred valued obligation and the execution of role: 'Morally everyone is a trustee to the public – to the All – for the use of all that he has' (Marshall, 1909: 464). Alfred favoured collective action where political intervention was essential for social progress: 'If the State work for this end, the State will gain. If we all work together for this end, we shall all gain together' (Marshall, 1873: 118). Alfred looked forward, most relevant of all, to a citizenship-based future in which 'the working classes [will] have been abolished' (ibid.). Alfred pinned his hopes on capitalism, enterprise and expansion while T.H. combined indispensable exchange with the conscious uplift of democracy and welfare. Citizenship is citizenship, however. Unrelated in any other way, still Alfred and T.H. were both of them the spiritual children of Toynbee, Toynbee Hall and T.H. Green.

8.1.4 The Evolution of Rights

There is a tradition in conjectural historicism which simplifies the transition.

Maine's status and contract (Maine, 1861), Spencer's militant and industrial society (Spencer, 1876. 1893, 1896), Durkheim's organic and mechanical solidarity (Durkheim, 1893), Schumpeter's capitalism and socialism (Schumpeter, 1942), Galbraith's original and revised sequence (Galbraith, 1967) – all these dichotomies refer to either/or trajectories, as uncompromising as *yesterday* versus *tomorrow* and as irreversible as the Marxian Apocalypse. Marshall as a historical sociologist seems to situate his own theory of evolution in the time-honoured tradition of developmental stages and destinations such as these.

Hegel's philosophy of progress is an imagined reconstruction of an undocumented passage. Marshall's law of rights, more pragmatic, is presented as an inference from the evidence that unbiased science has amassed. Marshall declares that his understanding of citizenship was 'dictated by history even more clearly than by logic' (Marshall, 1950: 8). Referring to his 'historical survey', pointing to its 'historical accuracy', Marshall said that he had confidence in his generalisations precisely because he had been 'digging for a while in the subsoil of past history' (ibid.: 13, 10, 7). Empiricism came first. The theory of citizenship was only an attempt to fit a schema to the facts.

Marshall's citizenship is first and foremost an interpretation of the British experience: 'The investigator who chooses his own society as his field of research is able to use the knowledge he can derive from intuition and investigation as a guide in his analysis. . . . The whole analysis will be made in the light of my knowledge of the society in which I live' (Marshall, 1934: 89). Confining himself to a single country, Marshall was precluded by his own methodology from claiming universality in the sense of Maine or Galbraith: 'The citizenship whose history I wish to trace is, by definition, national' (Marshall, 1950: 9). Writing of his homeland, however, he believed that there at least the theory had reasonable support from the record.

Marshall begins his story 'in early times', in feudal times, when the three entitlements were 'wound into a single thread' (ibid.: 8). No clear distinction could be made between civil, political and social rights where the same institution was at once a legislature, an executive and a court of law. Typically, the sense of nationhood was loose and diffuse: assemblies and councils tended to have a local base. Typically, different classes had different rights: the lord enjoyed privileges that the serf would never taste. Devolution and stratification built barriers and compartmentalised the membership. Except in the towns there was no strong sensation of a single band of brothers fighting as one to vanquish first Agincourt and then the slums, the ghettoes and the dark satanic mills.

Feudalism came first. It did not last. By about 1700, Marshall believed, gradual evolution had effectively tipped the scales in favour of the modern way. Centralisation took the place of *cuius regio*: the local and the specific gave way to the national and the standard. Equality before the law became the norm: all citizens regardless of class had to obey the rules. Functional differentiation occurred: the law courts, the legislature, the administration separated the functions that in medieval times had been operationally amalgamated.

By about 1700, the stage was set. All that remained for the unfolding of capitalism, democracy and socialism B was for the civil rights, the political rights and the social rights to come into their own. Marshall's rights are not eternal absolutes, *ex machina* and unbending, but rather Durkheimean relativities, conditioned and conditioning. Validated by consensus and shaped through agreement, rights are collective expectations even as they are individual consumables: 'Rights are not a proper matter for bargaining' (ibid.: 40). Civil rights, political rights, social rights: the evolution of rights is a trilemma that will be put under the microscope in the next three sections of this chapter.

8.2 CIVIL RIGHTS

Civil rights relate to protection, permission and law: 'The civil element is composed of the rights necessary for individual freedom – liberty of the person, freedom of speech, thought and faith, the right to own property and to conclude valid contracts, and the right to justice' (Marshall, 1950: 8). Civil rights are legal rights. The social institution most closely connected with them is the courts of law.

The 'first important step' (ibid.: 9) towards the *national*-isation of civil rights occurred in the twelfth century when royal justice began to defend the ordinary citizen against the land-owning nobleman. The rule of law was emerging, and with it the convention that all had an equal entitlement to due process. Even the State was expected to live within the laws.

The 'formative period' (ibid.: 10) of civil rights was the extended eighteenth century. It stretches roughly from the Revolution in 1688 to the Reform Act in 1832, from Habeas Corpus in the seventeenth century to Catholic Emancipation and the repeal of the Combination Acts in the nineteenth. Marshall's formative period coincides with the development of capitalism and the post-mercantilist take-off of the free market economy. The congruence is not a surprise. 'Intensely individual', property rights and enforceable contracts are 'indispensable to a competitive market economy' (ibid.: 40, 20). Without equality before the law, inequality in the marketplace would not appear legitimate and would not signal efficiency.

Marshall does not say if market capitalism was the cause or the effect of the new enforceability. Nor does he address the Hegelian objection that the documented co-variance only exists because *Geist*, through equality and individualism, served as the meta-parent that made events move. Marshall is weak on the chicken and the egg. Perhaps this is because his spiritual home was in the record room. A historian by training and temperament, all that Marshall wanted to show was that the extended eighteenth century had been the period in which Blackstone and Smith added up to security and growth.

8.2.1 De Facto and De Jure

The law is 'democratic' and 'universal' (Marshall, 1950: 12): all citizens de jure are guaranteed the shelter of the same umbrella. The position de facto is less precisely defined. The legal profession is recruited overwhelmingly from the privileged suburbs: the class monopoly must carry with it the threat of cultural monolingualism and even of unintended favouritism. Besides that, there is the financial commitment: the risk that the defendant's costs will be awarded against the plaintiff is in itself a good reason not to go to court. The pecuniary burden is an inequity as well as an obstacle. Income and assets make it disproportionately difficult for the poor to bring an action against the rich.

As for the cultural asymmetry, Marshall believes that this is less and less a concern: 'Impartiality as between social classes is firmly established in our civil justice' (ibid.: 22). Bias cannot be eliminated by statute: no attempt has been made. Education and the English tradition of even-handedness have certainly played their part; but so too has economic and social evolution in the all-including sense of Hobhouse and of Alfred Marshall. Because of the wealth of nations, Alfred had written, soon 'everyone who is not a gentleman will have himself alone to blame for it' (Marshall, 1873: 111). Because of the cultural convergence, T.H. continued, conspicuous universality has been associated with 'the spread in all classes of a more humane and realistic sense of social equality' (Marshall, 1950: 22). Every man is becoming a gentleman. Self-presentation, accelerated by social rights, makes it ever easier for a middle-class lawyer to treat his neighbour with respect.

Expense, however, remains a barrier. Hobhouse, writing of civil rights, had said that equal access would be a toothless tiger so long as the ability to pay was not ensured: 'Hence will come in time the demand for the abolition of the power of money to purchase skilled advocacy' (Hobhouse, 1911a: 12). Marshall did not see a need for a 'National Barristry' on the model of the National Health: 'Costs perform a useful function by discouraging frivolous litigation' (Marshall, 1950: 29). Means-tested legal aid was a different matter. Cutting off at a ceiling income and backed up by free advice from voluntary bodies, a sliding scale would at the very least price the disadvantaged back into law.

Marshall did not believe that a means test was always and everywhere a source of stigma: progressive tax and university grants are cases where the household is profiled but spoiled identity seldom if ever reported. Just as worrying as stigma is, however, the precedent of co-payment. Marshall acknowledges the possibility that fees for lawyers could open the way to charges for health. His conclusion is that the likelihood is not very great: 'The seriousness of the disease and the nature of the treatment required can be objectively assessed with very little reference to the importance the patient attaches to it' (ibid.). The law, on the other hand, is more volatile and more subjective.

Somehow the figures do not square. Practice variation shows that even doctors disagree; while it is a strange democracy that nets out the treatment rankings of the patient himself merely because uncultured lungs and kidneys have no civil right to a choice. If the law is a continuum, then so too is health.

Marshall has no solution to the deadweight of frivolous litigation. He does not explain who will denationalise the damages when the loser is too poor to pay. Nor does he consider market liberalisation as an antidote to the excessive charges of a restrictive profession. Entry and competition could attract back not just the chronically impoverished but also the middle-middle classes who are frightened off by the fees.

Fees are a hurdle but they are also an advantage. Healthcare itself might stand to gain from user charges on the model of the law. Marshall, concentrating on clinical best practice, ignores the economic functions (deterrence and signalling) that are fulfilled by price: Schumpeter would never have accepted that socialism could be effective so long as central planning was being economical with its exchange. Besides that, there is the cross-subsidy. Even if there does exist such a thing as an unambiguous need that cannot be reduced to naked Adam's untutored want, still that does not mean that the patient who can afford to pay should necessarily be exempted from the duty to share.

None of this, however, must be allowed to detract from Marshall's insistence that the law is a social service. Where the power to spend is unequally distributed, formal rights are toothless tigers in the absence of means-tested legal empowerment.

8.2.2 Labour

Labour is itself a sub-topic in civil rights. The 'basic civil right' in the modern labour market is 'the right to follow the occupation of one's choice in the place of one's choice, subject only to legitimate demands for preliminary technical training' (Marshall, 1950: 10). This freedom to choose and right to work is a modern acquisition. The Elizabethan Statute of Artificers confined certain occupations to certain classes. Other regulations reserved employment for locals, or limited wage negotiation, or treated apprenticeships as an entry barrier to new blood. Things were to change. As early as 1614, and certainly in the eighteenth century, the common law was attacking group monopolies and restrictive practices that stood between the maximising individual and the freedom of choice.

It is at this point that Marshall defends trade unions because they 'exercise vital civil rights collectively on behalf of their members' (ibid.: 26). Individuals have rights. Amalgamations of individuals have rights as well. Corporations with limited liability are one instance of the fictive and composite personality. Unions are another.

Unions, Marshall writes, promote the interests of their members 'through the use of contract in the open market, not through a minimum wage and social security' (ibid.). Political intervention and social rights are the functional equivalent. Historically speaking, the need for their firm hand has been that much less: 'The acceptance of collective bargaining was not simply an extension of civil rights; it represented the transfer of an important process from the political to the civil sphere of citizenship' (ibid.). Some unions may want to overthrow bloodsucking capitalism. The vast majority, however, only want to negotiate their just equilibrium within the framework of the proud Smithian game.

The doctrine Marshall is promulgating is not entirely clear. For one thing, pooled rights in Britain did not emerge in the eighteenth century but in the nineteenth and twentieth centuries. Restrictions on limited liability were lifted only in 1856. The Taff Vale Decision was in 1901. Packaging the corporations and the unions as a civil right is almost to treat them ahistorically as a step backward in time. Marshall ought perhaps to have created a separate (fourth) category for composite rights. At the very least he should have made a distinction between the early civil rights and the much later civil rights which followed them several generations on.

The sequence is important since collective rights did not evolve spontaneously. Man-made and not a natural growth, they were deliberately created by political authority in response to the multiple influences that have an impact upon accountable vote-seekers. Collective rights are the consequence of political rights and the child of an up-and-doing State. They are also an illustration of Marshall's moderation. Since politicians are creating the rights, they could just as easily be exercising them. Given political and social rights, some would say, there is no real need for civil rights to be granted to the blocs. Marshall is, however, like Galbraith, a sociological pluralist. In contrast to the centralisers, he wants the power-pools to continue their *collective* bargaining in the market.

Civil rights are universal. Composite rights, however, are polar. Limited liability favours the capital owners. Trade unions speak largely for the working class. Marshall does not mention the class bias or acknowledge the political linkages.

Capital, lobbying for profit, demands the discretion to hire and fire and a ban on the closed shop. Labour, exempted from the anti-monopoly laws, insists that unions be excused all liability for strikes and breakages. Marshall, who was not a Marxist, says little about systemic conflict between capital and labour. As far as he is concerned, the opposing interests can resolve their differences through supply and demand. His unions 'standardise' (ibid.: 42) the wage. They do not buck the market because the market's verdict is final.

Or is it? Perfect competition precludes price gouging but the push and shove of concentration is somewhat redder in tooth and claw. Marshall neglects the extent to which the redistribution of power is also a redistribution of income which is also a redistribution of the market's verdict which is always and everywhere final. Not least does he neglect the extent to which politicians are continuously reconfiguring the outcomes through laws and regulations which favour one horse over another in the race. The reallocation of power is an unexpected blind-spot in the political economy of an English author who knew about the Conservatives' campaign contributions and the Labour Party's union-sponsored Members. Here again, political rights have an impact upon civil rights in a way that the price-taking Enlightenment had not really been able to foresee.

Union governance confuses still further the meaning of rights. Not only are the composite rights vested in supraindividual bodies 'without formal collective responsibility' (ibid.: 26), the chiefs who make the decisions are not democratically elected by their constituents. Political rights legalised composite rights. The unions, however, saw no need for their own in-house nineteenth century. All things considered, it is hard to see how Marshall could have been so enthusiastic when he wrote as follows about the political–civil nexus: 'Trade unionism has . . . created a secondary system of industrial citizenship parallel with and supplementary to the system of political citizenship' (ibid.). It has done nothing of the sort.

Marshall's collectivism in civil rights, his movement 'from the representation of individuals to that of communities' (ibid.: 27), is especially problematic where composite rights cut across other principles and objectives. High wages favour incumbents over outsiders. A strike restricts the freedom of the manufacturer to make a profit. Repeated disruptions slow down the rate of growth. Marshall recognised that agglomerated power could go too far.

A theorist of duties as well as rights, Marshall believed that unions should have a 'lively sense of responsibility towards the welfare of the community' (ibid.: 41). The leadership was trustworthy and public-spirited. The rank-and-file, however, thought nothing of an unofficial strike. Their selfish particularism was threatening the living standards of their fellow-citizens. It had to be contained if civil rights were not to undermine the social interest: 'The government can no longer stand aloof from industrial disputes' (ibid.). Political rights engender composite rights. Political rights take them away again.

8.3   POLITICAL RIGHTS

The second set of rights is political rights. It is in essence 'the right to participate in the exercise of political power, as a member of a body invested with
political authority or as an elector of the members of such a body' (Marshall,
1950: 8). Referring at once to the guidance of authority and to the periodic
vote, it is clear that both of Schumpeter's two theories of democracy are
picked up by Marshall's definition. The institutions most closely connected
with political rights are Parliament and local government. The formative
period when the franchise became universal (except for women, whose rights
came in 1918) was the nineteenth century.

Parliament in earlier times exercised judicial functions on the feudal model
of the king's Curia Regis. Later these functions were handed over to the courts.
The judiciary became, Montesquieu-like, an independent branch. Political
rights remained for all that law-making and law-enforcing in nature. Only the
interpretation and the precedent had been hived off from the monopoly of
force.

Democracy is built around the values of loyalty, respect, service and cooperation. It presupposes integrity and audit: 'Citizens should have faith in the
honesty and efficiency of the system of government' (Marshall, 1963: 227). It
presupposes a 'we' and not a 'they': 'Nothing is more destructive of the true
essence of citizenship than the existence of a gulf between the governors and
the governed' (ibid.). It presupposes a civil service that recruits widely on the
equitable principle of access: 'It believes in equality, and its plans must therefore start from the assumption that every person is potentially a candidate for
every position in society' (Marshall, 1953b: 247). Democracy above all else is
dependent upon popular participation. Without information sharing, transparency and active consultation, the accurate representation of opinion will be
next to impossible to achieve.

Almond and Verba emphasise that internalised cognitions and attitudinal
capital make the democratic system not just an exercise in technocratic rationality but 'a humane and conservative way to handle social change': 'One
aspect of this new world political culture is discernible: it will be a political
culture of participation. If there is a political revolution going on throughout
the world, it is what might be called the participation explosion' (Almond and
Verba, 1963: 7, 3). Ordinary people want to speak and be heard. T.H. Marshall
had already thrown his weight behind Henry Dubb in the street. Democracy
must be *social* democracy for it to be called democracy at all.

Sensitive mirrors count. Local government will certainly have local knowledge. Marshall was aware that devolution could give the grass roots a greater
say. Extending the argument from rights to duties, he even added that free

riders will be less likely to shirk and litter where the 'limited loyalties' are those that they know and love: 'The national community is too large and remote to command this kind of loyalty and to make of it a continual driving force' (Marshall, 1950: 46–7). Marshall as a democrat was aware that an over-loaded centre had the option of politicisation to the periphery. Yet the local base was an option that he never fully endorsed.

Marshall had little interest in the public choice of Downs and the public knavery of Pareto: politicians and civil servants are not a separate interest group but the faithful servants of the Whole. He had in the circumstances little fear of the centralisation of a shared Westminster, of a monopoly D.C. It was precisely the same emphasis on the collectivity as a One that led him in the end to back away from local heterogeneity. Theorists of the *common* culture are never entirely at home with contra-Durkheimean breaking up. Regionalism can divide. Particularism can dilute: 'Political rights in a repre-sentative democracy can function at full strength only at one point, and through one institution, the national sovereign parliament. It is true that they function also, in a subordinate way, at the level of the local community, and more significantly at the level of the state in a federal system. But the ultimate power resides at the centre. The body politic, in short, has a single head' (Marshall, 1969: 141). A single body has a single brain. The organs are differ-ent but the head is one.

Citizenship might suggest a local base. It might also mean 'a sort of citizen-ship in the microcosm of the factory' (Marshall, 1963: 230): 'Industrial citi-zenship, devolving its obligations down to the basic units of production, might supply some of the vigour that citizenship in general appears to lack' (Marshall, 1950: 47). Democracy could usefully be extended from the State to the factory or office. G.D.H. Cole, socialist and guildsman, had argued that the reappraisal of self-government was long overdue: 'The right to elect the rulers is a recognised principle of democratic political theory. Is there any reason why such a principle should not be applied to industry also?' (Cole, 1913: 358).

Tom Bottomore concluded that it would have to be if the divided mind were not to suffer from intolerable confusion in a mixed-ethos society where sover-eignty was eulogised in the polity but totally repressed once the interchange-able part clocked on: 'It does not seem to me that a person can live in a condition of complete and unalterable subordination for much of the time, and yet acquire the habits of responsible choice and self-government which polit-ical democracy calls for' (Bottomore, 1993: 95). Aristotle said that the irre-deemably secondary-modern are born slaves and can never rise *en dessus de leur gare*: 'That one should command and another obey is both necessary and expedient. Indeed some things are so divided right from birth, some to rule, some to be ruled' (Aristotle, 1981: 67). Few in the Britain of the Marshall Lectures would have agreed with him.

Marshall knew that an era that had pinned its faith on personal judgment was bound to wonder why the economy too could not be made fully democratic. Flirting in places with decentralisation to the workplace or to the working group, he does seem about to come down in favour of participation as a logical extension of political rights. Then, perhaps surprisingly, he switches from Schumpeter's first theory to Schumpeter's second and decides not to press his case too far.

Leadership should be good: weeding out 'incompetence at the top', the firm should maximise the worker's 'confidence in the efficiency and disinterestedness of the management' (Marshall, 1963: 230). Leadership should be moderate: the worker will not take much pride in his little republic where he is made the victim of the 'excessive self-interest of his employer' (ibid.). Leadership should be open: managers should pass on information so that their workers can grasp what is happening and why. In all of these ways the governors should win over the rank-and-file by convincing them that best-possibles are being pursued and truthful explanations ungrudgingly provided.

Well and good – but listening and learning is not the same as political rights. It is here that Marshall becomes coy and even evasive. Above disclosure there is consultation – but, since the employers are not obliged to act on the opinions, 'there is no transfer of authority' (ibid.: 231). Above consultation there is 'joint control' – but, since any scheme for workers on boards has 'limited possibilities', 'the hopes sometimes placed in it may prove illusory' (ibid.: 231, 233, 232).

What it all comes down to is this: 'If the worker is to be happy in his work he must have confidence in his Government' (ibid.: 230). At the national level, he must believe that the State is on top of industrial shortcomings and social security. At the level of the firm, he must trust his decision makers to push back the frontiers and share out the gains. Putting the two together, what it all means is that the worker wants to be treated properly: 'He must know that he enjoys the full rights and dignity of a citizen' (ibid.). The worker wants to be governed well. Participative democracy is not needed for that.

Civil rights, logically as well as historically, were the necessary first step. Political rights were a 'secondary product of civil rights' (Marshall, 1950: 13). Since the freedoms of speech, assembly and association are classified by Marshall as civil and not political rights, there is a sense in which this is true by definition. Freedom of contract fanned the flames of equality and mobility. Individualism and ambition were set loose through market competition. In the heyday of British capitalism, inherited wealth was being challenged by achievement and choice. Universal suffrage was the political manifestation of that new and open road.

Marshall did not deny that there could be an unhealthy correlation between the affluence made possible by civil rights and the political power that the nineteenth century had legitimated through the great Reform Acts. Bribery, corruption, election expenses, all suggest that the opulent can be more equal than others; and so does the class snobbery that makes even Henry Dubb demand that his officers 'should be drawn from among the élites who were born, bred and educated for leadership' (ibid.: 22). A stately home can lead to a Woolsack. Even in a democracy, big money still talks big.

On the other hand there have been the palliatives. The secret ballot serves to prevent intimidation. The abolition of the poll tax and the payment of representatives both pluralise access beyond the propertied and the prosperous. The new spirit of the times, embodied in 'social education, and a change of mental climate' (ibid.), rejects the knee-jerk assumption that old Etonians have a natural right to lead. All things considered, it is democratisation that has won out in the end: 'Class monopoly in politics, unlike class monopoly in law, has definitely been overthrown' (ibid.).

It is just as well. Nowadays, increasingly, 'the sanctity of contract gives way to the requirements of public policy' (ibid.: 41). Civil rights are being pushed into second place by political rights. Only the validation of the governed can make the revised ranking legitimate and just.

8.4 SOCIAL RIGHTS

Third and last comes the drawing in and the bringing together. Marshall delimits the realm of social rights in the following words: 'By the social element I mean the whole range from the right to a modicum of economic welfare and security to the right to share to the full in the social heritage and to live the life of a civilised being according to the standards prevailing in the society' (Marshall, 1950: 8). The social element is evidently a menu of possibilities and not a single point: while 'a modicum' suggests the vestigial safety net, 'share to the full', 'civilised being' and 'standards prevailing' refer to social distance and generous levelling up. The institutions most closely connected with social rights are the educational and social services. The formative period was the late nineteenth and early twentieth centuries. It is 'conveniently marked' (ibid.: 28) by Booth's *Life and Labour* in 1889 and, in 1893, by the Royal Commission on the Aged Poor.

8.4.1 Social Rights before Civil Rights

In the Middle Ages the embryonic rights that then existed were derived from 'membership of local communities and functional associations' (Marshall,

1950: 14). Social intervention in forms such as wage regulation and poor relief was administered by the parts even where the obligation, national, was imposed by statute.

Wage regulation decayed in the eighteenth century. One reason was technical: 'Industrial change made it administratively impossible' (ibid.). Another reason was ideational: 'Wage regulation infringed [the] individualist principle of the free contract of employment' (ibid.). Social regulation was not compatible with the new civil rights that were emerging in tandem with the new economic devolution. Market value was coming in. Pay based on status or need seemed to have no further role.

Poor relief too collapsed as a consequence of a more competitive economy. The Elizabethan Poor Law, in common with the 'more primitive, but more genuine, social rights which it had largely superseded', had constructive and conservative objectives which made it 'something more than a means for relieving destitution and suppressing vagrancy': 'The Elizabethan Poor Law was, after all, one item in a broad programme of economic planning whose general object was, not to create a new social order, but to preserve the existing one with the minimum of essential change' (ibid.). The Elizabethan Poor Law sought to protect a social pattern which belonged increasingly to the past. It was 'utterly obnoxious to the prevailing spirit of the times' (ibid.: 15). It had to be dissolved.

It was matter followed by mind that produced the change. The last decades of the century of Adam Smith bore witness to 'a final struggle between the old and the new, between the planned (or patterned) society and the competitive economy' (ibid.: 14). Sunrise civil rights sided with creative destruction. Sunset social rights supported the time-out-of-mind. One way of interpreting the Speenhamland System of guaranteed income maintenance is to see it as the old order fighting back. Tradition did not stand a chance against steam. Social rights 'sank to vanishing point' (ibid.: 17) in the century of Bentham and Mill.

8.4.2   Social Rights in the Age of Laissez-faire

The Elizabethan Poor Law had been 'the aggressive champion of the social rights of citizenship' (Marshall, 1950: 15). The Poor Law of 1834 was more in tune with unequal wages and the free labour market. It offered outdoor relief only to the aged, the sick and the obviously incapable. The new Poor Law detached even the minimal aid it provided from the unquestioning status of citizenship: 'The Poor Law treated the claims of the poor, not as an integral part of the rights of the citizen, but as an alternative to them' (ibid.). Claimants ceased in practice to be citizens. Consigned to the workhouse, they lost both their civil liberties and their political franchise. Social support in such a scenario meant exclusion and stigma, not inclusion and community.

The early Factory Acts had the same tendency to divorce social intervention from citizenship status. Improved conditions and hours related to women and children only. They, of course, had fewer civil and no political rights. Men, as full citizens, were expected to make their own free contracts without the protection that only non-citizens and half-citizens were entitled to enjoy. Men did not have social rights. The reason was that they had civil and political rights instead.

8.4.3   The Revival of Social Rights

In the nineteenth century the older social rights were 'dissolved by economic change' (Marshall, 1950: 9). Simultaneously, however, political rights were emerging as an unintended consequence of civil rights. So was the 'modern national consciousness' (ibid.: 25) that cocooned the individual interests and the votes in a web of patriotism and belonging. The age of business was also the age of affect. The 'first stirrings of a sense of community membership and common heritage' (ibid.) were yet another unintended by-product.

Civil rights in that way led to the demand for social rights and to the political rights which were the channel: 'The normal method of establishing social rights is by the exercise of political power' (ibid.: 26). Civil rights would seem to point in two ways at once. Through the economy they validate the exchange of equivalents. Through the State, however, they validate the ascribed entitlement of which the 'content does not depend on the economic value of the individual claimant' (ibid.). Civil and political rights are individual. Social rights are collective. The former led to the latter. Democracy was the channel through which social welfare became a social fact.

8.4.4   Social Rights and Social Duties

Social rights are a citizenship charter and a unilateral transfer: 'Social rights in their modern form imply an invasion of contract by status, the subordination of market price to social justice' (Marshall, 1950: 40). Social rights in that sense are a request that cannot be refused: 'The claim of the individual to welfare is sacred and irrefutable and partakes of the character of a natural right' (Marshall, 1953b: 246).

Social rights are a stranger gift. They are also a multi-party contract and a loosely specified social exchange: 'Social rights imply an absolute right to a certain standard of civilisation which is conditional only on the discharge of the general duties of citizenship' (Marshall, 1950: 26). Marshall does not say that the right should be withdrawn if the duty is not fulfilled: he was too polite and too English to recommend that an incorrigible alcoholic should be stopped the dole. Even so, what he does say is very much in the spirit of the market mindset. His indication that bargains are not foreign to welfare is an important reminder that the distance between civil rights and social rights need not be a quantum leap.

Marshall writes as follows about 'the general social good' that must be given the final say: 'The Welfare State is the responsible promoter and guardian of the welfare of the whole community, which is something more complex than the sum total of the welfare of all its individual members arrived at by simple addition. The claims of the individual must always be defined and limited so as to fit into the complex and balanced pattern of the welfare of the community . . . That is why the right to welfare can never have the full stature of a natural right' (Marshall, 1953b: 247). From nine to five one has an obligation 'to put one's heart into one's job and work hard' (Marshall, 1950: 46). From five to nine one has a duty to 'live the life of a good citizen, giving such service as one can to promote the welfare of the community' (ibid.: 45). It is more like a well-ordered boarding school than it is the permissive society. But one does get the right to social services in return.

It is a Durkheimean consensus on spillovers, norms and the *sui generis*. It is a stern, judgmental socialism of externalities, conventions and fitting in. People who equate welfare with learned dependency, moral hazard and the taking posture must first refute Marshall's contention that acculturation and integration build up a regulatory barrier before which unlimited aspirations must perish and will. Marshall is in the tradition of the 'Dunkirk spirit' (ibid.: 46) and Adam Smith's *Moral Sentiments*. The result is that his social rights are rooted in pre-industrial community even as they are the third and final set that brings the evolution of rights to a close.

The principle is that rights come with duties attached: 'If citizenship is invoked in the defence of rights, the corresponding duties of citizenship cannot be ignored' (Marshall, 1950: 41). In the case of civil rights an illustration would be the unions. They should hold themselves back lest they impose the diswelfares of inflation and unemployment on their fellow signatories to the social contract. In the case of social rights, an illustration would be education: 'The right to education is a genuine social right of citizenship, because the aim of education during childhood is to shape the future adult. Fundamentally it should be regarded, not as the right of the child to go to school, but as the right of the adult citizen to have been educated' (ibid.: 16). There's no such thing as a free school dinner.

The Factory Acts in the nineteenth century protected children because children were *not* citizens. Compulsory education in the twentieth century empowers children because children must *become* citizens. Insisting upon education, the State 'is trying to stimulate the growth of citizens in the making' (ibid.). Society 'recognised that it needed an educated population' (ibid.: 37). Society recognised it. Society needed it. The supply of education was the collectivity's means-ends response.

The defence of education is clearly more than a defence of the individual who is hungry for a marketable skill. It is also the acknowledgment that the community *as a whole* has rights of its own which it has a composite right to enforce: 'The duty to improve and civilise oneself is therefore a social duty, and not merely a personal one, because the social health of a society depends upon the civilisation of its members' (ibid.: 16). Education is 'a necessary prerequisite of civil freedom': 'Civil rights are designed for use by reasonable and intelligent persons, who have learned to read and write' (ibid.). Education trains the manpower upon which the economy depends: international competitiveness presupposes human capital. Education is the precondition for responsible democracy: political rights do not identify authentic preferences where the voter is lacking in intellectual maturity. Civil rights and political rights may antedate social rights but they are also dependent on social rights for their own full flowering.

Education makes our nation what it is. Jones in the lower sixth is in that sense a national serviceman sent to the front for the All. The schoolboy has a private right to the lessons that are appropriate to his aptitudes and talents. Wedded to his *trivium*, however, he also has a public duty to his sponsors 'to develop all that is in him' (ibid.: 37). Fellow citizens expect a lad to make the most of his conjugations and his dissections, just as they expect his parents to be honest and above-board in declaring their tips for taxes. The nation is a rock-solid Us that lives in recollection and plans for posterity: 'Its culture is an organic unity and its civilisation a national heritage' (ibid.: 16). It uses education as an instrument to promote responsible attitudes and to keep to the minimum the waste of scarce potential.

Education was the watershed and the landmark. It was, in the British nineteenth century, the 'first decisive step on the road to the re-establishment of the social rights of citizenship in the twentieth' (ibid.: 16–17). To Marshall as to Tawney, it was the archetype of what good social policy was meant to be. Civil and political rights empower the individual to assert his essence. Social rights do that too, but simultaneously they do something more. They protect the whole against the solvent of the part who thinks he can go it alone.

8.5   THE IRON CAGE

Lindsay once said that 'indecisive wooliness is the curse of much modern democratic thought' (Lindsay, 1943: 263). As a university teacher, he will have known how important it is to be lucid, rigorous, precise and to the point. Reality is, however, the ultimate Everest for good social thought. If Lindsay had wanted to steer clear of indecisive wooliness, he should have made a choice to steer clear of the human condition itself. All of which is to say that, if Marshall on the law of evolution leaves a number of puzzles for the reader to solve, the fault might lie in the subject-matter and not with the social philosopher who is only trying to do his best.

Yet the fact remains that the message is opaque: 'The Marshallian legacy is in many respects ambiguous' (Rees, 1995: 343). Galbraith on mind and matter says precisely where self-expression stops and knee-jerk kicks in: 'Given a little time, circumstances will prove you either right or wrong' (Galbraith, 1958: 21). Schumpeter on the tendency to socialism says stoically that history must live out its fate: 'Things economic and social move by their own momentum ... The ensuing situations compel individuals and groups to behave in certain ways whatever they may wish to do' (Schumpeter, 1942: 129). Marx on political economy says confidently where he thinks the anatomy of civil society should be sought: 'It is not the consciousness of men that determines their existence, but their social existence that determines their consciousness' (Marx, 1859: 425). Then there was Marshall. Marshall knitted in wool because wool was all he had.

Marshall wove his cloth from the purest yes-but. His vision of an amicable handshake on the middle ground recalls Tocqueville's interpretation of free will as spontaneous choice situated within the iron cage of context: 'Providence has not created mankind entirely independent or entirely free. It is true that around every man a fatal circle is traced beyond which he cannot pass; but within the wide verge of that circle he is powerful and free; as it is with man, so with communities' (Tocqueville, 1840: II, 334). Marshall, like Tocqueville, wanted an action approach that would also be fully functionalist. The result was a mixed sociology that was so hyphenated that it papered over the cracks.

8.5.1   Ideals and Imperatives

Titmuss was a one-way moralist who believed that the altruism of welfare had to be ranked above the selfishness of exchange. The Titmuss tradition, Pinker states, 'has always implied that in a better ordered society the values of the social market would, as it were, take over and dominate those of the economic market. Titmuss's ideal of social welfare was based on a normatively unitary model of a good society' (Pinker, 1981: 15). Marshall, on the other hand, was a normative pluralist. He believed that in a hyphenated society it would be necessary to acknowledge and reconcile the claims of all three contributors to the free and tripartite order: 'Titmuss started from the protective institutions of social policy and worked outwards to the broader social structure. Welfare is at the centre of his universe. Marshall started, as a sociologist, with the total society, and he locates social policy among its several institutional parts' (ibid.). The truth is the three. All three must win. All three must have prizes.

That is why it is misleading to describe Marshall's final mix as a 'compromise': while blue mixed with yellow will compromise as green, Jill married to Jack is none the less Jill for becoming partnered into a duo. What is unique to Marshall, and what distinguishes him from Titmuss on the left or Friedman on the right, is his insistence on the coexistence of three sets of rights and practices. Individualism is civilised and sensitive. The free market produces the resources that pay for welfare. Collectivism is the expressed will of the democracy. Marshall was happy with what he saw. While the capitalists will call it socialist and the socialists will call it capitalist, Marshall probably saw the threesome as a model of tolerance in which different orientations, like different races, give and take peacefully and assist each other to unfold. The truth is the three. All three have a right to be there and a duty to exist.

That is why his discussion of evolution has a moral as well as a predictive dimension. Marshall expected the hyphenated society but he also welcomed it as good. Like Marx, he felt at home in the utopia that was becoming a fact of life. He praised Gaitskell and Crosland for making equality central and moving ownership to the fringe: 'With socialism redefined in this way, and nationalisation demoted to the status of a means, the hyphenated democratic–welfare–capitalist society became possible, or even inevitable' (Marshall, 1972: 105). He criticised Durbin and Schumpeter for using the language of extremes and for underplaying the useful role of gifts: 'Socialism, as seen by Durbin and Schumpeter, was the antithesis of capitalism, an antagonist with whom there could be no fusion or compromise. Neither of them said anything much about welfare' (ibid.). Neither of them understood that there had to be three.

Schumpeter 'examined socialism as a system for the management of a country's economic affairs rather than as a way of life' (ibid.). Schumpeter, Marshall believed, should have broadened his understanding of historical trends. Capitalism was not disappearing. It was, however, being amplified, augmented and rethought. Marshall was happy with the change. There were the ideals. There was the imperative. And there was Marshall, who knew that three standing side by side could be a civilised way to face the problems of the future.

8.5.2   The Linear Progression

First the civil rights, then the political rights, finally the social rights; Marshall's continuous unfolding has the character of a linear progression in the direction of a ratchet-effect betterment. Anthony Giddens contends that Marshall, 'based upon a long-term historical survey', genuinely felt he had

happened upon an 'irreversible trend of development', a 'one-way phenomenon': 'He writes as though the development of citizenship rights came about
as something like a natural process of evolution, helped along where necessary
by the beneficent hand of the state' (Giddens, 1982: 162, 172, 171).

Giddens stresses that the inference cannot be comparative or general
precisely because the evidence is country-specific: 'Being concerned mainly
with Britain, Marshall refrained from suggesting that it could be applied *en
bloc* to other countries in Europe, or to the USA' (ibid.: 162). Marshall would
have encouraged other scholars to conduct studies of their own countries in
order to enrich his hypotheses. He would not, however, have been discouraged
by other paths which were at variance with his expectations.

Bismarck relied on social rights to stifle the demand for political democracy. The Americans looked to charity to relieve destitution and saw no need
for a classless community. The Soviet Union guaranteed a welfare State but
offered few civil or political liberties. France fell back on revolution to overthrow an authoritarian autocracy. Singapore has thrived on the law of contract
but has shown less interest in Marshall's political and social entitlements.
Observations such as these make it difficult to say that Marshall's pattern is a
universal law, or to employ it for policy purposes in would-be developed societies. Rights can come and go out of sequence. Rights can become de-coupled
from other rights. Rights might not emerge at all. The world is a mixed economy and extremely queer. Giddens would nonetheless argue that Marshall
regarded his growth path as a reasonable approximation to the uniquely British
experience.

Giddens groups Marshall with the social evolutionists. Other thinkers are
not so sure. Thus Halsey, finding little evidence of mechanical automaticity,
makes the point that *histoire raisonnée* is a far cry from Marxian constraint:
'The assumptions and vocabulary of the doctrines of evolution and progress,
it must be conceded, may still be discerned in Marshall's writing. But the
thrust of his work is towards the importance of contingency in historical explanation and towards openness or voluntarism in any view of the future' (Halsey,
1984: 10). Pinker, again, looking beneath the superficial veneer of modernisa-
tion, notes that Marshall's three stages could be the footprint of 'fortuitous
changes of circumstance' and not the 'forces of historical necessity' at all:
'The balance is never more than precarious. Marshall was alive to the possibility of regress as to that of progress in social change, and he did not claim
that the rights of citizenship developed in immutable order' (Pinker, 1995:
110). Halsey discerns values and choices. Pinker highlights accidents and U-
turns. Neither accepts that Marshall is Marx all over again.

Turner, reading the schema, shares the view that it 'does not *necessarily*
entail some commitment to an immanent logic in capital; on the contrary, his
view of citizenship appears to rest on a contingent view of historical develop-

ment' (Turner, 1986: 45). This, Turner says, is fully borne out by 'Marshall's actual treatment of historical development', 'self-consciously in opposition to the evolutionary historical analysis of writers like L.T. Hobhouse and Morris Ginsberg' (ibid.: 46). Turner thinks that the three stages are optional. Giddens says that they are standard.

8.5.3   Affluence versus Welfare

Marshall in the Marshall Lectures was optimistic and confident. Eleven years on he seems to have been experiencing some doubts. Two papers on welfare and affluence, both dating from 1961, give the impression of a man who feared he had loved and lost. The British Welfare State, Marshall wrote in 1961, had been an accident, 'the product of an explosion of forces which chance and history had brought together in Britain's unique experience in the war and in the transition to a state of peace. As this situation dissolved, the society changed, and the thing to which we had first given the name of "Welfare State" passed away' (Marshall, 1963: 287). It was born in the caring 1940s. It passed away in the shop-till-you-drop of late Macmillanism. It did not last very long.

A welfare State must bubble up from the depths. Like any mutual-aid collective, it 'must be based, as regards its fundamental aims and principles, on unanimity and not on a majority vote' (ibid.). Welfare presupposes a popular commitment to 'genuine needs' over manipulated wants, to 'fair shares' (ibid.: 284) over aggressive egotism. The requisite consensus 'reigned unchallenged' (ibid.: 282) in the age of austerity. It was being 'smothered by the Affluent Society' (Marshall, 1961: 308). Marshall in 1961 seemed to be concerned that advertising and salesmanship were going to win the multi-party high ground while pooling and sharing would end up bearded and sandalled on the minority-interest fringe.

Marshall believed that Galbraith had been right to warn against the negativities of competitive consumption. He was therefore cautious about Crosland's insistence that material affluence was the friend and not the foe of the socialist ethic: 'When he says that this affluence favours personal freedom, social justice, an egalitarian society, democratic anti-paternalism, I find I have reservations. These blessings will not flow automatically from affluence' (Marshall, 1963: 315). Public policy waits on cooperative attitudes. Private acquisitiveness, however, depletes the moral capital. The conflict between the self-seeking and the community-spirited 'permeates some of the most important social problems of our age' (ibid.). Crosland was too quick to declare that social balance would carry the day.

Private pensions were coming in. State pensions were going income-linked. Charges and insurance were rationing healthcare by price. Miners and shop assistants were buying freehold detached. Crosland in 1956 treated the 1940s compromise ('a kind of capitalism softened by an injection of socialism') as a middle ground that had come to stay: 'It is for him a new kind of society, inspired by a new spirit' (ibid.: 284, 285). Marshall in 1961, while not expecting that welfare would actually be scrapped, inferred from the encroaching marketisation and the proletarian Conservatism that rights-talk could be a problem should the fickle kaleidoscope ever change its minds.

Marshall in 1961 recommended a guarded reappraisal: 'There is a need for a new model' (Marshall, 1961: 308). His own ideal remained a capitalist economy tempered by an interventionist State. This middle ground was indispensable precisely because there are 'some elements in a civilized life' which can only be nurtured by 'curbing or superseding the market' (Marshall, 1963: 284). Green and Hobhouse were the sine qua non. That was just the problem. Marshall in 1961 seemed to be frightened that conspicuous acquisitiveness was taking the edge off the march into social rights. It was a fear, fortunately, which seems to have receded as Britain settled into the white heat of the Harold Wilson years.

8.5.4 History to Come

Marshall's history is a selection of convenience. Civil rights for the unions came not before but after the democratisation of political rights. Social rights in the Middle Ages came before the civil rights in the Enlightenment that came before the social rights of Lloyd George that came before 1961. The social right to education is a complement both to the civil right to trade and to the political right to vote: history seems to be simultaneity and symbiosis even as it is a quasi-Hegelian progression towards a three-in-one End. Marshall's anecdotes do not always support his theories. As a historian who was also a social scientist, he must have known that his inductions and his deductions had a will of their own.

The harmonious articulation is itself too good to be true. A less convenient selection would bring into relief the inconsistencies and the discordances. The economic civil rights of the merchants and manufacturers were restricted by the ascribed social rights of the employees and the deprived. The freedoms of privacy and assembly were put on the defensive by new challenges such as terrorism and corporate fraud. Modern surveillance techniques and need-to-know disclosure have made information flows biased, unequal and even inadequate. Marshall understated the conflict of rights that had undermined and would undermine the three supports of his structure. The absences leave a hole in the iron cage

The past is a problem. The future is worse. Writing in places as if Marx, Schumpeter and Galbraith, Marshall gives the impression that he sees 'the present phase of the development of democratic citizenship' (Marshall, 1950: 49)

as the final equilibrium. It is, however, never safe to assume that any promises are set in stone. Rights are a Pandora's Box. Change being the only constant, the theorist is obliged to clear some space for the next phase in the flow. Marshall, trained as a historian, preferred to leave it to more speculative minds to guesstimate the *incognita* that had not yet been born.

One possibility is that old rights will be withdrawn. Welfare, especially fragile, might end up confined to the residuum because of a cost–benefit prudence that is hostile to malingering and lifestyle dependency, because of rising expectations that dismiss high taxes and deficit finance as a brake on further growth. Disillusionment, moreover, can tarnish the image. A more cynical generation might become so antithetical to the vote motive, class partiality and duplicitous spin that it favours the privatisation of healthcare and State schooling quite simply because political rights do not protect the little man against the mind games of his scheming emperors. Consensus is the source of all rights. There is no telling what consensus-to-come will demand: 'Rights are not as absolute as some people think' (Marshall, 1975: 205–6). At-risk minorities should live with their suitcase packed.

A second possibility is that new rights will be created. Whether an *ab initio* fourth set or a radical revision of an existing endowment, the crucial point is that new choices drive a coach and horses through the idea that history stopped once Mr Butskell had completed his scheme. Workers, attracted by universal suffrage, might demand active participation at work. They might also say that the employer owes them unearned perquisites such as job security and long-service increments because the NHS has taught them that their citizenship standards cut across his civil right to a market return. Women, given the vote, might interpret democracy to mean equal representation in parliaments and in executive positions. They might also say that they have a reproducer's right to paid maternity leave and childcare facilities because the profit-seekers cannot deny to their fellow citizens the freedom to multiply the nation's true wealth. Marshall is enough of a capitalist to believe that pay more or less settles the debt. What might happen instead is that staff demand a right to supplementary benefits consumed at the place of work on the basis that work, like citizenship, is an all-embracing thing.

Esping-Andersen, pointing to the 15 per cent daily absenteeism in the typical Swedish firm, says that, at least in the eyes of the employees, 'a very large share of what normally is regarded as labor time is in fact "welfare time" ' (Esping-Andersen, 1990: 156). The Swedish absentees were acting in accordance with their workplace-welfare rights. Such non-contractual rights, like women's reproducer's rights, do not figure in Marshall's iron cage of musts. What Esping-Andersen is arguing is that modern capitalism, at least in Sweden, nowadays acknowledges the currency of economic rights that transcend the 'pure exchange principle': 'The Swedes are relatively de-commodified: they do not just hand over their time to the employer; the employers' control of the purchased labor-commodity is heavily circumscribed' (ibid.). Voluntary absences are not a written-down entitlement. They are, however, a consensual expectation. That widespread acceptance, both to Marshall and to Durkheim, is enough to give them the legitimacy of the next valid right down the road.

The right to plan is itself a new right that Marshall did not anticipate. The State can, through democracy, claim the right to regulate hires, conditions and externalities into the corset prescribed for them by the median voter. Nationalising and commanding, the State can centralise even greater power still. The banks can be given their priorities. The steel mills can be assigned their quantities and markets. Efficient in the sense of Schumpeter or inefficient in the sense of Mises, the fact remains that the right to plan can be as legitimate a right as any other. The only condition is that it be an uncontested emanation from the whole that is greater than the sum of its parts. The 'great majority' of the people is the sole wellspring of all the entitlements: 'They become, as it were, details in a design for community living. The obligation of the state is towards society as a whole, whose remedy in case of default lies in parliament or a local council, instead of to individual citizens, whose remedy lies in a court of law, or at least in a quasi-judicial tribunal' (Marshall, 1950: 35).

The truth is the whole. That is what the 'democratic socialist state' is all about: the 'design for living' is primary, a social absolute to which 'individual rights must be subordinated' (ibid.: 35, 36). The fourth set of rights could therefore be communitarian rights, coordinated rights, balanced rights, bundled rights: 'Town planning is total planning' (ibid.: 36). Total planning is totalitarian planning. The rights of the whole are stronger than the rights of the part. That is what rights-talk by consensus means once the polish and the gloss have worn off.

It is a social contract in pursuit of the social interest. Peasants starve because industry needs cheap inputs. Production is relocated because customary networks must not be disrupted. Intelligent women breed with intelligent men because procreation is the people's bloodstock. Marshall said that everybody's business is Everybody's Business: 'Your body is part of the national capital' (Marshall, 1965a: 91). It is just as well that his dynamic plays itself out before new rights are created that, in a country with no written constitution and no bill of rights, could collectivise many of the liberties that Marshall held most civil. Marshall believed that Little England could safely rely upon tea, tolerance and common sense to serve as a cultural bulwark against invasive new entitlements that might go too far. Perhaps he was right.

9. T.H. Marshall: citizenship and social distance

Citizenship is a 'principle of equality' (Marshall, 1950: 20). Class, however, is a principle of distance. Marshall says that there is no a priori reason why economic layering has to be eliminated if capitalism is to be brought tolerably close to felt community: 'Status differences can receive the stamp of legitimacy in terms of democratic citizenship provided they do not cut too deep, but occur within a population united in a single civilisation; and provided they are not an expression of hereditary privilege' (ibid.: 44).

Marshall's first condition is that separation should not be excessive. Some inequality is 'necessary and purposeful': 'It provides the incentive to effort' (ibid.: 19). Too much inequality, however, is a pollutant, like a smoking chimney, that the 'social conscience' (ibid.: 20) deems to be an evil that must be abated.

The second condition is that there should be a unifying way of life. This is the internalised sense of 'community membership and common heritage', of 'common culture and common experience' (ibid.: 25, 44). It binds together the fellow participants through the ideas and the values that they share.

The third condition is that intergenerational inequities should be suppressed. People are willing to accept differences in income if opportunities are equal and selection is unbiased: 'Inequalities can be tolerated within a fundamentally egalitarian society provided they are not dynamic' (ibid.: 44). People are less receptive to unequal outcomes if the law is stratified, achievement unacknowledged, mobility blocked, privilege inherited. Citizenship is fully compatible with the 'inequalities of capitalist society' (ibid.: 20) provided that each contestant plays to the same set of rules. Citizenship is, on the other hand, absolutely 'incompatible with medieval feudalism' (ibid.: 19). Where the aristocrats, the serfs and the townspeople live and die in the class into which they were born, there it would be true to say that hierarchy gets in the way of solidarity and social distance splits one-nationhood into islands and inbreeds.

Social distance is the subject of this chapter. The discussion is divided into four parts. Section 1, 'Social class and social status', situates Marshall's endstate of dignity and respect in the context of structural patterning and the

Marxian factors of production. Section 2, 'Capitalism and inequality', and section 4, 'Socialism and inequality', explore the evolution of social distance in a mixed society where political economy brings together and market economics tears apart. Section 3, 'Socialism and social rights', probes the anatomy of the promise-making society. It shows that Marshall was vague about his shopping list, uncertain about resourcing, specificity and profession-alism, not always clear about path-dependence, not always reassuring about personal autonomy.

The social rights are underexplained. The principled stance is, however, what it is. Marshall believed that separation should not be excessive, that communication should not be impeded, that injustices should not be handed on. This chapter shows that Marshall on affluence and Marshall on interven-tion were in the end made one by a unifying conviction: 'Equality of status is more important than equality of income' (ibid.: 33). A citizen's a citizen for a' that. Like world peace and the East Mimms donkey sanctuary, it is a cause which every decent citizen will be only too happy to support.

9.1   SOCIAL CLASS AND SOCIAL STATUS

Marxism is about class consciousness and class conflict: 'The history of all hitherto existing society is the history of class struggles' (Marx and Engels, 1848: 79). It is, specifically, a late Ricardian's brutal diagnosis of an unavoid-able civil war between the surplus-snatchers who own the capital and the impoverished reserve army which has only its labour power to supply: 'Our epoch, the epoch of the bourgeoisie . . . has simplified the class antagonisms. Society as a whole is more and more splitting up into two great hostile camps, into two great classes directly facing each other – Bourgeoisie and Proletariat' (ibid.: 80). Economic interest and bitter resentment are the driving force. Soon it will all be over.

Marxian socialism is about a class system that stratifies its citizens along the lines of their pecuniary position. So is Weberian sociology. Max Weber, not a revolutionary, had little time for the bursting of the integument and the expropriation of the expropriators. Even so, the expectation that societal cladding would cling to economic contours was a shared affirmation that production produces origins and destinations and not just the goods and services that we buy and sell.

Weber defines social class almost exclusively in terms of the material base: 'We may speak of a "class" when (1) a number of people have in common a specific causal component of their life chances, in so far as (2) this component is represented exclusively by economic interests in the possession of goods and opportunities for income, and (3) is represented under the conditions of the commodity or labor markets' (Weber, 1922d: 181). To Weber as to Marx, it is the distribution of material resources and their allocation through market competition that determines an individual's class: ' "Class situation" is, in this sense, ultimately "market situation" ' (ibid.: 182). Asset-ownership maps a man out: '"Property" and "lack of property" are . . . the basic categories of all class situations . . . The factor that creates "class" is unambiguously economic interest' (ibid.: 182, 183).

They agreed on the economic interest. They disagreed on the perception and the self-perception. To Marx, the workers have class awareness and class loyalties that reflect the common experience of selling themselves. Living conditions and life chances, like the tight binding of ethnicity and religion, stamp the lumps of affinity with a single die. To Weber, however, market power and even unequal advantage are not enough to smelt the negatives of frustration and unfairness into the positives of resemblance and recognition: 'A class does not in itself constitute a community' (ibid.: 184). Economics does not in itself breed much consciousness. Honour and lifestyle tell a different story: 'In contrast to classes, *status groups* are normally communities' (ibid.: 186).

Status, because status-symbols cost money, may be correlated with economic variables like income and wealth: 'The possibility of a style of life expected for members of a status group is usually conditioned economically' (ibid.: 190). Sometimes necessary, never sufficient, the operative point is that possession and distinction are entirely separate things: 'Both propertied and propertyless people can belong to the same status group' (ibid.: 187). Marxian ownership relates to production and compensation. Weberian packaging relates to consumption and esteem. Possession is objective. Distinction is subjective. The two are not the same.

Status is an equal thing within the group: 'A specific *style of life* can be expected from all those who wish to belong to the circle' (ibid.). The members have the same rituals, totems, insignia and taboos. They have customs which are unique to themselves: 'Status groups are the specific bearers of all "conventions" ' (ibid.: 191). Socialising mainly with one another, prone to the practice of endogamy, they often evolve into a closed caste that is exclusive and separate. The microsociology can be an obstruction to the one-nationness of the whole. Weber gives the example of the Jews. A chosen people, they do not welcome outsiders as converts. One group speaking Latin and another group speaking Greek, where then is the common culture that makes every Marshallian a citizen and a gentleman and a valued end in himself?

Status groups can be as divisive as Latin and Greek, slums and suburbs. They can, however, also be as Us-defining as the Union Jack and the Church of England. Henry Dubb and the Earl of Muck will never be equal in terms of economic function, social influence and accumulated pelf. In the currency of status, however, they can wear the same fashions, eat the same hamburgers and jig to the same tunes. Alfred Marshall looked forward to the day when the whole nation would have overlap enough to see itself as a single status group. So did T.H. Marshall, who sought to mix the capitalism of Youth Culture with the socialism of the National Health in order to produce a Britain sufficiently homogeneous that both the proletarian and his boss might know that he had within his veins the same blood of Arthur that collectively had made them great.

9.1.1 Citizenship and Self-presentation

As a socialist and a sociologist, one would have expected Marshall to continue the historic quest into the self-perpetuation of structure. It was his perception that stratification was his principal research area at the LSE (Marshall, 1963: vii). His publications tell a different story. Describing his Marshall Lectures, he seems to be speaking as well for the rest of his work: 'Social class occupies a secondary position in my theme' (Marshall, 1950: 17). What was primary to him was not class but classification.

Bottomore writes that perception and presentation, signals and signifiers, seem more important to Marshall than the objective parameters that determine the social location: 'The impact of citizenship on social classes, rather than the impact of social classes on the extension of citizenship, was clearly his principal concern' (Bottomore, 1992: 55). This interpretation of Marshall as more like a Quaker than a Marxist is borne out by the following declaration, dating from 1938: 'There are two main roads to the classless society. One leads through the abolition (as far as possible) of the social differences between individuals – which is roughly the way of communism – and the other proceeds by rendering all differences irrelevant to social status – which is roughly the way of democracy' (Marshall, 1963: 172). Qualitative comparison, Marshall is suggesting, counts for more than do role, function or cash: 'Social classes are the identity groups existing for the sake of the internal contacts which identity makes possible' (Marshall, 1934: 110). Marx defines his classes in terms of external contacts. Marshall treats his classes as (culturally) self-sufficient: 'The borderline between my classes is defined by an attitude of comparison which recognises qualitative differences. The borderline between his classes is defined in terms of functional interaction' (ibid.). Consciousness and thought have exceptional power to reshape the world in the image that the mind finds the most congenial. As Barbalet concludes: 'It follows that class differences might be reduced, indeed eliminated, by altering social attitudes' (Barbalet, 1988: 55).

It is Max Weber on status over Marx–Weber on class. Cohesion and solidarity are clearly not impeded by zero-sum rivalries and power-perpetuating rules of the game. Integration and harmony are not put at risk by patterned antagonisms that only the suppression of the labour–capital divide can transcend. Inequality need not mean privilege and can just as easily mean productivity: 'It may be that the inequalities permitted, and even moulded, by citizenship, do not any longer constitute class distinctions' (Marshall, 1950: 44). In place of the old-style distance factors Marshall sees the gentlemanly alternatives of civil rights, political rights, social rights – and, of course, economic growth which gives all but the basement *residuum* a decent share in 'the concrete substance of civilised life' (ibid.: 33). The glaring and visible disparities fade away. What is out of sight is out of mind. The Marxists would call it false consciousness. Marshall calls it the true consciousness of a nation at peace.

Dahrendorf says that Marshall saw modern history as the perceived incompatibility between the equality of citizenship and the inequality of class. The evolution of rights would ultimately put an end to the dynamic of struggle. Dahrendorf summarises as follows the broader implications of Marshall's unstoppable homogenisation: 'If these suggestions are correct (which is open to dispute), then Marshall has shown that there *can* be no class conflicts in the Marxian sense in advanced industrial societies, because the structure of these societies is subject to a different law of development . . . It explains both why capitalist society was a class society and why there are no classes in post-capitalist society' (Dahrendorf, 1959: 102).

Dahrendorf is by no means satisfied with Marshall's account of society as a lake in which the separate tributaries dissolve their recognisable differences. Schumpeter compares class to an omnibus, 'always full, but always of different people' (Schumpeter, 1927: 248). Marshall, concentrating on the common experience shared by an ever-changing pool, neglects the fixity and the continuity of the seats arranged in rows which go on and on. In Dahrendorf's words: 'A clear distinction is necessary between social positions or roles and their agglomerations on the one hand, and the personnel of these units, the incumbents of such positions, on the other hand' (Dahrendorf, 1959: 108). Marshall does not make the requisite distinction between (the liberal's) recruitment and (the socialist's) structure. The consequence is that Marshall's contributions must 'remain marginal to our problem and cannot be considered as superseding the old theory' (ibid.: 125).

Lifestyle convergence does not mean the dissolution of class, while social mobility does not alter the hierarchy of destinations to which the ambitious can aspire. Wanting as a liberal to equalise individual citizens, it is probable that Marshall failed as a socialist to equalise the economic categories and the functional groups. Maybe people do *feel* equal and *look* equal once perception and presentation have submerged the big fish and the little fish alike in a common lake. Yet that does not mean that they *are* equal. Thinking, typically, cannot make the Gini coefficient go away. Power and property are not always all in the mind.

Power to Marshall normally derives from the political right to vote. Economics is a tougher nut to crack. There is in Marshall's evolutionism no Schumpeter-like break between the decentralised decision making of entrepreneurial capitalism and the concentrated control of its corporate successor. Where managers and bureaucrats are taking over, there is no reason to think that choices are being democratised or business authority levelled down.

Also, in terms of bank balances, capital ownership, middle-class socialisation or an inherited head start, Marshall's lifestyles do nothing to address the structural multipliers. Titmuss acknowledged the material underpinnings when he referred to the '*class* distribution of incomes and wealth' (Titmuss, 1962: 198, emphasis added). Status by itself would not be enough. The bulldog of class would have to be tamed.

9.1.2   Conflict

Marshall's citizenship, like Marx's communism, is a final equilibrium in which harmony and consensus rule. The end is concord. The means, however, is combat. People do not ask for – fight for – rights which they already possess.

Marshall writes that the evolution of citizenship is dominated by the 'struggle to win those rights'; that strikes under the Liberal Government reflected 'a concerted demand for social rights'; that capitalism and citizenship have traditionally been 'at war'; that the competition for entitlements 'springs from the very roots of our social order' (Marshall, 1950: 25, 40, 28, 49); that even the modern wage-bargaining mechanism, driven into the acrimony of the industrial dispute, can be 'about the very acceptability of the system itself' (Marshall, 1963: 30). Marshall writes that there can be intense hostility even on the middle ground: 'There are forms of conflict incorporated in the system itself; and there are other forms which attack the system and may even destroy it' (ibid.: 31). Passages such as these do not suggest endemic polarisation or a divide that must necessarily bring the house down. A marginalist and not a militant, Marshall would have felt that Turner was overestimating the bitterness when he stated that 'the critical factor in the emergence of citizenship is violence – that is, the overt and conscious struggle of social groups to achieve social participation' (Turner, 1986: 26). What Marshall's writings do make clear is that change does not come by itself. Change is interest-driven, deliberate and micro-motivated. History to Marshall is perceived discomfort and a group cry for help.

Marshall was not a functionalist who assumed frictionless articulation. He was fully aware that the excluded could regard the privileged as their oppressors and make common cause to secure their rights: 'Class conflict occurs when a common interest unites adjacent social levels in opposition to more distant social levels' (Marshall, 1963: 173). In contrast to Marx, however, Marshall saw the capital–labour dialectic neither as an insurmountable inconsistency nor as an outstanding and salient abuse. The capital–labour divide was only one species in the broader genus of rightlessness. If one had to single out the primum *primum mobile*, it would not be the working-class movement per se but rather the conflict between principles that excites the workers even as it inspires the intellectuals. As Barbalet explains: 'The struggle which Marshall refers to here is not necessarily social struggle, between groups or classes of people, but primarily struggle against established ways of doing things' (Barbalet, 1988: 30).

Struggle is just a way of describing the cumulative demand to get on board. The middle classes in the eighteenth century had to struggle with the feudal aristocracy for civil liberties and the right to vote. The working classes later on had to struggle with the middle classes for universal suffrage, social services and the unionised shop. Different groups struggle for different things. What is crucial is that they do so against a broad background of agreement on principles. The middle classes having already taken their stand on rights, they knew that they could not in all conscience refuse to their workers the foothold on the ladder that individualism and equality had effectively bought for the class before. The ramifications were not always anticipated: 'Political rights of citizenship . . . were full of potential danger to the capitalist system, although those who were cautiously extending them down the social scale probably did not realise quite how great the danger was' (Marshall, 1950: 25). The consequences were not always foreseen. That, however, is beside the point. The monarch gave way to the Lords. The Lords gave way to the Commons. Universal principles were in the air. Where all Englishmen thought as one, the system would adapt incrementally and peacefully. Violent revolution need not apply.

Because the consensus is sympathetic to individualism and equality, the intellectual conflict itself is more likely to reinforce the social mainstream than to challenge it. Civil and political rights were extended but not invented: struggle only meant that the haves were obliged to share. Social rights built upon the economist's notion of the plus-sum spillover: the struggle for human capital is also the struggle for economic growth. Conflict in Britain was kept within limits and put to good use. Background agreement ensured that Oxford Fabians and not wild anarchists would form the advance guard of reform.

Individualism and equality explain how social contradiction is managed through common values. Perhaps they do; but still the analysis is incomplete. Marshall postulates that the social ethic is all around. What he does not say is why.

Weber invoked the Protestant Ethic and the Christian Socialists preached Christ-like cooperation. Galbraith, on the other hand, argued that ideas are only the rubber stamp of events and that material constraint is ineluctably the cause of the cause. His economic determinism recalls Marx's contra-Hegelian contention that 'it is not consciousness that determines life, but life that determines consciousness' (Marx and Engels, 1845–6: 37): 'The mode of production of material life conditions the general process of social, political and intellectual life' (Marx, 1859: 425).

On the one hand there is thought: this is the case of an ex-colonial territory which emulates the Constitution and the Bill of Rights because that is what the first-year textbooks teach. On the other hand there is circumstance: this is the folk memory of a wartime enemy, the safety valve of an open frontier, the multiculturalism imported with the immigrants made necessary by an ageing population and a shortage of labour. In the middle there is T.H. Marshall who says that conflict is embedded in consensus but never really models the why. It is historical sociology without the historical sociology. The utopia is under-explained but at least it makes us all feel good.

9.2   CAPITALISM AND INEQUALITY

Capitalism and citizenship have developed side by side since the late seventeenth century. The conjunction is an unexpected one. Capitalism grades and sifts. Citizenship, however, is an endowment in common. Unexpected or not, Marshall states that the age of exchange has been the age of rights as well. Social distance has been affected both by the economics of achievement and by the politics of status. This section examines the links.

9.2.1   Contracts and Markets

Capitalism was and is dependent on enforceable agreements. The new economy agitated for equality before the law because without an impartial judiciary it would be difficult for the propertied classes to turn a profit. It also agitated for an equal right to vote because the bourgeoisie did not trust the aristocracy to legislate equitably and to tax. Protection of interest is 'indispensable to a competitive market economy' (Marshall, 1950: 20). Once the middle classes had secured their equality, it was only a matter of time before the working classes would put in their claim for *as much* and *as good*. The excluded became the included. The capitalist revolution had put the ball in play.

Capitalism equalised the protection of interest. Earning and spending were more of a problem. Capitalism is a meritocratic system which is happy to hand the prize to whichever runner happens to win the race. Such an even-handed allocation of rewards does not necessarily mean a compression of the income scale. All that it does is to introduce legitimacy into the differentials of supply and demand: 'The final outcome is a structure of unequal status fairly apportioned to unequal abilities' (ibid.: 38). This is not one-man-one-fish on the model of one-man-one-vote. It is, however, 'the equal right to be recognised as unequal' (ibid.). It is an equal chance to win first prize. That is social equality too.

Capitalism and distance go hand in hand. There is nothing wrong with that provided that discriminatory privilege does not put all the clocks wrong: 'Equalisation is not so much between classes as between individuals within a population which is now treated for this purpose as though it were one class' (ibid.: 33). Marshall has no objection to differentials per se. What he finds unacceptable is that opportunities should be unequal or that Muck Minor should be given special treatment merely because his parents are rich.

Marshall as a liberal has no objection to productivity being paid its bonus. Marshall as a socialist is, however, aware that excessive disparities can weaken the cohesion of citizenship. The duality of markets mixed with membership is a central tenet of his middle ground. It is also a question mark and a minefield of imprecision.

There is, Marshall writes, 'a kind of basic human equality, associated with full community membership, which is not inconsistent with a superstructure of economic inequality' (ibid.: 45). His phrase, 'not inconsistent', is somewhat less than a strong endorsement. Marshall implies as much when he says that 'the inequality of the social class system may be acceptable *provided* the equality of citizenship is recognised' (ibid.: 6, emphasis added). Marshall's *provided* is the ultimate hostage to fortune. *Provided* X is recognised, Y may be acceptable. If, however, X is not recognised, then the economist's Y is unlikely to command much support.

Tolerable inequality to Marshall derives its legitimacy from two intellectually separate clusters of principles. From liberalism it takes the idea of market-clearing distribution as if guided by a selfless, faceless arbiter. From socialism it adopts the notion that 'full community membership' must limit the distance that disparities can travel from the mean. *Provided* the principles are 'not inconsistent', income and wealth can safely be left to lie where they fall. The problem arises when the two principles do not coincide. It is this conflict of orientations that Marshall has in mind when he confesses that market and membership need not after all be mutual supports: 'In the twentieth century, citizenship and the capitalist class system have been at war' (ibid.: 18).

Where there are two polar principles, one of them must give way. Pigou famously said that the limit to equalisation should be determined by the discouragement to growth: 'Anything that either increases the dividend without injuring the absolute share of the poor, or increases the absolute share of the poor without injuring the dividend, must increase economic welfare' (Pigou, 1920: 645). Marshall echoes Pigou's meta-principle in the following *as far as*, where he seems to be warning his fellow socialists to keep their hands off the golden goose: 'In time, as the social conscience stirs to life, class-abatement, like smoke-abatement, becomes a desirable aim to be pursued *as far as* is compatible with the continued efficiency of the social machine' (Marshall, 1950: 20, emphasis added). Levellers may cream off the icing. Levellers must not cream off the cake.

Market capitalism, although essential, can generate disparities incompatible with the solidarity of citizenship. Where the distance is a pollutant, Marshall's answer is the State.

Marshall says that 'the basic equality' cannot be 'created and preserved without invading the freedom of the competitive market' (ibid.: 7). He is calling for bounded laissez-faire that 'functions – within limits' (ibid.) but he need not be endorsing intervention that violates the strict Pigovian standard. There would be no conflict of principles where a progressive income tax only creamed off a functionless quasi-rent while leaving unaffected the economic incentive to perform. The problem arises when the Pigovian meal fails to satisfy the integrationist's craving and Marshall's *as far as* is *not far enough*.

Marshall recognised that markets will sometimes point to one integer but membership to quite another: 'It may prove, therefore, that the inequalities permitted, and even moulded, by citizenship will not function in an economic sense as forces influencing the free distribution of manpower' (ibid.: 44). Social distance might necessitate the compression of the scale. Living standards, however, might presuppose a greater premium. There is here a 'basic conflict' (ibid.: 42) between values and opportunities that the growth economist's material *as far as* does little to resolve.

Marshall is unlikely to have thought that a trade-off between economy and society would raise its head very frequently. Moderation has its benefits as well as its costs. Where, however, a choice had to be made, there is no question as to what Marshall believed his court of appeal would have to be: 'the subordination of market price to social justice', 'the replacement of the free bargain by the declaration of rights' (ibid.: 40). Forced to make a choice, Marshall would have had to conclude that democratic engineering has the edge over market homeostasis. The conciliatory Marshall was a real socialist after all.

9.2.2 Mass Consumption

Economic evolution has meant assimilation and incorporation. As we all move up, so we all look more and more alike: 'There has been a progressive equalization of the quality of material culture so that, even though great differences remain between the top and the bottom, they are variations on a single theme and are linked in a continuous scale' (Marshall, 1963: 226). Capitalism has mass-produced us into a single status group. Affluence has buried the inequalities that used to make each class a 'unique species' (ibid.: 225), an island race cut off from the rest.

The classless national market delivers quantitative benefits in the form of economies of scale but also qualitative approximation through the narrowing of visible distance: 'Mass production for the home market and a growing interest on the part of industry in the needs and tastes of the common people enabled the less well-to-do to enjoy a material civilisation which differed less markedly in quality from that of the rich than it had ever done before' (Marshall, 1950: 28). Thanks to the adaptive upgrading made possible by rising incomes, the less well-to-do gain access to a way of life that previously they had known only from the glossies, the Sundays and the soaps: 'The components of a civilised and cultured life, formerly the monopoly of the few, were brought progressively within reach of the many' (ibid.). Once it was patriotism that integrated the tribe. Under capitalism the unification was the consequence of the general enrichment of 'material enjoyment' and of the 'concrete substance of civilised life' (ibid.: 28, 33).

The capitalist era had been the cause and effect of an unprecedented homogeneity: 'There has been going on, especially in the last fifty years or so, a steady fusion of class civilizations into a single national civilization' (Marshall, 1963: 225). This fusion has been made possible by the consensual State: witness the civil, political and social rights which have made equal treatment and respect their highly-valued goal. What socialists should never forget is just how much the fusion owes to 'material enjoyment' as well. The consumer culture has brought the citizens closer together. It has made national life more common for all.

Convergence is a panacea but it is also a mystery. If all classes are travelling confidently on the common escalator of growth, it is by no means obvious why the relatively deprived should ever catch up with the high-income passengers in front. Logically speaking, stratified earning should only perpetuate distinctive spending without any inbuilt tendency for the queue to jump itself. Marshall was, however, the man who said 'social status is judged in terms of social status alone' (Marshall, 1953a: 190). What he said was what he meant, that material differences are rapidly obscured by visible overlap and a similar way of life.

Off-the-shelf self-presentation is making every man a gentleman. A gentleman is a citizen who knows where to cluster around the norm. Of course the upper income groups will retain the freedom to spend their differential on a superior brand: South African sherry is *not* the same. Of course the lower income groups will have to second-best 'with a cheap and shoddy imitation of a civilisation that has become national' (Marshall, 1950: 19): Versace is not on prescription as if it were the National Health. Diversity amidst unity will remain the rule and Bond Street will never become a one-size bazaar. That, however, is not the point. In the era of conspicuous resemblance, 'the realities of life' play second fiddle to 'the shadows and the symbols' (Marshall, 1953a: 196). Real gold or fool's gold, we all wear gold today.

9.3   SOCIALISM AND SOCIAL RIGHTS

Socialism is Socialism B. Socialism B is social rights. It is there that the sea of treacle begins. Social rights are a mix: some favour the needy but some reward the successful. Social rights are selective: different people make different claims. Social rights are contingent: the consensus giveth and the consensus taketh away. Social rights are biased towards the whole: what *we* need is what *you* get. Social rights are resource-constrained: the cheque cannot be cashed where the funds cannot be raised. Social rights are subject to discretion: professionals decide because the grants economy presupposes the division of labour.

It is a sea of treacle and a kaleidoscope of kaleidoscopes. Section 9.4, 'Socialism and inequality', asks whether, and in what way, Socialism B is likely to narrow the social gap. The present section tries to put its finger on the pulse of Marshall's B. It concludes that B has more pulses than the section has fingers. In doing so, it takes its text from Marshall's *dictum*, 'Social behaviour is not governed by logic' (Marshall, 1950: 49). Marshall had nonetheless believed that good judgment and muddle-through would somehow save the day: 'A human society can make a square meal out of a stew of paradox without getting indigestion' (ibid.). The present section proves that he was right or wrong.

9.3.1   The Unfinished Agenda

Marshall never says precisely what he takes to be a social right. The value of his socialism is limited by his reluctance to draw up a list. Since his rights depend on consensus and since the median citizen is quintessentially unpredictable, one can sympathise with his need as a democrat to endorse an open-ended manifesto and put his name to a work in progress. Yet the fact remains that little can be said about socialism and inequality until the current value system makes known its bid. Provided that the aims and principles 'are fully understood and accepted by the great majority of the citizens, and progressively absorbed into their culture' (Marshall, 1975: 206), it is hard to think of any potential entitlement that could not be politicised by an elected government into an acceptable claim.

A social right is created, Marshall says, whenever society recognises 'the right of the citizen to a minimum standard of civilised living' (Marshall, 1950: 40). State intervention then occurs in order to convert that perception into a fact. Education, public housing, subsidised healthcare, income transfers and social work have, in Britain, all been popularly validated and passed through as rights. The problem is that the five social services have not been alone. Since all that is needed is a democratic spike, the category has been extended to include support to the arts, discretionary stabilisation, a minimum wage law, statutory maternity leave, reliable public transport, the health and safety inspectorate, subsidies to big business to facilitate R & D and subsidies to small business to protect long-established communities. All of human life is there. Almost anything could fit within the rubric.

Including, explicitly, a traditional differential. Embodying as it does 'the notion of status', a fair wage represents 'a social right and not merely a market value' (ibid.: 42). A long-established gap is 'a species of welfare' and a 'socialist' (Marshall, 1963: 280) fixed point in the social economy. It is an institution with a history that cannot be rejected out of hand merely because conservatism can slow down the rate of economic growth. The market is efficiency: that is why it pays a flexible premium for productivity and training. The market, however, is equity as well: a doctor earns three times as much as a dustman and twice as much as a nurse because folk memory demands that the expected hierarchy should not be economised into oblivion. Marshall's point is that, while economic inequality has a function, so too does sociological convention with which it will frequently be at variance.

Marshall as a democrat is obliged to rely on consensus to rank the conflicting principles. All he can do, as a sociologist, is to repeat with Durkheim that we are what *we* are. If market freedom does not like our customs and habits, it should go and live in Tocqueville's America where the locals love their anomie – and their innovation.

9.3.2 General and Specific Rights

Social rights are difficult because social rights are open-ended. Almost anything can be a social right. Social rights are difficult as well because social rights de facto can never be universal. Anyone can make a contract and everyone can vote. Only a sick person needs an operation, however, and only a musical child needs a conservatory. Until the universities admit 100 per cent of the cohort and every adult is assigned a parole officer just in case, social rights, as Barbalet explains, will never be other than specific: 'Social services have to be particular because social and economic disabilities are by their nature particular' (Barbalet, 1988: 70). We are all equal. Yet we are not all alike.

Tawney, relying partly on common sense and partly on the solid evidence of Sir Cyril Burt, recognised that talents and capabilities are not merely the Enlightenment's *tabula rasa* upon which experience writes. Because nature will still be grading and streaming long after nurture has been levelled down to the genetic drift, Tawney had this message for socialist egalitarianism and for the welfare State: 'Equality of provision is not identity of provision. It is to be achieved, not by treating different needs in the same way, but by devoting equal care to ensuring that they are met in the different ways most appropriate to them' (Tawney, 1931: 49). An academic boy needs an academic education. A manual boy needs a manual education. The social rights are equal because the collective involvement is appropriate. The financial commitment is, of course, not nearly the same.

Marshall shared Tawney's interpretation of equal as appropriate. With it, however, he also inherited the conundrum that equal rights will seldom mean an equal subsidy. The academic boy gets a law school. The manual boy gets a building site. Equal citizens with identical passports do not take home an equivalent social wage. It could be a recipe for bitterness and resentment. Here as elsewhere, however, it is the meta-arbiter of consent that puts the worm within to flight.

What Marshall is reasoning is that unequal benefit is acceptable provided that the democratic concord takes it to be good. No one would object to money spent on training a promising policeman or a nurse: to each according to *our* need is also a commitment to pay our share of the cost. The consensus, for the same reason, might be in favour of means-tested university grants: the inverse correlation would at least allow the poor to claw back a disproportionate part of the allocation. Progressive income tax is perhaps believed by Marshall to fulfil a no less redistributive function. The medical student takes out more when he is young but pays in more in the course of a high-income working life. It is an intertemporal social compact. It is a matrix of costs and benefits that derives its *ought to be* from consent.

The Rawlsian veil (Rawls, 1971) can be invoked to explain the thrust of particularism within universality. Where the citizens are ignorant because all dwell in the dark, they are better able to abstract from their blinkered private circumstances in order to form a consistent and impartial view of their nation's overall needs. Marshall could not have been a Rawlsian: his citizens are not ignorant but self-aware. Marshall would have had to be a Kantian. He would have had to cut his cloth by the moral principle that self-respect presupposes an equivalent respect for others and in the light of the Categorical Imperative that a decent democrat must honour the Golden Rule: 'Act in such a way that you always treat humanity, whether in your own person or in the person of any other, never simply as a means, but always at the same time as an end' (Kant, 1785: 96). Kantian or Rawlsian, the expectation is nonetheless that voters who want to do what their own private stake demands will take the welfare of strangers in some measure into account. Unknowledge in the Rawlsian case, social values in the particularism of Marshall – not all of agreement is current interest, narrowly defined.

9.3.3 Path Dependence

Marshall's consensus is path-dependent. As such it is trapped in the chicken-and-egg circularity of memories and mindsets. Social rights are the cause of integration and the confirmation that community exists: so long as Jack believes that his own dignity and requirements are being treated with respect, he will not want to exclude the drug addicts and the dialysis patients from their share in the national heritage. Social rights are also the effect of nationhood and the consequence of a common identity: so long as Jill recognises that her dole is an affirmation of status and not a declaration that she has failed, she will not feel dishonoured as a pariah since she will know that she is welcome in sickness as much as in health. Social rights, in other words, are both cause and effect. They come from consensus but also strengthen the bonds of the All.

Cumulative causation is momentum-driven. As with any gravitational field, however, it is crucially dependent on the initial Big Bang. Marshall emphasised the *deus ex machina* of the Second World War and the sheer Britishness of mutual aid and fair shares. Welfare institutions, he once wrote, are not just 'means to an end, but in a certain sense ends in themselves, a much-to-be admired feature of our society and the embodiment of the British way of life' (Marshall, 1963: 291). Dunkirk and decency are certainly a part of the story. By themselves, however, they leave the lift-off somehow vulnerable and underexplained. Something more is needed to account for the orbit. Perhaps that missing link is Schumpeter's second democracy, always one step in front of the crowd.

It may be that Marshall looked to the politicians for a leaderly injection of social rights. Consolidating the consensus, priming the pump, the demand for social democracy would follow the supply of social democracy once citizens became accustomed to social rights and discovered that they wanted more.

Tawney had understood that social engineering could be the precondition for the seamless web in which each is treated as one, no more and no less: 'Democracy,' he said, 'should be, not only a form of government, but a type of society and a manner of life' (Tawney, 1931: 196). Tawney believed that a welfare society would have to be experienced before people would have the self-confidence to believe in welfare rights. *L'appétit vient en mangéant.*

To Tawney, perceived social distance would have *first* to be reduced before all classes and sub-cultures would be able to convince themselves that they had a genuine stake. The first mover puts the ball in play. Bottomore states that the demand for social equality will be muted so long as citizens have not had the freedom *to* that raises them off their knees: 'Inequalities of wealth, of social rank, or of education and access to knowledge, should not be so considerable as to result in the permanent subordination of some individuals and groups to others in any of the various spheres of social life, or to create great inequalities in the actual exercise of political rights' (Bottomore, 1993: 100). What Bottomore, like Tawney, is saying is that the supply of social rights can shape the demand for social rights. Cumulative causation is a snowball. Someone or something must push the snowball on to its path.

That, however, is just the problem. Tawney and Bottomore will select one path. Hayek and Friedman will, however, choose another one. Marshall's path dependence is a preference but not a prediction. Should history travel down the right-hand file, then not a lot will survive of Marshall's chicken or of Marshall's egg. The recipients of social rights will see themselves as inferior and passive, stigmatised and second-rate. The winners in life's lottery will have no scruples about spoiling the identity of the also-rans who slipped and fell. Where one citizen thinks he has no rights save those he can buy, where another citizen understands he is a public burden and a drain, the likelihood is low that social rights will be extensive enough to mount a credible challenge. Only brothers can experience brotherhood. The outcome is social rights that are vestigial and grudging rather than comprehensive and generous. Social distance will be reduced. It is unlikely that it will be reduced very far.

9.3.4   An Organic Whole

Social rights can turn either left or right. Where they cannot turn is in. Social rights are *social* in their legitimation and in their function. The Noble Savage has got to learn that he cannot live for himself alone: 'Individual rights must be subordinated to national plans' (Marshall, 1950: 35).

The government governs for *us*. It does not govern for him or her: 'The obligation of the state is towards society as a whole . . . instead of to individual citizens' (ibid.). The singleton has rights. So, however, does 'the community, as a whole' (Marshall, 1953b: 252). The State has the duty of reconciling the preferences of the atom with the imperatives of the people: 'The maintenance of a fair balance between these collective and individual elements in social rights is a matter of vital importance to the democratic socialist state' (Marshall, 1950: 35). The task is not an easy one. Education shows how hard it is.

The nation has manpower needs and the individual wants suitable employment. The implication is that the State cannot make the access to qualifications entirely demand-led: 'If a boy who is given a Grammar School education can then get nothing but a Modern School job, he will cherish a grievance' (ibid.: 38). Resentment as well as misallocation is the result where more doctors and accountants are trained than there is work for them to do. Ambitious parents will not like it, but still social ceilings are inevitable. The *numerus clausus* is a fact of life.

Because prestigious skills should not be overproduced, streaming and competitive selection 'must remain with us to a considerable extent' (Marshall, 1953b: 264). So long as the procedures are impartial and latent capacities are not overlooked, a test such as Britain's Eleven-plus cannot be eliminated. The notion that it can 'seems to me to be a pipe-dream and not even a Utopian one' (ibid.: 254). Being realistic, therefore, filtered schooling will not mean parity of esteem. Hurdles and targets will impose stigma on those tested out and block the aspirations of children whose desires and aptitudes are assigned a low social priority. The individual's claim to a social right is no stronger than society's willingness to affirm that the demand is a valid one. It is cold comfort to a pensioner denied a transplant because his community does not regard him as an end in himself.

Social rights are limited by social needs. The right to a skill is not absolute but fragile and dependent: 'Expectations officially recognised as legitimate are not claims that must be met in each case when presented' (Marshall, 1950: 35). Starts must be rationed by merit. Being capped both by opportunities and by talents, it is unavoidable that the outcomes to which they lead will be uneven as well. It is unavoidable since inequality is precisely the product that is being manufactured and sold: 'The Welfare State is bound to pick the children of high ability for higher education and for higher jobs, and to do this with the interests of the community as well as the rights of the children in mind' (Marshall, 1953b: 264).

Intelligent genes breed intelligent offspring. Achieving parents produce achieving graduates. Marshall, speaking of education, concedes that 'a considerable part of the benefit went to the middle classes' (ibid.: 257). Social rights can be regressive. That's the way it is. The socialist State must use grants, subsidies and talent-spotting new initiatives to equalise the chances and make the most of scarce endowments. Outcomes, however, will be what they are. There is no expectation that socially-provided services will always and everywhere discriminate in favour of the poor: 'The dominant objective today is undoubtedly the maximization of welfare. This aims at the satisfaction of particular needs without specifying either that the beneficiaries should be in a state of poverty or that the effect should be to reduce social inequality. The former will often be the case and the latter may frequently be the result, but both are secondary to the central criterion by which policy is judged, namely that of need satisfaction' (Marshall, 1975: 201). If the nation wants the skills, then the nation will have to pay the price.

9.3.5   Budgets and Resources

Social rights are limited by manpower needs. They are limited as well by what the nation can pay. Affordability makes budgeting the science of the possible. If the money is not there, then social rights are as meaningless as any shopping expedition unsupported by effective demand.

Marshall acknowledges that advance in social rights 'depends on the magnitude of the national resources and their distribution between competing claims' (Marshall, 1950: 35). He gives the example of secondary and higher education in the early twentieth century, when underfunding spelled underprovision and ability was no guarantee of success: 'There was no pretence that all who could benefit from more advanced education would get it' (ibid.: 37). The right to vote is fixed. The right to welfare is variable. Barbalet observes that public finance in this way robs the whole theory of any sense of precision: 'The significance of this qualification is that the relationship between the institutional basis of social rights and the rights themselves is necessarily unstable' (Barbalet, 1988: 71).

Slower growth could mean insufficient tax: Marshall was too close to post-war expansion, too far from inflation and unemployment. Ironically the threat could originate in the welfare sector itself. Public borrowing and high interest rates damp down the investment multiplier. Permissive transfers blunt the necessity to work and save. Rising expectations raise the cost of quality and comfort. The vote motive can force through demand-led education that the nation does not need. Imperialistic bureaucracies can oversupply the paperwork and refuse to adapt. The superstructure undermines the basis. Even if the law promises 'best possible' to all, finance might dictate that the social right will have to be annulled.

9.3.6   Professionals and Administrators

Social rights, finally, do not speak for themselves but require the expert interpretation of the professional. The NHS member has a right, legally enforceable, to be registered for primary care. What happens next, discretionary differentiation within the infrastructure of universalism, is more difficult to predict. It might be a tablet or it might be an operation. The doctor will decide. The doctor knows best.

Marshall accepted, broadly speaking, that only good teachers can know what good teaching is. He was therefore prepared to put his faith in the professionals to allocate such resources as the politicians assign to them: 'Benefits in the form of a service have this further characteristic that the rights of the citizen cannot be precisely defined. The qualitative element is too great' (Marshall, 1950: 34). Administrators were not a threat. Like Weber and Schumpeter, Marshall took for granted an efficient and rational bureaucracy, committed to equal treatment for equal citizens and determined not to put its own estate interest first.

Marshall has confidence in the public service ethos of the career administrator. He encourages his fellow citizens to share his faith in the bureaucrat who only wants to do what is right: 'The citizen must learn to respect the authority of the official as something without which he could not discharge his responsibilities, but at the same time to regard him as his friend and his servant' (Marshall, 1949: 332). Marshall speaks of learning and regarding as if he were merely pointing to an unnoticed Grail. He also speaks of dialogue, however; and it is here that Schumpeter's first theory of bottom-up voice makes an unexpected appearance alongside Schumpeter's second theory of wise leaders shepherding a passive and satisfied flock.

Thus Marshall writes of two-way communication as an investment in popular accountability: 'Representative government will not create a true democracy if the citizen cringes before the official, or if he sullenly resents his authority. The establishment of a proper co-operative relationship between the public and the bureaucracy is a matter of vital importance' (ibid.). He does not say precisely how this 'proper co-operative relationship' is to be brought into being; but decentralisation is one option he explores. Local government 'makes it possible for those who run the services to be responsible to those who use them' (ibid.: 332–3). Social rights still retain the element of discretion which makes it so difficult to pin them down. At least, with decentralisation, the discretion exercised might be more in tune with the citizen in the street.

9.4   SOCIALISM AND INEQUALITY

Citizenship, through social policy, has an effect on social distance. Social rights, however, are a double-edged sword: 'The extension of the social services is not primarily a means of equalising incomes. In some cases it may, in others it may not' (Marshall, 1950: 33). The poor will be less poor. The rich, however, need not be less rich. Marshall's socialism is a civilised way of saying that rich and poor are all citizens and that all citizens should have what they deserve.

9.4.1   Poverty

Absolute deprivation, Marshall argued, was a problem not just in the Punjab but in Huddersfield and Glasgow as well. There were British families that, irrespective of rapid growth, were still lacking in 'the minimum necessary for decent living' (Marshall, 1950: 20): 'There still remains a substantial section of the population at the bottom of the scale that has been little affected by the change' (Marshall, 1963: 225). The desperate and the destitute were urgently in need of safety-net relief. The *as of right* of welfare was the ungrudging response to need.

The social minimum is assured through citizenship benefits in cash and kind: 'The state guarantees a minimum supply of certain essential goods and services (such as medical attention and supplies, shelter and education) or a minimum monthly income available to be spent on essentials – as in the case of old age pensions, insurance benefits and family allowances' (Marshall, 1950: 32). To these provisions must be added the rules and regulations, the food subsidies and the rent restrictions, the full employment policies and the equal opportunities laws that were deemed essential by the consensus if the vicious cycle of absolute deprivation was ever to meet with a much-needed check.

Poverty is challenged. Inequality is less certain. A hand in need through social rights 'was not an attack on the class system', only on 'its less defensible consequences' (ibid.: 20). Measures to raise the floor level of the basement did not alter the fact that it remained a basement – and that the upper stories of the structure were largely unaffected by the support. The supplementation of market income through social income, a life-saver though it was to the poor, can hardly be said to have been 'converting a skyscraper into a bungalow' (ibid.: 28).

Absolute deprivation is the more pressing concern. Yet relative deprivation too can be uncitizenly separation. Unpublicised disparities do no real harm. The harm is done when conspicuous consumption, flagrant and excessive, splits the national identity into malintegrated factions.

The relatively deprived stand out because they are lacking in the status symbols of 'clothes, houses, furniture, art and amusements' (Marshall, 1963: 225). Where the median citizen owns a house and a car, the sub-standard citizen will see himself, and be so seen by others, as a stranger on the fringe who has failed to achieve his way in: 'Property is or may be the certificate of membership of society ... The property-less man is an outcast, a parasite, a tramp. The man of property has a stake in the country' (ibid.: 238)

The need is not just to be fed but to be included. Citizenship, after all, means nothing if it does not mean the equality of respect: 'It is not a purely political conception but signifies full membership of a community' (ibid.: 230). Capitalism, raising spendable incomes and stimulating the rich to save, has narrowed the consumption gap that breeds the distinctiveness and the divisions: widening reference groups and generalised affluence have been the melting pot, the solvent that has made the 'class cultures dwindle to a minimum' (Marshall, 1950: 19). Just as capitalism is the evolution from status to contract, so it is the movement from contract to status as well. Socialism only supplies the *coup de grâce*. A few shillings more on the surtax, a grant-in-aid to an inner-city council: capitalism does the real work while *post festum* only sands down the rough edges that remain.

Policies that raise up the basement need not be policies that level down the penthouse. What is intriguing about Marshall on deprivation is the sense in which a rational rich man will do well to vote enthusiastically for reform.

Philanthropy of all kinds always defuses social tensions. Welfare or charity, it makes the class system 'less vulnerable to attack' (ibid.: 20). Social control aside, the relief of poverty is a money-spinning investment. State supplementation empowers the business interest to pay Marxian subsistence wages while still enjoying the services of a labour force robust enough to add solid value: 'The Poor Law was an aid, not a menace, to capitalism, because it relieved industry of all social responsibility outside the contract of employment, while sharpening the edge of competition in the labour market' (ibid.: 21).

Such welfare is not socialist but counterrevolutionary. Primary schooling was first designed with the same restabilising function in mind: 'It increased the value of the worker without educating him above his station' (ibid.). Skills raise productivity. Grading inculcates hierarchy. Transfers create demand. Social rights are everybody's rights. They are not a challenge to inequality so much as they are a complement to the market sector's status quo.

9.4.2   Merit

Equal life chances lead to unequal outcomes. Citizenship rights declare war on inherited status and on 'class distinctions . . . which have no appropriate economic function' (Marshall, 1950: 45). Birth swept out, however, brains surge in. Equality of access makes it possible for talent to occupy the same unaltered first-class suite: 'Citizenship operates as an instrument of social stratification . . . The status acquired by education is carried out into the world bearing the stamp of legitimacy' (ibid.: 39). Social rights make the new distance earned and meritocratic: each contender is seen to be given his just and appropriate reward. Yet impartial price in the modern age perpetuates the function of ranking and separating. Equitable or not, it is business as usual for the pyramid of success.

Marshall writes that 'citizenship is itself becoming the architect of inequality' (ibid.: 36). The divisive effects of welfare are especially clear in the case of intelligence-graded schooling: 'Educational competition has never been more intense ... It is associated directly in the public mind with the class barriers which break up the unity of our society' (Marshall, 1963: 286). The 'public mind' knows its hopeful high-flyers from its clock-watching dead end. The stigma of labelling does little to reinforce the close binding of socialism's class abatement.

Segregated secondaries, in the 'public mind', are associated less with 'parity of esteem' than they are with 'aggressive individualism' (ibid.). Their intellectual home is more nearly civil rights than social rights, their intellectual thrust more like competitive comparison than the wartime solidarity which had led to the 1944 Education Act. Assuming, however, that the aptitude-streaming Eleven-plus is a tolerably accurate measure of innate ability, then there is a cap to the resistance that a performance-oriented society can or should mount to what is consensually the social need: 'The more confident the claim of education to be able to sift human material during the early years of life, the more is mobility concentrated within those years, and consequently limited thereafter' (Marshall, 1950: 38). This may be fairness and it may be efficiency, but it is less likely to be the uninhibited mingling that makes felt citizenship something more than societal joint stock.

Marshall was weak on the stigmatising meritocracy of the brains-tested grammars. He was weaker still on the *lack* of meritocracy that held the ancient independents in its dead-hand grip. Marshall in 1950 must have known that there was Apartheid in darkest Goldalming and even in Kent. Yet he made not a single proposal for tearing down the walls. His silence is not *obiter dictum* but the words and the tune. Marshall was a decent man who practised live and let live because the alternative was Hobbes. Destructive levelling down came harder to him than did constructive levelling up. Democratic tolerance casts a long shadow before.

9.4.3   A Middle-class Welfare State

It is often said that social rights are socialist rights in the sense that they empower the disadvantaged to pull themselves up. The badly off are certainly valued claimants in Marshall's 'to each according to his need'. The same must be said, however, of the prosperous and the privileged who are chauffeured to Harrod's in a latest-model Mercedes-Benz. Citizenship does not turn away a brother cherub merely because he is rich.

Marshall's universalism extends an invitation to all the income groups to take what is seemly. Bright children from poor families are assisted to leave behind the handicap of their birth. Bright children from rich families are given taxpayers' money to enhance their existing lead. The poor catch up. The rich speed up. Socialism through welfare has implications for income inequality. The nature of the link is, however, unpredictable and obscure.

The National Health illustrates the indeterminacy. The NHS, clearly, confers real benefits on the deprived. The suppression of the payment nexus means that there is no longer a price deterrent to keep them out, while the citizenship entitlement does away with the stigma of the means test and the shame of the pauper's ward. There is in addition a qualitative gain in the form of the 'class fusion' that is bred and shaped by 'a new common experience' (Marshall, 1950: 33). Council housing is adequate but segregated. The NHS is common surgeons, a single queue and one professional ethic for all.

The deprived secure real benefits from the NHS. The non-deprived, however, get well-being from welfare too. The middle classes used to pay good money for health. Since 1948 they have been able to divert the resources into private consumption and investment: 'The direct effect is in part to increase the inequality of disposable incomes' (ibid.). Even their non-essential extras, their 'frills' and 'luxuries' (ibid.: 34), will sometimes come within the permitted minimum. Top-ups, where allowed, can make a standard service more special: consider a private room (analogous to an add-on pension) just off a citizenship-mixed ward. Flat-rate contributions, without the cross-subsidy of progressive tax, mean that the poor pay percentagewise more: earmarking without pooled supplementation has a perverse effect on the ratio of an identical package to a lopsided income.

It all sums up to a blank. Marshall knew that the net effect of social rights on social distance could not be known since the long-term multipliers were too complex: 'Our ignorance of this matter is profound' (ibid.: 44). Yet he also appreciated that someone had to hazard a guess if welfare and inequality were not to become immobilised in the Gordian knot of directionless agnosticism.

9.4.4   Socialism and Citizenship

Marshall cut the Gordian knot. He announced that economic inequalities were becoming less and less: 'The preservation of economic inequalities has been made more difficult by the enrichment of the status of citizenship. There is less room for them, and there is more and more likelihood of their being challenged' (Marshall, 1950: 45). Marshall acknowledged that skills, incentives and native mother-wit would introduce a trade-off between the economics and the sociology: 'There are limits inherent in the egalitarian movement' (ibid.). At least until those limits were reached, however, the trend of history was on the side of the smaller dispersion. Marshall did not give his reasons.

Marshall was making a conjecture when he guessed that the differentials were becoming less. He was on the firmer ground of the liberals and the

Liberals when he predicted that the differences were becoming just. Citizenship, passing through three stages, has 'provided the foundation of equality on which the structure of inequality could be built' (ibid.: 21). The end result, Marshall said, will not be a 'classless society' but it will be 'a structure of unequal status fairly apportioned to unequal abilities' (ibid.: 36, 38). It will be unequal finishes made equitable through equal starts as if guided by Samuel Smiles on the golden road to gold. Yet it will also be socialism – since it will be social rights that put teeth into market capitalism's promise of hard work repaid.

Although civil rights do legitimate reasonable distance, the three sets of rights taken together have undeniably led to an 'enrichment of the status of citizenship', of the 'concrete substance of civilised life' (ibid.: 45, 33). Tolerance and acceptance become second nature in a society committed to equal opportunities, transparent governance, common services, upgraded consumption, overlapping references, cultural integration – a society, in other words, in which 'the classes cooperate more closely than at present to the common benefit of all' (ibid.: 36). The classes cooperate. Prosperity and fraternity are the result. Three sets of rights make us all one citizenship at last.

10. T.H. Marshall: welfare on the middle ground

Schumpeter, reluctantly, regretfully, anticipated a top-down future in which 'the superior rationality of the socialist plan' (Schumpeter, 1942: 196) would regiment the uncoordinated and the uninformed into an efficiency maximum that would end the dominion of hunger and want, class exclusion and wasted talent. Adam Smith, who had learned from Rousseau about the repressiveness of the Bastille and from Quesnay about the idle drones who gobbled up the patrimony of the poor, felt it would be better to 'open the floodgates' (Smith, 1776: II, 18) in order to entrust the wealth of nations to the private vice that would at least supply the public good. Schumpeter predicted that prosperity would come to mean compulsion. Smith recommended a decentralised order where each individual would be a king. Hayek was absolutely clear that the either/or put an end to the debate: 'We face here a real alternative . . . There is no third possibility' (Hayek, 1944: 94).

Where there are two peaks and that is all, the subtleties and the modifications fall by the wayside. Schumpeter saw a role for small-firm enterprise, flexible pricing and humanitarian welfare because value added does not satisfy the hungry soul. Smith was in favour of the Usury Laws, the Navigation Acts and a State-run Post Office that would make good profits to keep the tax rates down. The ideologues showed as little interest in Schumpeter's autonomy that escaped the plan as they did in Smith's paternalistic leadership that civilised the snatching hand. The bipolar constituency had no real need to inquire too deeply into a middle ground that could not, would not survive. East is East and West is shopping. The bipolar constituency bought the symbol Schumpeter and the symbol Smith that it needed to model its future. The line-by-line exegesis it left behind for the academics and the intellectuals who while away their anonymity by counting up the semi-quavers in the *Pathétique*.

The doctrinaire believe that there is a barren void between the two snowy peaks. Most people are not so confident. Schumpeter and Smith themselves were far too practical, too flexible to fall into the trap of believing that extreme positions exhaust the political landscape. Marshall and Crosland were mix-and-match who shared the interest in open-minded search. Anthony Crosland was speaking for everyone who wanted the best of leadership in partnership with the best of commerce when he argued as follows in support of common sense and a blend: 'On the one side the harsh pressing overweighted regime of Soviet Russia, where the state has run riot, & individual freedom has been swallowed up in the orgy of planning . . . On the other hand, America, where the executive is so weak, so timid, that at the slightest sign of crisis it disintegrates into impotence. The world doesn't want to choose between these alternatives. It wants a middle way' (Crosland, unpublished speech to the Oxford Union, n.d., probably 1946, in Crosland Papers, Box 13/21).

The world wants a middle way. This chapter is concerned with two models that build in the fertile valley and not on the barren peaks. Section 10.1, 'The hyphenated society', shows that T.H. Marshall in the seven papers of his last three decades fleshed out his earlier triad of civil rights, political rights and social rights with an amplifying triangle made up of the City, the Commons and the welfare-dependent who are our brothers and sisters too. Section 10.2, 'Crosland', demonstrates that Marshall's vision of socialism as social services rather than a nationalised plan was shared by his distinguished contemporary, whose *Future of Socialism* was about successful businessmen in outdoor cafés even as it was about the interventionist's progressive quest for equality and welfare. Section 10.3, 'Labour's Liberals', builds on a felicitous phrase first used by *The Economist*. It tries to summarise the intellectual position of the British Centre-Left using the examples of Marshall and Crosland. It reaches the conclusion that a home without a Hobhouse can never be a We.

10.1   THE HYPHENATED SOCIETY

The hyphenated society is a three-legged stool. Calling it 'democratic-welfare-capitalism', Marshall defines his chemical compound to be that matrix of complementarities which exists 'when a country with a *capitalist* market economy develops *democratic* political and civil institutions and practices out of which emerge a mixed economy including both private and public capitalism similarly organised and using the same calculus, together with that complex of public social services, insurances and assistances which is the eponymous element in what all the world knows as the *welfare* state' (Marshall, 1972: 104, 107).

The hyphenated society is a fusion of principles. It is an amalgam of three independent sub-systems, all three retaining their 'separate identities', all three enjoying an 'equal contributory status': 'The golden calf of democratic socialism has been translated into a troika of sacred cows' (Marshall, 1981: 124, 129). The three sub-systems have different values and do different things. Out of that functional pluralism a fruitful collaboration evolves. The whole is stronger than the sum of the parts.

10.1.1   The Capitalist Market Economy

The starting point is the individual. Marshall was attracted by gain-seeking exchange because of its association with civil liberty. He believed that, for the greater part of men, 'the essence of freedom consists in the right and power to choose and to act according to one's choice' (Marshall, 1965b: 157). Schumpeter's Plan might deliver the goods for passive citizens who do not mind being told what to do. Most of us, however, want to have at least some input in the shaping of our fate: 'Socialists have maintained that capitalism treats labour as a *commodity*. Of course it does, and that is its contribution to freedom, for the alternative was to go on treating the *labourer* as a commodity, and that meant slavery and serfdom' (ibid.: 163).

The textbook market is freedom to supply and freedom to demand. The Marxians object that the long-term unemployed have no choice but to comply; and that wages cannot be negotiated up lest capital take the place of labour. Oligopolistic competition, bureaucratic hierarchies and non-transferable pensions all reduce the power of the self to codetermine the situation. Want creation and the lack of workplace democracy seem to some to be a new form of servitude dressed up as the citizen's right to move on to more of the same. Marshall was familiar with criticisms such as these. His reply was an invitation to take allocation as it is and not as it ought to be. Everything is relative. The civil and political rights which evolved in the optimistic Enlightenment are better exercised under market capitalism than under economic command which makes unfreedom the rule.

The capitalist economy means a high standard of living. That in itself is a good reason for a hyphenated consensualist to speak in defence of exchange. Yet there is something more: 'The superstructure of welfare can be firmly built only on the foundation of a viable economy' (ibid.: 169). Market and welfare set themselves the same task, 'that of satisfying the needs and wants of the population' (Marshall, 1981: 133). The market takes on an additional task as well. It must generate the resources that pay for the gifts. The market is the friend, not the enemy, of welfare.

Speaking of Germany in the 1950s, Marshall observes that it was the 'economic miracle' which enabled that country 'to take in her stride the high costs of top-grade social services and social security' (Marshall, 1972: 106). Speaking of Britain in the 1970s, he comments that it was slow growth even more than the revival of libertarian ideologies which called into question the truce on universalism: 'Capitalism is most dangerous when it is weak and frightened, not when it is strong and confident' (ibid.: 120). Speaking of the human family as a whole, he expresses the view that even the most self-denying censor of the marginal futilities of opulence ought to defend steady expansion if he wishes also to defend generous welfare. Growth produces the funding that makes possible the collective consumption. Growth at the same time promotes the caring ethic without which there would be no demand. At once the way and the will, growth is statist and the future turns left.

Marshall sees growth as both the necessary and the sufficient condition: 'If new resources are created, the pressure to spread the benefits is likely, in the long run, to be irresistible' (Marshall, 1965a: 93). Welfare, he writes, 'represents the natural reaction of the majority to a rising standard of living': it receives 'the powerful support of collective action in favour of common enjoyment' (Marshall, 1966a: 61). Marshall normally reasons that altruism experiences a high income elasticity of demand even in a prosperous new world of widening choice-sets and the steady appeal to interest. His mentor is Durbin: 'Prosperity often moves the English electorate towards the left. The British people appear to feel more optimistic about reform, and less fearful of change, when they are doing well' (Durbin, 1940: 144). His proof is the record. Social evolution is what social evolution does.

As a historian, Marshall had a tendency to fall back on the facts. The problem was that the facts were Delphic and the correlations obscure. Thus, surveying the third stage of social rights, Marshall was able to report that deprivation and contrast had become their own turning-points: 'The men and women of the twentieth century came to feel that where there was wealth there should be no poverty' (Marshall, 1981: 39). Interpreting the rebarbarisation of the 1950s, however, he was clearly less convinced that good times had meant good fellowship as well. Whatever the 'men and women of the twentieth century' had felt, the men and women of 'you've never had it so good' had decided that 'in times of prosperity increased productivity should enable nearly all the people to meet nearly all their needs out of their own pockets and through the mechanism of the market, thus reducing free or subsidised welfare provisions once more to the level of a peripheral affair' (Marshall, 1961: 307). On the one hand the 'common enjoyment' of the 'twentieth century', on the other hand the 'peripheral affair' of the Affluent Society that he believed he was seeing in the early 1960s – Marshall appealed to the facts and the facts failed to speak with a single voice. As well as on 'good nourishing history' (Marshall, 1963: 5), Marshall could usefully have relied more heavily on a theoretical schema to help him elucidate the intertemporal relationship between the way and the will.

Marshall praised the capitalist market both because it satisfied consumers' wants and because it produced the surplus that paid for the State. The capitalist market was a case of *non est disputandum*. No other mechanism allocated scarce goods and services so well: 'The incentives provided by and expressed in competitive markets make a contribution to efficiency and to progress in the production and distribution of wealth which cannot, in a large and complex society, be derived from any other source' (Marshall, 1981: 135).

The market for labour is no exception to the rule. It proportions the price of a productive input to the economic value that visible performance has been able to add. Achievement-oriented and open, it combines economic growth with that 'full membership of a community' (Marshall, 1950: 6) that takes the sting of illegitimacy out of distance. Marshall in 1950 was arguing that 'equality of status' and 'equal social worth' need not be 'inconsistent with the inequalities which distinguish the various economic levels in the society' (ibid.: 33, 24, 6). Civil, political and social rights were tasked with ensuring 'the foundation of equality on which the structure of inequality could be built' (ibid.: 21). Provided that they successfully delivered their freedom *to*, there was no reason to fear that market-determined differentials would threaten the fabric of social cohesion.

Marshall said that differences should not be unjust: ' "Fair shares" does not mean equal pay; it implies that some inequalities are fair and acceptable, and others are not' (Marshall, 1975: 111). In *Citizenship and Social Class* he seemed to be confident that unequivocal rights would make unequal accomplishments fully 'fair and acceptable'. By the affluent 1960s, narrowing the condition, he was shifting his emphasis from the liberal's starts to the socialist's finishes: 'Equality of persons is compatible with inequality of incomes *provided the inequality is not too great*' (Marshall, 1966a: 65, emphasis added). Marshall in the age of indulgence was less certain about the sociology of supply and demand. He was beginning to doubt whether the unguided market would after all limit the disparities to those that pass through the needle's eye of his *'provided the equality of citizenship is recognised'* (Marshall, 1950: 6, emphasis added).

The older Marshall states bluntly that 'the capitalist market economy can be, and generally has been, a cause of much social injustice' (Marshall, 1981: 135). He confesses that the vital question of whether it is possible to secure more equity without a worrying sacrifice of efficiency 'has not yet been answered' (ibid.). He even hints that the answer to the clash between markets and morals might have to be the State: 'It is clear that, although unequal incomes and differential earnings are accepted as legitimate, there is no general agreement about the principles by which the inequalities and the differences should be regulated. Both the major political parties in Britain today talk about the need for an incomes policy' (Marshall, 1966a: 64). In 1950, the political parties were talking about Smithian deregulation. In 1966, they were talking about Galbraithian hands-on. The labour market had changed. The unions in particular seemed to have been abusing their concentrated power to such an extent that reformers were wondering if the Taff Vale Decision might not have run its course.

The younger Marshall of the *Citizenship* had welcomed the collective use of civil rights (Marshall, 1950: 26). He had made the traditional differential into 'a social right and not merely a market value' (ibid.: 42). The older Marshall of *The Right* was somewhat more sensitive to the possibility that the cat might bell the mice. The older Marshall was concerned about the bullying tactics of strong unions which increase pushfulness in preference to productivity (Marshall, 1965b: 164), which elbow the weak out of their rightful place in the queue (Marshall, 1972: 109), which refuse to obey the mandate of the sovereign Parliament because their members have given them a mandate of their own (Marshall, 1981: 155–6). Speaking of the unions, Marshall said that 'freedom, if it is not to be anarchy, must be built upon a foundation of law' (ibid.: 172). The unions had challenged the social contract which circumscribes the market mechanism. Incomes policy was what the democracy had to use in order to defend its constitution against the lawless who wanted to break in and steal.

Marshall says 'the capitalist market' but what he means is the 'mixed economy' (Marshall, 1972: 107;1981: 52, 123, 124, 131, 135). As a middle-ground thinker who looked to diversity for stability and tolerance for concord, it was his wish to combine the complementarities in order to 'strike an acceptable balance': 'All human situations are psycho-social . . . In the matter of welfare, I contend, the emphasis should be bang in the middle, on the hyphen' (Marshall, 1965a: 102;1966b: 81). Marshall's hyphenated society is the sum of its hyphens. Not much is found in Marshall's political economy save where it is present in a compound.

Marshall found elements of social responsibility even in capitalist exchange. An illustration would be the market for labour, where an other-encompassing consensus makes possible a radical narrowing of the market-clearing disparities: 'It is futile to imagine that differentials can be made acceptable simply by scaling them down, however necessary this may be. It can be done only by changing the attitude towards them' (Marshall, 1972: 119). All that the traffic will bear would give us more. Personal responsibility makes us settle for less.

Just as attitudes in the labour market can twist supply and demand into generous self-abnegation, so attitudes in the welfare market can mean that the milk of human kindness will be diluted with a good measure of brass-knuckled expediency. This is the mix that Marshall has in mind when he writes that 'social insurance is . . . a hybrid of welfare and capitalism and a bridge between them' (ibid.: 113). On the one hand the old-age pension is the same school uniform for all: it bears witness to the 'fundamental principle of the welfare state that the market value of an individual cannot be the measure of his right to welfare' (ibid.: 107). On the other hand the State pension is earnings-related (even if subject to a ceiling cap). Replicating past disparities, it will inevitably be responsible for 'subordinating welfare to some extent to market value' (ibid.: 113).

Pensions policy is hyphenated policy. Marshall, like other Wilsonian centrists who wanted to build beyond Beveridge, was prepared to accept that there would be one evaluatory standard for entitlement and a different heuristic for amount. Equality would coexist with inequality, one nation with two. Yet the only way to moderate the variance in life's final act would be to tamper with the incentive-bearing allocative efficiency of men and women still at work: 'Social insurance has become a part of incomes policy. It is no longer a bearer of the welfare message' (Marshall, 1981: 132). Things like this must be expected once institutions become mixed and the hyphen sets in.

The hyphenated order is a multifaceted order for the further reason that each social actor has internalised within his world-view more than a single normative orientation. It is mind as well as matter that is as ambidextrous as a centipede and as heterogeneous as a cross-breed. Too much diversity is, of course, latent conflict threatening to turn malign: 'It is obvious that an acute incompatibility of values prevalent in different sectors may cause intolerable friction or possibly the destruction of one value system by another' (ibid.: 129). A reasonable degree of diversity, however, is no threat to conflict management but rather a simple statement of the way things are: 'This kind of ethical relativity has been a feature of very nearly every society since civilisation began' (ibid.).

The ethos of the capitalist market is an individualistic, competitive, acquisitive, self-regarding fixation which is forever focused on its bottom line. Its concentration on 'a man's value in the market (capitalist value)' to the exclusion of 'his value as a citizen (democratic value)' and of 'his value for himself (welfare value)' (Marshall, 1972: 119) means that it is at variance with other axial principles in the tripartite mix. The record shows that normative pluralism is possible without a destabilising struggle for normative supremacy: 'A hyphenated relationship between church and state is a much commoner historical occurrence than either a theocracy or a totally secular social order' (Marshall, 1981: 129). What the record also shows is that not everyone is as multiaxial as the Good Society demands.

Consider the doctors, nurses and other caring professionals who went on strike in the winter of 1978–9 because the money was not enough (ibid.: 132). Consider the students and their middle-class parents who squeeze the taxpayers (the great majority of whose children will never command a graduate salary) for 'the last legitimate penny with complete disregard of the general community interest' (Marshall, 1972: 115). Consider the legalised scrounging in the form of tax avoidance (ibid.). Consider the fraudulent welfare claims, happily 'relatively rare' (ibid.; see also 1965a: 90). Consider the union militants who think that socialism is for losers who cannot extract the market price. Acknowledging exception after exception, Marshall would seem to have harboured real fears for the future of the multiaxial compromise under assault from the capitalist ethos that has no time for hyphens since it is heavily into cash.

Marshall in his later years was prepared to acknowledge that triple-think was not for all seasons. Market hegemony or even Durkheimean anomie could be the unappealing successor to a hyphenated ethic that had lost its hold. Yet Marshall nonetheless believed that the civilised mix could retain its rightful place. Its future, he wrote just before his death, was crucially dependent on two social conditions. The first was understanding: the community must recognise that 'both the welfare sector and the mixed economy are contributing to the creation of welfare in the broad, non-technical sense of the word' (Marshall, 1981: 131). The second was validation: the division of responsibility between the various spheres must receive the 'measure of acceptance or approbation which is normally accorded to decisions reached through the processes of democratic government' (ibid.). The striking doctors and the fraudulent claimants, the union barons and the corporate executives will do right to tremble before the force of Marshall's conditions. The hyphenated ethic is still in with a chance.

10.1.2   The Democratic Polity

The consultative system of one person, one vote and majority rule was the great conquest of nineteenth century radicalism. It emerged just after the capitalist market on which it is unequivocally dependent: 'I am one of those who believe that it is hardly possible to maintain democratic freedoms in a society which does not contain a large area of economic freedom' (Marshall, 1981: 135). Economics is decentralised power. Economics is initiators who break the mould.

Economic freedom in collaboration with political freedom means that authority will be diffuse and decision making ubiquitous. Civil rights responsibly exercised are in truth the best bulwark against the totalitarians and the despots. The principle is a simple one: 'If the dictator chops one head off, a new one is likely to grow in its place' (Marshall, 1965b: 142). Events 'seem to testify more to the resilience of democracy than to its vulnerability' (Marshall, 1981: 154). Events seem to testify even more to the popularity of capitalism with which it shares its hyphenated throne.

Yet politics is coercion since in Utopia there would be no State. Marshall could have adopted Schumpeter's first theory and said that in a democracy all constraint comes directly from the consensus. Instead he opted for

Schumpeter's second theory and said that elected representatives are in office to serve the wider interests of the whole: 'Though we may boggle at Rousseau's idea that citizens in a democracy "will be forced to be free", we can accept more easily the view that they may be induced to be healthy' (Marshall, 1965a: 91). Politics is paternalism. Little would be left of the grants economy if accountable leaders supplied no more than the vote-winning bundle: 'The welfare principle cannot be derived from the principle of majority rule; its duty is to provide not what the majority want but what minorities need' (Marshall, 1981: 126).

The social interest is a powerful thing. Citizens may be induced to be healthy. Dysfunctional parents get what battered babies need. Schooling is made compulsory even if good kitchen hygiene is merely encouraged from the top (Marshall, 1966b: 68). Democratic legitimation is, however, what Evan Durbin declared to be 'the indispensable means, the *fons et origo* of all our social hopes' (Durbin, 1940: 271). A blood-bred elite will make an attempt to trick poor old Dubb into voting for its own selfish interest: 'What social classes are particularly good at defending is privilege' (Marshall, 1969: 139). The attempt will fail. Ascribed status or achieved reputability, no leaders will be selected or reselected for long if the social interest which they promulgate is seriously out of line with the needs that the voters ultimately know to be right. Uxbridge does not have to be Oxbridge to see that its children belong in school.

Power is not a problem so long as the major-general is a committed democrat. That nice Mr Attlee conformed nicely to Schumpeter's second theory even if not to Schumpeter's first. The Prussian Bismarck, on the other hand, saw little role for the Common Man. The Iron Chancellor acted as if a great man could do great things only so long as civil and political rights minded their own business: 'Bismarck had made the first experiment in national social insurance in order, as he said, by satisfying the legitimate claims of the working classes, to discourage them from pressing their illegitimate ones' (Marshall, 1966a: 59). Bismarck used welfare to buy out democracy. The experiment paid off. Under his tutelage the rustic yokels of *Hänsel und Gretel* became the *Wirtschaftswunder* of *Made in Germany* and the fearsome killers of the Western Front.

Bismarck put progress before participation. The experiment is being replicated today in those countries, principally in the Third World, where 'planned economic development and social welfare are put before effective democracy and personal freedom' (Marshall, 1965b: 169). Development and welfare given from above may, Marshall conceded, 'stunt the growth of liberty' (ibid.): treating citizens as clients and takers rather than as creators and doers, such 'social rights are no danger to totalitarian regimes, and indeed flourish in them' (Marshall, 1969: 141). No one would deny, Marshall argued, that 'state action carried to excess can destroy individual liberty' (Marshall, 1965b: 158). What he also said is that *fays ce que voudras* can be in excess as well: 'Individual liberty in a developed or developing society is possible only under the cover of state action' (ibid.). Our hired custodians know what to do. Our trusted dentist will not let us down.

To ask is not to receive. In the welfare sector at least, the supply side determines the flow: 'Although it must take careful note of expressed desires, it does not simply react to or obey them. Its responsibility is to satisfy needs, which is a different undertaking' (Marshall, 1972: 107). Oliver wants gruel. The beadle wants rule. Anyone who has ever asked a doctor for a sleeping pill will understand precisely what this means.

Citizens accustomed to active involvement in shopping and voting will feel deflated and disoriented if the supply side refuses to take their revealed preferences into account. Provision without consultation, Marshall writes, 'is what I call welfare without citizenship' (Marshall, 1965b: 170). Apparently, however, he felt that the silence was a fact of welfare life since he made few if any proposals to put the citizen back in. One searches in vain for the parent–teacher associations, the claimants' unions, the pensioners' action groups, the housing committees that would give the end user the chance to be a participant and not just a spectator. As with industrial democracy in the market sector, so with consumer consultation in the caring services: Marshall never saw the need to found a school for democrats in order to rescue Schumpeter's first theory from the dream world of Morris's Nowhere.

One reason for the neglect is the elementary truism that 'the right to choose, if it is to have real substance, must include the right to choose wrongly and to take the consequences' (ibid.: 157–8). A person who spends out of income has the right to make his own mistakes. Not so a person who spends out of the taxpayer's transfers. Money earmarked for food must not be spent on drink: that is the message of Durkheim's *conscience* when the whole tells the part that dependency has opened his books for public inspection. It is the task of the politician to ensure that the right to welfare is the right of the consensus and not of the consumer who only contributes his homelessness, his profligacy or his disease.

A related reason for the neglect is the premium on 'balance and proportion' in a welfare world where resources are finite and efficiency counts: 'You cannot make the optimum use of scarce skills and resources in a nation-wide service open to all if you allow every applicant for its help to pick and choose as he pleases' (Marshall, 1972: 114). The system must husband well its economies of scale and coordinate its competing priorities in order that maximum welfare might be squeezed from a limited public budget. In doing this it has to rely heavily on advice from the professionals, the experts and the administrators. They have the training and the *anno domini* in the field.

Discretion must, of course, be 'sustained by publicity, accountability, supervision and, finally, the right of appeal': 'The right of appeal implies that the claimant is the subject of welfare, not merely the object of it' (Marshall, 1965a: 89, 96). The right of appeal guarantees some social rights even to a welfare-dependent not covered by a watertight contract. It reduces the extent to which democratic practices encouraged in two sub-systems might be trodden under foot in the third.

10.1.3   The Welfare State

It is not easy to say what T.H. Marshall understood by the welfare State. His exploration of the terminological maze in his textbook on *Social Policy* by no means produces a definitive map. Marshall in his book explains that social policy 'does not lend itself to precise definition'; that its meaning in a particular context 'is largely a matter of convenience or of convention'; that in trying to pinpoint its nature the community should look 'not simply at the measures adopted, since these are but means to an end, but at the nature of the end itself' (Marshall, 1975: 11). Social policy, Marshall writes, sets out to 'achieve results which the economic system would not achieve on its own' (ibid.: 15). Interventionist, collective, corrective, conscious, it is 'guided by values other than those determined by open market forces' (ibid.). Social policy is not kismet fatalism or the self-correcting thermostat. Instead it is the man-made determination to plan and redefine.

Social policy is not effective demand so much as it is validated redirection: 'A "needs test" . . . in the broadest sense of the term, is the foundation of every benevolent welfare service' (ibid.: 88). Social policy is supraeconomic supply. The five social services clearly come within its elastic ambit. They are, however, by no means alone: 'In my estimation welfare must be envisaged as an integral part of the whole apparatus that includes social security, education, public health, the medical services, factory legislation, the right to strike, and all the other rights and legitimate expectations which are attached to modern democratic citizenship' (Marshall, 1966b: 81). Welfare is money for the arts and Our Man in Dubai who smoothes the passage of British exports. Welfare is 'community services for the preservation and development of the physical, social and cultural environment' (Marshall, 1981: 135). Welfare is subsidised staples and public utilities that ordinary people can afford: 'Why . . . should housing and school meals be run as quasi-social services and not gas and electricity?' (ibid.: 134). Welfare, in short, is all around. If the democracy calls it welfare, then welfare it must be.

In *Citizenship and Social Class*, Marshall had defined his needs-based *desiderata* as the whole range of rights from 'a modicum of economic welfare' to 'the life of a civilised being' (Marshall, 1950: 8). In *The Right to Welfare* he filled in the gaps in his Socialism B when he associated his middle-ground mix quite explicitly with 'a specific historical social system – the one which evolved in Britain and most of Western Europe in the first 20 years or so after the war' (Marshall, 1981: 123). Accused of quantifying the qualitative with the aid of a rubber yardstick, Marshall would reply that he is describing *what is* rather than proposing *what ought to be*. He would show his grainy newsreels from the first 20 years or so after the war. He would say that the facts from Attlee to Wilson effectively put the kibosh on the demand for the minimal State.

The facts in Mr Butskell's Britain speak eloquently for libraries and museums, sewers and parks. So, importantly, do the facts in Joseph Chamberlain's Birmingham, where pre-Boer Liberalism was proudly municipalising the levelling infrastructure and taking upon itself the duty to care. Chamberlain himself was happy to call his social reforms by the name that virulent nationalisers had used to attack market enterprise: 'Of course it is Socialism ... Every kindly act of legislation by which the community has sought to discharge its responsibilities and its obligations to the poor is Socialism' (cited in Freeden, 1978: 27). So was Chiozza Money: 'Wherever two or three men are gathered together for mutual help, Socialism is in the midst of them. A crusade against Socialism would be a crusade against the better part of human nature' (ibid.: 49). So was Hobhouse: 'The ideas of Socialism, when translated into practical terms, coincide with the ideas to which Liberals are led when they seek to apply their principles of Liberty, Equality and the Common Good to the industrial life of our time' (ibid.: 47). And so was T.H. Marshall. He, like Mr Butskell and Mr Chamberlain, treated the right to welfare as the invitation to belong.

The welfare nexus, 'social in origin' (Marshall, 1965a: 91), is inseparable from affiliation. It is embedded in the concentric circles of membership: the family, the neighbourhood, the community, the nation (Marshall, 1966b: 82). In peasant societies the kinsfolk and the locals look after the retarded and the incapable. In the industrial system, mobile and anonymous, there is no friend of last resort but the State.

The residual supplier in that sense is indispensable if the poorer countries are to modernise and grow: 'This process of emancipation from familial power, like the other freedoms, *can only take place* if the society, through its government, provides for the individual outside his group the security and the opportunities he previously enjoyed within it' (Marshall, 1965b: 165, emphasis added). *Can only take place*: the words are a subjectivist's concession that structure has its imperatives and that functions have got to be performed.

Social rights evolve because there is no close substitute: State pensions are needed because blood ties become loose. Need on its own is not, however, enough. There must also be demand – since Marshall's vision, not of philanthropy but of 'mutual aid on the basis of common citizenship' (Marshall, 1966b: 71), is incapable of realisation in the absence of society's proud affirmation that it has a 'collective responsibility to seek to achieve welfare' (Marshall, 1965a: 88). Commitment is essential. Without felt citizenship 'there could be no welfare state' (Marshall, 1972: 113).

Welfare is mutual aid. In that sense it has a double meaning, at once across-the-board service and the relief of acute distress. The general meaning derives unprejudiced access from 'a direct sense of community membership based on loyalty to a civilisation which is a common possession' (Marshall, 1950: 24). Because welfare is All, all classes will have an interest in State schooling and national insurance. The specific meaning is more focused, more selective and more sectional. Welfare being in this second case not All but Some, sharing is indicative in effect of a 'genuine concern for the sufferings of the poor, and . . . personal devotion to their service' (Marshall, 1966b: 73). Even a stockbroker will regard the National Health as mutual aid. A hostel for abandoned derelicts, on the other hand, he will see more commonly as a shared cost than as a shower shared.

Welfare is common interest but it is also a helping hand for the poor. Where it has the downward bias, where it 'favours the weaker at the expense of the stronger' (Marshall, 1965a: 88), it can only be regarded as 'help given by the privileged to the under-privileged' (Marshall, 1966b: 71). It cannot realistically be seen as a dormitory bed for which today's stockbroker anticipates an imminent need. Welfare is clearly not just the pooling of resources but also the redistribution of responsibilities. The stockbroker is being asked to pay money despite the high probability that he will receive no consumable in return. However much 'democratic voting is egotistic', the affluent and the self-supporting must nonetheless be prepared to sacrifice taxes for transfers at the expense of their own private well-being: 'Welfare decisions depend on altruism – both concern for others and mutual concern for one another' (Marshall, 1972: 108).

There must be sociability and there must be agreement: 'Without a foundation of near-consensus, no general social welfare policy would be possible' (ibid.: 109). The citizens must see eye-to-eye on the charter and on the statutes. In modern Britain at least they certainly do so. In modern Britain 'a very high degree of consensus exists about the aims of the welfare services' (ibid.: 113). A very strong sense of affiliation 'permeates the whole life of the society and penetrates the consciousnessness of its members' (Marshall, 1966b: 71). Welfare both general and specific has been the entirely functional response to social need.

Marshall puts his faith in the moral consensus. Yet he also resists the temptation to speculate on the long-lost causes of the other-regarding norms: 'It is
impossible to say exactly how these ethical standards arise in a society or are
recognised by its members' (Marshall, 1972: 109). We today are the beneficiaries of a valuable capital. History has not left a comprehensive account of
the peasant communities, the parental educators, the high-minded philan-
thropists who accumulated it for us to use.

Marshall seems to think that Darwinian instinct and the Kantian Imperative
have played a pivotal role. He writes that welfare is much in debt to a 'natural
reaction' which he calls 'the urge to sociability within the group': 'So when
modern welfare policy set itself to breach the barrier of shame and replace it
by the bridge of sympathy, it did not have to plant new instincts in the human
psyche, but primarily to enlarge the human group' (Marshall, 1966b: 73).
Capitalist evolution, building outwards from the biological constants, has
made all of Britain into a giant *Gemeinschaft*. Welfare in this scenario is the
unintended consequence of the autonomous and the non-social. Marshall
knew that there were other scenarios as well. Seeing no way to test the
untestable, he preferred to leave the peasants and the Darwinians to their own
devices and to start from the present because the present is all around.

Welfare is all around – and the consensus is bound to grow more caring still
over time. Private provision stratifies fellow citizens into separate facilities:
'Medical care and education . . . are areas in which differences of opportunity
and experience, and particularly an institutionalised dual standard (which
would inevitably follow), do more to create and sustain class distinctions than
any other' (Marshall, 1972: 112). Common provision, on the other hand, integrates the beneficiaries because the gatekeeper becomes real need alone and
not the divisiveness of the ability to pay: 'I imagine . . . that when you are
weighing a naked baby on a pair of scales, the idea of social class does not
obtrude itself unduly' (Marshall, 1966b: 78). Consensus creates the demand
for welfare. The 'new common experience' creates the feel-good 'class fusion'
(Marshall, 1950: 33) that deepens the consensus and thereby reinforces the
State.

Welfare is its own best friend. It is by its very nature a levelling force in that
it applies a single and a citizenship standard: 'A common standard cannot, of
course, be an absolute one, but it is relative, not to the individual concerned,
but to the level of civilisation of the society' (Marshall, 1966b: 78). Marshall
says that welfare, rejecting 'the lowest that is tolerable' in favour of 'the highest that is possible' (Marshall, 1966a: 59), is committed to service that is optimal and not minimal. Trying simultaneously to improve the absolute success
rates in the schools and the hospitals, welfare has an obligation to ensure that
no child, no patient, be given a product which is radically inferior to that of the
median.

The moral consensus favours the integration of the whole. The moral consensus at once encourages the individuation of the part. Being British is a full-time job. An ideological Liberal as well as an ideological socialist, Marshall was adamant that the I should not be forgotten merely because the We is today at the cutting edge of reform.

Marshall was concerned that the economies of Schumpeterian, Galbraithian size were severely restricting the freedom of choice. Mass production, mass communication, mass consumption were having the standardising effect of making all of us, 'more or less, members of the same crowd' (ibid.: 61). It would be easy enough for universalistic welfare to conform to the capitalist trend. It would be easy enough for national schools, say, to operate 'in the same way, at the same time, and with the same content on the minds of all those within range of their influence' (ibid.: 62). Some assimilation is the very essence of the life in society. Too much assimilation, however, is a threat to self-respect. Even welfare dependants do not want to be treated as inter-changeable parts.

Both to countervail the depersonalisation of the market and to differentiate the non-standard self, Marshall recommended that the welfare sector wherever possible should distribute 'a highly individualized product' (Marshall, 1975: 14). Planned diversity was a vote for the 'free development of personality' (Marshall, 1966a: 63). It sent a free man's message to the corporate bureau-crats and the welfare chiefs that no unique beneficiary may legitimately be forced into a Procrustean box because the made-to-measure is not to the taste of his producer sovereigns: 'Welfare, like peace, is indivisible. However specialised the services it offers, it must always keep in view, and pay respect to, the integrity of the whole person. And it is only this kind of individualism of the whole person that can resist the assault of the mass society against the individual personality' (ibid.: 62).

Socialism means that I am I. It is an attractive defence, but also one that sits uneasily with the I am We that is socialism as well. Marshall may have been too confident that welfare pluralism would not jeopardise the common expe-rience: variety in the Health Service can mean that pay-bed patients never share their mealtime anecdotes with the ward. He may, again, have underesti-mated the extent to which differentiated access can prove a 'great architect of inequality' (Marshall, 1972: 119) at the end. As always, the intelligence-tested grammar schools are a good example of State welfare that divides.

Grammar schools signify separateness and reinforce condescension. So a fortiori do the historic public schools. If streaming by intelligence is divisive, then so a fortiori must be streaming by cash. Marshall in 1950 had acknowl-edged that the Etons and the Harrows were the breeding grounds for class soli-darity, 'inter-class difference', 'intra-class similarity' (Marshall, 1950: 34). He was aware that the Headmasters' Conference, despite the post-feudal pledge of life chances allocated class-at-birth blind, continued to account for a dispro-portionate number of Britain's bank managers, bishops and senior civil servants (Tawney, 1931: 77). He had learned from Tawney that it was a real danger for social decision making to be entrusted to blue blood that had never queued for a bus, to commanding drawing-rooms that had never seen at first hand 'the conditions of life and habits of thought of those for whose require-ments . . . they are engaged in providing' (Tawney, 1943: 65).

Titmuss followed Tawney in questioning the shopkeeper logic that the class that can pay has a civil right to buy the privilege: 'Until we, as a society, can rid ourselves of the dominating influence of the private sector of education we shall not have the will to embark on an immensely higher standard of provi-sion for all those children whose education now finishes when it has hardly begun' (Titmuss, 1964: 24). Tawney and Titmuss were concerned about the sale at auction of accent, contacts, teaching, facilities. T.H. Marshall was concerned as well. Concern, however, was all. Aware as he was that a free market for outputs does not necessarily imply a free market for starts, he nonetheless came down on the side of conservative replication, libertarian choice. Like Tawney and Titmuss, he in the 1950s and the 1960s made no actual proposal to put right an injustice that British reformers had long believed to be an especial cause for concern.

Marshall in the 1970s returned to the problem of the opted-out alternative that was selling above-average life chances to a privileged elite. Marshall the ideological socialist recognised that the dual system had to go: 'The two cannot coexist indefinitely in their present form' (Marshall, 1972: 112). Marshall the ideological liberal knew, however, that personal freedoms had to be respected: the independent sector could not be abolished so long as a sizable minority preferred it to the State. The compromise that Marshall proposed was designed to meet the double requirements of his Janus-faced constituency.

State schooling was not to push out private schooling but it was to become 'potentially comprehensive' (ibid.). Well funded, academically successful, it must guarantee a place for every child who, 'for financial or other reasons' (ibid.), wishes to return from civil to social rights. The door must always be open: that is why parents who pay school fees should not be given a tax credit against the local alternative that is forever their own. The State must do its best. At the end of the day, however, there is nothing the politicians can do or should do to vandalise 'a private sector of acceptable size and scope' (ibid.: 113).

Marshall's welfare is a marriage of the benefit and the cost: 'Every right to receive implies an obligation to give' (Marshall, 1965a: 92). Marshall's rights are Marshall's duties. Marshall was a Good Samaritan who was a Good

Contractarian as well. More often than not he expected a citizenship gift in return.

In places Marshall seems to be expressing a belief in irrevocably ascribed entitlements, in 'rights created by the community itself and attached to the status of its citizenship' (ibid.: 88): 'The old morality stressed obligations more than rights; in the new it is the opposite' (Marshall, 1981: 175). The velvet glove must not be mistaken for the iron fist. Defending the gift without the fee because no decent doctor can refuse to patch up a drunk, Marshall is also arguing that no decent citizen can take pride in his status if he knows he is free riding on his collectively valued commitments: 'If you concede to a poor person an absolute, unconditional right to relief, the question then arises how to deny him the right to become poor if he so wishes. The obligation of the community to relieve destitution must somehow be matched by a duty of the individual not to become destitute, if he can help it' (Marshall, 1965a: 90).

Even status absolutes cannot fully be separated from social exchange. Marshall made this clear in his *Citizenship and Social Class*: 'Social rights imply an absolute right to a certain standard of civilisation which is conditional only on the discharge of the general duties of citizenship' (Marshall, 1950: 26). Marshall's insistence upon the 'conditional only' is a reminder that he is telling only a part of the story when he declares, as he so frequently does, that social rights are a reflection of 'the strong individualist element in mass society' (Marshall, 1969: 141). In the early freedom *from* of Locke versus the tyrant, rights were deemed to be 'inherent in the individual and not created for him by the society of which he was a member' (Marshall, 1965a: 91). We today tend to see rights more as the obligation of equal citizens to one another: 'The modern rights to education and health are . . . not merely recognised by all as being social in origin, but are part of the mechanism by which the individual is absorbed into society (not isolated from it) and simultaneously draws upon and contributes to its collective welfare' (ibid.). The old individualism was natural rights. The new individualism is the freedom to play one's part.

Marshall says that welfare rights are the property of 'individuals as consumers, not as actors' (Marshall, 1969: 141). The citizen because he is a citizen has the right to see a doctor. His child because he is a citizen has the right to go to school. Yet Marshall also makes clear that the surrounding collectivity holds an additional claim on the asset and its state of repair: 'It would be dishonest to pretend that there is not about welfare policy decisions something intrinsically authoritarian or . . . paternalistic' (Marshall, 1972: 109). Things change once the citizen is poked in the ribs to see how much work he can do. Your body is not just *your* body. Your children are *our* children as well.

What Marshall is saying is that citizens acquire social duties at the same time that they are granted social rights. In some cases the rights and the duties are effectively the same. Health is one instance, because it 'is in large measure a form of public discipline': 'Your body is part of the national capital, and must be looked after, and sickness causes a loss of national income, in addition to being liable to spread' (Marshall, 1965a: 91). Education is another, because it 'is a process by which citizens are made': 'Education is of such vital importance for the health and prosperity of a nation, that it is regarded as something of which the individual has a duty to avail himself, to the extent that his natural abilities warrant' (ibid.: 90–91). Health and education are means as well as ends. A child has a right to go to school. A nation has a right to a good supply of skill.

Much of welfare is social investment. Much of welfare, however, is unproductive consumption: 'It cannot be said that society needs happy old people in the same way that it needs a healthy and educated population' (ibid.: 91). In the case of the unemployable and the senile, the likelihood of a return gift is negligible and the payback not worth the cost: 'The most that one can say is that the handicapped have a moral duty to try to overcome their misfortunes as far as in them lies' (ibid.: 92). Where the benefits stream approaches zero, the widows and orphans will look to Heaven and the chronically incapable to 'compassion rather than interest' (ibid.). Welfare is 'your duty to your neighbour' (Marshall, 1966b: 67). Without the democratic acknowledgment of that duty the chronically incapable would have to beg and maybe die on the street.

Such welfare is unreciprocated. Being pure Samaritanship, it is somehow not quite as good: 'Though compassion (or "the impulses of common humanity") may create a right, having almost the force of law, to minimal subsistence, it cannot establish the same kind of right to the benefit of services which are continuously striving to extend the limits of the possible' (Marshall, 1965a: 92). Marshall seems to have believed that there was a hierarchy of social rights. Some citizens evidently have a stronger claim than others. Even in the welfare State it is a good selling point to be able to pledge promise and potential in exchange for a kidney transplant or a university place.

Whether up and coming or over the top, it is a central tenet of the welfare State that the needs of the deprived will wherever possible be met. Gifts or exchanges, no one who needs welfare will ever be sent away.

Much of poverty is the absolute distress of the hungry and the homeless: 'The common factor in the state of the poor is the urgency of their need' (Marshall, 1972: 117). Much of poverty is, however, the spoiled identity and the loss of face that is the shame and stigma of life left behind by the crowd. Relative deprivation is second-class citizenship and self-presentation that hurts. Just as a decent society must spread a safety net for its schizophrenics sleeping rough, so it has to build a floor such that no child faces his peer group without some at least of the emblems of defensive consumption.

Relative deprivation means an intolerable distance between the needy and the normal. It does not mean that envy and malice can pass themselves off as virtues when in truth they are sins: 'If this means that poverty is relative to the standard of civilisation of the country concerned, it is beyond dispute. If it means that I may not say that A is poor, but only that he is poorer than B, I cannot accept it' (ibid.: 116–17). Levelling up is a virtue. Cutting down to size is a sin. In the hyphenated society the spread of incomes is what makes the whole thing work: 'In such a society poverty is a disease, but inequality is an essential structural feature' (ibid.: 117).

Inequality is here to stay. Crushing hardship, defined as 'a sub-minimal social condition' relative to a respectable national norm, is not: 'The comparison made here is not in fact with an average, but with a minimum . . . Poverty is a condition of life which lies below the minimum which that particular civilization can accept as part of itself' (Marshall, 1975: 185, 184). People must have the material wherewithal that makes it possible for them to live as gentlemen and present themselves as citizens. Upgrading is needed, and that means a policy mix. The task 'must be undertaken jointly by welfare and capitalism; there is no other way' (Marshall, 1972: 117). The fringes and the tails cannot deliver the goods. The middle ground, on the other hand, has made the Englishmen think of their homeland as their home: 'Our particular type of social system has got nearer to achieving this objective than any that has gone before or now exists' (ibid.: 117–18).

Thus 'low wages and irregular employment' (Marshall, 1981: 40) are being driven into the history books by rapid growth and Keynesian economics. The stagnation and the joblessness of the 1930s have been put to rout by the business dynamic smoothed into steady progress by the Treasury and the Bank. Owing both to aggregate demand and to statutory intervention, there has been 'a trend towards the greater protection of the individual against the fluctuations of the market' (ibid.: 52). It is 'a trend which many would argue is an expression of the spirit of the welfare state' (ibid.).

Prosperity has made fellow citizens more receptive to social distance. So has the welfare-formed consensus that is tolerant towards incomes so long as the distribution seems just. Marshall writes that scaling down differentials ('however necessary this may be') will never be enough unless it is complemented by cultural relegitimation, by 'changing the attitude towards them': 'The problem is structural in origin, but there is no purely structural solution to it' (Marshall, 1972: 119). The decent society must be seen ex ante to 'substitute prevention of poverty for relief of poverty' (Marshall, 1981: 132). This will mean the equality of life chances and the social reformers' freedom *to*: 'Nineteenth-century individualism was rooted in rights, but only in certain rights . . . Nineteenth-century individualism, in fact, did not fully recognise, or realise, the individual' (Marshall, 1966a: 62). The decent society must be seen

ex post to 'patch the wounds inflicted by the social system' (Marshall, 1981:
133): income maintenance and a council flat are a soft landing for a craftsman
whose skills lose their market value because of change. Ex post or ex ante, in
other words, the welfare society makes the minnows more accepting of the
pike precisely because their own position is more secure.

The welfare society in any case is a one-class train. Rich and poor alike
share in the same kinds of benefits and wrestle with the same kinds of procedures. Income inequality is more visible and more resented where the successful can buy their way into a superior product while the paupers are condemned
to a 'second-class service for second-class people' (Marshall, 1966b: 79).
Income inequality by the same token pales into a background fact of life where
'welfare-consciousness' (Marshall, 1965a: 89) has been instilled by universality and separate facilities have been rejected because they stigmatise and
divide. Common services do not preclude a means test such that the rich pay
more. What is essential is simply that the services be common, classless and
open to all. The comprehensive principle is 'an intrinsic characteristic of twen-
tieth-century civilisation' (Marshall, 1966b: 79). It is the socialism that helps
the capitalism to give us all a good standard of life.

Tony Rees says that the citizenship was crowded out by the gain-seeking as
Marshall grew older in a Britain he had not designed. Marshall, Rees avers,
'seems to have lost faith in the concept in the end': 'It merely takes its place
among a plurality of often competing values and organising principles' (Rees,
1995: 360). Britain had changed. The hyphenated social democrat had
changed as well: 'Marshall was (or became) a rather convoluted apologist for
capitalism' (ibid.: 359).

This section reaches a different conclusion. Small modifications had to be
made: labour relations were said to have worsened, incomes policy to have
become the democratic alternative to antinomian greed. The overall structure,
however, remained precisely what it was. The hyphenated society is a mix of
capitalism, democracy and welfare. It can reconsider its relative position
within the middle band. What it cannot do is to renege on the fellowship of the
three.

10.2   CROSLAND

On the Marxian Left there is the insistence that democracy and exchange will
not produce the equitable society so long as private profit-seeking and wasteful market anarchy are left uncorrected: 'Where planning attempts mainly to
alleviate poverty, distress and squalor, it will perpetuate rather than transcend
the capitalist mechanisms which continually create such social injustice'

(Holland, 1975: 34). On the libertarian Right there is the contention that non-discriminatory impartiality is defensible both as a moral end in its own right and as the prerequisite for sustained economic adaptation: 'Equality before the law and material equality are therefore not only different but are in conflict with each other' (Hayek, 1960: 87). On the middle ground there was Charles Anthony Raven Crosland (1918–77), Oxford economist, Gaitskellite moderate, Member of Parliament for Grimsby, Secretary of State for Education (1965–7), President of the Board of Trade (1967–9), Foreign Secretary (1976–7). Crosland was an intellectual in politics who, in his classic work *The Future of Socialism* (1956) and in its successor essays, sought to chart a pragmatist's middle course between the barren extremes of militant Labour and self-satisfied Conservatism: 'Socialism is about the pursuit of equality and the protection of freedom – in the knowledge that until we are truly equal we will not be truly free' (cited in Hattersley, 1987: 254).

Crosland, like Marshall, believed that absolute and relative deprivation, not public ownership and the Plan, had to become the priority concerns of social reformers in the post-scarcity sunrise of affluence and efficiency. Attlee's nationalisations, State regulation of restrictive practices, the expert adjustment of aggregate demand, the sheer dynamism of capitalism itself had all contributed to a standard of economic performance unanticipated in the 1930s by apocalyptic socialists like Strachey, Laski, Bevan and the Webbs: 'The contemporary mixed economy is characterised by high levels both of employment and productivity and by a reasonable degree of stability' (Crosland, 1956: 105).

The economy was doing what was expected of it. The society, however, was not. Writing in 1956, Crosland said of Britain that it was 'the most class-ridden country in the world' (ibid.: 277). Writing in 1974, he continued to complain of a splintered nation, 'conspicuous for its persistent and glaring class inequalities' (Crosland, 1974a: 23). A socialist of social distance rather than of market failure, Crosland made it his mission to reorient Labour towards opportunity and outcome and away from capitalist production and allocation which had shown themselves to be sound: 'The purpose of socialism is quite simply to eradicate this sense of class, and to create in its place a sense of common interest and equal status.' (Crosland, 1952: 62).

10.2.1 Opportunity

British people in the 1950s were in broad agreement on the need for an equal start and an open road. 'I suppose that most liberal people would now allow that every child had a natural "right" as a citizen not merely to "life, liberty, and the pursuit of happiness", but to that position in the social scale to which his native talents entitle him: should have, in other words, an equal opportunity for wealth, advancement, and renown' (Crosland, 1956: 208). Free marketeers

have long made a virtue of earned status in place of a self-reproducing conservatism that closes the doors to new talent. So, importantly, have social democrats like Anthony Crosland, who wrote of the competitive race that 'life itself
is a selective process' – 'but we must allow that process to work fairly'
(Crosland, 1966: 199): 'The essential thing is that every citizen should have an
equal chance' (Crosland, 1956: 218).

Crosland wanted to see the elimination of ascription and directive. Like
Smith, like Hayek, he believed that ambition and improvement should be set
free from the fetters of impediment and preference. Emancipation was essential; but it would not be enough. What society needed in order to clear the
backlog of neglect was, in the words of Tawney, 'the possession of powers'
and not just the 'freedom from restraints'; the 'presence of abilities' and not
just 'the absence of disabilities' (Tawney, 1931: 103). Without positive support
and public-sector empowerment, Tawney argued in the actively interventionist spirit of Green and Hobhouse, the winners and the losers could not realistically be said to have received their just deserts: 'It would be as reasonable to
hold that the final position of contenders in a race were an accurate indication
of their physical endowments, if, while some entered fit and carefully trained,
others were half-starved, were exhausted by want of sleep, and were handicapped by the starters' (ibid.: 116). The libertarian looks to personal ambition
plus the constable for the open road. The reforming democrat looks to enablement and hard cash: 'Equality and higher public expenditure are what divide
us from the Tories' (Crosland, 1974a: 58).

Crosland, like Tawney, feared that the promise of opportunity might be
little more than talk: 'The distribution of rewards and privileges still appears
highly inequitable, being poorly correlated with the distribution of merit,
virtue, ability, or brains' (Crosland, 1956: 116). Declaring his commitment to
'a political framework of freedom for the individual' (ibid.: 104), he
demanded 'an improvement in our social capital' in order to ensure that 'the
less well-off have access to housing, health and education of a standard
comparable, at least in the basic decencies, to that which the better-off can buy
for themselves out of their private means' (Crosland, 1971a: 71).

The better-off can pay and the worse-off cannot. Corrective spending in
such a perspective is evidently not incompatible with the libertarian vision of
the self-made man. On the contrary, as Galbraith points out, it is the precondition for the accomplishment of the libertarian's task: 'It is extraordinary how
little in economic discussion we hear of the greatest of liberties, which is
having some money to spend. Or how little of the way liberty is circumscribed
by poverty' (cited in Bartel, 1983: 124). Where children are too hungry to
learn, where good education is economically inaccessible, where tuberculosis
and glaucoma affect performance at work, no one would say that all citizens
have an equal chance of reaching the top.

Education, not unexpectedly, took on an especial importance for Crosland: 'The school system in Britain remains the most divisive, unjust, and wasteful of all the aspects of social inequality' (Crosland, 1956: 258). It was divisive because segregation in the formative years breeds 'contrasts in social manners' which, carried on into adult life, 'remain a conspicuous index of class location' (ibid.: 234). It was wasteful because overconcentration on high achievers means that we as a nation do not make the 'best use of our beta resources also' (ibid.: 215). It was unjust because some schools were better funded than others, better placed to offer the good back-up facilities and the low pupil–teacher ratios that contribute so much to examination success. Wanting more equitable finishes, Crosland was convinced that life chances had to be reformed in the schools.

Many Labour egalitarians had been very negative about private education. Tawney, educated at Rugby, was among the most vocal: 'A special system of schools, reserved for children whose parents have larger bank accounts than their neighbours . . . is socially disastrous, for it does more than any other single cause, except capitalism itself, to perpetuate the division of the nation into classes of which one is almost unintelligible to the other' (Tawney, 1931: 145). Crosland, educated at Highgate, shared Tawney's assessment of the golden ghettoes where money talks. The historic public schools, he wrote, were too arrogant and too exclusive to satisfy any but the shopkeeper's sense of what is right when unequal starts are sold: 'These commanding heights of private privilege and social separatism (far more commanding than the steel or the chemical industry!) are a flagrant denial of the most elementary democratic claim to equal opportunity' (Crosland, 1961: 182).

The ancient independents traded in superior coaching and signalled the 'crucial advantages of the right accent, manners, and dependability of character' (Crosland, 1956: 208). Their visible and their invisible curriculum, taken together, had made them 'a major determinant of occupation, and hence of income, power, and prestige' (ibid.). Crosland as a socialist would very much have liked to see the inequality merchants put out of business. The problem was that his socialism was built upon the fundamental principle that tastes and preferences were to be treated with respect. Torn between his collectivism and the individualism that made the socialism worthwhile, Crosland was in no doubt as to the product that he had to pick: 'The values of solidarity, community, and even traditional neighbourliness may well threaten the opposite (and equally "socialist"!) values of freedom, autonomy and critical revolt . . . I personally hold the latter values higher.' (Crosland, 1962: 210). What that meant was that, in the tolerant society, the boarding schools were safe from the State: 'To prohibit all private fee-paying . . . would be an intolerable restriction on personal liberty' (Crosland, 1961: 182).

Like T.H. Marshall, Crosland wanted purchasing power to be corrected through tax and the State schools steadily upgraded until they were clearly the best. Like T.H. Marshall, however, he also accepted that sovereign choice must in the last analysis be ranked above the negation of the educational inequity: 'A democracy cannot forbid people to found schools and charge for going to them.' (cited in Crosland, 1982: 149). A democracy cannot stray too far from the moral commitment that makes market economics another name for doing good: 'The consumer is the best judge of how to spend his money; and even if he were not, the principle of individual liberty would still require that he should be left free to spend it, subject only to . . . social service considerations' (Crosland, 1956: 504–5).

The consumer should be left free to choose, subject only to the standard Pigovian constraint of social service and social disamenity. Mill's rule of thumb in deciding when the frontiers of autonomy should be closed to initiative had been his community-regarding cut-off 'to prevent harm to others' (Mill, 1859: 58). Crosland employed the same criterion ('provided only that no nuisance is caused to others') when he contended that even the public schools had an Englishman's right to exist: 'A flat proscription is undesirable on libertarian grounds . . . It is out of tune with the temper of the country' (Crosland, 1956: 262).

It was a curious conclusion, given that he had already shown the purchase of privilege to be a smoking chimney. Trapped between the noxious externalities and the spillovers of unfreedom, Crosland clearly sensed how difficult it will always be to recognise a polluted stream. The commanding secondaries enjoyed tax concessions and charity status. He did not even recommend that the injured nation should withdraw its fiscal welfare. Henry Dubb pays a purchase tax when he forks out for 20 Woodbines. Eton and Harrow pocket a public subsidy when they train the heir to the throne and the future House of Lords. Regressive though the transfers will be, a breach with 'the temper of the country' would be a greater pollutant still.

The public schools were a public nuisance that could not be put right. State education, however, was a different matter: 'If it's the last thing I do,' Crosland once said, 'I'm going to destroy every fucking grammar school in England' (cited in Crosland, 1982: 148).

The wartime coalition had, through the Education Act of 1944, put in place a streamed system of secondary schooling. It relied on a test taken at age 11 (the 'Eleven-plus') to decide if a child were better suited to the intellectual challenge of the grammar school or to the vocational bias of the secondary modern. Almost immediately, Labour's socialist wing decided that a mistake had been made. It reasoned that the intelligence test was fallible and biased; that separate institutions were a poor breeding ground for the common culture; that a superior option would be the 'common school life' of the 'comprehensive high school' (Cole, 1952: 108). Crosland was an educational radical who wanted education to be community-based, non-judgmental and inclusive. He was convinced that comprehensive schooling was essential if Marshall's felt citizenship was ever to become a fact.

Negatively speaking, the Eleven-plus had a tendency to sift out not just talents and aptitudes but surroundings and upbringing as well: 'What the 11-plus is doing is this: it penalizes the working-class boy not necessarily for innate stupidity but partly for his social background, for his less educated parents, his larger family, his crowded home, his slum neighbourhood, his generally less favourable environment' (Crosland, 1966: 197–8). Positively speaking, the local comprehensive would be the forcing house for 'uninhibited social mixing', 'goodwill', 'breadth of personal experience' (Crosland, 1956: 237), just as the omnibus high school had been a cause as well as a consequence of social harmony in the relatively classless conditions of the mobile United States. In the United States, Crosland reported, the schools have 'none of the fissiparous effect on society produced by the British system': 'The huge majority of the population . . . share the same educational experience up to the time when they leave school' (ibid.: 253). He obviously believed that a united Britain would do well to follow the good example of a melting-pot nation that had educated itself into One.

He had less to say about academic excellence or the possibility that the quality of the throughput would sink to the lowest common floor. He may or may not have recognised that the equalisation of experience might also mean a debasement of standards. What is clear is that achievement was never a serious consideration for him: 'Really clever children are going to stay clever, and get ahead and educate themselves, or be educated almost regardless of the kind of school they go to' (Crosland, 1974b). Clever *in spite of* their education, really egg-headed children, frustrated by the remorseless dumbing down, are likely to wonder why even a minority that likes books should not be treated with respect. Crosland saw no reason to sacrifice the neighbourhood in order to satisfy the gifted. Private schooling was always there if really clever parents felt that their democracy had let them down.

Crosland expected the institutions to be comprehensive. Not so the syllabus or the content of the lessons: 'I certainly don't think Ministers or civil servants are competent to interfere in detail' (Crosland, in Boyle and Crosland, 1971: 173). Crosland's communalisation of educational delivery was evidently not to mean that the curriculum should be nationalised into propaganda. We as a State school will not be compelled to learn about the constitution, to pledge allegiance to God, to read three plays by Shakespeare, to sing the national anthem. State prescription is not the answer. The educator knows best.

Moderate on course content, Crosland was no less moderate on the pace of reform. He was aware that constructing new comprehensives would impose a heavy financial burden. He accepted that not all teachers and laboratories matched up to the best-practice norm. He knew that the British tradition of educational autonomy meant that the local authorities would have to be wooed and won. He acknowledged that neighbourhood comprehensives would not be a good cross-section so long as housing within the catchment area was not a representative microcosm of the whole. It was presumably because of reservations such as these that Crosland in Government proceeded so slowly and cautiously. Put in charge of the comprehensive revolution, he issued the vacillating circular 10/65 and then left it to history to grow his gradualism into shape. Democracy would produce welfare in the end. But it would take time.

Public housing, like State education, is merit infrastructure that permits and enables. Crosland made it a 'basic right of citizenship' that every member of the community should expect to enjoy a 'minimum civilized standard of dwelling, adequate for a decent, comfortable and private household life' (Crosland, 1971b: 117–18). Sometimes owner occupation and commercial rentals will be enough to give the consumer his valued freedom of choice. Often, however, 'the need for housing is ... markedly at variance with the effective money demand' (Crosland, 1962: 189); and then there will be no one there but the State.

Housing is a valued consumable, an end in itself. Like education, however, it is also an investment in opportunity and an opener of roads. Cold, damp, crowded conditions do nothing to encourage the unfolding of potential, while mobility to level one's family up is frequently impossible in the absence of an affordable roof: 'The choice the Tories are offering you is this. Either you have a home on the dole in Lincoln, or a park bench with a job in the South East' (Crosland, unpublished speech to a by-election meeting at Lincoln, 1972/3, in Crosland Papers, Box 13/24). A council house, a rent rebate, a regulated rent, even (albeit studiously confined to the standard band) the mortgage interest allowance are all ways in which a well-articulated society guarantees meaningful freedom to every citizen who needs a gentle push in order to better his condition. Such assistance, whether through provision, subsidisation or control, makes possible a shift out of welfare dependency. It gives the left-behind an entry point into the virtuous spiral.

Yet there is a case for income maintenance too. The working poor are inexorably vanishing from the economic landscape owing to growth, full employment and the upgrading of skill: 'Most wage-earners, happily, are now comparatively well-off' (Crosland, 1962: 11). Secondary poverty, however, is here to stay. In the case of the old–elderly, the abandoned with children, the released prisoner whom no one wants, the undernourished reserve army when the macroeconomy crashes towards its trough, self-supporting employment is not an option. Relief in cash is all that keeps distress and hardship from the door.

Crosland stressed that the socialist is an instinctual Samaritan, committed on principle to 'the poor, the unfortunate, the "have-nots", and generally to those in need' (Crosland, 1956: 113). The socialist is a supraeconomic altruist who wants to render unstinting service to 'the deprived and generally the under-dog' (Crosland, 1975: 2). Yet that does not mean there is no element of multi-party exchange in his transfers. If the pensioner desperate for a cold-weather payment is not expected to add value in return, the position is different where the involuntarily unemployed go on benefits in order to search responsibly for the best paid, the most productive opening. Improving life chances as well as dispensing free prescriptions, there is clearly a sense in which the humanitarian impulse can be good business as well.

Transfers facilitate new starts and alleviate intolerable misery. Doing so, they also make the distribution of purchasing power less extreme. Income maintenance is at the interface between opportunity and outcome. Welfare is egalitarian. Selective provision of cash levels up the relatively deprived.

Crosland made need 'a social or cultural concept', a topic in context-dependent 'conventional necessities' (Crosland, 1956: 129) and not simply an emergency palliative for the desperate and the lost. Income maintenance was about interdependence and citizenship. It was about one-nation-building and financial approximation. It was about the uplifting of the forgotten in the direction of the social mean: 'What we can do is both raise the incomes of the poorest 20 per cent *relative* to those of the remaining 80 per cent and at the same time so markedly increase their *absolute* incomes that any person of compassionate common sense would agree that poverty had diminished' (Crosland, 1974a: 16).

Social casework and generous allowances narrow the gap. Benefits in kind make the nation more integrated and more just. Welfare is egalitarian, and it is the people's choice. Crosland was convinced that the British people shared his commitment to socialism as social services. The following gives the feel of his optimism and confidence: 'If people were asked "Do you think it more important to devote resources to developing electrical hair brushes or to providing sheltered housing for the elderly?", they would want to help the elderly. It is Labour's job to give them that choice' (Crosland, 1976: 14). Those words were written in 1976. Three years later, Mrs Thatcher was at No.10.

10.2.2   Outcome

Crosland was a leveller and an interventionist. In sympathy with the libertarians on the ethics and the economics of an equal start, he was persuaded as well by the socialists' insistence on managed endstates in preference to the cold-hearted indifference of free-market luck-of-the-draw. Crosland had little time for the primitive communism of the early Christians and the common-pot kibbutz: 'I am sure that a definite limit exists to the degree of equality which is desirable. We do not want complete equality of incomes, since extra responsibility and exceptional talent require and deserve a differential reward . . . I do not myself want to see *all* private education disappear . . . nor the Queen riding a bicycle . . . nor the House of Lords instantly abolished' (Crosland, 1956: 217). Crosland did not believe in the drab uniformity of the Cultural Revolution. What he did demand was a reasonable reduction in the divisive distance that was an unintended outcome of directionless automaticity.

Income was a high-profile prize. It was not a finish that Crosland took to be prima facie unjust. Different aptitudes and endowments merit different compensation since the payoff to the community is different as well: 'Superior talent deserves some rent of ability' (ibid.: 210). Differential rewards are the necessary stimulus to effort in a society that is not prepared to buy its equal pay at the cost of its rising prosperity: 'Some danger point must evidently exist at which equality begins to react really seriously on the supply of ability . . . and hence on economic growth' (ibid.: 213). The scatter will always be with us. Differences and differentials are the way the system works.

Incomes would never be the same; but that did not mean that great disparities should ride free merely because moderate disparities were the financial spur. Crosland, trained as an economist, knew the difference between the fat and the meat. Looking at his own British dispersion, he conceded that natural endowments might be reaping an excessive windfall: 'It seems unjust and unwise to reward or penalise people to quite such a prodigious extent for inherited characteristics' (ibid.: 212). Besides that, referring to the possibility that surplus remuneration could be masquerading as the minimum supply price, he admitted that the measured variance might not be a functional necessity: 'I am not convinced that the present 20:1 spread in post-tax incomes is really essential to incentive' (ibid.: 213). Much of the fat had been trimmed off by progressive tax. Much, however, was still alive and well and living in Weybridge.

Crosland had definite reservations both about the biological free gift and about the pecuniary drive. As a socialist, he must have been tempted to call for higher surtax rates and further chopping down. As a moderate, however, he was a man of minimax who did not want to stifle the growth that paid for welfare. In the end it was the moderate who won. The scope for higher direct tax, he concluded, had, in Britain at least, become very limited: 'It is clear that we have now reached saturation-point as far as taxation of income is concerned' (Crosland, 1950: 13).

Wealth, however, was a different matter. Douglas Jay, in *The Socialist Case*, had made property and its usufruct the core target in his non-Marxian revisionism: 'The traditional socialist belief that unearned incomes are the main removable cause of poverty and inequality is true and of dominating importance' (Jay, 1937: 237). Almost 20 years on, his fellow Gaitskellite had to report that even a Labour Government had not managed to terminate the inequity: 'The unequal distribution of property is still the major cause of inequalities in spending power' (Crosland, 1956: 296). It was assets far more than incomes that were streaming the nation into posh Bond Street and proletarian Grimestead Road.

Sociologically speaking, property was a cause of distance. The social barriers might be called a necessary evil if ownership still retained its historic function. Evolution, however, was calling the old logic into question. For one thing, the Schumpeterian corporation had no room for the Smithian capitalist who threw his whole being into his new combinations: 'To-day, over the bulk of industry, ownership and management have become divorced . . . The owner, from being an active entrepreneur, has become the familiar passive shareholder, neither in fact controlling his firm, nor capable of doing so' (ibid.: 352). Also, ethically suspect because it was cut off from current sacrifice, the asset stock was even more suspect where it was an inherited bequest and not the tangible proof of achievement, frugality, and the man's own hard work: 'This offends against the principle that every citizen should have an equal chance of attaining the highest rewards, and confers a differential advantage related solely to the accident of birth, and not in any way the "fruit of the man's own labour" ' (ibid.: 296). It is the Lockean labour justification through and through. Marx on surplus value contributes nothing to the delegitimation that to Crosland was solely the consequence of giant corporations and the family trust: 'Our classic conception of the class-struggle as being between the property-owning and the property-less class must go overboard' (Crosland, unpublished letter to P.M. Williams, 19 January 1941, in Crosland Papers, Box 3/26, Part I).

Crosland was concerned about functionless portfolios and intergenerational transmission. His response was to put forward proposals for higher estate duties (since windfall legacies are unearned accidents that inequitably distance the well-born from the asset-poor), an annual wealth tax (since a stock is as harmful as a flow to the esprit de corps of a nation that wants to be a Toynbee Hall) and a capital gains tax (since speculators are pirates who incur no marginal cost when their paper appreciates passively in the sense of hallowed Henry George). Unaffected by the concessions he had to make to the rent of ability and the incentive to effort, the fiscal engineering that he endorses would both level down the offensive peaks and generate new monies for public spending: 'Socialism and equality require a relative transfer of resources from private consumption to public expenditure' (Crosland, 1974a: 26).

The levelling down is likely to have been the more potent consideration. The new taxes which he recommends are seldom major revenue earners. Least of all are they likely to generate significant new funds when they are imposed at rates that are intentionally moderate, not at all confiscatory: 'The socialist aim is the removal of extremes of wealth, not the reduction of all to the lowest common standard' (Crosland, 1956: 307). Crosland did not want to bash the rich. He only wanted to make the haves a little bit more like the rest of us on the crowded old Clapham bus. The highest surtax rate in his time was 83 per cent for earned income, 98 per cent for interest and dividends. It might be the last straw for Adam Smith's accumulators and Schumpeter's entrepreneurs. Crosland's self-image and Crosland's policy recommendations did not always square.

Unexploited land is an especially interesting case of enablement through disempowerment. Many socialists have argued for a development levy on the basis that site value is merely a demand-determined surplus. Crosland had no objection to a fiscal levy on 'private value due to public causes' (Crosland, 1974d: iv). Even so, it was not his preferred solution: 'Taxation doesn't give you one of the advantages of public ownership, that is that ownership does enable [you] to plan much better' (Crosland, 1974b). Crosland at the end of his life was moving to the conclusion that the bounty of growth should be nationalised and State-run. Labour's moderates were not *as if* dead sheep. Sometimes even the middle ground does the unexpected and hits its target hard. Crosland, had he lived, would almost certainly have become Chancellor of the Exchequer in the next Callaghan reshuffle.

Just as income and wealth drew fellow citizens apart, so too did power. G.D.H. Cole, while still a guild socialist had made clear that he believed in the 'democratic administration of industry' (Cole, 1913: xvi) even as he believed in the representative House of Commons: 'Higher wages will not make less dreary or automatic the life of the worker who is subjected to bureaucratic expert control and divorced from all freedom and responsibility' (Cole, 1917: 53). Beatrice Webb, a Fabian elitist and an admirer of the Weberian bureaucracy, had reached rather a different verdict on the active involvement of muddle-headed Henry Dubb: 'We have little faith in the "average sensual man", we do not believe that he can do much more than describe his grievances, we do not believe that he can prescribe the remedies . . . We wish to introduce into politics the professional expert' (Webb, 1948: 120). Crosland was influenced both by the participative individualism of socialists like the Coles and by the leaderly paternalism of socialists like the Webbs. The result, not uncharacteristically, was a mix.

On the one hand Crosland accepted that the 'authoritarian power' of the boss, whether a capitalist profit recipient or a salaried corporate executive, was distasteful and alienating: 'I believe that social justice would be improved if it were to be still further diminished, and the power of the worker at the point of production correspondingly increased' (Crosland, 1956: 210). On the other hand he insisted that the workers themselves had no strong desire to go to meetings or pore through complicated balance-sheets: 'All experience shows that only a small minority of the population will wish to participate' (Crosland, 1968: 65). Only a small minority will reveal a preference for the Coles' self-government. The vast majority will cast its vote for the Webbs' prudent leaderliness because even the citizen in the street will find Schumpeter's first democracy a bit of a bore.

Crosland as a democrat knew that he had to respect the people's will. Crosland as a *social* democrat was, however, determined to make the exercise of power more diffuse and less concentrated. His proposals for greater equality in the way collective choices are made fall into two groups.

First, eschewing formal mechanisms like the Germans' statutory *Mitbestimmung*, he put his faith in casual conversation, union representation and 'enlightened personnel management' (Crosland, 1959: 226). Comprehensive schooling, shared wards and meritocratic authority will no doubt make it easier for master and servant to communicate openly in the one-class washroom or on the works' excursion. Welfare in that sense plays a useful role in making stiff industrial relations into amicable human relations that are less likely to fail.

Second, there is the State, the dependable dentist, the 'guardian of the public welfare' (Crosland, 1974a: 42). The State speaks for the nation as a whole whereas the miner or postman only speaks for himself: 'Workers' control is not the same as social control' (ibid.: 52). Syndicalism is *un*democratic, not least if the surplus the economy needs for investment is frittered away on wages and consumption. The government is a better bet. The equalisation of power balances the politicians and the bureaucrats against the capitalists and the managers. It does not require the average sensual citizen to become active and involved.

Culture, alongside income, wealth and power, was a fourth and final endstate which Crosland believed should not be allowed to put up walls. Here, as so often in his work, it was Tawney who had gone before. Tawney felt that the needed convergence in ideas, attitudes and modes of self-presentation presupposed a 'a large measure of economic equality' (Tawney, 1931: 43) and a high degree of overlap in real-world experience. It was a degree of intimacy that the State alone could ensure. Crosland took up and adapted Tawney's insights on the social engineering that was the precondition for the common sense of self.

The comprehensive school unifies a jumble of backgrounds. Public housing integrates and upgrades. Income maintenance raises up the relatively deprived. Asset taxation trims down the excessively privileged. Making it all happen is the State. Crosland was confident that power sharing through politics would lead to other-regarding laws that discriminate and restructure. One Nation would be the result. State intervention would be an agency that unites.

The State protects the Us by shutting down the grammar schools. Yet economic growth too can be an agency of national unity. Rising living standards, well-polished skills and full employment of labour mean that even the relatively deprived can secure a significant presence in the mass consumption market. The high savings of the rich suggest that exceptional earnings need not be showcased as conspicuous ostentation that would be a focus for envy and resentment. Cheaper alternatives are decent substitutes for the real thing: 'Bourbon is almost as palatable as Scotch, South African as Spanish sherry, and tinned as fresh asparagus' (Crosland, 1956: 283). The classlessness of *embourgeoisement* is in the air. The dynamic of capitalism is making every man a gentleman, as perceptive Alfred Marshall had predicted it would.

As the absolutes rise, Crosland hypothesized, so the relativities lose their perceived distinctiveness: 'Seen and felt disparities in personal living standards are a function not only of income-distribution, but also of the absolute level of average real income. That is, the higher the level of average income, the more equal is the visible pattern of consumption, and the stronger the subjective feeling of equal living standards . . . almost regardless of the distribution of total income' (ibid.: 278). Marx treats the capitalist economy as the cause of sub-cultural class identity. Crosland treats it as the solvent. Where the lower deciles can go on holiday to the Azores, the Matisse-owning deciles will not appear too deviant if they buy a yacht.

Crosland is not saying that the statistical distribution must move in step with the subjective perceptions. What he is saying is that the 'seen and felt', smiling on citizenship, is taking the sting out of the measured relativities that still survive: 'An unemployed family before the war, living in extreme poverty, resented bitterly the fact of inequality; a prosperous working-class family today, with a car, a refrigerator and a new house, is comparatively indifferent to the fact that others are wealthier still' (Crosland, 1960: 13). The workers today feel no urgent need to storm the Winter Palace now that their living standards are good and their Health Service good enough. Socialism has to move with the times. Crosland believed that the democratic Left had no choice but to follow the median citizen into lifestyle convergence. It had to hand over the confrontational and the zero-sum to the historians of ideas who make a study of the past.

The red flag and Soviet Russia cease to be at the heart of the socialist model. Frank Sinatra and the Fourth of July move in to take their place. Asa Briggs, expecting Keir Hardie and finding musak hedonism, concluded that the *Future* was a Valhalla of eating and drinking in which 'the sociology overshadows the Socialism': 'The Statue of Liberty and the super-market figure more prominently in Mr. Crosland's thinking than Marx's *Kapital* or Owen's New Lanark' (Briggs, 1956: 8). It is a clean, attractive, drip-dry socialism, imbued with the materialism of the leading capitalist nation and promising no pain, only gain, all the way into fraternity: 'Generally I have never been able to see why high consumption and brotherly love should be incompatible – why should not the brothers be affluent, and the love conducted under conditions of reasonable comfort?' (Crosland, 1955: 975). Equality need not be Edinburgh's Knox. Surfing the Internet can be the citizenship culture that binds.

Socialism has often attracted the austere and the self-denying. Collini describes their earnest Victorian ideal of an 'organized, ascetic, closely integrated community pursuing the noblest aims' as 'a kind of moral keep-fit camp' (Collini, 1979: 70). Whereas a Puritanical Tawney or a judgmental Galbraith could be sharply critical of Smith's 'trinkets and baubles' (Smith, 1776: I, 439), of Carlyle's 'Midas-eared Mammonisms' (Carlyle, 1843: 24), not so Anthony Crosland, who put so much emphasis on respect for persons that he was prepared to trust even quite uneducated consumers with the right to be the best judge of their own tastes and preferences. Demand-led supply is validated by the commitment to individualism. It is also the precondition for Crosland's socialism. Should eternal dissatisfaction be superseded by a hunger stilled, the Plymouth Brethren of Crosland's restrictive youth will claim a moral victory but public spending will languish, since there will no longer be a painless increment to pay for an improvement in social balance. Redistributive public spending must necessarily be inadequate in the absence of rapid growth: 'I do assert dogmatically that in a democracy low or zero growth wholly excludes the possibility' (Crosland, 1971a: 74). Socialism must necessarily be a near-impossibility in the absence of the consumer culture and the crowded shopping mall.

10.2.3 Policy and Performance

Socialism, like economics, is about who gets what: 'The fundamental divide between Left and Right, socialists and non-socialists, has always been about the distribution of wealth, power, and class status' (Crosland, 1975: 2). The market is one mechanism that socialists use to allocate the trophies. It is especially prominent in Crosland's validation of income, power and culture. The State is the proactive alternative that socialists employ when they want design and not the throw of the dice to reconsensualise the outcomes. It is the knight of last resort to which Crosland appeals for a moderate redistribution of wealth and for the perpetuation of uncompromising income tax. The knight seems not to have been given much socialism to do. At the level of opportunity the State was expected to be creative and engaged. At the level of outcome, however, it was more frequently to exchange than to authority that Crosland turned for a fair attribution of the rewards.

The crux is the chance. Not opposed to ex post tinkering once the race had been won, Crosland assumed nonetheless that it would be good starts and good rules that would in the long run bring about the greater levelling up: 'Equality of opportunity is the best guarantee of eventual equality of income' (Crosland, 1949: 11). His contention is that meaningful freedom *to* is the complement to tolerable freedom *from*. He believes it will lead to a beneficial clustering of fellow-citizens in the vicinity of the Hotelling mode.

As with Marshall, however, there is somehow a missing step. Putting the have-nots on the escalator does not necessarily mean that the gap will narrow between them and the haves who have had a head start. Genes, contacts, family aspirations and family assets may all protect an established dispersion. The past can remain the future even where surface self-presentation is made more standard-size by growth.

Room at the top is a further constraint. Should the supply of apex positions not keep pace with the supply of talented meritocrats, what is likely to happen is not so much an equalisation of prizes as the win/lose redistribution of a zero-sum pot. Those promised positional goods and then informed that the show is sold out will experience the disillusionment of the graduate who hawks coconuts on the beach. Those forced into the escalating waste of defensive qualifications will share with Hirsch the profound regret that 'the race gets longer for the same prize' (Hirsch, 1977: 67). Equality of opportunity does not mean, cannot mean, that every voter is automatically handed a marshal's baton. All it means is that those who can, do and those who cannot clean the streets in Grimestead South.

Crosland's statism is too polite to go the whole hog. Much of public spending is skewed towards the affluent and the vocal – an argument for means testing of university fees and selective discrimination in order to fine-tune the take-up. Much of business opportunity is by the same token hedged about with stereotypes, prejudices and biases – an argument for controls, quotas and access schemes to make the world of work ever more like a giant comprehensive. Welfare and capitalism by themselves are not enough to produce a substantive equalisation of condition. If equality of outcome is to mean more than merely clothes and music, then the State may have to become more regulatory, more directive, more prescriptive – more socialist – than is compatible with Crosland's tolerant middle road.

Crosland's proposals might not go far enough. Ironically they might also go too far. Crosland's socialism is absolutely dependent on the dynamic economy, at once the cause of a convergent consumer culture and the source of an expanding fiscal dividend. Rapid growth does not automatically lead to equality: for that, opportunity and welfare will be required as well. What is clear, Crosland said, is that a buoyant economy is the sine qua non. That is why the feedback of his socialism on his socialism is such an important topic. It is worrying that the overall impact is all but impossible to predict.

Some of Crosland's proposals are likely to have a favourable effect on growth: education builds up the stock of human capital and informal consultation is an investment in employee attachment at work. Others of his proposals are, however, more controversial. The comprehensive revolution might blunt the edge of skill. State regulation can distort information flows. Taxes can make market signals unreliable. What it all means is that sluggishness and stagnation can be the unwelcome result of doing too much. Slow growth is not conducive to the realisation of Crosland's objectives. It is a limit to equalisation that, ironically enough, can be the consequence of equalisation as well.

10.3   LABOUR'S LIBERALS

Collini says that Hobhouse was the servant of two masters: 'He wants both to have his cake of Socialism and to eat it in accordance with Liberal principles' (Collini, 1979: 134). His favourite colour may have been tartan but he was not alone. Marshall and Crosland, *in* Labour but not *of* Labour, shared with him the ideological middle ground where the borders are ill-defined, where changing circumstances forever redefine the parameters and where coexistence, as Churchill so strongly believed, is the only response to empirical evidence and the falsifiable hypothesis: 'No man can be a collectivist alone or an individualist alone. He must be both an individualist and a collectivist. The nature of man is a dual nature. The character of the organisation of human society is dual' (cited in Freeden, 1978: 161). The real world is thoroughly mixed. Even a grand theoretician has to live in the real world.

Labour at the time of the *Citizenship* and of the *Future* was still committed, through Sidney Webb's historic Clause 4, to the 'common ownership of the means of production, distribution and exchange'. It called itself a *labour* party despite the fact that leading figures like Gaitskell and Dalton were clearly not working class. It insisted that it was not a social democratic party, not a classless coalition for welfare and cohesion. It sang the 'Red Flag' to the tune of 'Der Tannenbaum' and regularly commemorated its capital-martyred dead. It received funding from the unions. Its Members of Parliament were often sponsored. Its roots were in the industrial manual grades who did not want to be pushed around. Its heart was in militancy, assertiveness, strikes and even corporatism – the reason why the one-nation Hobhouse refused to join: 'The trade union organization . . . is essentially sectional in its structure and has all the blindness and collective selfishness characteristic of sectionalism' (cited in Collini, 1979: 99). Hobhouse, a social market democrat, was a Liberal because Labour was labour. Marshall and Crosland, no less sympathetic to the ideal of a democratic social market, joined Labour because Labour was socialist. Socialism, they felt, could not be rejected merely because the party had its flaws.

Marshall and Crosland wanted to have their socialist cake but they also wanted to have their liberal principles. The result was a mixed perspective, 'more of a synthesis than a compromise' (Freeden, 1978: 116). Marshall and Crosland, caring but cautious, held a vision of the pragmatic centre that sought to combine the best of Left and Right. Marshall's hyphenated analytic is a useful macroscope with which to examine the complexities of the middle ground that they shared.

10.3.1 The Capitalist Market Economy

Both Marshall and Crosland had a strong attachment to the prosperity-enhancing mutuality of self-interested competitiveness. The market itself is a mode of self-development in so far as it makes the gain-seeking rational, independent and self-reliant. They become sensitive to others' wants since it is alertness and creativity that identify the sector where money is to be made. They become rich in self-control since it is deferred gratification and not impulsive indulgence that purposefully maximises the stream of goal-attainment. Most British people in the 1940s and 1950s believed in freedom within the law, efficiency, initiative, hard work, responsibility and choice. Marshall and Crosland would not have been prepared to go against the consensus even if they had thought that dictatorship and authoritarianism would necessarily improve the common man's standard of life.

Marshall and Crosland did not in any case see an economic argument for a national plan. Like Hayek and unlike the Webbs, they felt that the open society would better address the problem of dynamic and allocative efficiency while Russian totalitarianism or Schumpeterian direction would lead unavoidably to inertia and waste. Profit maximisation and enlightened selfishness make the butcher, the brewer and the baker the obedient servants of T.H. Green's 'common good'. They are the reason why even Henry Dubb can afford a semi-detached and a car.

The norm is private property and profit-seeking exchange. Only when the market fails should the government step in to show the experts how to run the shop.

Nationalisation is not the socialist utopia. The Fabians believed in the bureaucrats and Schumpeter predicted that the managers would be managed by the State. Crosland, on the other hand, saw no reason to upset the apple cart so long as it was so remarkably successful in meeting the community's needs:

'A higher working-class standard of living, more effective joint consultation, better labour relations, a proper use of economic resources, a wider diffusion of power, a greater degree of co-operation, or more social and economic equality – none of these now primarily require a large-scale change in ownership for their fulfilment' (Crosland, 1956: 475). The bias is in favour of the market. The market has made possible the progress that the community expects.

Socialisation was desirable in the case of public utilities like gas, water and power generation, public services like health, museums and libraries, infrastructure like the roads and the railways, commanding heights like iron, steel, coal and the Bank of England, where natural monopolies and uncredited externalities mean that private automaticity had a social or an ethical flaw that the post-capitalist alternative would be able to put right. By the time of Marshall and Crosland, however, the obvious industries had already fallen to the State. Further nationalisation should not be feared merely because residual Spencerians had an obsessive attachment to radical laissez-faire. On the other hand, there were no obvious boundaries that still had to be rolled back. Any rational redesign would have to be selective, microscopic and carefully considered.

The past should not be privatised nor the present enlarged. Banking, sugar and even the British Match Corporation could remain in private hands. Regulation, however, was indispensable. Crosland, a democrat and a politician, made clear that he was looking to Parliament to defend the public interest: 'No one today (except for a lunatic fringe in the United States) believes that the economy should be wholly unregulated and the pattern of production entirely dictated by market forces' (Crosland, 1962: 50).

Crosland praised the work of the Monopolies and Mergers Commission (which limited conspiracies in restraint of competition) and the Industrial Reorganisation Commission (which brokered mergers in order to secure cost-cutting efficiencies of scale). He was in favour of town and country planning and, like Marshall, an incomes policy. Child-labour laws and health and safety legislation were in. The minimum wage and compulsory strike ballots were, however, out. Neither Marshall nor Crosland put forward proposals extreme enough to force employers to pay a Hobhouse-like living wage or to prevent union leaders from behaving irresponsibly, as both social levellers knew that they might. For all that, regulation was essential on the middle ground. Ownership could remain capitalistic but the administration of the assets was to be under the scrutiny of the consensus and the democratic State.

10.3.2 The Democratic Polity

Crosland, in common with Marshall, was unwilling to cut corners on pluralism, accountability, consultation and the multi-party system: 'Underlying all our beliefs is a profound concern for liberty, democracy and the rule of law. We refuse to accept that socialism has any meaning except within a framework of liberty for the individual and representative democracy' (Crosland, 1975: 3). Socialism is about equality. One person, one vote is precisely what individualistic socialism must stand for and achieve.

The bias is for the unit actor, both in enterprise and in altruism. Liberty being an end as well as a means, the activist State should only be up and doing where individuals are seen to have left the job undone. Too much compulsion would weaken initiative, sap energy and violate the core value of human worth. Too little intervention would, however, create social problems of its own: just as no one would want to live forever in the unfreedom of the barrack room, so no one will say that the nation is maximising its gains from mutual dependence where contracts are unenforceable, borders undefended, talents underdeveloped and distress unrelieved. Trapped between too little and too much, between the Cobdenites and the Webbs, the society has to choose a middle course. Democracy is the sole reliable procedure that gives the ordinary citizen the chance to reveal the preferences that mark him out as unique.

Democracy charts the course. Crucially, however, it is democracy in the sense of Schumpeter's *second* theory upon which both Marshall and Crosland relied. Neither put much faith in works councils or wanted the client to name the welfare that best suited his needs: social rights, Marshall warned, are 'not designed for the exercise of power' (Marshall, 1969: 141). What Marshall and Crosland expected was the freedom of speech ex ante, the chance to approve or reject ex post. In between there was to be a realm of discretion where the leaders tease out the social interest because that is what the leaders are there to do.

The social interest, as Hobhouse explains it, is the interest of an embedding community that transcends the cut-off self: 'A right is nothing but what the good of society makes it . . . The curtailment of the liberties of some, then, may mean the maximum of liberty upon the whole' (cited in Collini, 1979: 69, 70). The State must be responsive to the whole and not just to the parts – the reason why Crosland's State has a moral licence to shut down the darned grammar schools. The State must also do what is right for the higher self without being seduced by the easy win – the reason why Green's State legislates against drunkenness in order to protect the backslider from his own weak will. In areas such as spillover education or deficient self-control, the State has a duty to be parental since the citizens must be forced to be free. The re-election of the rulers is the proof that the democracy correctly prescribed the medicine that made the patient feel good.

Both Marshall and Crosland trusted the State. Implicit in their parliamentary socialism is the idea of incorruptible politicians and well-informed bureaucrats serving as faithful agents for their principals and putting the public good above their own private gain. Government, as in the world-view of Weber and Schumpeter, has its professional ethic and its moral code. An unwritten but binding constitution ensures that even the leaders will be self-policed thanks to multi-period standards and will obey the rules of the game.

The capitalist class does not sabotage the sensitivity of the system. The working class as well as the rich has a fair chance to stamp its will upon the laws. Intimidation, vote rigging, favour buying, peerages and beerages are anathema to our spokesmen in government. The parties are not special pleaders. Consultation is not cynical window dressing. Public choice and its vote motive are for foreigners who do not understand that the State *is* the people and is not the enemy. In Britain at any rate, public-spiritedness is all around.

The government is bound by the social contract. The citizens too are bound. Marshall in so many words, Crosland more subtly, took it for granted that decent people would want to do their share.

Society is a matrix of rights and duties. It is an extended contract within which taking and giving mean very much the same. The dole is not a serious threat to work: socialised citizens know that assiduity and thrift are preferable to laziness and sponging. Industrial relations on balance are peace and not war: bosses and workers alike take a personal pride in a fair day's work for a fair day's wage. Marshall and Crosland may have been too confident but at least they were too confident about all the right things. Citizens have a Lockean contract with their democratic State. Circumscribing that contract and giving it legitimacy are the Smithian moral sentiments and the Durkheimean social compact that the social partners have made with one another.

10.3.3 The Welfare State

Crosland redefined socialism to mean the unifying equality of status and the humanitarian relief of need (Crosland, 1956: 112). Economic allocation and economic growth, by and large, can be left to business. Social disharmony and material deprivation, unrealised capacities and hard-core destitution are, on the other hand, the inalienable responsibilities of a morally-minded government that spends freely on justice and interdependence.

Welfare spending both succours the residual and releases human potential. On the one hand it is the safety-net of last resort when discretionary philanthropy proves inadequate. On the other hand it is the removal of artificial obstacles, socioeconomic as well as legal, that prevent the upwardly mobile from maximising their value added: 'The function of the State is to secure conditions upon which its citizens are able to win by their own efforts all that is necessary to a full civic efficiency' (Hobhouse, 1911a: 76). The betterment is cumulative. As the less privileged become better integrated into the mainstream, they become better placed to pay back the start-up capital that was advanced to them in the name of common humanity. Welfare is a shrewd business investment for Britannia Inc that sows and reaps. Socialism, like Liberalism, is not man *versus* the State. Rather, it is man *together with* the State for the benefit and the development of all.

Marshall and Crosland were Labour's Liberals because they saw socialism as social-ism and progress as comradely good-neighbourliness. Many on the Left have been attracted by the grand inevitabilities of determinism, necessitarianism and historicism, by the confident predictions of Marx, Darwin and Galbraith. Marshall and Crosland, less certain than Hegel or even than Schumpeter, preferred to build their world-view around free will, abstract principles, conscious choice and normative commitment. It is a characteristic of the mixed perspective that man is seen as both active and passive, as both the author and the agent: 'The theory that social structures interact with rather than determine individual character is fundamental to ethical socialism' (Dennis and Halsey, 1988: 239). Cultural values precede current choices. It is conservative socialism, sociological socialism. It is incremental socialism that cannot make a revolution without at the same time destroying the roots that sustain it.

Labour's Liberals were not rootless mould-makers *ab initio*. They were the products of an old country that had a rich tradition of membership and custom. Their socialism – gradual adaptation, political piecemealism, a fair chance for all, a compromise between innovation and affirmation – is the national character of an in-between country that had practised *Manchestertum* in Manchester but also cooperation in Rochdale, self-help through the friendly societies, voluntary work through the Charity Organisation Society, fellowship at Dunkirk. The Britishness, even the patriotism, cannot be emphasised too strongly. The British middle is not Muscovite cosmopolitanism. It is the clear image of home.

It is also the religious values which even atheists like Marshall and Crosland had absorbed when they were young. Cobbett took his Church of *England* as literally as Adam Smith took his Wealth of *Nations*. The church is a single communion, a living organism. The church is a classless society in which all are equal in the sight of God. The church is a compassionate community which praises the altruistic Samaritan because he did what was right. The church is Marshallian rights welded into Marshallian duties. Christianity to the British middle meant not just monastic withdrawal and biblical exegesis. It also meant chiropodists in geriatric wards and non-contributory family benefits because no child should grow up dirty, hungry or afraid.

Marshall and Crosland grew up English and grew up Christian. Their combination of enterprise, democracy and welfare (of economics, politics and social policy) would have evoked resonances in the pubs and the common rooms of a going Jerusalem that had continuous experience of markets with values. Whether it can travel is another matter. Russian new money in the normless 1990s will have read Labour's Liberals with almost total incomprehension. What will globalisation and dynamism mean for a world-view which is an idealisation of the remembered, the socialised and the shared?

11. Titmuss: welfare as good conduct

The subject of this chapter is the duty to care. It is an essay in social economics in the tautological sense that resources must be allocated and choices have to be made. Yet it is also an essay in ethical values, in functioning communities and the right relationships upon which they depend. Richard Titmuss was an interventionist who wanted the State to provide a dense and comprehensive network of welfare services available to all on the basis of a citizenship shared. He was also a believer in normative holism who wanted the State not just to correct a market failure but also to actualise a consensual striving. To Titmuss the welfare State was another name for good conduct, for neighbourliness and the freedom to share. His philosophy of fraternalism, neither the private vice of cupidity nor the arrogant bossiness of all-knowing Webbs who know best, is a middle ground with a mission. It cannot be captured by the stark Hayekian polarities of liberty versus collectivism.

The chapter is divided into three sections. Section 11.1, 'The evolution of the vision', traces Titmuss's development as a political sociologist of democracy beyond exchange from the inadequate birth rates of the stunted 1930s to the solidarity through service of the Second World War, to the demand for taxes and the gift of blood that typified generous Britain at its post-Attlee summit. Section 11.2, 'The intellectual system', guessing at the completed puzzle that Titmuss himself never fully assembled, argues that Titmuss on welfare is the mix of five core and interdependent concepts: consensus, integration, dignity, compensation and expediency. Section 11.3, 'Good conduct and political economy', asks whether socialism or capitalism is more in tune with the statism by consent of Titmuss's responsible society. It concludes that both economic orders stand to make a valuable gain. Titmuss's Categorical Imperative is a plus-sum world in which the only victim is the moral vacuum that is crushed under foot.

11.1 THE EVOLUTION OF THE VISION

The approach is consistent. Titmuss was Titmuss even in the four books that he wrote before the Blitz. The theme is the stranger-gift. Titmuss never wrote on any subject not related in some way to the unilateral transfer made because altruism makes us family, each with all.

11.1.1   Poverty and Population

Richard Titmuss was born on 16 October 1907. His father had been a small
farmer who had moved from Bedfordshire to London when his farm was
broken up under the Government's plan to resettle soldiers after the First
World War. Morris Titmuss tried his hand at haulage. His business failed. By
1926 he was dead. A drinking problem and a wife who felt she had married
beneath herself must have contributed to his early death. One consequence
was that Richard, still not yet 20, became the family breadwinner. His mother
was dependent on him, financially and emotionally, until her own death in
1972.

Richard left school in 1921. He attended a six-month course in bookkeep-
ing and then entered Standard Telephones and Cables Ltd as an office boy. He
moved on to the post of clerk at County Fire Insurance Office, becoming a
London Inspector in 1939 when he was only 32. Insurance brought him into
contact with real people who had lost everything and with the investment policies of giant institutionals. It gave him an on-the-job education in the 'careful
computation of statistics about social groups and life-chances' (Oakley, 2001:
12). It also taught him how it felt to lose an entitlement. When he left County
Fire in 1942, 35 years of age, he lost 16 years of non-transferable pension
contributions.

Titmuss in the 1920s joined the Hendon Young Liberals and also practised
public speaking at St Bride's Institute. Few people in the 1930s (the age of the
dictators, of mass unemployment, of Keynes's *General Theory*, Macmillan's
Middle Way, the Webbs' *Soviet Communism: A New Civilisation*) could have
failed to come under the spell of politics. Besides that, Titmuss in 1937
married Kathleen (Kay) Miller. Not educated beyond a secretarial course but
with a social conscience, she was working in London clubs for the unemployed. She told Richard what she had seen. He said later that it had helped
him to visualise the human distress of threadbare people who were looking
actively for jobs at a time when there were not enough jobs to go around. The
story of Richard and Kay is told by Ann Oakley in *Man and Wife* (Oakley,
1996), her attempt to trace out the early years of her parents' marriage.

Titmuss in 1937 joined the Eugenics Society. He was still a member at the
time of his death. This unusual organisation, not well-known today, was in its
time prominent and influential. It had been set up to discuss the subject of
genetic inheritance, including the intergenerational transmission of defective
traits. Titmuss, working in his spare time while employed at County Fire,
presented papers to the Society, published in its journal, served as editor of its
Eugenics Review and went on the Council of the Society. Contacts were an
unexpected benefit. Among the people he met through the Society were David
Glass, Lord Horder, Eva Hubback and Alexander Carr-Saunders.

It was in this period that Titmuss's first four books were written. Their theme is good conduct to see off the evils of depopulation and war.

Poverty and Population was published by Macmillan in 1938. The fact that Lord Horder, physician to the royal family, contributed the preface must have been a strong recommendation. So was the subject. Titmuss said that his book was an investigation into 'social waste'. By waste he meant people. The British population was declining. One reason was premature death that was claiming 50 000 British lives a year. Involuntary unemployment was visible on every street-corner in the demand-deficient Depression years that Titmuss much later praised the Keynesians for having made a thing of the past: 'Improved health, better nutrition, lessening of class consciousness, the reduction of gross poverty, fewer inequalities – owe more to Full Employment than anything else or all the social services' (Titmuss, unpublished lecture, n.d., in Titmuss Papers, Box 3/370). War, however, was on the horizon and the nation needed its citizens.

Titmuss in his book showed that 'war is always dysgenic' (Titmuss, 1938: 16). It is, clearly enough, the males most fitted to survive who are the most likely to be sent to the Front and be killed. The loss of top-quality material is a serious threat to a nation that wishes to maximise its economic and military potential. Some comfort may be found, however, in the knowledge that valuable genes remain unexploited in the social residuum that has not yet been tapped. Many of the most promising specimens were not being given the chance to develop their inborn endowments because of nurture that choked off the flowering of the seeds that nature had supplied: 'Satisfactory diet allows valuable hereditary qualities to assert themselves' (ibid.: 88). Humanitarian reform, morally an end in itself, would expand the public good of talent and capacity. Better housing and medical care would be an investment in collective performance, economic and military. We as a nation want the spillover. We as a nation must contribute to the cost.

In 1939, on the eve of war, Titmuss's Penguin Special on *Our Food Problem* appeared. His second book, it was written with F. Le Gros Clark. As before, it was about malnutrition, social class and national defence. It argued that, in peace or at war, Britain needs a 'lively and vigorous population' (Titmuss and Clark, 1939: 91–2).

Physical stamina is a part of the nation's production function. Inadequate calcium causes pregnant women to bear sickly children. A vitamin deficiency means a labour force that cannot do its best. Tawney, studying poverty at the Ratan Tata Foundation, had grasped what the vicious circle meant: 'Bad wages produce bad work' (Tawney, 1914: 113). *Our Food Problem*, recognising with Tawney that it is a wonderful thing when 'the bent stalk gradually straightens, the crushed leaves unfold' (ibid.: 101), therefore made a strong case for a social income paid proudly in kind. Staple foodstuffs should be heavily subsidised. All children should be given free school meals, a pint of milk and an apple a day.

Physical stamina is a part of the nation's vigour. Yet social stamina too is an investment in a going concern. Workers will strain every sinew and soldiers give their life on the field provided that, in their own estimation, 'society is organically constructed to serve the common good of all' (Titmuss and Clark, 1939: 94). They will be less willing to make a real commitment where they believe that the rich and powerful are eating up the lion's share of the gains: 'If there is one thing few men can stomach to-day, it is the growing divergence of interest between rich and poor and the suspected inequality of sacrifice' (ibid.). Diet is an ingredient in national welfare since it makes the citizens strong. Equality is the social equivalent of nutritious food since division is the corrosive that prevents the gears from meshing with the whole.

Parents Revolt (jointly authored with Kay) was published in 1942. Its subject was the Europe-wide decline in the birth rate and, specifically, the fact that the British population was not reproducing itself. Parents were in revolt against their country. The middle classes especially had selfishly defaulted on their debt: 'If the common people had restricted the size of their families in the same way as the well-to-do, Hitler's *Wehrmacht* might by now be goose-step-ping down Whitehall' (Titmuss and Titmuss, 1942: 18).

Birth control was depriving Britain of its Britons. The effect would be a threat to survival: there would ultimately be too few workers, too few soldiers, too few consumers, too few taxpayers, to support social costs like old-age dependency and to keep the economies of size in business. The cause would be an internal contradiction every bit as real as Marx's proletarian unrest or the anarchy of production: *turpe lucrum*'s me-first rapacity makes post-Malthusian couples unwilling to contribute their share. Thus does the rootless economy in the end depopulate the collectivity that embeds it: 'Capitalism is a biological failure' (ibid.: 116). It was at about this time that Titmuss left the Liberals and joined the Labour Party. Always a moderate centrist, he probably felt that Labour would nationalise the commanding industries and do more to strengthen the ties of affinity. The Liberals, social reformers though Lloyd George and Asquith had made them, possibly remained too Gladstonian for the metaphysics of a whole that was more than the sum of its parts.

It is striking just how directly *Parents Revolt* sought to address the norma-tive disequilibrium of narrow-horizoned catallactics. As before, it contained an attack on absolute deprivation which, like birth control, kills the people and shrinks the nation. Poverty relief is an investment in all of us, not just in the poor. Mainly, however, the book was about competitive, possessive commer-cialism which makes children an 'expensive liability' (ibid.: 67) in a society where people are judged more by their conspicuous consumption than by their role-playing for the group. Tawney had led the way by deploring the sickness of a marketing culture in which the 'economic egotism which snatches private gains at the cost of neighbours or the community' (Tawney, 1937: 190) was leaving little room for the higher moral worth of cohesion, commitment and the 'bond of service to a common purpose' (Tawney, 1921: 79). *Parents Revolt* was in the spirit of Tawney's communitarian socialism that embedded rights in the matrix of our shared place in the sun.

The problem, the book declared, was the sickness of an acquisitive society and the need for self-actualisation through good conduct: 'We have got to progressively eradicate the profit-motive from society; we have got to go forward to a real economic democracy based on co-operative values and we must offer something more compelling than the goal of economic prosperity' (Titmuss and Titmuss, 1942: 112). Parents had already shown that they were capable of altruism. Limiting family size, they were already concentrating their resources on a smaller number of better-provided-for children. It was at the social level that their altruism was not manifesting itself. Exchange was in the air. Citizens saw no reason to donate unremunerated fertility in order to enrich the body politick as a single entity *sui generis*.

What is needed, Titmuss says, is 'a feeling of nationality, a sense of belonging to a national group' (ibid.: 92). This identification of the individual with the people would be the ultimate prophylactic against contraception: 'The individual *must not only feel but know* that he is working and living not for himself alone but for the community' (ibid.: 120). For purposive breeding to be seen as the privilege of stewardship, there must come into being a new set of values and a new set of institutions: 'We must look at things in terms of men and women, and not in terms of money' (ibid.: 13). That in turn presupposes an ambitious agenda for reform. *Parents Revolt* concentrates on the welfare sector: it calls for family allowances in order to acknowledge the group-good externality. Implicit in the discussion is, however, the need for a more cooperative economic order that does not rely on blinkered voracity to the exclusion of the citizenship drive.

Birth, Poverty and Wealth, published in 1943, was the fourth and last of Titmuss's four early books. As in all of his early work, he recognised that genes could account for much of origins and destinations. What he warned against once more in 1943 was the weeding out of good genes by man-made contingencies, largely preventable: 'In all the major causes of death in this country there is little or no evidence of *important* hereditary factors' (Titmuss, 1943: 68). Although a genetic disposition to cancer is inherited, tuberculosis and rickets are a function of the environment that can be corrected through public housing.

Titmuss in *Birth, Poverty and Wealth* showed that the mortality rate of the lowest occupational group exceeded that of the highest occupational group by 161 per cent (ibid.: 33). The gap was even greater in the more depressed North. Native predispositions could not have accounted for so great a dispersion. Chronic malnutrition, unhygienic drinking water and slum doctoring must have played a major part. The result was that the nation as a whole was losing out on a valuable asset that it could not afford to neglect: 'Wealth opens the door of opportunity while poverty keeps it closed from the cradle to the grave' (ibid.: 15). The Eugenics Society supported publication of the book. The Leverhulme Trust had funded the research through a small grant. Through his books and papers Titmuss, still at County Fire, was making a name for himself. He had become a consultant to the Ministry of Education and the Ministry of Health. He was also, from 1941, advising the Ministry of Economic Warfare on the effect of bombing on German morale.

11.1.2 War as Good Conduct

Titmuss in the Second World War was exempted from conscription because of his occupation as an insurance inspector. He was visiting bombed-out houses and talking to the victims of a catastrophe that was a non-discriminating plague. All citizens are at war. Some citizens lose their homes. Private insurance alleviates the burden. Still the collectivity must owe something to those random unfortunates who have been disproportionately afflicted. A social organicist, Titmuss as an insurance inspector is likely to have sensed that the costs of the national emergency could not be allowed to lie where they fell.

The British Government had decided that the civil history of the Second World War should be written while the events were still unfolding. It assembled a team of historians under the Cabinet Office. The leader of the group was Keith (later Sir Keith) Hancock, an economic historian at Birmingham University. Eva Hubback, Principal of Morley College, had met Titmuss in the Eugenics Society. She suggested his name for the volume on the social services. County Fire denied him unpaid leave and, in 1942, he resigned. He remained in the Cabinet Office until 1949.

Titmuss's monumental book, *Problems of Social Policy*, was published in 1950. Meticulously documented and carefully researched, its conclusion was that a shared contingency evokes a collective response. War pools resources because the risks too are pooled: the means test for personal failure is clearly unacceptable where rich and poor, the East End and Buckingham Palace and Titmuss in Pimlico himself were equally exposed to one enemy from without. War means discipline, politicisation, leadership, forbearance that is 'only tolerable if – and only if – social inequalities are not intolerable' (Titmuss, 1963: 85). War is a school for collective solidarity to the extent that it allows discrete cells the opportunity 'to play an active part within the community', the chance to feel that purposeful work serves the common cause: 'The civilian war of 1939–45, with its many opportunities for service in civil defence and other schemes, also helped to satisfy an often inarticulate need; the need to be a wanted member of society' (Titmuss, 1950: 347). War revealed the low physical standards of rejected conscripts: it showed that inadequate access to nutrition and shelter could be a negative externality that spread the contagion of an inability to protect the nation as a whole. War, in short, was the academy that educated the consensus in the value of integration and equality. It was not an accident but the proof of the thesis that free school milk was introduced within a week of the Dunkirk evacuation.

War to Titmuss was always the single most important cause of the British welfare State: 'War, as a total experience, has done more to shape the evolution of social policy in Britain – and to greatly extend the role of Government – than any other major historical set of causal agents' (Titmuss, unpublished lecture, 1970, in Titmuss Papers, Box 3/370). It was 'the war-warmed impulse of people for a more generous society' that had led directly to Bevan's National Health Service, to Attlee's cradle-to-grave precisely because We are We and domestic division, like the Hun at the gate, threatened our ability as a network memory to survive: 'If dangers were to be shared, then resources should also be shared' (Titmuss, 1950: 508).

War was the swing to the left. Peace was to prove the greater problem. In 1950, Titmuss seemed to think that welfare as good conduct was a ratchet *accompli*. By 1970, the Huns replaced by the monetarists and even Labour in two minds about the high cost of inclusion, he was not so sure: 'In the absence of war and the solidarities, the compassion, the "Garments of Hardship" (Winston Churchill), what takes its place as an ethical driving force?' (Titmuss, unpublished lecture, 1970, in Titmuss Papers, Box 3/370). By 1970 he was beginning to think that the self-reinforcing momentum of the comprehensive schools and the Rawlsian vested interest in a free National Health might not be enough to keep the dynamic alive. The stockbroker comes in. The social worker goes out. *Problems of Social Policy* seems to imply that an accident brought about good conduct. By 1970, Titmuss was beginning to fear that business as usual could all too easily mean bad conduct again.

While working on the *Problems*, Titmuss wrote (with Fred Grundy, Medical Officer of Health) the *Report on Luton*. It had been commissioned by the Luton Borough Council and was published in 1945. The *Report* made use of a sample survey of the Luton population to identify salient deficiencies in areas of infrastructure such as housing and health. Venturing from fact gathering into policy, the authors called upon the State to spend freely in order to transform the market's failure into a de facto citizenship right: 'Policy should not be determined mainly according to money resources. It may, indeed, be argued that if we cannot afford these services we must have them; if we could easily afford them, many would be unnecessary' (Titmuss and Grundy, 1945: 125). The *Report on Luton* was in the spirit of the Beveridge Report on Social Insurance which in 1942 had exhorted the nation to declare war on the five 'giants' of Want, Disease, Ignorance, Squalor and, recalling the 1930s, Idleness 'which destroys wealth and corrupts men, whether they are well fed or not' (Beveridge, 1942: 170). Coincidentally the new Labour Government came into office in the same year that Titmuss was spotlighting the shortcomings in Luton that only the State could put right. The employment guarantee, the core nationalisation, the National Health all became part of the British landscape while Titmuss was still a civil servant completing his contribution to Hancock's 30-volume series.

11.1.3 Community and State

By 1949 *Problems of Social Policy* was on its way to the publisher and Titmuss had to decide what to do next. He was 42, working (as Deputy Director) with Jerry Morris in the Social Medicine Research Unit of the Medical Research Council. All Souls' or Nuffield were possibilities although he was acutely aware of his general lack of university culture. In 1950, however, new professorships were being created in Birmingham and London to provide intellectual support for the welfare services that had so recently been expanded. Titmuss in 1950 was appointed to the new Chair of Social Administration at the London School of Economics. He was supported by Hancock and well respected by T.H. Marshall, Professor of Social Institutions. The Director of the LSE, Sir Alexander Carr-Saunders, knew Titmuss from the Eugenics Society. The discipline was a new one. Not only could Titmuss shape it as he liked once he was appointed, there were few other strong contenders for the post.

Titmuss took over a staff of 13 social administrators, mainly social workers. Their status in the School was low as they were believed to be mere practitioners, *how to* tradesmen unable to handle an academic *why*. At first they resented their new professor who had no background in casework and no personal experience of clients trapped in the paperchase. He won their support through his obvious commitment to real people in need of no-fault sympathy and support. Titmuss set up the first course in Britain in development administration and pushed through innovations such as the admission of older applicants without formal qualifications. He had left school at 14 and still had no degree himself. Later he was to be awarded five honorary doctorates. These were from the University of Wales (1959), Edinburgh (1962), Toronto (1964), Chicago (1970) and Brunel (1971). He was made a Commander of the Order of the Dannebrog in Denmark in 1965 and a Fellow of the British Academy in

1972. He accepted a CBE in 1966 but turned down the life peerage that he was offered by Harold Wilson. Moderate social distance was acceptable to him: his daughter Ann (Oakley) (born 1944) was educated at a direct grant school and later at Oxford. Too much social distance, however, creates caste distinctions and should be avoided.

The welfare State was already in place in 1950. What it lacked was a theoretical schema, a set of legitimations and justifications that would build on Tawney's *Equality* of 1931 and Durbin's *Democratic Socialism* of 1940 but would also make a practical contribution to British reconstruction and current debate. The Conservative, Liberal and Labour parties were in broad agreement about the institutions. What were missing were the reasons. As is so frequently the case in public policy, events had moved faster than the explanations that made sense of them. Titmuss provided the explanations. He had to be original. There was not much authority in 1950 on which he could build.

Titmuss dominated the new discipline from 1950 until his death from cancer on 6 April 1973, aged 65. He worked closely with Brian Abel-Smith, Tony Lynes and Peter Townsend, trained followers and successors like Della Nevitt and John Greve, and served as a kingmaker who was able to keep his tradition alive. What is curious is what happened then. Little more than a decade after his death his books, not hallowed as classics and canonical contributions, quietly went out of print. Students learned only fragments of his ideas, often from secondary sources.

One reason for the decline in interest is that his disciples sank into applied research and let the broad vision slip. Another reason is that students of social policy wanted tools they could use rather than the ethical uplift of Green and Hobhouse who had sought both to save the body and to protect the soul. The monetarist counterrevolution and supply-side economics called into question the economic viability of social rights, not subjected to a cost–benefit appraisal, that crowd out private investment and pay for self-inflicted sloth. New Labour, pragmatic and prudent, showed less interest in remoralising the unequal society than in making the economic market function with ever greater efficiency. By the 1980s, the Titmuss constructs were going into an eclipse which is in sharp contrast to the status they enjoyed in the 1950s, the 1960s and the 1970s. In that period – optimistic, fully employed, consensual, Butskellite, rapidly growing – to say social policy was, in Britain, to say Titmuss.

Titmuss was active not just inside the LSE but in the nation as a whole. He advised the Labour Party on policy issues such as superannuation. He was a member of the One Parent Family (Finer) Committee. He served on the Community Relations Commission (1965–71) and the Supplementary Benefits Commission (1966–73). Abroad, he was a consultant to the governments of Mauritius (on income transfers and population containment) and Tanganyika (on healthcare and public policy). The two reports were published as *Social Policies and Population Growth in Mauritius* (1961) and *The Health Services of Tanganyika* (1964).

Most of all, however, it is the books and the papers which in the long run will be Titmuss's greatest legacy to social thought. That is why it is so frustrating that the threads were never woven together into a web. Titmuss, publishing widely as he did, never produced the sweeping overview that would unify his disparate insights in a general theory of welfare. There is no single volume that can be set alongside Schumpeter's *Capitalism*, Marshall's *Citizenship*, Crosland's *Future* or Galbraith's *New Industrial State*. After his death Kay and Brian Abel-Smith published some of his lecture notes as *Social Policy* (1974). The book clarifies some of the hidden links despite the fact that it was never polished or refined. Yet it is not the missing textbook that Titmuss never wrote. Perhaps he did not want to write it. Perhaps he died before he felt ready to draw together the whole of his synthesis.

Titmuss at the LSE was the author of seven books. The first of these (written with Brian Abel-Smith) was *The Cost of the National Health Service* (1956). This was a largely statistical account of what the Health Service was costing the nation, together with an economist's reminder that it was a relatively inexpensive way to deliver medical care.

After that there was *Essays on 'The Welfare State'*. First published in 1958 and reprinted in 1963 with the text of Titmuss's Fabian Tract on *The Irresponsible Society* (1959), it is a collection of loosely connected articles on topics such as health, pensions, war and industrialisation. The book is particularly interesting since it includes the Eleanor Rathbone Memorial Lecture of 1955 on 'The Social Division of Welfare'. In that lecture Titmuss recommended that social welfare should be seen not as the nation's only subsidy but as one among three systems of public support: the other two were fiscal welfare (such as mortgage-interest relief or tax-free lump sums) and occupational welfare (well-known fringe benefits being company cars, company pensions and private healthcare). Some will feel that Titmuss should have added to his list the valuable categories of microeconomic welfare (grants to declining areas, child-labour restrictions, health and safety legislation) and intra-family welfare (including the contribution made by women to the network of care even at the cost of their own careers and financial independence). Society is a labyrinth of gifts and transfers. It is never easy to know when an act of socialism is being committed, or by whom.

Social Policies and Population Growth in Mauritius appeared in 1961. It was written with Brian Abel-Smith and Tony Lynes. The background was geometric birth rates and high unemployment in a less developed country.

James Meade was making proposals to accelerate economic growth and the aid agencies were insisting on family planning. Titmuss took as his primary focus the incentive effect of selective welfare. An augmented pension should be paid to a woman of 65 who had given birth to no more than three live-born children: the benefit would tempt money-minded mothers to call a halt. No family allowance should be offered to a couple for their first or second child: the cost would discourage young people from burdening their nation with more mouths to feed. The use of contraception was not to be the precondition for support: 'The tolerances and courtesies of a liberal society must be prac- tised by all. The illiberalities of some must not thrive on the courtesies of others' (Titmuss *et al.*, 1961: 187). What was to be the precondition was the collection of information: to be eligible for benefits the parents had to show that they had a basic knowledge of what prevention could do. Economics teaches that money talks. Titmuss advised the Mauritians that welfare too can appeal to the same narrow horizons to bend private interest to the collective need.

In 1962, there was *Income Distribution and Social Change*. This is an empirical social scientist's tour de force. Titmuss displays a comprehensive knowledge of tax tables, tax shelters, educational covenants, separate assess- ments, fringe benefits, family trusts, unequal incomes and avoidable contri- butions. He does not justify his investigation by saying that inequality is discordant, high incomes unfair. What he does is to show that, more than a decade into the welfare State, the rich had found ways to shield their concen- trated wealth and pass on their inherited privilege.

In 1964, Titmuss (with Abel-Smith and other colleagues) published *The Health Services of Tanganyika*. Of course its theme was doctoring. What a poor country desperately needed was detailed advice on how to set up an inte- grated national health service that would deliver preventive and curative care through a coordinated network extending upwards from semi-trained auxil- iaries in the villages to high-standard teaching hospitals at the top. Yet its theme was also the need for locality, identification and *social* growth that is more than productive efficiency alone. As Titmuss wrote: 'We want to see a health service developing which will not be separate and aloof from the life of the nation but an expression and reinforcement of national unity' (Titmuss *et al.*, 1964: 214).

In 1968 came *Commitment to Welfare*. Once again a collection of occa- sional pieces (often demand-led by invitations to speak), the book covers issues such as the nature of social administration, the scope for community care, redistribution in national insurance and the role of the family doctor. Many of the essays in the book are good illustrations of Titmuss's propensity to juxtapose the inefficiencies and inequities of the (American) market to the smooth functioning and generosity of the (British) State. Unlike Marshall and even Galbraith, he never accepted that the market could complement welfare and need not be its enemy.

At the end there was the masterpiece. *The Gift Relationship* was first published in 1970. It was reprinted in 1997 with five new assessments by social scientists who had grown up in its shadow.

The Gift Relationship is a remarkable attempt to combine factual evidence with moral philosophy. Taking as its point of departure a Manichean bipolarity in which 'the grant, or the gift or unilateral transfer . . . is the distinguishing mark of the social', 'exchange or bilateral transfer . . . the mark of the economic' (Titmuss, 1968: 22), it presents empirical evidence to show that, at least in the case of blood, unremunerated voluntarism delivers better results than does the self-seeking quid pro quo. In communist Russia and capitalist America supply is a function of cash. The consequence is infected blood from Skid Row drug addicts, prohibitive expense (Soviet donors demanding as much as half a month's pay for one session), operations 'postponed daily' (ibid.: 149) because of lack of blood. In middle-ground Britain, on the other hand, good-quality blood is available free of consumer charge precisely because 'the conscience of obligation' (Titmuss, 1970: 159) inspires well-integrated citizens to do their part. Altruism and social responsibility get the job done. Egotism and the cash nexus leave the nation in the lurch. The statistics speak with a single voice. Private virtues, not private vices, are the more effective means of supplying the textbook economist's public good.

Community-spirited men and women, a representative cross-section and not an impoverished 'blood proletariat' (ibid.: 245), make a stranger-gift because as individuals they have a 'biological need to help' (ibid.: 198). Darwin had associated the survival of the fittest with the self-sacrifice of the other-regarding singleton: the exemplar would be the watching deer who sounds the alarm but draws the predator's attention to himself. Titmuss, building on the sociobiologist's notion that the satisfaction of a biological need can be a source of superior utility in itself, made much of the fact that socialised decision makers greatly valued their freedom to choose to care: 'To "love" themselves they recognized the need to "love" strangers' (ibid.: 239). Wanting to 'affirm a sense of belonging' (ibid.: 240), they wanted also to make themselves complete and whole. The free rider is much to be pitied. He could have enjoyed the benefits of a transfusion without the time and discomfort of the gift. Abstaining, however, he would have missed out on the 'essential human right' (ibid.: 13) to respond to the ritual and to reinforce the bonds. In the words of Aneurin Bevan, explaining why he believed that the National Health made every citizen better off: 'What more pleasure can a millionaire have than to know that his taxes will help the sick?' (Bevan, 1958: col.1389).

The case study of *Parents Revolt* used the sensitive sample of children.

The case study of *The Gift Relationship* used the comparative indicator of blood. In the latter book as in the earlier one the warning is stark, that informal support is badly undersupplied where Economic Man lives for himself alone: 'If the bonds of community giving are broken the result is not a state of value neutralism. The vacuum is likely to be filled by hostility and social conflict' (Titmuss, 1970: 199). Organicism and holism, building up the muscles of attachment, clearly protect the group not just against too few children and too little blood but also against lying, shoplifting, littering and the rapid depletion of the environment that the unborn future as well as the self-centred present has a legitimate right to enjoy. Privatisation, on the other hand, means that bad ethics drives out good once the moral choice to give life to an anonymous other is shorn away: 'A decline in the spirit of altruism in one sphere of human activities will be accompanied by similar changes in attitudes, motives and relationships in other spheres' (ibid.: 198). In the end old ladies will be mugged in Piccadilly and no one will care.

11.2   THE INTELLECTUAL SYSTEM

Titmuss's legacy is uncompromising documentation accompanied by a sense of purpose. It is in the solid British tradition of Arnold Toynbee, Charles Booth, the Webbs, the Oxford historical economists who treated fact-gathering as the complement to policy studies in the service of ideals and improvement. Titmuss, like Marshall and Crosland, was a quintessentially British author. His mixed ethos shows the influence of Mill on individualism and tolerance, an unwritten constitution which allows for discretion as well as rules, the popular resistance to panaceas and extremes, the public-service ethos of consensual politicians and obedient bureaucrats, the philanthropy of the caring aristocracy and the informal reciprocity of the working-class mesh. The nation that had bred and shaped him was the community of discourse that provided a focus for his neighbourly culture: 'Being English was for Titmuss stronger than his feeling for class. The inequalities of class were to be rectified in the name of the larger community of England' (Rose, 1981: 488).

Just as the intellectual system is an English summer's day, so it is the footprint of a half-forgotten Christianity absorbed semi-consciously as a child. Titmuss, his daughter recalls, saw himself as an agnostic (but not an atheist) and 'never personally went to church': 'He held no belief in any sort of God at all' (Ann Oakley, cited in Reisman, 1982: 81). Even so, there cannot be many social scientists of the last hundred years who have devoted themselves so single-mindedly to Jesus's dictum 'Be compassionate as your Father is compassionate' (Luke 6: 36), to St Paul's invocation 'A body is not one single organ, but many ... If one organ suffers, they all suffer together' (1 Corinthians 12: 15, 26).Trevor Huddleston, speaking at the memorial service at St-Martins-in-the-Fields, described him as a 'true Christian'. Never going so far as to legitimate equality with the justification that all men are gift cherubs in the Maker's sight – capitalist institutions are 'not so much un-Christian as anti-Christian' (Tawney, 1937: 170), the Christian statist Tawney had declared – Titmuss preached the duty of the part to the whole as if explaining guilt, sin, communion and redemption in a church.

Titmuss must have known that he was sheltering in the shadow of giants such as the saint who warned that belief and hope would not be enough: 'Though I have the gift of prophecy, and understand all mysteries, and all knowledge; and though I have all faith, so that I could remove mountains, and have not charity, I am nothing.' (1 Corinthians 13: 2). Very occasionally he even said as much, as where, speaking of 'mutual, neighbourly help in the contingencies of industrial, city life', he stated that the friend in need was 'surely a Christian idea' (Titmuss, unpublished lecture, 1953, in Titmuss Papers, Box 3/374). Titmuss believed that values have consequences: 'Human welfare is an ethical concept' (Titmuss, 1963: 223). What is striking is the extent to which his own personal values were coloured by a half-forgotten Christianity at least as much as they were by the market failure of the Great Depression. He in that way raised the moral tone of the debate on the gaps in the social fabric.

The intellectual system bears the imprint of Ealing-comedy England and the best of parish rallying round, the marches from Jarrow and the beneficent interventionism that had demand-managed the idleness into a chicken in every pot. What it cannot accommodate is class conflict, workplace alienation, surplus value. Titmuss showed no interest in the strident certainties of Marx. He saw no reason to brand parliamentary socialism a sham, to impute internal contradictions to capitalist processes, to make matter and not mind the driving force in social evolution. The Marxists wrote of capital and labour. Titmuss wrote of the ins and the outs. The Marxists expecting revolution, Richard Titmuss engineering *camaraderie*, the two world-views lived in their own separate worlds. There was no way that the parallel lines could ever cross.

Titmuss never laid out his system. Tracking down the links and teasing out the connections is an exercise that well repays the effort. Titmuss's welfare was not the piecemeal and the ad hoc but rather a unified whole made one by an encompassing analytic. The focal concepts in that vision are consensus, integration, dignity, compensation and expediency. Together they make up the best available framework for conceptualising the social services and for situating the beneficiaries in an interpersonal context that generalises beyond the discrete.

11.2.1 Consensus

Policy towards people who require unilateral transfers both springs from the value consensus and helps to reinforce it: 'All collectively provided services are deliberately designed to meet certain socially recognized "needs"; they are manifestations, first, of society's will to survive as an organic whole and, secondly, of the expressed wish of all the people to assist the survival of some people' (Titmuss, 1963: 39).

The first condition is the security of the structure. The social services are not 'things apart', not 'phenomena of marginal interest, like looking out of the window on a train journey': 'They are part of the journey itself. They are an integral part of industrialization' (ibid.: 8–9). In the pre-industrial village the extended family looked after its own. In the anonymity of modernism, urban and mobile, public services will often be all that stands between orderly change and social undersupply: 'The "gales of creative destruction" (to use Schumpeter's words) have to be matched by agencies of social equilibria' (Titmuss, unpublished lecture, n.d., possibly 1968, in Titmuss Papers, Box 3/370). Children must go to school as otherwise they would not have the skills our industries require. Epidemics must be prevented as otherwise there would be avoidable absences from work. The unemployed must be given food as otherwise the destitute, starving, would turn to crime. In calling for welfare, what we as a community are saying is that *our* existence as a well-tuned engine must be protected and enhanced. The rule is 'to each according to *our* needs' (Titmuss, 1974: 141). In thinking of the dependent, we are thinking of the non-dependent as well.

The first condition is survival. The second condition is agreement. Help is offered – the wish is 'expressed' – not simply because there is an objective locus of need. It is offered because fellow citizens experience a subjective sensation that distress exists and that they want to do something about it. Felt sympathy and spontaneous generosity lie at the root of the out-of-pocket donation for hurricane relief and of the tax-funded State service alike. It is the freedom to refuse as well as the freedom to sacrifice that makes the gift of welfare a genuinely *moral* choice. Income maintenance is legitimate because it is the 'expressed wish' of the independent that malnutrition and disease should not be allowed to lie where they fall. The National Health is legitimate because 'the demand for one society' (Titmuss, 1968: 19) validates the universalism and makes it our social pact. T.H. Marshall was prepared to economise on convergence at the mean where it was obviously the State that had the better purchase on the non-expressed need (Marshall, 1972: 107). Titmuss in his theory was less willing to use command and control as his social safety valve. Where public opinion is indifferent, divided or hostile, there the nationalisation of good conduct cannot legitimately be made a public policy concern.

Representative attitudes define the specific boundaries. Welfare systems reflecting 'the dominant cultural and political characteristics of their societies' (Titmuss, 1974: 22), collective responsibility, value-driven, must always be the creature of time and space. It 'cannot be discussed or even conceptualised in a social vacuum' (ibid.: 16). Titmuss for his own part uses 'welfare' to mean the five areas of State education, public healthcare, subsidised housing, income maintenance and personal social services. He also believes that the desire for welfare is itself a consequence of the welfare experience. Supply creates its own demand. Children of different races attend the same local schools. Common hospitals narrow the perceived social distance between rich and poor. The consensus validates the intervention. The social engineering validates the consensus. The end result is a national ideology that is different from what it was at the start. Cumulative causation is fully democratic, uncompromisingly so. Still, however, the *conscience collective* has been sociomandered and representative attitudes stand not quite where they did.

11.2.2 Integration

Edmund Burke was a social conservative who saw what the 'sophisters, oeconomists and calculators' did not, that the 'whole chain and continuity of the commonwealth' (Burke, 1790: 170, 193) is an intergenerational partnership that possessive individualism is wrong to make into the simple agglomeration of its parts. Lasting partnership gives men a home. Divisive selfishness tends to tear up the roots: 'It is a community of purpose that constitutes society. . . . Without that, men may be drawn into contiguity, but they still continue virtually isolated . . . . Christianity teaches us to love our neighbour as ourself; modern society acknowledges no neighbour' (Disraeli, 1845: 75–6).

Disraeli, diagnosing the sickness of a Britain adrift, blamed the shopkeepers and the money-men for the chasm that separated the two nations of comfort and hardship. There were, he wrote, 'two nations; between whom there is no intercourse and no sympathy; who are as ignorant of each other's habits, thoughts, and feelings, as if they were dwellers in different zones, or inhabitants of different planets' (ibid.: 77). Disraeli could not accept that a society was healthy where it left its citizens so insensitive to their shared inheritance that it was as if they were visitors from different worlds. Nor could Tawney who, like Burke and Disraeli, made everyday understandings the badge of place and blood: 'What a community requires, as the word itself suggests, is a common culture, because, without it, it is not a community at all' (Tawney, 1931: 43).

That in turn, to Tawney, meant the State. What was needed was 'equality of environment, of access to education and the means of civilization, of security and independence, and of the social consideration which equality in these matters usually carries with it' (ibid.). What was needed was social policy to smooth down the sharp contrasts that drove a wedge between equal citizens and Burke's intertemporal chain. What was needed was a welfare community that was an acknowledgement of a common destiny and the embodiment of the felt wish to care. In the words of Evan Durbin:

> The social services are, for all their deficiencies, a primitive recognition of human solidarity, a crude realization of the splendid idea of corporate responsibility for individual disaster, of the profound social truth that we are all members one of another. In America these services are called 'social security' measures. They are well named, for they are not only measures for the security of men in society but measures for the security of social relationships, of social order among men. (Durbin, 1940: 145)

Membership and inclusion were not new when Titmuss threw in his lot with the social conservatism of 'I am We'. He immediately recognised in the continuing struggle of *Gemeinschaft* versus *Gesellschaft*, universal good fellowship versus the greedy peddler principle, the threat to the welfare society that it was the specific mission of social policy to contain. On the one hand there was the tight binding of Tanganyikan communalism before the Fall: 'Towns and villages which have been long established have, like the houses of which they consist, often developed characteristics which favour the maintenance of a satisfactory community structure within them' (Titmuss *et al.*, 1964: 171). On the other hand there was the unanchored exchange and fleeting liberty of the amorphous United States: 'More prosperity and more violence may be one of the contradictions in a system of unfettered private enterprise and financial power oblivious to moral values and social objectives' (Titmuss, 1963: 218). Intemperance is incompatible with belonging. Stasis, however, is incompatible with entrepreneurship. Social policy plays a small but vital role in confining the path-dependence to the middle ground where social growth and economic growth make their valued contributions side by side.

Richard Titmuss made it the special concern of social policy to study 'those social institutions that foster integration and discourage alienation' (Titmuss, 1968: 22). He also said that it was the social mission of the welfare services to reinforce the skein of interconnected memberships even as they relieve the unique human being's private and personal distress: 'It is now (or should be) an objective of social policy to build the identity of a person around some community with which he is associated' (Titmuss, 1974: 38). The psychology is in line with Maslow on the hierarchy of needs that begins with passive consumption but evolves upwards into activity, esteem, self-actualisation and involvement with others: 'The human being is simultaneously that which he is and that which he yearns to be' (Maslow, 1962: 26). The techniques are profoundly in the tradition of Tawney who did not want nation building and horizontal standardisation to be crowded out by shifting sands and the self-interested swap.

On the side of spendable resources, reasonable levelling is essential in order to narrow the cultural divide: 'History suggests that human nature is not strong enough to maintain itself in true community where great disparities of income and wealth preside' (Titmuss, 1967b: 358–9). Levelling up, the single parent, the village simpleton, the new immigrant with nowhere to go, are to be given welfare transfers sufficient to alleviate their absolute poverty and to reduce the relative gap. Whether the redistribution makes the excluded feel wanted and loved or simply leaves them less hungry and less cold is, of course, a matter for debate. Levelling down, what Titmuss is proposing is a high rate of income tax (he raises no objection to the peak marginal rate in Britain in his LSE years) and of inheritance duties (he sees no reason to spare the intergenerational multiplier merely because it perpetuates the family that is his basic building block). Such confiscation is desirable and democratic. It confers the neighbourhood benefit of approximation precisely because it imposes a de jure levy on the pollutant of social distance. That is why, logically speaking, the rate of the levy would have to be high. A small equalisation in purchasing power is unlikely to make fellow citizens look and feel the same.

So swingeing a levy on success, a punishment and not a reward, is a strange way of acknowledging the contribution of initiative and assiduity to the sustained rise in across-the-board living standards. While invidious comparison can undoubtedly be demoralising, it would clearly make sense for the also-rans to keep their resentment within bounds lest they retard their own rate of economic advance. The resentment of the left-behind would in any case be matched by the estrangement of the alert and the talented when they perceive that envy and revenge are being given an institutional outlet that in the private sector would be the basis for a fist fight or a lawsuit. Disincentives and a new source of rejection are a strange way of producing an integrated society. To say that 'all the people' are in agreement about welfare is to neglect the fact that the majority might want to Robin Hood the rich but that the wealthy themselves, demanding equality of respect despite the fact that they are very few, might not want to share.

On the side of collective consumption, the model is the National Health Service, free-on-demand and as-of-right. Allocating by need alone and indifferent to the ability to pay, the National Health is the guarantor of 'one publicly approved standard of service, irrespective of income, class or race', in place of the free market's 'double standard which invariably meant second-class services for second-class citizens' (Titmuss, 1968: 195). Hindus and

Muslims, riff-raff and toffs, sit in the same waiting room to consult the same best-practice physician. Blacks and whites, bishops and Buddhists, have neighbouring beds in a non-discriminatory ward and select meals from a menu that caters for all of their tastes. The doctoring and the nursing aside, what equal citizens such as these take away from the medical encounter is the feel of a common experience. Their treatment teaches them that nationality, not just a passport, is a church, a family and a fraternity as well.

The first of July 1948 made all of us one: 'The most unsordid act of British social policy in the twentieth century has allowed and encouraged sentiments of altruism, reciprocity and social duty to express themselves' (Titmuss, 1970: 225). The NHS set free the freedom to love. We learn acceptance by living acceptance. We learn brotherhood by living brotherhood. The norms become flesh because the effect, self-strengthening, becomes the valued cause of more of the same.

State schooling is widely believed to be a uniform curriculum in the service of a cohesive community. The National Health is often called an investment in equality of respect and learned integration. Welfare is expected to condition a transferable reflex. The citizen is expected to carry the welfarist mindset into the non-welfare world of market-driven differentials and unequal outcomes. Titmuss is convinced that the means will produce the mix. Others, more sceptical, will accuse him of exaggerating his case. Schools and hospitals bring the dependent together only for a self-liquidating purpose that might not be enough to produce a permanent transformation. Cash benefits would have to be exceptionally generous to raise up the relatively deprived to the standard of the median. Public housing is not a representative cross-section of the multi-class community. Welfare, in short, might serve a humanitarian purpose but still be inadequate to produce the sense of an Us that is at the root of Burke's sociology and that of Disraeli.

Welfare could go further than the moderate Titmuss was prepared to recommend. Unlike Crosland, he says little about the stigma of the dratted 'Eleven-plus'. Unlike Tawney, he is too much of a liberal to recommend that the public schools be bought out by the State. Unlike Bevan, he does not demand the phasing out of pay beds in citizenship-affirming hospitals despite the socialist's belief that 'a free health service is pure Socialism' (Bevan, 1952: 106). He is too responsive to middle-class resistance to recommend that the dependent be resettled through rent rebates not in council estates but in leafy suburbs. He is too sensitive to business vested interest to insist on compulsory apprenticeships and in-house reskilling as an alternative to State education, on safety inspections and a works clinic as an alternative to the NHS. Titmuss never forces welfare into the earning life through affirmative action, the wage floor or subsidies to unemployment black spots where loss of one's job would be stigma in itself. Titmuss was a moderate. He was too much of a middlegrounder to do what would have been deemed necessary by less complacent interventionists on the Left.

The Right will be even less attracted by the One Nation paradigm of the NHS. Free marketers will maintain that one of the most potent sources of the common culture has been growth, *embourgeoisement*, television serials, popular music; while traditional conservatives will argue that what Hitler called *Einheit* depends not so much on welfare as on the monarchy, the established church, national service, State-manipulated propaganda and our own side's triumph in the World Cup. Radical individualists, meanwhile, will feel threatened on principle by the implication that political democracy means social homogeneity. The NHS or the patriotic rally, they will say, my home is not your castle and my reference points are not yours to commandeer.

11.2.3 Dignity

A gift cherub is there not to be evaluated but to be esteemed: 'When men have this feeling for equality it expresses itself principally as an awareness of the worth of their neighbour and of the need to cherish him for himself' (Titmuss, unpublished lecture, n.d., probably 1960s, in Titmuss Papers, Box 3/370). Cherishing one's neighbour as an end in himself means in turn that he should be spared the shame of stigma, the 'spoiled identity' that makes him, in Goffman's words, 'a blemished person, ritually polluted', a contaminated thing, 'disqualified from full social acceptance' (Goffman, 1963: 9, 11). Respect for persons dictates that the dependent should not be made to experience a humiliating loss of status when extreme need forces them to ask for help.

Titmuss in the circumstances recommended that welfare transfers and services should be provided without the imposition of a personal means test. Such a test would be perceived by the needy as a debasing confirmation that they had defaulted on the work ethic and let themselves down. The poverty test tends to 'foster both the sense of personal failure and the stigma of a public burden' since it is the very function of the gatekeeper 'to keep people out; not to let them in. They must, therefore, be treated as applicants or supplicants; not beneficiaries or consumers' (Titmuss, 1968: 134). The long-term unemployed who never get an interview, adult asylum seekers without a full contributions record and discharged mental patients unable to cope are trapped in a multiplicity of vicious circles from which no rate of economic growth will grant them release. Compassion demands that their self-esteem at least should be protected and that they should not have to beg.

The personal means test, moreover, is incompatible with the policy aim of universal services for integrated citizens. Where the down-at-heel and the out-of-luck are shunted into 'separate, Apartheid-like structures' (ibid.: 114) intended for paupers, the consequence of safety net facilities is at once a perceived expression of disapproval and an inferior standard of provision: 'Separate discriminatory services for poor people have always tended to be poor quality services' (ibid.: 134). Both the psychological damage and the second-rate standards are avoided where all classes make use of the same welfare infrastructure. That is why it is desirable that the middle classes should not practise their own private means-test and opt themselves out of the encompassing welfare web. Their continuing participation in State health and education convinces less privileged groups that 'citizenship-based' does not mean 'residual'. Involvement brings with it quality control. Their insistence on the best confers a positive externality on the inarticulate who might be afraid to ask.

Universalism in place of means testing is by design a wide-open door. Titmuss did not believe that access without deterrence would very frequently lead to abuse. There is little in his philosophy about manipulative scroungers who collect their dole while moonlighting in a pub; about teenage mothers who succumb to moral hazard because the State will provide; about deliberate indolence, debilitating drug addiction and health-threatening smoking that impose on one's fellow-citizens the third-party bad of slower growth. Titmuss seems almost to be defending the feckless and the self-centred against the claim of the self-reliant and the hard-working that moral men and women are being taken for a ride. Humanitarian and tolerant, Titmuss has no answer to the objection that the good conduct of the many is subsidising the dependency culture of the few; or that the consensus from which all legitimacy comes might be unprepared to say that malingering without retraining is a lifestyle choice that the social contract is obligated to rubber-stamp. Perhaps some stigma ought unashamedly to be the moralist's choice. Ostracism and rejection will have a social function where they protect the interdependent organism from free riders and cheats who have detached themselves from the responsible collectivism of the whole.

Titmuss saw things differently. Starting from here and not from fault, he believed that it was better for a handful of self-serving parasites to get through the system than for a needy old person to die of hypothermia because he once spent all his savings on himself and now has to depend on total strangers for food. Titmuss was the product of a less permissive Britain where most people, upright, independent and honest, regarded employment as honourable and cared uncomplainingly for their kin. It is this implicit conviction that only a minority will abuse the system that underlies his belief that no one should be asked to put his hand up and declare that he is poor.

11.2.4 Compensation

Libertarians, associating perceived self-worth with purposive self-help, treat it as the duty of individuals to buy life for themselves and their dependants. They criticise welfare theorists for championing the stranger gift that challenges the moral primacy of achievement through exchange. Titmuss finds their trade-off between charity and equity a false and misleading duality. Atomists blame the individual for the things that go wrong. Organicists are more inclined to blame the rules, the setting and the game for the inconvenience that the parts must experience in order that the whole might thrive. Where it is society that imposes the externalities, Titmuss says, it must be society that looks after the victims of the whole's net advance.

Consider new technology that raises living standards for the mainstream in work but prematurely ends the career of 40-something team-mates afflicted with obsolete skills. Consider the children evacuated in the Blitz whose own children will inherit the fear and the insecurity bequeathed by yesterday's national emergency. Consider the coal miner living in sub-standard accommodation who is invalided into unemployment by pneumoconiosis, tuberculosis or a disabling accident. In cases such as these, it would clearly be wrong to expect the innocent and the swept-along either to absorb unaided the full costs of social development or to settle gratefully for benevolence and bleeding hearts when their real claim is for justice and enforceable rights. The losers have drawn the blanks that enable the majority to draw the benefits. That is why, encasing the gift relationship in the cast-iron quid pro quo, the nation must pay welfare compensation to the victims of its social facts lest they, forgotten and discarded, end up 'the social pathologies of other people's progress' (Titmuss, 1968: 157).

Titmuss is reluctant to blame the individual for social facts like geographical mobility that breaks up the family network or lengthened life expectancy that makes old age a more costly liability: 'The devil in this particular piece seems to have more of the character of Bentham than of Freud' (Titmuss, 1963: 109). What he emphasises instead is the diffuse nature of the causality, impossible to pin on a single tort-feasor or to put right through the courts. Titmuss insists that social welfare 'represents some element of compensation for disservice caused by society' (Titmuss, 1974: 89). Not redistribution but re-redistribution, the function of welfare damages is to restore the status quo ante level of felt well-being. Redress being the objective, it would clearly be an inequity to stigmatise the beneficiary through a means test or a second-rate service. The victim of economic change is like a war hero. We have a responsibility to look after our wounded comrades. They, after all, have done their bit for us.

The model is Pigou on the smoking chimney and the polluted stream, the 'uncompensated services and uncharged disservices' (Pigou, 1920: 191) that separate the private from the social return. Agreed on the split, still there is disagreement as to the solution. Titmuss believes that public finance should be used after the event to clean up the neighbourhood disamenity that private production has caused. Pigou, however, wants taxes and subsidies to be fine-tuned in advance in order to contain the toxins before the citizen falls ill. Titmuss says nothing about legislation to outlaw noxious emissions, about the internalisation of third-party costs by means of filters, about an NHS surcharge levied on industries known to cause a supernormal drain. What he says instead is that welfare must be in place so that the spillovers do not lie where they fall. The focus is macrosociological: *we* want economic growth, *we* want to look after the fallen. The focus is not microsociological: *he* wants the profits, *he* wants *us* to pay for *his* refuse. Pigou told the businesses that they had to stop poisoning the fish. Titmuss told the businesses that 'if one organ suffers, we all suffer together'.

11.2.5 Expediency

Titmuss felt surrounded by market economists who were indifferent to compassion, justice and integration. It was a discovery of great significance to him that private enterprise was inferior to social provision in key areas such as insurance, medical care and blood, where both market and State had a presence and direct comparisons could be made (Reisman, 2001: 203–40). He had little interest in industry and trade. There, possibly, he felt that the rank-ordering of deontology and consequentialism would be reversed.

Quality is a first success indicator: blood bought from donors with a financial incentive to conceal is more likely to pass on the unwanted gift of hepatitis or AIDS, a fee-for-service doctor despite his professional ethic more likely to merchant unnecessary treatment for profit. Quantity is a second: blood-selling does not ensure adequate supplies, whereas selflessness and attachment are the guarantee that the surgeons will never run short. Choice is a third: insurance companies (accountable only to shareholders) deny policies to non-standard applicants, actuarially unascertainable, whereas social insurance (pooling risks on a national basis and policing bureaucrats through an appeals mechanism) promises equal citizens that none will be left without cover.

A fourth success indicator is price. Coordination in the British National Health contrasts favourably with the wasteful randomness of semi-duplicate private hospitals, typically with excess capacity such as an underutilised scanner, that is a feature of the business-minded United States. Administration costs are less in Britain, not least because the providers have no need to sell and bill. The doctor–patient relationship is less likely to degenerate into mistrust, malpractice litigation, defensive medicine, second opinions or multiple tests. Prevention is linked up with cure, treatment with sickness benefits, income maintenance with hospices and hostels. There is a good geographical spread of service and expertise. Blood is free. The National Health is a responsible custodian of the nation's scarce resources. The market is less effective because it has tried to cut corners and has priced out the freedom to care.

Titmuss develops his social economics in his own selective way. Different ad hocs would suggest different inferences. Non-transferable pensions, loss of survivor's rights, uninsurable haemophiliacs in the *homo homini lupus* of commerce are snookered by doctor shortages, lightning consultations, early retirements and long waiting times in the NHS. The contention that private doctors exploit information asymmetry and underinvest in primary care is shouted down by the assertion that State bureaucrats are ambitious empire builders, that cynical politicians put vote-value before hidden need, that organisational rigidities respond disproportionately to producer-side lobbies. There is no mention of the Hayekian discovery process as a way of introducing innovation into care. There is no role for internal markets, bought-in services, Walrasian price signals, welfare vouchers in order, the money following the client, to make public facilities more cost-conscious through competition. Anecdotes, horror stories and bad blood do not prove that the State is efficient and the market lags behind. All they prove is that Titmuss was a social philosopher who selectively plucked those roses that had no thorns.

A model that eulogises good conduct because private virtues maximise economic throughput is, however, a model with an exposed flank. Should it turn out that the market consistently delivers a better product than the State, the economical moralist is faced with a difficult choice. Is it preferable to save more lives through an appeal to pecuniary self-love or to settle for inferior provision because a joint venture with the Devil cannot reasonably be considered? Convinced that benevolence of intent leads to best-attainable welfare, Titmuss at least could never be tempted by the poisoned chalice.

11.3   GOOD CONDUCT AND POLITICAL ECONOMY

Titmuss believed in welfare. He also believed in the welfare *State*. The politicisation of good conduct is not an obvious road for a preacher to select. Titmuss's reasons for the centralisation rather than the devolution of other-regarding ethics are best understood in the context of comparative economic orders.

11.3.1   Welfare Socialism

Socialism, Titmuss said, is about belonging and continuity even as it is about the reduction in social distance: 'Socialism is about community as well as equality. It is about what we contribute without price to the community and how we act and live as socialists' (Titmuss, 1968: 151). The immature child expects treats without the privilege of the countergift that completes the circuit. The grown-up society knows that putting in is at least as much a welfare right as is taking out: 'Socialism is also about giving' (Titmuss, 1970: 187).

Socialism is the gift of progeny, of war service, of blood for transfusion. It is the 'expressed wish' of all the people to contribute taxes that will empower the more needy to regain their self-esteem. Socialism by that definition is helping a blind person to cross the road, arranging an outing for a local school, participating in log rolling and barn raising on the American frontier. Socialism is self-help like Alcoholics Anonymous, mutual aid like the trade union with an emergency fund, 'a variety and diffusion of genuine voluntary agencies' (Titmuss, unpublished letter to J.H. Robb dated 21 September 1959, in Titmuss Papers, Box 2/130) that have made British welfarism a special topic in getting involved. The family is a socialist cooperative: it cares for the very young and the very old, the autistic and the mentally disturbed. So are the collective farm and the monastery, the factory that keeps on an over-the-hill worker and the restaurant that slips free coffees to the down-and-out because the weather has turned cold. There are few decent people who do not manifest some socialism every day of their adult lives.

Socialism is altruism, but it is also the State. That is the black box. Titmuss was a commune-ist and a social-ist. What has to be explained is why the good neighbourliness made him a welfare *statist* as well.

The first reason is clearly the economic benefit. State coordination maximises the welfare that can be squeezed from a limited budget. Long runs mean economies of scale. Giant organisations have countervailing power. Duplication is planned away. Professionalism takes the place of opportunism. The State is economical. We need the State because it is too expensive to allow private enterprise to lie where it falls.

The second reason for the State is viable differentiation within the bounded domain of democratically delimited homogeneity. Private business means multiple histories and separate compartments. Collective provision means common memories and unstratified adventures. Socialism is overlap. Capitalism is plurality. Titmuss, aiming at a tolerant compromise, made clear that it was the task of the welfarist State to deliver a combination that would satisfy the citizen even as it was consolidating the community.

Titmuss, commemorating the tenth anniversary of the NHS, said on the BBC that British socialism was inseparable from 'a respect for the unique value of each individual and his or her need for self-respect': 'Cultural diversity in the instruments of welfare is a precious asset in a world of more and more standardised products' (Titmuss, unpublished lecture, 1958, in Titmuss Papers, Box 2/130). What this might mean is that there are Muslim prayers in a universalist school but not segregated schools, single sex or single faith.

What this cannot mean is that a rich pensioner buys an organ transplant that the consensus has earmarked for a working-age beneficiary. The rich pensioner, like the equal citizens denied euthanasia or an abortion because their fellow socialists are resolutely pro-life, will complain that such a tyranny of the median over the tails is not what he understands by 'unique value', by 'need for self-respect'. Titmuss has no answer to this objection. Diversity within homogeneity is the second welfare function of the State. Confronted with a conflict of orientations, it is nonetheless the majority and not the minority view that must be the socialist choice.

The third reason for the State is social equity in the maelstrom of market failure. All mutual-aid pooling involves an element of intended cross-subsidisation. In insured healthcare, this takes the form of a transfer from the well to the sick. In pay-as-you-go it is superannuation subscribed by the young so that the old might draw a non-actuarial stream. State-pooled welfare alone has an explicit charter to bring about redistribution from the rich to the poor, and to do so without shaming judgment or the loss of face. Positive discrimination to an educationally deprived locality benefits the broad grouping but singles out no individual miscreant. Dynamised pensions redirect social resources to the retired who typically stand disproportionately in need of help. No personal means test is needed and no invasive investigation is conducted. The market has little time for good citizens who cannot pay. The State is in the circumstances the better way to institutionalise the collective commitment to mutual aid without fault or guilt.

11.3.2 Welfare Capitalism

The Marxists say that socialism and capitalism are radical opposites, strictly either/or. Titmuss sees them not as substitutes but as complements that add up to a whole: 'More equality in income and wealth, education, and the enjoyment of the decencies of social living might conceivably be a democratic precondition of faster economic growth' (Titmuss, 1964: 9–10). Because our State supplies welfare, therefore our profit-seekers are better placed to supply the goods and the jobs that our democracy demands.

Titmuss knew that infrastructure was the precondition for development: 'Good drains mean good business' (Titmuss, unpublished lecture, n.d., probably 1950s, in Titmuss Papers, Box 3/370). Welfare was a part of the social overhead that a market economy had to have. Looking to the past, he, like Schumpeter and Galbraith, reached the conclusion that welfare had been 'a major force in denying the prediction that capitalism would collapse into anarchy' (Titmuss, 1967a: 100). Looking to the future, he made it his objective to ensure that State altruism would continue to support the free marketeer's indulgence in order that both together might contribute to the public good of growth: 'I consider that social policy ... must function as an instrument for the encouragement of economic flexibility' (Titmuss, unpublished lecture, n.d., probably 1950s, in Titmuss Papers, Box 3/369).

State schooling equalises opportunities: it trains potential meritocrats from all classes (thereby minimising wastage and defusing resentment) and delivers a free gift to the employers (thereby absolving the profit seekers from the unprotected expense of on-the-job training). The National Health gets down-time manpower back to value-adding activity, stems costly epidemics that wipe out time and talent, and patches up damaged workers not offered gloves and visors by a miserly boss. Council housing means low-cost accommodation close to the place of work. Unemployment benefits make dismissals in a changing economy that much less painful. The organicist ethic of attachment and harmony itself massages away social tensions that could be a threat to morale. Where latent conflicts are functional and productive, the tranquilliser of welfare will be seen by some as brainwashing, window dressing and the manipulation of symbols. Others, however, will argue convincingly for the social-services truce. A factory owner would have to admit that moderate statism does a lot to ease the flow of trade.

Titmuss says that welfare can make a 'positive contribution to productivity as well as reinforcing the social ethic of human equality' (Titmuss, 1965: 355). It is a sobering thought that good conduct, an end in itself, can also be the means to the economic end of wealth and dividends. We succeed in Maine's contract because we have a home in Maine's status. There are few rational capitalists who do not demand some 'We-ness' because they sense that it increases their gain.

Richard Titmuss was one of a kind. It is impossible to situate him in the standard division of academic labour. Titmuss was a social administrator, a political economist, a conservative, a socialist, a social-ist, a sociologist, a philosopher, a democrat, a leader and a visionary. The reader who approaches the 14 big books and the numerous occasional pieces with the notion that Titmuss was just another social scientist will be seeing only the tip of the iceberg. The reader who is sensitive to the moral commitment, the secular spiritualism, the poetic imagery, the uncompromising sense of purpose will be more likely to put down any of Titmuss's major works with the feeling that he or she has been exposed to the inspiring prospect of a whole that looks after its parts, to a demonstration that even data on birth rates and blood supply can be put at the service of democracy, of exchange and of the duty to care.

12. Conclusion: Adam Smith on market and State

Rothbard believed that Smith, at best 'a plodder in tune with the Zeitgeist' (Rothbard, 1995: 464), at worst 'a retrogression and deterioration, rather than an advance' (ibid.: 417), had shunted the car of gain-seeking activity on to the line that leads to the managed market and not to individual freedom: 'In *Wealth of Nations* ... *laissez-faire* becomes only a qualified presumption rather than a hard-and-fast rule, and the natural order becomes imperfect' (ibid.: 465). Adam Smith had written of capital invested in domestic industry that the self-interested atom 'is in this, as *in many other cases*, led by an invisible hand to promote an end which was no part of his intention' (Smith, 1776: I, 477, emphasis added). Smith had observed of the profit motive and the market outcome that the myopic calculator can also prove the ultimate visionary: 'By pursuing his own interest he *frequently* promotes that of the society more effectually than when he really intends to promote it' (ibid.: I, 477–8, emphasis added). Warren Samuels had no doubt as to the conclusions that followed from the 'in many other cases', from the 'frequently', that seemed to him to convert the libertarian's principled *always* into the pragmatist's contingent *we'll see how we go*: 'Notice the merely tentative properties attributed by Smith to market results ... There is no presumptive optimality of market solutions' (Samuels, 1977: 703, 704). Murray Rothbard was not disposed to disagree with this assessment. Adam Smith, he wrote with regret, had 'introduced numerous waffles and qualifications into what had been, in the hands of Turgot and others, an almost pure championing of *laissez-faire*' (Rothbard, 1995: xi–xii). In the process he had made himself nothing less than 'a necessary precursor of Karl Marx' (ibid.: xii).

Rothbard, like Samuels, saw Smith as an advocate of economic engineering and not simply as the ideologue of supply and demand. So did Richard Musgrave, who stressed that 'Smith was no economic anarchist. Governmental activity forms an inherent part of his system of natural liberty' (Musgrave, 1976: 296). So did Alec Macfie, who found that the scattered interventions summed up to 'a formidable state autocracy: a socialist spread of controls which would make some modern socialists' eyes pop' (Macfie, 1967: 348). The present chapter reaches the same broad conclusion as did Macfie and Musgrave, Samuels and Rothbard . The conclusion is that there is State as well as market in the world-view of an Enlightenment eclectic who found a single dimension neither to his taste nor to his measure. Divided into five sections dealing, respectively, with 'Market efficiency', 'Government failure', 'The protective State', 'The productive State' and 'Public finance', the discussion confirms that Smith was indeed free from what Coats calls 'that species of single-mindedness which makes a virtue of consistency' (Coats, 1975: 219). Road to serfdom or road to welfare, it was the *via media* of middle and mix which Adam Smith selected when he set off for the wealth of nations. The sixth section of this chapter, 'Democracy and exchange', says that Smith was not alone in wanting a middle way that would take the best from both market and State.

12.1   MARKET EFFICIENCY

As early as 1755, the young Adam Smith was declaring a preference for the spontaneous process: 'Projectors disturb nature in the course of her operations on human affairs, and it requires no more than to leave her alone and give her fair play in the pursuit of her ends that she may establish her own designs . . . Little else is required to carry a state to the highest degree of affluence from the lowest barbarism but peace, easy taxes, and a tolerable administration of justice; all the rest being brought about by the natural course of things' (cited in Rae, 1895: 62). In 1759, in the *Moral Sentiments*, the Glasgow professor returned to the theme of a beneficent order that established itself without conscious direction as the unintended consequence of self-love – 'hunger, thirst, the passion which unites the two sexes, the love of pleasure, and the dread of pain' (Smith, 1759: 78) – held in check by the countervailing virtues of justice and benevolence. He praised the 'Author of nature', also called 'an invisible hand', for having created a social machine that was suited so admirably to the task of ensuring 'the universal happiness of all rational and sensible beings' (ibid.: 105, 184, 237).

In 1776, writing in the *Wealth of Nations* quite specifically of material advance, the mature philosopher and sociological economist arrived at the following proposition in support of individual liberty and the free market system: 'All systems either of preference or of restraint . . . being thus completely taken away, the obvious and simple system of natural liberty establishes itself of its own accord. Every man, as long as he does not violate the laws of justice, is left perfectly free to pursue his own interest his own way, and to bring both his industry and capital into competition with those of any other man, or order of men' (Smith, 1776: II, 208). Adam Smith was early on taken to be a committed libertarian whose last word on economic policy was believed to be the following: 'Open the flood-gates, and there will presently be less water above, and more below, the dam-head, and it will soon come to a level in both places' (ibid.: 18). His emphasis on the stream and not the dam ought to have appealed strongly to a later contractarian like Murray Rothbard, who was unstinting in his support for the voluntary, his opposition to the coerced: 'When the society is free and there is no intervention, everyone will always act in the way that he believes will maximize his utility, i.e. will raise him to the highest possible position on his value scale . . . The fact that each man, in pursuing his own self-interest, furthers the interest of every one else, is a *conclusion* of economic analysis, not an *assumption* on which the analysis is grounded' (Rothbard, 1962: II, 766, 768).

Smith's defence of the market mechanism makes much of its allocative efficiency. He contrasts the competitive bidding for a limited stock with a maximum price law that has counterproductive consequences. He gives the sad example of the corn dealer who is prevented by decree from minimising distress:

> If by not raising the price high enough he discourages the consumption so little, that the supply of the season is likely to fall short of the consumption of the season, he not only loses a part of the profit which he might otherwise have made, but he exposes the people to suffer before the end of the season, instead of the hardships of a dearth, the dreadful horrors of a famine. (Smith, 1776: II, 30)

Smith is not seeking to defend the morality of the businessman – witness his unambiguously negative attitude to 'the mean rapacity, the monopolizing spirit of merchants and manufacturers' (ibid.: I, 519) – but only to show that private vices in a competitive environment can in practice deliver public benefits:

> Every individual is continually exerting himself to find out the most advantageous employment for whatever capital he can command. It is his own advantage, indeed, and not that of the society which he has in view. But the study of his own advantage naturally, or rather necessarily leads him to prefer that employment which is most advantageous to the society. (Ibid.: 475)

The stress is, however, on the competitive environment. Only significant numbers can ensure independent action. Only same-side rivalry, as in the case of the corn dealers, can protect the public from abuse: 'The inland dealers in corn . . . are necessarily more numerous than the dealers in any other commodity, and their dispersed situation renders it altogether impossible for them to enter into any general combination' (ibid.: II, 32). Smith had little appreciation of significant fixed-capital overheads. He did not anticipate that markets freed from State intervention would come under the control of corporations and cartels such as had built the bureaucratic dysfunctionalities of carelessness and profusion into private sector organisations like the East India Company (ibid.: II, 278). Given the large number of small competitors that he took to be the norm, Smith believed that mutual benefits and reciprocal assistance would automatically be the rule. He was considerably less sanguine about self-declared humanitarians and the deontology of the visible hand: 'I have never known much good done by those who affected to trade for the public good' (ibid.: I, 478).

All systems of political preference and State restraint cause scarce resources to be employed less economically than would otherwise have been the case. Allocative inefficiency, unattractive in itself to a severe moralist who valued productivity and looked down on waste, thus had the further disadvantage that it acted as a brake on growth:

> Every system which endeavours, either, by extraordinary encouragements, to draw towards a particular species of industry a greater share of the capital of the society than what would naturally go to it; or, by extraordinary restraints, to force from a particular species of industry some share of the capital which would otherwise be employed in it; is in reality subversive of the great purpose which it means to promote. It retards, instead of accelerating, the progress of the society towards real wealth and greatness; and diminishes, instead of increasing, the real value of the annual produce of its land and labour. (Ibid.: II, 208)

Economic growth means rising living standards for the lower classes, checks and balances in society and State, a Protestantisation of the Catholic monopoly. It also means a humanisation of character since fellow-citizens will no longer have the need to fight each other over each crust of bread. Selling-points like these strongly recommended the wealth of nations even to a judg-mental ascetic who, unlike Rothbard no uncompromising champion of the consumer's right and sovereignty, was prepared to dismiss some revealed preferences as 'trifling' and 'frivolous' (ibid.: I, 368), some material welfare as a 'deception' (Smith, 1759: 183). Economic growth was the key to social progress in the work of Adam Smith. That is why he was so intolerant of any allocative inefficiency that would curb profits, limit accumulation and disturb 'the natural balance which would otherwise have taken place among all the different branches of British industry' (Smith, 1776: II, 119). Wanting rapid advance, Smith made himself the scourge of wasteful misallocation: 'Every derangement of the natural distribution of stock is necessarily hurtful' (ibid.: 148). Wanting rapid growth, Smith proposed the delegation of good husbandry to the self-interested who stood most directly to gain:

> The natural effort of every individual to better his own condition, when suffered to exert itself with freedom and security, is so powerful a principle, that it is alone, and without any assistance, not only capable of carrying on the society to wealth and

prosperity, but of surmounting a hundred impertinent obstructions with which the folly of human laws too often incumbers its operations. (Ibid.: 49–50)

Smith believed that the market mechanism could safely be trusted to deliver consumables and to stimulate growth. An important reason for his confidence was his conviction that the free enterprise system was fully in line with the natural order, at once self-enforcing in the sense of Canute and morally legitimate in the sense of Locke. Smith was at all times aware of the real-world constraint represented by the momentum inherent in matter: 'In the great chess-board of human society, every single piece has a principle of motion of its own, altogether different from that which the legislature might chuse to impress on it' (Smith, 1759: 234). Smith took the view that human behaviour in exchange situations was demonstrably in keeping with the principles and the motions that had to be respected.

Thus the division of labour is natural: it is 'not originally the effect of any human wisdom' but is rooted instead in the inbred and instinctual drive to 'truck, barter and exchange' (Smith, 1776: I, 17). The exchange nexus is natural: 'Man has almost constant occasion for the help of his brethren, and it is in vain for him to expect it from their benevolence only. He will be more likely to prevail if he can interest their self-love in his favour' (ibid.: 18). The pursuit of approbation and 'sympathy' is natural: 'Nature, when she formed man for society, endowed him with an original desire to please, and an original aversion to offend his brethren' (Smith, 1759: 116). The 'uniform, constant, and uninterrupted effort of every man to better his condition' (Smith, 1776: I, 364) is natural: it 'comes with us from the womb, and never leaves us till we go into the grave' (ibid.: 362–3). The impulse that leads to inquiry is natural: 'Wonder . . . is the first principle which prompts mankind to the study of Philosophy, of that science which pretends to lay open the concealed connections that unite the various appearances of nature' (Smith, 1795: 51). Specialisation, negotiation, conscience, rank, discovery – Smith would appear to have put his faith in the natural order in preference to the man-made substitute which regrettably 'made that a crime which nature never meant to be so' (Smith, 1776: II, 429). An economist as well as a Lockean, Smith was always in favour of the natural order and the market adjustment. Except, of course, when he was not.

12.2 GOVERNMENT FAILURE

Smith was friendly to the market. Smith was critical of the State. The previous section showed that Smith was attracted by the ideal of efficiency through liberty. The present section shows that he at the same time had serious reservations about the wisdom of direction and guidance. Smith could have said that control was tolerable but that exchange was normally the more effective means. What he said instead was that the two roads could not be seen as leading to the same destination. The *quid pro quo* led to economic growth. Management meant stagnation. The choice was a real one and the case against the State the following.

First, the government was ignorant of trade. Parliaments were 'conscious to themselves that they knew nothing about the matter' (Smith, 1776: I, 455). The outcome had been ill-considered enactments leading to low-return allocations. Statistics in Smith's time (despite the early attempts at data collection made by King, Petty, Davenant and others) were hardly as full as they were later to become: Smith's objection to tinkering in the dark, his sceptical 'I have no great faith in political arithmetic' (ibid.: II, 42), may in that sense be interpreted as the acknowledgment of a conditional constraint rather than the endorsement of a general principle. Hayek, on the other hand, has found in Smith an 'Austrian'-type awareness that intelligence is always and everywhere dispersed: 'Adam Smith was the first to perceive that we have stumbled upon methods of ordering human economic cooperation that exceed the limits of our knowledge and perception' (Hayek, 1988: 14). In support of Hayek's assessment is Smith's declaration that 'the sovereign ... must *always* be exposed to innumerable delusions' in the execution of a task 'for the proper performance of which *no* human wisdom or knowledge could *ever* be sufficient' – namely that of 'superintending the industry of private people, and of directing it towards the employments most suitable to the interest of the society' (Smith, 1776: II, 208, emphasis added). Where the State must *always* be deluded, *no* argument for economic management can *ever* be very convincing.

Second, the government was wasteful of capital. Courts are notorious for their love of luxury and 'insignificant pageantry' such as 'not only prevents accumulation, but frequently encroaches upon the funds destined for more necessary expences' (ibid.: I, 468). Popular governments are no closer to the prudent frugality of the mercantile and manufacturing classes: witness 'the thoughtless extravagance that democracies are apt to fall into' (ibid.: II, 342). Relying heavily on his definition of service labour as unproductive and sterile, Smith arrived at the following conclusion concerning the involvement of the State: 'Great nations are never impoverished by private, though they sometimes are by public prodigality and misconduct. The whole, or almost the whole public revenue, is in most countries employed in maintaining unproductive hands' (ibid.: I, 363).

Market economists will object that priced services are no less value added than are priced commodities: they will say that Smith trivialises the intrinsic wastefulness of the public sector by placing undue emphasis on the composition of employment. Social democrats will comment that a wise Solon (mentioned with respect in Smith, 1759: 233) can do great good even if a scheming Borgia (mentioned with contempt in Smith, ibid.: 217) can indeed be an 'insidious and crafty animal' (Smith, 1776: I, 490): they will point with approval to Smith's concession that 'we talk of the prudence of the great general, of the great statesman, of the great legislator' (Smith, 1759: 216). Marketeers and interventionists will take issue with the detail of Smith on the wasteful steward. They will not, however, be in any real doubt as to the message that Smith was trying to get across. Britain at any rate 'has never been blessed with a very parsimonious government' (Smith, 1776: I, 367). Kings and ministers in that country should therefore contribute to the wealth of nations by taking to heart the following piece of sound advice: 'Let them look well after their own expence, and they may safely trust private people with theirs. If their own extravagance does not ruin the state, that of their subjects never will' (ibid.).

Third, the government was vulnerable to the 'clamorous importunity of partial interest' (ibid.: I, 494), to the special pleading of 'particular tribes', that was threatening to introduce 'real disorder into the constitution of the state' (ibid.: 495). Like Anthony Downs, Smith (referring explicitly to mercantilist trade diversion and the artificiality of the colonial system) stated that it had been the producers and not the consumers 'whose interest has been so carefully attended to': 'The interest of the home-consumer has been sacrificed to that of the producer . . . A great empire has been established for the sole purpose of raising up a nation of customers.' (ibid.: II, 180). Like Karl Marx, Smith (opposed to wage fixing lest the natural justice of the many be ranked below the profit on capital that accrued to the few) warned that the State had seldom been an impartial arbiter in the claims between the classes: 'Whenever the legislature attempts to regulate the differences between masters and their workmen, its counsellors are always the masters' (ibid.: I, 158–9). Smith believed that the government, disproportionately sensitive to the needs of 'shopkeepers' (ibid.: II, 129), 'the rich and the powerful' (ibid.: 161), and at the same time all too prepared to countenance the neglect or oppression of 'the poor and the indigent' (ibid.) had come to speak for a small section of the wider community rather than for the British people as a whole. Laissez-faire could not be more biased. Perhaps it would be more even-handed.

Fourth, the government, like any other large organisation, is dependent on a network of salaried officials. Such bureaucrats cannot but prove 'idle and profligate' (ibid.: 357), 'negligent, expensive, and oppressive' (ibid., 347). Their reward being independent of their efforts, they have 'acted as their situation naturally directed' (ibid., 158). The result has been a slippage in prudence and care that is a world away from the public service ethos of Weber and Schumpeter, Marshall, Crosland and Titmuss.

The incentives and institutions are the cause of the inefficiency, not the civil servants themselves. What this means in practice is that there ought to be a significant reduction in the number of functions entrusted to agents without a financial stake in the outcome: 'Public services are never better performed than when their reward comes only in consequence of their being performed, and is proportioned to the diligence employed in performing them' (ibid., 241). Smith does not discuss in detail what policies would be required to restructure the game. Clearly, however, the expedient of privatisation should be explored wherever possible. The example he gives involves the sale of the Crown Lands (ibid., 349). Small farmers can be trusted to make things grow. An absentee's bailiff has no analogous reason to be industrious.

Mismanagement is, however, no less to be expected from private-sector bureaucrats than it is from civil servants on a salary. Smith was quick to recognise the family resemblance between the executive in a corporation and the cog from the Ministry: 'The directors of such companies ... being the managers rather of other people's money than of their own, it cannot well be expected, that they should watch over it with the same anxious vigilance with which the partners in a private copartnery frequently watch over their own' (ibid., 264–5). Such 'negligence, and profusion', such 'folly ... and depredations' (ibid., 268), does not lead by the shortest possible route to the wealth of nations. It is, however, precisely what an economist would predict where big businesses are run by managers and ownership is 'divided among an immense number of proprietors': 'An unremitting exertion of vigilance and attention ... cannot long be expected from the directors of a joint stock company.' (ibid., 267, 278). Privatisation, however necessary, would evidently not be sufficient unless and until the managerial revolution were effectively to be reversed.

Smith, as has been argued in this section, had four reasons for being critical of the State. How he would have reacted had governments been better informed, more economical, more independent of interest groups (had the private sector in addition been less competitive, more Schumpeterian) can only be a matter for conjecture. Such speculation, as Andrew Skinner has observed, need not be either fair or accurate in respect of a historically minded social scientist who lived so long ago: 'It is not appropriate uncritically to translate Adam Smith's policy *prescriptions* from the eighteenth to the twentieth century – moreover, it is quite inconsistent with Smith's own teaching' (Skinner, 1996: 206). What is clear, however, is that much of Smith's hostility to government was relative and not absolute. He was quick to acknowledge the outstanding success of public enterprise in certain foreign republics: witness his recognition that the government of Berne did a flourishing trade in loans to other States while the government of Hamburg ran a public pawnshop, wine-cellar, apothecary and bank (Smith, 1776: II, 342, 344). The problem would seem to be not all government in general so much as the eighteenth-century British government in particular. No one would deny that the 'orderly, vigilant, and parsimonious administration' in Venice or Amsterdam had been able intelligently to carry out commercial projects. Whether the 'slothful and negligent profusion' and the 'thoughtless extravagance' of the eighteenth-century British government could, however, 'be safely trusted with the management of such a project, must at least be a good deal more doubtful' (ibid., 342).

We start from *here. Here* can move on. It is not a watertight defence of anything at all. Murray Rothbard knew that he could never feel comfortable with the contingencies of expediency. Convinced that the State must always be 'the inherent and overwhelmingly the most important enemy of . . . the rights of person and property' (Rothbard, 1973: 47), he argued on principle for the devolution of choice from 'oligarchs – in practice, government bureaucrats' (ibid.: 35) – to purposive actors with a resistance to coercion: 'Only individuals have ends, and can act to attain them. There are no such things as ends or of actions by "groups", "collectivities", or "States", which do not take place as actions by various specific individuals' (Rothbard, 1962: I, 2). Rothbard would have been pleased to have found in Smith a kindred spirit with an uncompromising attachment to market exchange. What he found instead was a costing, benefiting cautiousness that looked 'Open the flood-gates' prudently in the mouth and tested Venice and Amsterdam for soundness of wind. Expecting an *always* and finding a *sometimes*, Rothbard had in the end to accept that Smith was looking to the State even as he was eulogising the market: 'The list of exceptions Smith makes to *laissez-faire* is surprisingly long' (Rothbard, 1995: 465).

12.3   THE PROTECTIVE STATE

Adam Smith believed in natural liberty. It was natural liberty, he said, that had revealed to him the true and proper functions of the State: 'According to the system of natural liberty, the sovereign has only three duties to attend to; three duties of great importance, indeed, but plain and intelligible to common understandings' (Smith, 1776: II, 208). A book at least as long as the *Wealth of Nations* would be required to explain Smith's unwarranted confidence in his 'only', his 'plain', his 'intelligible' and his 'common'. Be that as it may, Smith defined the scope for active State intervention in terms of the three duties of defence, justice and public works that are the subject of this section and of the next. The present section is concerned with defence and justice.

These constitute James Buchanan's 'external "governor" ' or 'protective state' (Buchanan, 1975: 95).

12.3.1 Defence

Smith assigned to the government 'the duty of protecting the society from the violence and invasion of other independent societies' (Smith, 1776: II, 208). This is the duty of national defence. It is a responsibility which goes beyond the maintenance of 'a well-disciplined standing army' (ibid., 307) to embrace economic policy as well.

In that spirit, exceptionally, bounties should be paid to encourage the exportation of British-made sailcloth and gunpowder: the artificial inflation of the vent would then stimulate the expansion of these strategic industries at home, even if the commodities in question could otherwise have been purchased more cheaply abroad (ibid., 28). Also the Navigation Acts – 'perhaps, the wisest of all the commercial regulations of England' (ibid.: I, 487) – should be resolutely preserved: they confined much of British trade to British ships regardless of cost, but they also ensured that Britain would have a good supply of experienced sailors in the event of a sea war. All in all, Smith wrote, 'defence . . . is of much more importance than opulence' (ibid.). It was a conclusion which led him to endorse both the standing army itself and the economic policy that could be shown to back it up. Smith seems not to have appreciated just how open-ended the category of defence-related activity could ultimately become in the hands of a gain-seeking private pleader.

Once, Smith said, the public good of defence had been supplied directly by means of a people's militia. No less recently than the '45 rebellion, he recalled, some 'four or 5 thousand naked unarmed Highlanders took possession of the improved parts of this country' (Smith, 1766: 540–1). Their initiative testifies eloquently to the efficacy of a popular force. Economic evolution was, however, taking its course. While voluntary action could be a realistic option in the hunting, pastoral or agricultural stages, the fourth or commercial stage imposed a logic of its own such that 'the martial spirit of the great body of the people . . . would not, perhaps, be sufficient for the defence and security of any society' (Smith, 1776: II, 307).

Opulence and luxury excite the envy of the foreigner. Simultaneously, they make our own people 'effeminate and dastardly' (Smith, 1766: 540), 'incapable of defending themselves' (Smith, 1776: II, 220). The division of labour makes military technique a specialised study: it also debases the ordinary workman into a state of 'mental mutilation, deformity, and wretchedness' (ibid., 308) so extreme that in him the 'heroic spirit is almost utterly extinguished' (Smith, 1766: 541). The public good of defence can, Smith said, be supplied on a voluntary basis in a pre-commercial society. Unlike Ferguson and Kames, however, he denied that individual action still remained a realistic option given the modern mode of productive activity. The market economy breeds State intervention and selective nationalisation. The standing army is the effect and cause of flourishing enterprise.

Smith believed that public sector authority was the precondition for private sector autonomy: 'That degree of liberty which approaches to licentiousness can be tolerated only in countries where the sovereign is secured by a well-regulated standing army' (Smith, 1776: II, 229–30). Rothbard, needless to say, was considerably less confident about so massive a concentration of weaponry and violence: 'A government that has a permanent standing army at its disposal will always be tempted to use it . . . Any standing army, then, poses a standing threat to liberty' (Rothbard, 1973: 82, 83). Smith accepted that a standing army held a monopoly of power that was by its very nature an invitation to abuse. In his perspective, however, the threat was first and foremost a threat to the ruling government on the precedent of Caesar or Cromwell.

Recognising as he did the possibility of a military *coup d'état*, he proposed to contain the problem by ensuring that 'the sovereign is himself the general' and the commanding officers 'those who have the greatest interest in the support of the civil authority' (Smith, 1776: II, 229). Such an interleaving of loyalties is an imaginative curb to the standing threat in the sense of Smith. Not so, however, to the standing threat in the sense of Rothbard, who has in mind not the standing threat to Sir but rather the standing threat to you and me: 'To guard against private criminals we have been able to turn to the State and its police; but who can guard us against the State itself? No one' (Rothbard, 1973: 47). Rothbard views Smith on defence as incompatible in the long run with Smith on justice. Living in a Smith-type society, Rothbard the libertarian would live in fear of the abrogation of the constitution and the knock on the door.

12.3.2   Justice

The second duty is 'the duty of establishing an exact administration of justice' (Smith, 1776: II, 209).

Smith was in no doubt that the 'negative virtue' of justice (the abstention from harm to the person, property or reputation of others) was of far greater immediacy than the 'positive virtue' of benevolence: 'Justice . . . is the main pillar that upholds the whole edifice. If it is removed, the great, the immense fabric of human society . . . must in a moment crumble into atoms' (Smith, 1759: 86). He was also convinced that the task of protecting every member of the society 'from the injustice or oppression of every other member of it' (Smith, 1776: II, 231) could only be the natural monopoly of the government or 'civil magistrate': 'The liberty, reason, and happiness of mankind . . . can flourish only where civil government is able to protect them' (ibid., 325). On the one hand there was the war of each against all that would be the consequence of radical individualism: then the nation 'would become a scene of bloodshed and disorder, every man revenging himself at his own hand whenever he fancied he was injured' (Smith, 1759: 340). On the other hand there was the material security that must forever be unattainable without the nationalisation of force: 'It is only under the shelter of the civil magistrate that the owner of that valuable property, which is acquired by the labour of many years, or perhaps of many successive generations, can sleep a single night in security' (Smith, 1776: II, 232). Trapped between anarchy and Leviathan, Smith believed that he had no choice but to make his peace with the State.

James Buchanan shares with Smith the middle-ground position that the lesser liberty will have to be sacrificed to authority if the greater liberty is indeed to be enjoyed by exchange. He has written as follows about Smith on the privatisation too far: 'Adam Smith was far too realistic to argue that markets would emerge and would function effectively in the absence of a legal framework. One of the most important lessons of the 1776 masterpiece is the linkage between the *general* security of property (including the enforceability of contracts) and the functioning of markets, a security that could only be provided by the vigilant protection of the sovereign' (Buchanan, 1976: 273).

Buchanan acknowledges that 'modern libertarian anarchists, sometimes called property-rights anarchists' – 'they are best exemplified by Murray Rothbard' (ibid.: 272) – take the view that even law and order can dependably be supplied along the lines that Smith endorsed when he penned his famous defence of expediency through interest: 'It is not from the benevolence of the butcher, the brewer, or the baker, that we expect our dinner, but from their regard to their own interest. We address ourselves, not to their humanity but to their self-love, and never talk to them of our own necessities but of their advantages' (Smith, 1776: I, 18). Buchanan is insistent that Smith never expected his eulogy of collective action through market exchange to be extended to the infrastructure of the collectively itself: 'Is Rothbard the modern analogue to Adam Smith? Little or no exegesis is required to answer such a question emphatically in the negative' (Buchanan, 1976: 273). Rothbard would reluctantly have to agree with this verdict. It would be yet another reason why he would hold Smith in part responsible for the betrayal of 'self-ownership' that was to follow: 'The nineteenth-century laissez-faire liberals came to use laissez-faire as a vague tendency rather than as an unblemished yardstick, and therefore increasingly and fatally compromised the libertarian creed' (Rothbard, 1973: 27, 31).

Unlike the libertarians, Smith did not expect voluntary enforcement to evolve spontaneously in the absence of the State. The example of the Dark Ages confirmed to him that contracts for law and order, like all other contracts, would not dependably be concluded until the government had assumed its responsibilities as the guarantor of the public good: 'Among the barbarous nations who over-run the western provinces of the Roman empire, the performance of contracts was left for many ages to the faith of the contracting parties' (Smith, 1776: I, 107). Unlike the libertarians, moreover, Smith took the view that the private administration of justice could not realistically be made compatible with the central consideration of impartiality. Relying once again on evidence from the past, he made the point that justice for sale was not justice at all: 'The person, who applied for justice with a large present in his hand, was likely to get something more than justice; while he, who applied for it with a small one, was likely to get something less' (ibid.: II, 237).

Smith's instance is the market for bribes. Rothbard's reply would be that Smith, here as elsewhere, is simply uncovering a public-sector failure and blaming it on exchange. A corrupt civil servant can sell to the highest bidder because his monopoly is unchallenged through a 'built-in corrective mechanism'. A private competitor rivalled by substitute arbitrators cannot afford to let his honesty slip: 'The very life of the court, the very livelihood of a judge, will depend on his reputation for integrity, fair-mindedness, objectivity, and the quest for truth in every case. This is his "brand name". Should word of any venality leak out, he will immediately lose clients' (Rothbard, 1973: 235). The same is true of the butcher, the brewer or the baker when he gives short measure or pockets the change. Rothbard criticised Smith for opening the flood-gates and leaving them half-closed all the same.

Smith was in favour of State-sponsored law and order because he believed the alternative to be the teeth and the claws. Yet he also recognized that the decentralised order could itself contribute much to the war against the *bellum*.

Profit-seeking could cordialise the economy. The butcher needs the brewer as much as the brewer needs the baker. Mutual need is a convincing reason for them to keep their hands to themselves. Smith wrote that 'commerce . . . ought naturally to be, among nations, as among individuals, a bond of union and friendship' (Smith, 1776: I, 519). His contention, that interdependence is likely to have a dampening effect on aggression and injustice, recalls Schumpeter's assessment that non-rational impulses like 'the need for self-glorification and violent self-assertion' have, in richer societies, 'outlived their usefulness': 'Capitalism is by nature anti-imperialist' (Schumpeter, 1918/19: 148, 164, 194).

There is a Spencerian side to Smith. Confusingly, however, there is a Lockean side as well. Locke wrote that whatever natural harmoniousness there might once have been had been destroyed forever by accumulation and inequality: 'The preservation of property [is] the end of government, and that

for which men enter into society' (Locke, 1689: 186). Smith followed Locke
in arguing that the contract that creates the State is also the proof that harmonious exchanging is not enough to keep the peace: 'Civil government, so far
as it is instituted for the security of property, is in reality instituted for the
defence of the rich against the poor, or of those who have some property
against those who have none at all' (Smith, 1776: II, 236). Commerce is a
bond of union. Ownership of property is a source of division. Interdependence
means that we need the State less. Bank accounts mean that we need the State
more. Smith because of Locke made at any rate a conscious choice not to go
as far as he might have done down the road that makes law-abiding conduct a
direct consequence of the capitalist order.

Exchange aside, there is another reason why Smith could with greater
confidence have put his trust in the decentralised order. That is the moral sentiments. Man 'has a natural love for society . . . The orderly and flourishing state
of society is agreeable to him, and he takes delight in contemplating it' (Smith,
1759: 88). Man has a humanising capacity to empathise and imagine: 'How
selfish soever man may be supposed, there are evidently some principles in his
nature, which interest him in the fortune of others, and render their happiness
necessary to him, though he derives nothing from it except the pleasure of
seeing it' (ibid.: 9). Man conforms to the rule-governed order because he has
instinctively internalised his society's standards of right and wrong: 'Nature
. . . has not . . . abandoned us entirely to the delusions of self-love. Our continual observations upon the conduct of others, insensibly lead us to form to
ourselves certain general rules concerning what is fit and proper either to be
done or to be avoided' (ibid.: 159). Moral sentiments such as these (the
attribute of sympathy, the pull of convention, the accumulation of social capital) suggest that the sensitive social actor will automatically gravitate to his
society's normative guidelines. He will behave with justice as if guided by an
invisible hand.

The market itself appeals directly to these pressures and proclivities. The
ambitious climber is eager for standing and not just possession: 'Place . . . is
the end of half the labours of human life' (ibid.: 57). The risk-chasing adventurer knows by the same token that bankruptcy will cost him more than money
alone: being seen to fall and fail is in itself a 'humiliating calamity' (Smith,
1776: I, 363). A man who glories in his successes 'because he feels that they
naturally draw upon him the attention of the world' (Smith, 1759: 51) would
not, in the Smithian perspective, feel other than a fraud and a cheat if others
knew, and he himself knew, that he had broken the rules of justice en route to
his goal. The sheer success of market capitalism will make that much less
pressing the need to violate the code.

Smith seems to be saying that markets and morals make social life that
much less bloody. On balance, however, he remained a Hobbesian and a

misanthropist – a frightened theorist who expected that the sociable proclivities of compassion, generosity and fellow-feeling would always be at risk from 'envy, malice, or resentment' (Smith, 1776: II, 231), from the pride of man which 'makes him love to domineer' (ibid.: I, 412), from the 'anger, hatred, envy, malice, revenge . . . which drive men from one another' (Smith, 1759: 243). Smith was in favour of State-sponsored law and order because he recognised the law of the jungle in every self-interested individualist and feared the worst from 'so imperfect a creature as man' (ibid.: 25). A more confident moralist would have relied more extensively on societal sanctions and the wealth of nations for that cordiality in conduct that the true libertarian will always rank above the coercion of the State.

Smith wanted the State to protect. He did not want the State to invade. Believing, indeed, that the State in the past had overstepped the mark, he often presented the case for economic liberalisation in the language of righting a previous wrong. Opposing the Settlement Laws, he declared that they were inequitable and not simply inefficient: 'To remove a man who has committed no misdemeanour from the parish where he chuses to reside, is an evident violation of natural liberty and justice' (Smith, 1776: I, 157). Attacking the colonial system, he invoked the rights of man as well as the allocation of things: 'To prohibit a great people . . . from employing their stock and industry in the way that they judge most advantageous to themselves, is a manifest violation of the most sacred rights of mankind' (ibid.: II, 95). Defending the grain trade, he said that freedom was ethical and not only expedient: 'To hinder, besides, the farmer from sending his goods at all times to the best market, is evidently to sacrifice the ordinary laws of justice to an idea of public utility, to a sort of reasons of state' (ibid.: 48). Adding up the 'natural liberty', the 'sacred rights', the 'ordinary laws of justice', what emerges is the diagnosis of 'real encroachments' (ibid.: I, 493). Such infringements of person, property and reputation are impossible to reconcile with the duty of justice that would seem all too often to have fallen victim to the temptation to invade.

Smith believed it to be in the interests of justice to roll back the frontiers of the State. To that end he proposed the abolition of laws guaranteeing primogeniture and entails; he opposed the chartered monopolies and the statutes of apprenticeship; and he supported the phasing out of the export bounties and the import duties. The State, he maintained, ought to substitute simple protection for unwarranted direction in instances such as these where moral boundaries had been infringed. The Settlement Laws were 'a plain violation of this most sacred property' (ibid.: 136) which every man has in his own labour; while the grant of a monopoly privilege was 'contrary to that justice and treatment which the sovereign owes to all the different orders of his subjects' (ibid.:

II, 171). A 'sacred property' and a commitment to impartiality had been violated. It cannot be justice for the State to make laws which invade a private realm which ought to have been left alone.

Justice must be served through the repeal of bad laws. Economic expansion, coincidentally, will be an additional gain. A free market in land would stimulate productivity whereas a caste of hereditary absentees 'would soon degrade the cultivation' (ibid., 357). Occupational and geographical mobility would channel labour into its best-paid outlets and eliminate the man-made unemployment that can so easily exist where the law comes between the workman and an opportunity 'in another trade or in another place' (ibid.: I, 493). Freedom of trade would mean that Scottish resources need not be plunged in Scottish grapes because foreign grapes could be imported more cheaply on the basis of absolute advantage: 'If a foreign country can supply us with a commodity cheaper than we ourselves can make it, better buy it of them with some part of the produce of our own industry, employed in a way in which we have some advantage' (ibid.: 478–9). The looser rein, right and proper in itself, is clearly conducive to economic growth. Both ethics and economics are in agreement on the need to roll back the law.

Smith saw justice as a 'negative virtue', but there were exceptions. There were, more specifically, at least three sets of circumstances in which Smith, attracted as he was by the principle of 'Open the flood-gates', turned not to restraint removed but to restraint imposed for the protection of the public good.

The first instance is that of legislation to contain the spillovers. The argument is the familiar one that non-contracting outsiders must bear no burden, that 'the greatest good of the greatest number' (ibid., 344) must in exceptional circumstances override any natural rights that the individual may possess: 'Those exertions of the natural liberty of a few individuals, which might endanger the security of the whole society, are, and ought to be, restrained by the laws of all governments' (ibid., 345).

Laws can do it and enterprise will not. Thus the State must prevent a market failure in respect of fire-resistant construction and prudent banking practice: 'The obligation of building party walls, in order to prevent the communication of fire, is a violation of natural liberty, exactly of the same kind with the regulations of the banking trade which are here proposed' (ibid.). The State must accept that free enterprise is powerless in the face of a contagion or an epidemic: it must itself therefore invest 'the most serious attention' in order to 'prevent a leprosy or any other loathsome and offensive disease, though neither mortal nor dangerous, from spreading itself among . . . the great body of the people' (ibid.: II, 308). The State must even be prepared to 'correct whatever was unsocial or disagreeably rigorous' in the morals of small religious sects where competition between them regrettably did not dissipate 'that melancholy and gloomy humour which is almost always the nurse of popular superstition and enthusiasm' (ibid., 317, 318).

The State is in and the market is out – or perhaps Smith simply threw in his cards without appreciating just how much the push and pull of interest could rise to the challenge. The builders and the banks will be drawn by an invisible hand to quality control and deposit protection because paying customers will be attracted by safety and security. The insurance companies will have a commercial incentive to stop the spread of disease because preventable illness can unnecessarily sap their profits. The religious sects will lose their followers where they teach an asceticism that in a consumer culture will have only a minority appeal. Insisting that private enterprise is indeed the equal of the party walls and the loathsome diseases, warning that alarmist threats 'which might endanger the security of the whole society' (ibid.: I, 345) can easily be taken by a dictatorial prince as grounds for preventive detention or a stranglehold on the press, a libertarian like Rothbard would no doubt complain that Smith on spillovers would have done well to turn to the protective market and not to the State that would only make things worse.

A further instance of restraint imposed is that of legislation to set a ceiling limit to the interest rate. The Usury Laws, imposing a maximum, interfered with the individual's freedom to trade in loanable funds at the best price he could negotiate. Smith believed that the Usury Laws were good laws and that 'the present legal rate, five per cent., is perhaps, as proper as any' (ibid., 379). Smith knew that a lender with money was in a position to command eight or even ten per cent for his funds. As far as he was concerned, that market-clearing bargain had definitely to be blocked off by the State lest a scarce social resource be misallocated by the invisible hand. At eight or ten per cent, Smith wrote,

> the greater part of the money which was to be lent, would be lent to prodigals and projectors, who alone would be willing to give this high interest . . . A great part of the capital of the country would thus be kept out of the hands which were most likely to make a profitable and advantageous use of it, and thrown into those which were most likely to waste and destroy it. (Ibid.)

They would squander the wealth of our nation. We don't want that.

Smith could dismiss certain consumables as mere 'trinkets and baubles' (ibid., 439) but he generally stopped short of sumptuary legislation in support of his personal consumer sovereignty. With respect to the interest rate the position was different. There, as Rothbard observes, he did not hesitate to impose upon the community his 'Calvinist contempt for luxury consumer spending' and to put teeth into his 'hostility to free market time-preference between consumption and saving' (Rothbard, 1995: 467, 500). Justice was to be impartial. Spendthrifts and prodigals were nonetheless to be supplied with a personalised discrimination, tailor-made.

Smith is oblivious to the possibility that the extravagant and the speculative will obtain their funds illegally, and at even higher interest rates. Nor does he take into account the man-made scarcity of savings that Bentham in his *Defence of Usury* was in 1787 to predict would be a consequence of a self-defeating policy: Smith's reply to Bentham would only be, anticipating the *General Theory*, that the relevant supply schedule is not very interest-sensitive. Intolerance and inconsistency are serious charges, but so are hunger and unemployment. In China, the common people, 'begging employment' (Smith, 1776: I, 80), are forced to dine off 'any carrion, the carcase of a dead dog or cat, for example, though half putrid and stinking' (ibid., 81). In Britain, the wages of labour are 'evidently more' than the subsistence minimum and the complaint is common that 'luxury extends itself even to the lowest ranks of the people' (ibid., 82, 87). China is stationary and stagnant. Britain is growing rapidly. The growth of nations is the sine qua non for the diffusion of well-being.

Popular well-being is an end that to a utilitarian serves as its own legitimation: 'No society can surely be flourishing and happy, of which the far greater part of the members are poor and miserable' (ibid., 88). Yet growth and betterment wait upon the accumulation of capital. Adam Smith wrote: 'Every prodigal appears to be a public enemy, and every frugal man a public benefactor' (ibid., 362). The freedom of the prodigal is the freedom of an enemy within. That is why Smith, sacrificing natural liberty in order to procure the greatest happiness, was confident that he had to side with the Usury Laws.

A final instance is that of legislation to perpetuate selected positions of monopoly. Smith described monopoly as 'a great enemy to good management' (ibid., 165), the monopoly price as regrettably in excess of the 'natural and proper price' (ibid.: II, 169). Rejecting the dogma of credentialism, he criticised the single route of the university degree: 'When a man has learnt his lesson very well, it surely can be of little importance where or from whom he has learnt it' (Smith, 1774: 174). Rejecting protection for infant industries, he observed that the nation would have grown faster still 'had both capital and industry been left to find out their natural employments' (Smith, 1776: I, 479). Smith wanted to model the positive on the natural law. He wanted to 'Open the flood-gates', to take restraint away.

He also expressed his support for 'a monopoly of the trade for a certain number of years' where a 'company of merchants undertake, at their own risk and expence, to establish a new trade with some remote and barbarous nation' (ibid.: II, 277). He defended ('the public is afterwards to reap the benefit') the system of patents and copyrights according to which 'a temporary monopoly ... of a new machine is granted to its inventor, and that of a new book to its author' (ibid., 278). He was enthusiastic about 'premiums given by the public to artists and manufacturers who excel in their particular occupations' (ibid., 29) despite the fact that the State accolade differentiates extraordinary workmanship in a way that the rational market is paid to do. In favour of competition, Smith could also come down decisively in favour of restriction.

Nor can Smith be described as the impatient advocate of immediate free trade. Barriers should be reduced gradually rather than all at once lest the revolution of cheap imports too abruptly 'deprive ... many thousands of our people of their ordinary employment' (ibid.: I, 491). Tariffs can be reimposed as a retaliatory measure or to persuade other countries to remove their own obstructions: 'The recovery of a great foreign market will generally more than compensate the transitory inconveniency' (ibid., 490). Export prohibition can be converted to 'a legal exportation subject to a tax' in order to afford 'a revenue to the sovereign' (ibid.: II, 172). At the end of the day there is the compromise with expediency and the triumph of the second best: 'To expect, indeed, that the freedom of trade should be entirely restored in Great Britain, is as absurd as to expect that an Oceana or Utopia should ever be established in it' (ibid.: I, 493). Some positions of imperfection were clearly to continue protected, some prices charged to the consumer to remain supracompetitive. Life is like that on the middle ground.

12.4 THE PRODUCTIVE STATE

Over and above the protective functions of defence and justice, Smith assigned a third duty to the State. This was 'the duty of erecting and maintaining certain public works and certain public institutions, which it can never be for the interest of any individual, or small number of individuals, to erect and maintain' (Smith, 1776: II, 209). Nothing is less certain than 'certain' unless it be 'never'. Alexander Gray knew a bottomless pit when he saw one: 'This third duty throws open what the Treasury used to call a "serious door" ... Heaven knows what far-flung activities might not be pressed under this capacious umbrella' (Gray, 1976: 541).

Smith's criterion is that the projects be in the public interest (although how this is to be defined and by whom he does not explain) and that they be unattractive to private enterprise (and thus demonstrably at variance with the 'natural order' and the 'invisible hand'). One example would be the compulsory registration of leases (Smith, 1776: II, 359). Another would be 'the sterling mark upon plate, and the stamps upon linen and woollen cloth' (ibid.: I, 136). In cases such as these the State sets out to give the consumer a guarantee of security and quality. Reliable intelligence is as much the precondition for effective exchanging as is the protective enforcement of contracts (ibid., 107) once the buyer and the seller have concluded their deal.

The State takes over the precondition, Smith is saying, because 'it can never be for the interest' of the private sector to deliver the service for itself. Since gain-seeking registrars would have the incentive of fees, since commercial certifiers could make assaying and stamping into a profit-seeking business, it is possible that Smith, falling back on the done thing simply because it was there, was too quick to pronounce a sentence of 'never' on supply and demand. He might, of course, have meant *never satisfactorily* when he wrote 'never'. He might have had in mind the shortcomings of natural monopoly and conflict of interest which on a calculus of costs and benefits might have added up for him to the State. It is likely that it was relative performance and not 'never' that Smith had in mind in respect of the registering and of the benchmarking. That, however, is not what he said. A crucial step in the argument was, here as elsewhere, missed out for publication by a nervous recluse who was reluctant to be too precise.

Smith's 'never' is even more of a problem in the case of the Royal Mint and of the Post Office. The Mint belongs in the State sector because it is a money maker in more ways than one: coinage 'not only defrays its own expence, but affords a small revenue or seignorage to the sovereign' (ibid.: II, 246). The Post belongs in the State sector because it is even more of a success than the Mint: 'Over and above defraying its own expence, [it] affords in almost all countries a very considerable revenue to the sovereign' (ibid.). The Post Office, Smith reported, was not 'never' but *almost always* a source of profit for its owner, the State: 'It is perhaps the only mercantile project which has been successfully managed by, I believe, every sort of government. The capital to be advanced is not very considerable. There is no mystery in the business. The returns are not only certain, but immediate' (ibid., 343). Smith is here defending the State-run business in the language not of 'never' but of money. Libertarians will seize upon the same evidence when they call for privatisation and not for the State.

A further instance of public provision involves the nation's infrastructure: 'good roads, bridges, navigable canals, harbours' (ibid., 245). Here the standard of 'never' is seen quite explicitly to stand for *never very well*: 'At many turnpikes, it has been said, the money levied is more than double of what is necessary for executing, in the completest manner, the work which is often executed in a very slovenly manner, and sometimes not executed at all' (ibid., 248). Commercial turnpikes had shown a single-seller's indifference to value for money. The private sector had not provided a good quality service. The public sector had been obliged to become the residual supplier by default.

Even so, State infrastructure was wherever possible to be rendered self-financing through tolls. User charges would at once generate funding for the facilities and ensure that they were 'made only where . . . commerce requires them' (ibid., 246). Should tolls prove insufficient for the service a subsidy should be paid in recognition of the spillover. The tax to finance it should, however, be as local and provincial as the benefit. It should not be a national burden: 'It is unjust that the whole society should contribute towards an expence of which the benefit is confined to a part of the society' (ibid., 339). An even closer approximation of the expense to the benefit would, of course, have been secured through the market-clearing price.

Market failure can be a failure of demand and not of supply. Smith's most literal and irreducible 'never' refers to just such a case. It relates to the failure of 'the labouring poor, that is, the great body of the people' (ibid., 303) to demand even a modest level of schooling: 'These are the disadvantages of a commercial spirit. The minds of men are contracted and rendered incapable of elevation [and] education is despised or at least neglected' (Smith, 1766: 541). Nature herself is at fault, for on the one hand she endowed man with the propensity to specialise while on the other she condemned him to 'gross ignorance and stupidity' (Smith, 1776: II, 308) as a direct consequence of the division of labour. Nature herself is evidently to blame for the existence of a large working class that, brutalised and irrational, can easily prove a threat to the stability of the whole.

That is, 'unless government takes some pains to prevent it' (ibid., 303) – unless the State, in other words, deliberately tinkers with the course of events through the provision of the 'most essential parts of education' to 'those who are bred to the lowest occupations' (ibid., 305). Such education will not overcome the alienating effects of overconcentration, but it will possibly raise the productivity of the operative. This will happen where he is taught to read, write and account, and is also exposed to 'the elementary parts of geometry and mechanics' (ibid., 305, 306). More important, however, elementary education will make the workman 'less liable . . . to the delusions of enthusiasm and superstition', 'less apt to be misled into any wanton or unnecessary opposition to the measures of government' (ibid., 309). These ideological spillovers (complemented by the slight equalisation of opportunity associated with the moderate investment in skill) are of value to the nation as a whole. The benefit being non-specific, the cost, Smith said, 'may, therefore, without injustice, be defrayed by the general contribution of the whole society' (ibid., 340).

We need it and we must pay. Murray Rothbard was always on his guard when the collectivists of *sui generis* appealed not to the *each* but to the We: 'There is no existing entity called "society"; there are only interacting individuals' (Rothbard, 1973: 35). In the case of Smith on education he was in no doubt that it was manipulation and propaganda that was being proposed. The

State was being made responsible for 'governmental education in order to inculcate obedience to it among the populace – scarcely a libertarian or *laissez-faire* doctrine' (Rothbard, 1995: 466). The State was being invited to create the citizens that Smith thought the We ought to have. Rothbard felt that Smith should have put his trust in the invisible hand instead.

Rothbard was opposed to nationalisation: State-run schooling '*requires* the imposition of uniformity and the stamping out of diversity and individuality in education' (Rothbard, 1973: 126). Rothbard was in favour of competition: the free market throws up 'a host of diverse schools . . . to meet the varied structure of educational demands by parents and children' (ibid.: 128). In respect of Oxford education, Smith's prescription of private provision, competitive choice was more or less in line with that of the later libertarian. Prohibited from receiving any 'honorary or fee' (Smith, 1776: II, 284) from their pupils, promised a salary for life irrespective of their work, some of the Oxford tutors had retreated into the 'exploded . . . [the] antiquated . . . [the] useless . . . [and the] obsolete', while others – the 'greater part' – had 'given up altogether even the pretence of teaching' (ibid., 284, 294, 301). Things would be better at Oxford, Smith reflected, if, consumer choice restored, the incomes of the teachers were to be made dependent upon their ability to attract paying students.

As with the Oxford don, so with the village dominie. The schoolmaster should be 'partly, but not wholly paid by the public; because, if he was wholly, or even principally paid by it, he would soon learn to neglect his business' (ibid., 306). Unlike Oxford education, the schoolteacher was to be 'partly' paid by the community even if 'partly' paid by his customers. The syllabus was to be to some extent prescribed since society as a whole had a strong interest in order. The authorities were to offer 'small premiums, and little badges of distinction' to inspire the 'children of the common people' (ibid.) to take their lessons seriously. The authorities were also, where small inducements were seen to have failed, to 'impose upon almost the whole body of the people the necessity of acquiring those most essential parts of education' (ibid.). Subsidies and prizes, prescription and conscription: Smith on education for the common people is clearly less 'Open the flood-gates' than is Smith on education for the privileged elite who know what they need.

In one area of public policy at least, Smith and Rothbard were in complete agreement. Writing of income maintenance and welfare, Rothbard had this to say about the relief of destitution: 'What, then, *can* the government do to help the poor? The only correct answer is also the libertarian answer: Get out of the way' (Rothbard, 1973: 162). It is a recommendation with which Smith would not have wanted to take exception. Smith barely mentioned the Poor Laws. He evidently took the view that it had been even poorer laws such as the laws of settlement and apprenticeship which, impeding the mobility of labour, preventing a 'super-abundance' in one sub-market from coming to the relief of a 'scarcity of hands' (Smith, 1776: I, 157) in another, had forced self-respecting men involuntarily 'to come upon the parish' (ibid., 151).

A freer labour market and a rapidly growing economy are themselves the best form of poor relief. The economy is fully employed: consider the 'hundred thousand soldiers and seamen' absorbed with 'no sensible disorder' at the end of the Seven Years' War in 1763 (ibid., 492). Total demand is not likely to fall short: 'What is annually saved is as regularly consumed as what is annually spent, and nearly in the same time too' (ibid., 359). There are real jobs for all. There is no need for discretionary make-work to generate opportunities for the slack. The poor, 'begging employment', lived in China where the economic climate had frozen up. In a post-mercantilist Britain the able-bodied would not find it difficult to earn their own welfare by means of the quid pro quo.

Alfred Marshall's *residuum* remained, however, on the outside looking in. Smith had little to say about the desperate and the incapable. No doubt he was assuming that, so frequently cared for in the family, they would benefit at one remove from the dynamism of upgrading. Besides that, rising living standards would make possible the translation of instinctual benevolence into private charity: 'Before we can feel much for others we must in some measure be at ease ourselves' (Smith, 1759: 205). Private charity to Smith, like blood donation to Titmuss, is a voluntary gift that fills a market void: 'The relief and consolation of human misery depend altogether upon our compassion for . . . the poor and the wretched' (ibid.: 225–6). The State is not the first step and not even the last. When private giving fails, Smith wrote, the widows and orphans can console themselves with the hope of justice in Heaven and the dream of the 'life to come' (ibid.: 91).

The widows and orphans are directed to stoicism and acceptance. Equally in keeping with Smith on benevolence (and on security) would, however, be the alternative vision of a welfare government that fills the vacuum. Smith in 1759 and 1776 could not have anticipated the misery of the early nineteenth century. Faced with the urbanisation, the overcrowding, the disease, the unemployment, the hunger, the child labour, it would have been entirely in character for the pragmatic interventionist to have treated the Dickensian imperatives of the Industrial Revolution as the analogue to the party walls that had to be regulated, the lower-class education that had to be empowered. Laissez-faire was not, after all, general and universal in Smith's political economy. Rather, it was the particular prescription for a particular disease.

It would therefore be correct to conclude, with Jacob Viner, that *The Wealth of Nations* was in no small measure 'a tract for the times, a specific attack on certain types of government activity which Smith was convinced, on both

a priori and empirical grounds, operated against national prosperity ...
Smith's primary objective was to secure the termination of *these* activities of
government ... Everything else was to a large degree secondary' (Viner, 1928:
139). Everything else was to a large degree *possible*, including the welfare
parish and the government that gets involved.

12.5 PUBLIC FINANCE

Smith established two objectives for the science of political economy. The first
of these concerns rising income per head of the population – 'to provide a
plentiful revenue or subsistence for the people, or more properly to enable
them to provide such a revenue or subsistence for themselves' (Smith, 1776:
I, 449). The second relates to public finance – 'to supply the state or commonwealth with a revenue sufficient for the public services' (ibid.). The latter
topic, the subject of the present section, takes up almost a third of *The Wealth
of Nations*. It is the subject of Book V, the longest of the five component
books. The page count in itself is a reminder of the extent to which Smith, the
successor to Petty and the contemporary of Steuart, regarded his work as a
manual of statecraft.

Rothbard recognised that public finance was effectively the mirror image
of the protective and productive State: 'There has ... been a great amount of
useless controversy about *which* activity of government imposes the burden on
the private sector: *taxation or government spending*. It is actually futile to
separate them, since they are both stages in the same process of burden and
redistribution' (Rothbard, 1962: II, 793). Rothbard accepted that Adam Smith
had devoted considerable attention both to the plus side and to the minus. He
complained, however, that the result had not repaid the investment.

With respect to public expenditure, Smith had made no estimate of the
overall burden: 'If, for example, as in the case of Smith, the government is
supposed to supply public works, *how many* should it provide and how much
should be spent? There have been almost no preferred criteria' (Rothbard,
1995: 469). With respect to public finance, moreover, Smith had vacillated
between the obvious and the erroneous: 'Like the rest of his work, it was a
confused mixture of the banal and the fallacious' (ibid.: 470). Rothbard is here
referring especially to the four central maxims around which Smith structured
his theory of tax. The first maxim incorrect, the other maxims inconsequential,
it was Rothbard's view that all four principles could usefully be scrapped in
favour of the following meta-principle which said it all: 'Regardless of popular sanction ... Taxation is Robbery.' (Rothbard, 1973: 24, 25). Convincing or
not to a libertarian such as Rothbard, Smith's four central maxims at any rate
are as follows.

First, equality: 'The subjects of every state ought to contribute towards the support of the government, as nearly as possible, in proportion to their respective abilities; that is, in proportion to the revenue which they respectively enjoy under the protection of the state. The expence of government to the individuals of a great nation, is like the expence of management to the joint tenants of a great estate, who are all obliged to contribute in proportion to their respective interests in the estate' (Smith, 1776: II, 350).

Smith would seem here to be making the Lockean assumption that the citizen's stake in his country is proportional to the property which he holds and wishes to protect. Simultaneously, however, he accompanies his reference to 'respective interests' (the benefits) with another, quite separate, reference to 'respective abilities' (the costs). Musgrave, examining the dual criterion as presented in the maxim, all but accuses Smith of using words to hide the ambiguity: 'The "that is" clause nicely begs the issue since if ability-to-pay depends on income, and income is earned under the protection of the State, the two versions may be said to yield the same result' (Musgrave, 1976: 367). Respective interests might be in excess of respective abilities: this would be the case where person or reputation was abnormally at risk but where net worth was modest. Also the stock of property might not be a good proxy for ability-to-pay: the revenues of the tradition-bound landowner will be less in proportion to his estate than will be the returns of the maximising merchant to an equivalent capital. Smith would presumably have treated such occurrences as exceptions and mere *curiosa*. To him it was the interchangeability of the 'that is' that was expected to be the rule.

Smith's first maxim was proportional sacrifice. One illustration of its use would be his observation, concerning taxes on consumables, that they redistribute wealth in defiance of neutrality: 'They do not always fall equally or proportionately upon the revenue of every individual' (Smith, 1776: II, 426). Yet proportional sacrifice was not, apparently, a hard and fast rule, since Smith in some places actually welcomed a rising scale as equitable and good: 'It is not very unreasonable that the rich should contribute to the public expence, not only in proportion to their revenue, but something more than in that proportion' (ibid., 368). Smith is here recommending the introduction of higher tax rates for larger houses for the simple reason that larger houses are occupied by wealthier tenants. He goes even further when he calls for the imposition of discriminatory tolls (cross-subsidising the transportation of necessities) upon 'carriages of luxury'. In this way 'the indolence and vanity of the rich is made to contribute in a very easy manner to the relief of the poor' (ibid., 246).

The case of the turnpike tolls shows that Smith was prepared not only to bash the rich but to bash their revealed preferences as well. His attack on 'luxury', 'indolence' and 'vanity' – ascetic, Calvinist and judgmental in its thrust – implies a philosophical standard which identifies fairness with function and not with even-handedness. It is the same criterion which led Smith to defend the Usury Laws lest the idle fritter away on frivolities the capital that the parsimonious would have committed to productive labour. The criterion is growth and, with growth, 'the relief of the poor'. The maxim, however, is equality. The two considerations need not yield the same result.

Second, certainty: 'The tax which each individual is bound to pay ought to be certain, and not arbitrary' (ibid., 350). Smith's second maxim of taxation is an argument for impersonal assessment. It is a rejection of the 'insolence' as well as the 'corruption' and the 'power of the tax-gatherer' (ibid., 351, 350), which had so often made fiscal policy so random and so unjust. Smith's second maxim is a call for impartial rule-enforcement in place of administrative discretion. It is hard to believe that anyone but the bribable and the evasion-minded could object to that.

Third, convenience: 'Every tax ought to be levied at the time, or in the manner, in which it is most likely to be convenient for the contributor to pay it' (ibid., 351). It is convenient for taxes on rents to be collected after the rents themselves have duly been received. It is convenient for taxes on consumables to be demanded at the time when the shopper pays for the purchase. It is inconvenient, on the other hand, for the tax bill to arrive before cash flow has generated the wherewithal for settlement. You cannot get blood from a stone. Tax inspectors should not expect the impossible from their charges.

Fourth, economy in collection: 'Every tax ought to be so contrived as both to take out and to keep out of the pockets of the people as little as possible, over and above what it brings into the public treasury of the state' (ibid.). Smith is here concerned that time should not be wasted 'by subjecting the people to the frequent visits and odious examination of the tax-gatherers'; that no obstruction to industry should result that would cost 'great multitudes' their 'maintenance and employment'; and, of course, that so many tax-inspectors should not be set to work as would 'eat up the greater part of the produce of the tax' (ibid., 352, 351). The threat from the transaction cost obviously limits the extent to which taxes can be made proportional to the ability-to-pay. In that sense there would seem to be a tension between Smith's fourth maxim of taxation and his first.

The four maxims are, of course, separate and discrete. Smith does not see any need to integrate his principles, to resolve the tensions or to specify the ideal. The result, as Alan Peacock has pointed out, is a classificatory schema but not a programme or a mix: 'What is noticeably missing from his exposition is any attempt to weight the importance of each maxim, so that no final conclusion is drawn either about the relative merits of different forms of taxation or about the "package of taxes" which would best accord with

Smith's own normative propositions' (Peacock, 1975: 562). Nor should it be supposed that Smith's four maxims necessarily exhaust the relevant considerations. Referring specifically to Smith's surprising neglect both of revenue maximisation and of political acceptability, Stigler has concluded that a Chancellor of the Exchequer would be hard-pressed to find what he needed in Smith's four rules: 'They form a wholly inadequate basis for judging individual taxes' (Stigler, 1971: 130).

Smith himself, interestingly, did not stop short at the four. Four maxims were made explicit. The fifth is only identifiable from the shadow on the wall. The fifth is engineered reallocation. Directive, manipulative, unfree, Smith's implied fifth maxim confirms Rothbard's suspicions that public finance can easily degenerate into private serfdom.

Smith was prepared to see taxes levied not only to generate finance for defence, justice and public works but also to contain certain choices, to stimulate others. The taxation of alcohol illustrates the scope for discouragement. The taxation of rent illustrates the contribution of the constructive hand up.

In the case of alcoholic drink, Smith supported a tax to restrict the number of outlets: 'It may to many people appear not improper to give some discouragement to the multiplication of little alehouses' (Smith, 1776: II, 380). Different rates of tax could simultaneously be introduced in order to fine-tune the micro-choices within the framework of the whole: 'Spirituous liquors might remain as dear as ever; while at the same time the wholesome and invigorating liquors of beer and ale might be considerably reduced in their price' (ibid., 422). Smith knew that the market had reached a decision concerning the consumption of the commodity. Preferring a tax to a prohibition, he was proposing a revision of the incentive structure in order to induce the market to think again.

Selective taxation of rent is an instance of paternalism not to reduce but rather to expand. A Pigovian abatement could be offered to an improving landowner who ploughed back his rent in drains and manure or even moved into cultivation himself: 'His capital is generally greater than that of the tenant . . . The landlord can afford to try experiments' (ibid., 357). The rent in kind could be taxed at a higher rate than the rent in cash in order to price out a practice which deprived farmers of their productivity-boosting surplus: in this way 'a practice which is hurtful to the whole community might perhaps be sufficiently discouraged' (ibid.). A rise in rent in place of an even greater lump-sum fine upon renewal of the lease could be made more attractive by a two-tier tax that penalised the latter system, so little compatible with investment and activity: 'By rendering the tax upon such fines a good deal heavier than upon the ordinary rent, this hurtful practice might be discouraged' (ibid., 356).

All taxation of rent, more generally, is in the end a burden on the landowner. The windfall nature of the demand-led surplus makes such taxation at once legitimate and welcome: 'A tax upon ground-rents would not raise the rents of houses. It would fall altogether upon the owner of the ground-rent, who acts always as a monopolist, and exacts the greatest rent which can be got for the use of his ground' (ibid., 370). Discriminatory treatment would be a violation both of equality as proportionality (Smith's first maxim) and of justice as impartiality (Smith's promise of protection). On the other hand, 'no discouragement will thereby be given to any sort of industry' (ibid.) and the wealth of nations counts above the frivolity of the indolent.

The landowner will claim that he is being mugged by the State for no better reason than the fact that he 'shudders with horror at the thought of any situation which demands the continual and long exertion of patience, industry, fortitude, and application of thought' (Smith, 1759: 56). Rothbard will come to the defence of this resolute individualist, thrown to the dogs by his government because he has no wish to play with the team. Smith, however, will be less permissive, less prepared to 'Open the flood-gates' to an equilibrium that is a waste. Smith saw market and State as alternative routes, as competing means and not as absolute ends. Rothbard would reply that with friends like Smith, the market need have no fear of the social democrats at the door.

12.6   DEMOCRACY AND EXCHANGE

Schumpeter and Marshall believed that democracy and exchange had grown up together. Historically speaking, they were in agreement with Durbin that the 'political institution of government responsible to, and replaceable by, the people' had been associated with an unprecedented rise in the quality of life: 'Judged by results, the democracies have established the most efficient productive systems in the world' (Durbin, 1940: 32, 215). There the paths diverged. Schumpeter felt that the supersession of capitalism might or might not lead to the redundancy of democracy. Marshall, however, anticipated a hyphenated society in which the market economy and the democratic polity would exist side by side. Each pillar of the arch would reinforce the other. Each wheel of the cart would enable the vehicle to advance.

Marshall welcomed the affluence. He also welcomed the consultation. Durbin had said that democracy is not just the gilt on the gingerbread. Instead it is 'as air to breathing, as coal to fire, as love to life': 'The sources of life for a tree are its roots, not its fruits; and the roots of democracy lie deeply buried in the attitude to each other of people who disagree with each other, not in the benefits arising from social peace' (ibid.: 271, 262). Marshall and Durbin did not see democracy merely as the means to a material end. They saw it as an integral part of human decency when tolerant people debate and decide.

Marshall and Titmuss, like Durbin and Tawney, would not compromise on the articulation of the heart's desire. That is an important reason why Durbin was prepared to say farewell to exchange: 'Socialism is necessary to democracy,' Durbin wrote, while 'capitalism is incompatible with democracy' (ibid.: 271). The past had granted unprecedented freedom to the butcher, the brewer and the baker. The future would have to socialise and shape. Schumpeter, ranking events above ideas, was certain that anarchic capitalism would give way to the plan. In contrast to Durbin, however, he saw no reason why democracy after that would necessarily have any role to play.

Galbraith shared the inevitability but not the plan. Like Marshall, he anticipated a hyphenated society. He was certain that the masses would elect the Kennedys and the McGoverns who would do what the circumstances demand. Adam Smith was less confident that the voters could be trusted even with Schumpeter's second theory of democracy, let alone with Schumpeter's first. Smith feared that the rule of the people would upset the steady progress that was the great conquest of market exchange. He also feared that a powerful State might threaten the initiative and the autonomy upon which the wealth of the nation depends. Smith therefore defended exchange while pointing out that there were pitfalls both in Durbin's democracy that 'gives to the great majority of people what they want' (ibid.: 88) and in Schumpeter's Ministry that might in the end be telling all of us what to do.

It is often said that the authoritarian–bureaucratic State produces the best outcomes in the economy. Sen is not prepared to generalise from selective successes to a universal rule. For every Singapore with an exemplary record of growth there is a North Korea that is not a good advertisement for paternalism and hierarchy, while 'the best record of economic growth in Africa . . . can be seen in Botswana, which has been an oasis of democracy' (Sen, 2001: 11). Sen concludes that he can find no real link either in favour or against: 'There is, in fact, no convincingly general evidence that authoritarian governance and the suppression of political and civil rights are really beneficial in encouraging economic development' (ibid.: 12). What he does say is that elections, oppositions, security and expression have done much to alleviate hunger: 'No substantial famine has ever occurred in any independent and democratic country with a relatively free press' (ibid.). There must be something in democracy, he is saying, that makes the market and the State perform.

Economics in any case is not the whole of human development.

Individualism is a funny animal. Sometimes what people want is a job and a meal and a few designer labels: 'Thus God and Nature link'd the gen'ral frame/And bade self-love and social be the same' (Pope, 1733–4: 535). Sometimes what people want is the freedom to donate blood or to help disadvantaged children on to the ladder of success: 'Man, like the gen'rous vine, supported lives/The strength he gains is from th' embrace he gives.' (ibid.). Capitalism is freedom. Welfare is freedom. Democracy gives ordinary citizens the chance to say what kind of freedom they would like to have.

References

Allen, R.L. (1991), *Opening Doors: The Life and Work of Joseph Schumpeter*, 2 vols, New Brunswick: Transaction Publishers.

Almond, G.A. and S. Verba (1963), *The Civic Culture: Political Attitudes and Democracy in Five Nations*, Newbury Park: Sage, 1989.

Arblaster, A. (1994), *Democracy*, 2nd edn, Buckingham: Open University Press.

Aristotle (1981), *The Politics*, trans. T.A. Sinclair and T.J. Saunders, Harmondsworth: Penguin.

Asch, S.E. (1952), *Social Psychology*, Oxford: Oxford University Press, 1987.

Bagehot, W. (1867), *The English Constitution*, London: Collins, 1963.

Barbalet, J.M. (1988), *Citizenship: Rights, Struggle and Class Inequality*, Buckingham: Open University Press.

Bartel, R.D. (1983), 'The anatomy of power', *Challenge*, **26**; reprinted in J.R. Stanfield and Jacqueline Bloom Stanfield (eds) (2004), *Interviews with John Kenneth Galbraith*, Jackson: University of Mississippi Press.

Becker, G.S. (1985), 'Pressure groups and political behavior', in R.D. Coe and C.K. Wilber (eds), *Capitalism and Democracy: Schumpeter Revisited*, Notre Dame: University of Notre Dame Press.

Bell, D. (1965), *The End of Ideology*, rev. edn, Cambridge, MA: Harvard University Press, 1988.

Bentham, J. (1789), *An Introduction to the Principles of Morals and Legislation*, ed. J.H. Burns and H.L.A. Hart, London: Methuen, 1982.

Bergson, A. (1938), 'A reformulation of certain aspects of welfare economics', *Quarterly Journal of Economics*, **52**, 310–34.

Bevan, A. (1952), *In Place of Fear*, London: MacGibbon and Kee, 1961.

Bevan, A. (1958), 'Speech in the House of Commons, 30 July', *Parliamentary Debates* (UK), vol. 592, cols 1382–98.

Beveridge, W.H. (1942), *Social Insurance and Allied Services*, Cmd 6404, London: His Majesty's Stationery Office.

Bosanquet, B. (1895), 'The reality of the general will', in B. Bosanquet, *Aspects of the Social Problem*, reprinted in D. Boucher (ed.) (1997), *The British Idealists*, Cambridge: Cambridge University Press.

Bosanquet, B. (1899), *The Philosophical Theory of the State*, London: Macmillan.

Bottomore, T. (1992), 'Citizenship and social class, forty years on', in T.H. Marshall, *Citizenship and Social Class*, London: Pluto Press.

Bottomore, T. (1993), *Elites and Society*, 2nd edn, London: Routledge.

Boyle, E. and C.A.R. Crosland (1971), *The Politics of Education*, Harmondsworth: Penguin Books.

Brennan, H.G. and J.M. Buchanan (1985), *The Reason of Rules*, Cambridge: Cambridge University Press.

Briggs, Asa (1956), 'Socialism and society', *The Observer*, 30 September, p. 80.

Buchanan, J.M. (1975), *The Limits of Liberty*, Chicago: University of Chicago Press.

Buchanan, J.M. (1976), 'Public goods and natural liberty', in T. Wilson and A.S. Skinner (eds), *The Market and the State: Essays in Honour of Adam Smith*, Oxford: Clarendon Press.

Burke, E. (1774), 'Speech at Mr. Burke's Arrival in Bristol, 3 November', reprinted in I. Kramnick (ed.) (1999), *The Portable Edmund Burke*, Harmondsworth: Penguin Books.

Burke, E. (1790), *Reflections on the Revolution in France*, ed. C.C. O'Brien, Harmondsworth: Penguin, 1968.

Carlyle, T. (1843), *Past and Present*, London: Chapman and Hall.

Catephores, G. (1994), 'The imperious Austrian; Schumpeter as bourgeois Marxist', *New Left Review*, **205**, 3–30.

Challenge (1973), 'Conversation with an inconvenient economist', *Challenge*, **16**, reprinted in J.R. Stanfield and Jacqueline Bloom Stanfield (eds) (2004), *Interviews with John Kenneth Galbraith*, Jackson: University of Mississippi Press.

Coats, A.W. (1975), 'Adam Smith and the mercantile system', in A.S. Skinner and T. Wilson (eds), *Essays on Adam Smith*, Oxford: Clarendon Press.

Cole, G.D.H. (1913), *The World of Labour*, Brighton: Harvester Press, 1973.

Cole, G.D.H. (1917), *Self-Government in Industry*, London: G. Bell & Sons.

Cole, M.I. (1952), 'Education and social democracy', in R.H.S. Crossman (ed.), *New Fabian Essays*, London: Turnstile Press.

Collini, S. (1979), *Liberalism and Sociology: L.T. Hobhouse and Political Argument in England 1880–1914*, Cambridge: Cambridge University Press.

Crosland, C.A.R. (1949), 'The way towards more socialist equality', *Tribune*, 19 August, p. 11.

Crosland, C.A.R. (1950), 'Function of private enterprise,' *Socialist Commentary*, February.

Crosland, C.A.R. (1952), 'The transition from capitalism', in R.H.S. Crossman (ed.), *New Fabian Essays*, London: Turnstile Press.

Crosland, C.A.R. (1955), 'The arrogance of austerity', *The Listener*, **54**, 8 December, pp. 975–7.

Crosland, C.A.R. (1956), *The Future of Socialism*, London: Jonathan Cape.

Crosland, C.A.R. (1959), 'Industrial democracy and workers' control', *Encounter*, **12**; reprinted in *The Conservative Enemy* (Crosland, 1962).

Crosland, C.A.R. (1960), 'Socialism in a prosperous world,' *New Leader*, 29 February, p. 13.

Crosland, C.A.R. (1961), 'The public schools and English education', *Encounter*, 16; reprinted in *The Conservative Enemy* (Crosland, 1962).

Crosland, C. A. R. (1962), *The Conservative Enemy*, London: Jonathan Cape.

Crosland, C.A.R. (1966), 'Comprehensive education', speech delivered at the North of England Education Conference on 7 January; reprinted in *Socialism Now* (Crosland, 1974c).

Crosland, C.A.R. (1968), 'Socialists in a dangerous world', *Socialist Commentary*, November, reprinted in *Socialism Now* (Crosland, 1974c).

Crosland, C.A.R. (1971a), 'A social–democratic Britain', Fabian Tract 404, reprinted in *Socialism Now* (Crosland, 1974c).

Crosland, C.A.R. (1971b), 'Towards a Labour housing policy', Fabian Tract 410, reprinted in *Socialism Now* (Crosland, 1974c).

Crosland, C.A.R. (1974a), 'Socialism now', *Socialism Now* (Crosland, 1974c).

Crosland, C.A.R. (1974b), 'Interview with George Cole', London Broadcasting Radio, 25 April.

Crosland, C.A.R. (1974c), *Socialism Now*, London: Jonathan Cape.

Crosland, C.A.R. (1974d), 'Socialism, land and equality', *Socialist Commentary*, March, pp. iii–vii.

Crosland, C.A.R. (1975), 'Social democracy in Europe', Fabian Tract 438, Fabian Society London.

Crosland, C.A.R. (1976), 'Battle for the public purse,' *Guardian*, 24 March, p. 14.

Crosland, C.A.R., unpublished papers, in the British Library of Political and Economic Science, London School of Economics; cited by permission of Mrs S. Crosland.

Crosland, S. (1982), *Tony Crosland*, London: Jonathan Cape.

Dahl, R.A. (1956), *A Preface to Democratic Theory*, Chicago: University of Chicago Press.

Dahl, R.A. (1961), *Who Governs? Democracy and Power in an American City*, New Haven: Yale University Press.

Dahl, R.A. (1985), *A Preface to Economic Democracy*, Berkeley: University of California Press.

Dahrendorf, R. (1959), *Class and Class Conflict in Industrial Society*, London: Routledge and Kegan Paul.

Dennis, N. and A.H. Halsey (1988), *English Ethical Socialism: Thomas More to R. H. Tawney*, Oxford: Clarendon Press.

Disraeli, B. (1845), *Sybil or The Two Nations*, London: Peter Davies, 1927.

Downs, A. (1957), *An Economic Theory of Democracy*, New York: Harper and Row.

Downs, A. (1967), *Inside Bureaucracy*, Boston: Little, Brown and Co.

Durbin, E.F.M. (1940), *The Politics of Democratic Socialism: An Essay on Social Policy*, London: Routledge and Kegan Paul.

Durkheim, E. (1893), *The Division of Labor in Society*, trans. W.D. Halls, New York: The Free Press, 1984.

Durkheim, E. (1897), *Suicide: A Study in Sociology*, trans. J.A. Spaulding and G. Simpson, New York: The Free Press, 1951.

Durkheim, E. (1912), *The Elementary Forms of Religious Life*, trans. K.E. Fields, New York: The Free Press, 1995.

Durkheim, E. (1924), *Sociology and Philosophy*, trans. D.F. Pocock, London: Cohen and West, 1965.

Durkheim, E. (1925), *Moral Education*, trans. E.K. Wilson and H. Schnurer, New York: The Free Press, 1961.

Eastern Economic Journal (1988), 'A conversation with J.K. Galbraith', *Eastern Economic Journal*, **14**; reprinted in J.R. Stanfield and Jacqueline Bloom Stanfield (eds) (2004), *Interviews with John Kenneth Galbraith*, Jackson: University Press of Mississippi.

Esping-Andersen, E. (1990), *The Three Worlds of Welfare Capitalism*, Cambridge: Polity Press.

Freeden, M. (1978), *The New Liberalism: An Ideology of Social Reform*, Oxford: Clarendon Press.

Frey, B. (1982), 'Schumpeter, political economist', in H. Frisch (ed.), *Schumpeterian Economics*, New York: Praeger.

Friedman, M. (1953), 'The methodology of positive economics', in M. Friedman, *Essays in Positive Economics*, Chicago: University of Chicago Press.

Friedman, M. (1962), *Capitalism and Freedom*, Chicago: University of Chicago Press.

Fukuyama, F. (1992), *The End of History and the Last Man*, New York: The Free Press.

Fukuyama, F. (2004), *State-Building: Governance and World Order in the 21st Century*, Ithaca: Cornell University Press.

Galbraith, J.K. (1952a), *American Capitalism*, Harmondsworth: Penguin Books, 1967.

Galbraith, J.K. (1952b), *A Theory of Price Control*, Cambridge, MA: Harvard University Press.

Galbraith, J.K. (1954), *The Great Crash 1929*, Harmondsworth: Penguin Books, 1961.

Galbraith, J.K. (1958), *The Affluent Society*, Harmondsworth: Penguin Books, 1973.

Galbraith, J.K. (1964), 'Economics and the quality of life', *Science*, 10 July; reprinted in *Economics, Peace and Laughter* (Galbraith, 1971c).

Galbraith, J.K. (1965), *Economic Development*, Cambridge, MA: Harvard University Press.

Galbraith, J.K. (1966a), 'An agenda for American liberals', *Commentary*, **41** (June), 29–34.

Galbraith, J.K. (1966b), 'The starvation of the cities', *The Progressive*, December; reprinted in *A View from the Stands* (Galbraith, 1986).

Galbraith, J.K. (1967), *The New Industrial State*, Harmondsworth: Penguin Books, 1974.

Galbraith, J.K. (1969a), 'The big defense firms are really public firms and should be nationalized', *New York Times Magazine*, 16 November 1969, pp. 50, 162–75.

Galbraith, J.K. (1969b), *How to Control the Military*, Garden City: Doubleday.

Galbraith, J.K. (1970a), *Who Needs the Democrats*, Garden City: Doubleday.

Galbraith, J.K. (1970b), 'Foreign policy: the plain lessons of a bad decade', *Foreign Policy*, December; reprinted in *Economics, Peace and Laughter* (Galbraith, 1971c).

Galbraith, J.K. (1970c), 'The economics of beauty', lecture to the Danish Society of Industrial Design; reprinted in *A View from the Stands* (Galbraith, 1986).

Galbraith, J.K. (1971a), 'The American Left and some British comparisons', Fabian Tract 405, Fabian Society London.

Galbraith, J.K. (1971b), 'United States', *Sunday Times Magazine*, 7 November, pp. 91–9.

Galbraith, J.K. (1971c), *Economics, Peace and Laughter*, Harmondsworth: Penguin Books, 1975.

Galbraith, J.K. (1973a), *Economics and the Public Purpose*, Harmondsworth: Penguin Books, 1975.

Galbraith, J.K. (1973b), 'Power and the useful economist', *American Economic Review*, **63**, 1–11.

Galbraith, J.K. (1974), 'Richard Nixon', *The Boston Globe*, 18 August; reprinted in *A View from the Stands* (Galbraith, 1986).

Galbraith, J.K. (1975a), 'Gunnar and Alva Myrdal', lecture at the City University of New York; reprinted in *A View from the Stands* (Galbraith, 1986).

Galbraith, J.K. (1975b), 'Will the answer be controls?', *The Listener*, **93**, 30 January, pp. 130–31.

Galbraith, J.K. (1977a), *The Age of Uncertainty*, London: British Broadcasting Corporation and André Deutsch.

Galbraith, J.K. (1977b), 'A very specific guide to the economic folkways of American business and businessmen', *Fortune*, August; reprinted in *A View from the Stands* (Galbraith, 1986).

Galbraith, J.K. (1978) (with Nicole Salinger), *Almost Everyone's Guide to Economics*, Boston: Houghton Mifflin.

Galbraith, J.K. (1979), 'Barbara Ward: in admiration', *The Washington Post*, 2 September; reprinted in *A View from the Stands* (Galbraith, 1986).

Galbraith, J.K. (1980), 'Two pleas for our age', *The New York Review of Books*, 17 July; reprinted in *A View from the Stands* (Galbraith, 1986).

Galbraith, J.K. (1981), *A Life in Our Times*, Boston: Houghton Mifflin.

Galbraith, J.K. (1982), 'The St. Pierre syndrome', *The New York Times*, 1 January; reprinted in *A View from the Stands* (Galbraith, 1986).

Galbraith, J.K. (1983a), *The Voice of the Poor*, Cambridge, MA: Harvard University Press.

Galbraith, J.K. (1983b), *The Anatomy of Power*, Boston: Houghton Mifflin.

Galbraith, J.K. (1983c), 'George Kistiakowski', talk at a Harvard memorial service; reprinted in *A View from the Stands* (Galbraith, 1986).

Galbraith, J.K. (1984a), 'Russia', *The New Yorker*, 3 September; reprinted in *A View from the Stands* (Galbraith, 1986).

Galbraith, J.K. (1984b), 'John Maynard Keynes', *The New York Review of Books*, 22 November; reprinted in *A View from the Stands* (Galbraith, 1986).

Galbraith, J.K. (1986), *A View from the Stands*, Boston: Houghton Mifflin.

Galbraith, J.K. (1987), *A History of Economics*, London: Hamish Hamilton.

Galbraith, J.K. (1988) (with Stanislav Menshikov), *Capitalism, Communism and Coexistence*, Boston: Houghton Mifflin.

Galbraith, J.K. (1992), *The Culture of Contentment*, Harmondsworth: Penguin Books, 1993.

Galbraith, J.K. (1994), *A Journey Through Economic Time: A Firsthand View*, Boston: Houghton Mifflin. (published in Great Britain as *The World Economy Since the Wars: A Personal View*, London: Sinclair-Stevenson, 1994).

Galbraith, J.K. (1996), *The Good Society: The Humane Agenda*, Boston: Houghton Mifflin.

Galbraith, J.K. (1998), *The Socially Concerned Today*, Toronto: University of Toronto Press.

Galbraith, J.K. (1999), *Name-Dropping: From F.D.R. On*, Boston: Houghton Mifflin.

Giddens, A. (1982), *Profiles and Critiques in Social Theory*, London: Macmillan.

Goffman, E. (1963), *Stigma: Notes on the Management of Spoiled Identity*, Harmondsworth: Penguin, 1968.

Gray, A. (1976), 'Adam Smith', *Scottish Journal of Political Economy*, **23**; reprinted in J.C. Wood (ed.) (1984), *Adam Smith: Critical Assessments*, London: Croom Helm, vol. I.

Green, T.H. (1879), *Lectures on the Principles of Political Obligation*, London: Longmans, 1941.

Green, T.H. (1881), 'Liberal Legislation and Freedom of Contract', reprinted in R.A. Epstein (ed.), *Classical Foundations of Liberty and Property*, New York: Garland, 2000.

Halberstam, D. (1967), 'The importance of being Galbraith', *Harper's Magazine*, November, pp. 47–54.

Halsey, A.H. (1984), 'T.H. Marshall: past and present 1893–1981', *Sociology*, **18**, 1–18.

Halsey, A.H. (1998), 'T.H. Marshall and ethical socialism', in M. Bulmer and A.M. Rees (eds), *Citizenship Today: The Contemporary Relevance of T.H. Marshall*, London: UCL Press.

Hattersley, R. (1987), *Choose Freedom*, Harmondsworth: Penguin Books.

Hayek, F.A. (1944), *The Road to Serfdom*, London: Routledge and Kegan Paul, 1976.

Hayek, F.A. (1960), *The Constitution of Liberty*, London: Routledge and Kegan Paul.

Hayek, F. A. (1988), *The Fatal Conceit*, London: Routledge.

Held, D. (1996), *Models of Democracy*, 2nd edn, Cambridge: Polity Press.

Hirsch, F. (1977), *Social Limits to Growth*, London: Routledge and Kegan Paul.

Hirschman, A.O. (1970), *Exit, Voice, and Loyalty*, Cambridge, MA: Harvard University Press.

Hobbes, T. (1651), *Leviathan*, Oxford: Basil Blackwell, 1957.

Hobhouse, L.T. (1911a), *Liberalism*, in L. T. Hobhouse, *Liberalism and Other Writings*, ed. J. Meadowcroft, Cambridge: Cambridge University Press, 1974.

Hobhouse, L.T. (1911b), *Social Evolution and Political Theory*, New York: Columbia University Press.

Holland, S. (1975), *The Socialist Challenge*, London: Quartet Books.

Jay, D.P.T. (1937), *The Socialist Case*, London: Faber and Faber.

Kant, I. (1785), *Groundwork of the Metaphysic of Morals*, trans. H.J. Paton; reprinted in H.J. Paton (ed.) (1961), *The Moral Law*, London: Hutchinson.

Keynes, J.M. (1936), *The General Theory of Employment, Interest and Money*, London: Macmillan, 1973.

Lindsay, A.D. (1943), *The Modern Democratic State*, London: Oxford University Press.

Lenin, V.I. (1920), *Left-wing Communism, an Infantile Disorder*, Moscow: Progress Publishers.

Lipset, S.M. (1960), *Political Man: The Social Bases of Politics*, Garden City, NY: Doubleday.

Lively, J. (1975), *Democracy*, Oxford: Basil Blackwell.

Locke, J. (1689), *Second Treatise of Government*, in his *Two Treatises of Government*, reprinted in M. Goldie, (ed.) (1993), London: Dent.

Macfie, A. L. (1967), 'The moral justification of free enterprise: a lay sermon on an Adam Smith text', *Scottish Journal of Political Economy*, **14**; reprinted in J.C. Wood (ed.) (1984), *Adam Smith: Critical Assessments*, London: Croom Helm, vol. I.

Macpherson, C.B. (1966), *The Real World of Democracy*, Oxford: Clarendon Press.

Macpherson, C.B. (1973), *Democratic Theory: Essays in Retrieval*, Oxford: Clarendon Press.

MacRae, D.G. (1982), 'Tom Marshall 1893–1981: a personal memoir', *British Journal of Sociology*, **33**(3), iii–vi.

Maine, H. S. (1861), *Ancient Law*, London: Oxford University Press, 1954.

Marshall, A. (1873), 'The future of the working classes'; reprinted in A.C. Pigou (ed.) (1925), *Memorials of Alfred Marshall*, New York: Augustus M. Kelley, 1966.

Marshall, A. (1885), 'The present position of economics'; reprinted in A.C. Pigou (ed.) (1925), *Memorials of Alfred Marshall*, New York: Augustus M. Kelley, 1966.

Marshall, A. (1890), *Principles of Economics*, 8th edn (1920), London: Macmillan, 1949.

Marshall, A. (1909), 'Letter to Lord Reay', 12 November 1909, published in A.C. Pigou (ed.) (1925), *Memorials of Alfred Marshall*, New York: Augustus M. Kelley, 1966.

Marshall, T.H. (1934), 'Social class – a preliminary analysis', *Sociological Review*, **26**; reprinted in T.H. Marshall, *Citizenship and Social Class and Other Essays*, Cambridge: Cambridge University Press, 1950.

Marshall, T.H. (1949), 'Review of W. Beveridge, *Voluntary Action*', *Political Quarterly*, **20**; reprinted in *Sociology at the Crossroads* (Marshall, 1963).

Marshall, T.H. (1950), *Citizenship and Social Class*, London: Pluto Press, 1992.

Marshall, T.H. (1953a), 'The nature and determinants of social status', *Yearbook of Education*, **1**; reprinted in *Sociology at the Crossroads* (Marshall, 1963).

Marshall, T.H. (1953b), 'Social selection in the welfare state', *Eugenics Review*, **45**; reprinted in *Sociology at the Crossroads* (Marshall, 1963).

Marshall, T.H. (1961), 'The welfare state – a comparative study', *European Journal of Sociology*, **2**; reprinted in *Sociology at the Crossroads* (Marshall, 1963).

Marshall, T.H. (1963), *Sociology at the Crossroads*, London: Heinemann Educational Books (published in the United States as *Class, Citizenship, and Social Development*, Chicago: University of Chicago Press, 1977).

Marshall, T.H. (1965a), 'The right to welfare', *Sociological Review*, **13**; reprinted in *The Right to Welfare and Other Essays* (Marshall, 1981).

Marshall, T.H. (1965b), 'Freedom as a factor in social development', in India International Centre (ed.), *Freedom and Development*; reprinted in *The Right to Welfare and Other Essays* (Marshall, 1981).

Marshall, T.H. (1966a), 'Welfare in the context of social development', in J.S. Morgan (ed.), *Welfare and Wisdom*; reprinted in *The Right to Welfare and Other Essays* (Marshall, 1981).

Marshall, T.H. (1966b), 'Welfare in the context of social policy', in J.S. Morgan (ed.), *Welfare and Wisdom*; reprinted in *The Right to Welfare and Other Essays* (Marshall, 1981).

Marshall, T.H. (1969), 'Reflections on power', *Sociology*, **3**; reprinted in *The Right to Welfare and Other Essays* (Marshall, 1981).

Marshall, T.H. (1972), 'Value problems of welfare-capitalism', *Journal of Social Policy*, **1**; reprinted in *The Right to Welfare and Other Essays* (Marshall, 1981).

Marshall, T.H. (1973), 'A British sociological career', *International Social Science Journal*, **25**, 88–100; reprinted in part in the *British Journal of Sociology*, **24**, 1973, 399–408.

Marshall, T.H. (1975), *Social Policy in the Twentieth Century*, 4th edn, London: Hutchinson University Library.

Marshall, T.H. (1981), *The Right to Welfare and Other Essays*, London: Heinemann Educational Books.

Marx, K. (1844a), *Economic and Philosophical Manuscripts of 1844*, London: Lawrence & Wishart, 1970.

Marx, K. (1844b), 'Critique of the Hegelian Philosophy of Law: Introduction'; reprinted in T.B. Bottomore and M. Rubel (eds) (1963), *Karl Marx: Selected Writings in Sociology and Social Philosophy*, Harmondsworth: Penguin Books.

Marx, K. (1859), 'Preface to *A Contribution to the Critique of Political Economy*'; reprinted in L. Colletti (ed.) (1975), *Karl Marx: Early Writings*, Harmondsworth: Penguin Books.

Marx, K. (1867), *Capital*, vol. I, London: Lawrence & Wishart, 1965.

Marx., K. and F. Engels (1845), *The Holy Family*; reprinted in *Karl Marx and Friedrich Engels: Collected Works*, vol. 4, New York: International Publishers, 1975.

Marx, K. and F. Engels (1845–6), *The German Ideology*; reprinted in *Karl Marx and Friedrich Engels: Collected Works*, vol. 5, New York: International Publishers, 1976.

Marx, K. and F. Engels (1848), *The Communist Manifesto*, Harmondsworth: Penguin Books, 1967.

Maslow, A.H. (1954), *Motivation and Personality*, 2nd edn, New York: Harper and Row, 1970.

Maslow, A.H. (1962), *Toward a Psychology of Being*, 2nd edn, Princeton: Van Nostrand, 1968.

Matthews, D. (1978), 'Advice to Exxon', *Challenge*, **21**; reprinted in J.R. Stanfield and Jacqueline Bloom Stanfield (eds) (2004), *Interviews with John Kenneth Galbraith*, Jackson: University Press of Mississippi.

Matthews, R.C.O. (1985), 'Competition in economy and polity', in R.C.O. Matthews (ed.), *Economy and Democracy*, London: Macmillan.

McClaughry, J. (1973), 'Galbraith and his critics', *Business and Society Review*, **8**; reprinted in J.R. Stanfield and Jacqueline Bloom Stanfield (eds) (2004), *Interviews with John Kenneth Galbraith*, Jackson: University Press of Mississippi.

Medearis, J. (2001), *Joseph Schumpeter's Two Theories of Democracy*, Cambridge, MA: Harvard University Press.

Merton, R.K. (1968), *Social Theory and Social Structure*, rev. edn, New York: The Free Press.

Michels, R. (1911), *Political Parties: A Sociological Study of the Oligarchical Tendencies of Modern Democracy*, trans. E. and C. Paul, Glencoe: The Free Press, 1949.

Mill, J.S. (1859), *On Liberty*, ed. G. Himmelfarb, Harmondsworth: Penguin Books, 1974.

Mill, J.S. (1861), *Considerations on Representative Government*; reprinted in J.S. Mill, *Utilitarianism, Liberty, Representative Government*, London: Dent, 1910.

Mills, C.W. (1956), *The Power Elite*, Oxford: Oxford University Press.

Mises, Ludwig von (1949), *Human Action*, 3rd edn, Chicago: Contemporary Books, 1966.

Mitchell, W.C. (1984a), 'Schumpeter and public choice, part I: precursor to public choice?', *Public Choice*, **42**; reprinted in J.C. Wood (ed.) (1991), *J.A. Schumpeter: Critical Assessments*, London: Routledge, vol. IV.

Mitchell, W.C. (1984b), 'Schumpeter and public choice, part II: democracy and the demise of capitalism: the missing chapter in Schumpeter', *Public Choice*, **42**; reprinted in J.C. Wood (ed.) (1991), *J.A. Schumpeter: Critical Assessments*, London: Routledge, vol. IV.

Montesquieu, Charles de Secondat, Baron de (1748), *The Spirit of the Laws*, trans. A.M. Cohler, B.C. Miller and H.S. Stone, Cambridge: Cambridge University Press, 1989.

Morris, W. (1886/7), 'A Dream of John Ball', in *Three Works by William Morris*, New York: International Publishers, 1968.

Mosca, G. (1896), *The Ruling Class*, trans. H.D. Kahn, New York: McGraw-Hill, 1939.

Mueller, D.C. (2003), *Public Choice III*, Cambridge: Cambridge University Press.

Musgrave, R.A. (1976), 'Adam Smith on public finance and distribution', in T. Wilson and A.S. Skinner (eds), *The Market and the State*, Oxford: Clarendon Press.

Nisbet, R.A. (1967), *The Sociological Tradition*, London: Heinemann.

Niskanen, W. (1971), *Bureaucracy and Representative Government*, Chicago: Aldine.

Oakley, Ann (1996), *Man and Wife: Richard and Kay Titmuss*, London: HarperCollins.

Oakley, Ann (2001), 'The family, poverty and population: commentary', in P. Alcock, H. Glennerster, A. Oakley and A. Sinfield (eds), *Welfare and Wellbeing: Richard Titmuss's Contribution to Social Policy*, Bristol: The Polity Press.

Olson, M. (1965), *The Logic of Collective Action*, Boston: Harvard University Press.

Olson, M. (1982), *The Rise and Decline of Nations*, New Haven and London: Yale University Press.

Orwell, G. (1941), *The Lion and the Unicorn: Socialism and the English Genius*, London: Secker & Warburg.

Paine, T. (1792), *The Rights of Man*, part II; reprinted in *T. Paine, Political Writings*, ed. B. Kuklick, Cambridge: Cambridge University Press, 2000.

Pareto, V. (1966), *Vilfredo Pareto: Sociological Writings*, ed. S.E. Finer, trans. D. Murfin, London: Pall Mall Press.

Peacock, A. (1975), 'The treatment of the principles of public finance in "The Wealth of Nations" ', in A.S. Skinner and T. Wilson (eds), *Essays on Adam Smith*, Oxford: Clarendon Press.

Pierson, C. (1998), *Beyond the Welfare State?*, 2nd edn, Cambridge: Polity Press.

Pigou, A.C. (1920), *The Economics of Welfare*, 4th edn, London: Macmillan, 1932.

Pinker, R. (1979), *The Idea of Welfare*, London: Heinemann Educational Books.

Pinker, R. (1981), 'Introduction' to T.H. Marshall, *The Right to Welfare and Other Essays* (Marshall, 1981).

Pinker, R. (1995), 'T.H. Marshall', in V. George and R. Page (eds), *Modern Thinkers on Welfare*, Hemel Hempstead: Prentice-Hall.

Plamenatz, J. (1973), *Democracy and Illusion*, London: Longman.

Plato (1961), *The Laws*, trans. A.E. Taylor, in E. Hamilton and H. Cairns (eds), *The Collected Dialogues of Plato*, Princeton, NJ: Princeton University Press.

Pope, A. (1733–4), *An Essay on Man*, reprinted in J.W. Butt (ed.) (1963), *The Poems of Alexander Pope*, London: Methuen.

Pratson, F.J. (1978), *Perspectives on Galbraith*, Boston: CBI Publishing Company.

Rae, J. (1895), *Life of Adam Smith*, New York: Augustus M. Kelley, 1965.

Rawls, J. (1971), *A Theory of Justice*, Oxford: Oxford University Press, 1972.

Rees, A.M. (1995), 'The other T.H. Marshall', *Journal of Social Policy*, **24**, 341–62.

Reisman, D.A. (1982), *State and Welfare: Tawney, Galbraith and Adam Smith*, London: Macmillan.

Reisman D.A. (2001), *Richard Titmuss: Welfare and Society*, 2nd edn, Houndmills: Palgrave.

Reisman, D.A. (2004), *Schumpeter's Market: Evolution and Enterprise*, Cheltenham, UK and Northampton, MA, USA: Edward Elgar.

Richter, M. (1964), *The Politics of Conscience: T.H. Green and His Age*, London: Weidenfeld.

Riesman, D. (with N. Glazer and R. Denney) (1950), *The Lonely Crowd: A Study of the Changing American Character*, New Haven: Yale University Press, 1969.

Rose, H. (1981), 'Rereading Titmuss: the sexual division of welfare', *Journal of Social Policy*, **10**, 477–501.

Rothbard, M.N. (1962), *Man, Economy, and State: A Treatise on Economic Principles*, 2 vols, Princeton, NJ: Van Nostrand.

Rothbard, M.N. (1973), *For a New Liberty*, New York: Libertarian Review Foundation, 1978.

Rothbard, M.N. (1995), *Economic Thought Before Adam Smith: An Austrian Perspective on the History of Economic Thought*, Aldershot, UK and Brookfield, US: Edward Elgar, vol. 1.

Rousseau, J.-J. (1755), 'A discourse on the origin of inequality', trans. G.D.H. Cole, in J.-J. Rousseau, *The Social Contract and Discourses*, London: Dent, 1913.

Rousseau, J.-J. (1762), *The Social Contract*, trans. G.D.H. Cole, in J.-J. Rousseau, *The Social Contract and Discourses*, London: Dent, 1913.

Samuels, W.J. (1977), 'The political economy of Adam Smith', *Ethics*, **87**; reprinted in J.C. Wood (ed.) (1984), *Adam Smith: Critical Assessments*, London: Croom Helm, 1984, vol. I.

Samuels, W.J. (1985), 'A critique of *Capitalism, Socialism, and Democracy*', in R.D. Coe and C.K. Wilber (eds), *Capitalism and Democracy: Schumpeter Revisited*, Notre Dame: University of Notre Dame Press.

Schumpeter, J.A. (1906), 'Über die Mathematische Methode der Theoretischen Ökonomie', *Zeitschrift für Volkswirtschaft, Sozialpolitik und Verwaltung*, **15**; reprinted in *Aufsätze zur Ökonomischen Theorie* (Schumpeter, 1952b).

Schumpeter, J.A. (1908), *Das Wesen und der Hauptinhalt der theoretischen Nationalökonomie*, Leipzig: Duncker und Humblot.

Schumpeter, J.A. (1912a), *Theorie der Wirtschaftlichen Entwicklung*, Leipzig: Duncker und Humblot.

Schumpeter, J.A. (1912b), *The Theory of Economic Development*, trans. R. Opie from the 1926 (revised) edition of *Theorie der Wirtschaftlichen Entwicklung*, London: Oxford University Press, 1961.

Schumpeter, J.A. (1918), *The Crisis of the Tax State*; reprinted in *Economics and Sociology* (Schumpeter, 1991).

Schumpeter, J.A. (1918/19), 'The sociology of imperialisms', *Archiv für Sozialwissenschaft und Sozialpolitik*, **46**; reprinted in *Economics and Sociology* (Schumpeter, 1991).

Schumpeter, J.A. (1919), 'Speech to the 24th session of the Austrian National Assembly, 4 July', in *Aufsätze zur Wirtschaftspolitik* (Schumpeter, 1985).

Schumpeter, J.A. (1920/21), 'Sozialistische Möglichkeiten von Heute', *Archiv für Sozialwissenschaft und Sozialpolitik*, **48**; reprinted in *Aufsätze zur Ökonomischen Theorie* (Schumpeter, 1952b).

Schumpeter, J.A. (1926/7), 'Steuerkraft und nationale Zukunft', *Der Deutsche Volkswirt*, **1**; reprinted in *Aufsätze zur Wirtschaftspolitik* (Schumpeter, 1985).

Schumpeter, J.A. (1927), 'Social classes in an ethnically homogeneous environment'; reprinted in *Economics and Sociology* (Schumpeter, 1991).

Schumpeter, J.A. (1932), 'Das Woher und Wohin unserer Wissenschaft'; reprinted in *Aufsätze zur Ökonomischen Theorie* (Schumpeter, 1952b).

Schumpeter, J.A. (1936), *Can Capitalism Survive?*; reprinted in *Economics and Sociology* (Schumpeter, 1991).

Schumpeter, J.A. (1939), *Business Cycles: A Theoretical, Historical and Statistical Analysis of the Capitalist Process*, 2 vols, New York: McGraw-Hill.

Schumpeter, J.A. (1941), *An Economic Interpretation of Our Time* (the Lowell Lectures), reprinted in *Economics and Sociology* (Schumpeter, 1991).

Schumpeter, J.A. (1942), *Capitalism, Socialism and Democracy*, 3rd edn, London: George Allen and Unwin, 1976.

Schumpeter, J.A. (1943), 'Capitalism in the postwar world', in S.E. Harris (ed.), *Postwar Economic Problems*, reprinted in *Essays* (Schumpeter, 1951).

Schumpeter, J.A. (1946), 'The future of private enterprise in the face of modern socialistic tendencies', English translation of 'L'avenir de l'entreprise privée devant les tendances socialistes modernes', in Association Professionelle des Industriels (ed.), *Premier Congrès Patronal*; reprinted in *Economics and Sociology* (Schumpeter, 1991).

Schumpeter, J.A. (1948), 'There is still time to stop inflation', *Nation's Business*, **36**; reprinted in *Essays* (Schumpeter, 1951).

Schumpeter, J.A. (1949), 'The Communist Manifesto in sociology and economics', *Journal of Political Economy*, **57**; reprinted in *Essays* (Schumpeter, 1951).

Schumpeter, J.A. (1950a), 'American institutions and economic progress' (the Walgreen Lectures, uncompleted); reprinted in *Economics and Sociology* (Schumpeter, 1991).

Schumpeter, J.A. (1950b), 'The march into socialism', *American Economic Review*, **40**; reprinted in *Capitalism, Socialism and Democracy* (Schumpeter, 1942).

Schumpeter, J.A. (1951), *Essays on Entrepreneurs, Innovations, Business Cycles and the Evolution of Capitalism*, ed. R.V. Clemence, Brunswick, NJ: Transaction Publishers, 1989.

Schumpeter, J.A. (1952a), *Ten Great Economists*, London: Routledge, 1997.

Schumpeter, J.A. (1952b), *Aufsätze zur Ökonomischen Theorie*, ed. E. Schneider and A. Spiethoff, Tübingen: J.C.B. Mohr.

Schumpeter, J.A. (1954), *History of Economic Analysis*, London: George Allen and Unwin.

Schumpeter, J.A. (1985), *Aufsätze zur Wirtschaftspolitik*, ed. W.F. Stolper and C. Seidl, Tübingen: J.C.B. Mohr.

Schumpeter, J.A. (1991), *The Economics and Sociology of Capitalism*, ed. R. Swedberg, Princeton: Princeton University Press.

Sen, A. (2001), 'Democracy and social justice', in F. Iqbal and Jong-Il You (eds), *Democracy, Market Economics, and Development: An Asian Perspective*, Washington, DC: The World Bank.

Simon, H.A. (1957), *Models of Man*, New York: John Wiley and Sons.

Skinner, A.S. (1996), *A System of Social Science: Papers Relating to Adam Smith*, 2nd edn, Oxford: Clarendon Press.

Smith, A. (1759), *The Theory of Moral Sentiments*, ed. D.D. Raphael and A.L. Macfie, Oxford: Clarendon Press, 1976.

Smith, A. (1766), *Lectures on Jurisprudence*, ed. R.L. Meek, D.D. Raphael and P.G. Stein, Oxford: Clarendon Press, 1978.

Smith, A. (1774), 'Letter to William Cullen, 20 September', in E.C. Mossner and I.S. Ross (eds), *The Correspondence of Adam Smith*, 2nd edn, Oxford: Clarendon Press, 1987.

Smith, A. (1776), *The Wealth of Nations*, ed. E. Cannan, 2 vols, London: Methuen, 1961.

Smith, A. (1795), *Essays on Philosophical Subjects*, ed. W.P.D. Wightsman and J.C. Bryce, Oxford: Clarendon Press, 1980.

Spencer, H. (1860), 'The social organism', *Westminster Review*, January; reprinted in H. Spencer, *Essays: Scientific, Political, and Speculative*, vol. I, London: Williams and Norgate, 1891.

Spencer, H. (1876, 1893, 1896), *Principles of Sociology*, London: Macmillan, 1969.

Stewart, A. (1995), 'Two conceptions of citizenship', *British Journal of Sociology*, **46**, 63–78.

Stigler, G.J. (1971), 'Smith's travels on the ship of state', *History of Political Economy*, **3**; reprinted in J.C. Wood (ed) (1984), *Adam Smith: Critical Assessments*, London: Croom Helm, vol. I.

Swedberg, R. (1991), *Joseph A. Schumpeter: His Life and Work*, Cambridge: Polity Press.

Tawney, R.H. (1914), *The Establishment of Minimum Rates in the Chain-Making Industry under the Trade Boards Act of 1909*, London: G. Bell and Sons.

Tawney, R.H. (1921), *The Acquisitive Society*, London: Collins, 1961.

Tawney, R.H. (1931), *Equality*, 4th edn, London: George Allen and Unwin, 1964.

Tawney, R.H. (1934), 'The choice before the Labour Party', *Political Quarterly*, **3**; reprinted in R.H. Tawney (1953), *The Attack and Other Papers*, London: George Allen and Unwin.

Tawney, R.H. (1935), 'Christianity and the social revolution', *New Statesman and Nation*, November; reprinted in R.H. Tawney (1953), *The Attack and Other Papers*, London: George Allen and Unwin.

Tawney, R.H. (1937), 'A note on Christianity and the social order'; reprinted in R.H. Tawney (1953), *The Attack and Other Papers*, London: George Allen and Unwin.

Tawney, R.H. (1943), 'The problem of the public schools', *Political Quarterly*, **14**; reprinted in R.H. Tawney, *The Radical Tradition* (1964), ed. Rita Hinden (1966), Harmondsworth: Penguin Books.

Tawney, R.H. (1949), 'Social democracy in Britain', in W. Scarlett (ed.), *The Christian Demand for Social Justice*; reprinted in R.H. Tawney, *The Radical Tradition* (1964), ed. Rita Hinden (1966), Harmondsworth: Penguin Books.

Thucydides (1972), *History of the Peloponnesian War*, trans. R. Warner, Harmondsworth: Penguin.

Tiebout, C.M. (1956), 'A pure theory of local expenditures', *Journal of Political Economy*, **64**, 416–24.

Titmuss, R.M. (1938), *Poverty and Population*, London: Macmillan.

Titmuss, R.M. (1943), *Birth, Poverty and Wealth*, London: Hamish Hamilton Medical Books.

Titmuss, R.M. (1950), *Problems of Social Policy*, London: His Majesty's Stationery Office and Longmans, Green.

Titmuss, R.M. (1962), *Income Distribution and Social Change*, London: George Allen and Unwin.

Titmuss, R.M. (1963), *Essays on 'The Welfare State'*, 2nd edn, London: George Allen and Unwin.

Titmuss, R.M. (1964), 'Introduction' to R.H. Tawney, *Equality*, 4th edn, London: George Allen and Unwin.

Titmuss, R.M. (1965), 'Goals of today's welfare state', in P. Anderson and R. Blackburn (eds), *Towards Socialism*, London: Fontana.

Titmuss, R.M. (1967a), 'The welfare state: images and realities', in C.I. Schottland (ed), *The Welfare State*, New York: Harper Torchbooks.

Titmuss, R.M. (1967b), 'Social welfare and the art of giving', in E. Fromm (ed.), *Socialist Humanism*, London: Allen Lane.

Titmuss, R.M. (1968), *Commitment to Welfare*, London: George Allen and Unwin.

Titmuss, R.M. (1970), *The Gift Relationship*, London: George Allen and Unwin.

Titmuss, R.M. (1974), *Social Policy*, ed. B. Abel-Smith and Kay Titmuss, London: George Allen and Unwin.

Titmuss, R.M., unpublished papers, in the British Library of Political and Economic Science, London School of Economics, cited by permission of Ann Oakley.

Titmuss, R.M. and B. Abel-Smith (1956), *The Cost of the National Health Service*, Cambridge: Cambridge University Press.

Titmuss, R.M., B. Abel-Smith and Tony Lynes (1961), *Social Policies and Population Growth in Mauritius*, London: Methuen.

Titmuss, R.M., B. Abel-Smith, G. Macdonald, A. Williams and C. Ward (1964), *The Health Services of Tanganyika*, London: Pitman Medical Publishing.

Titmuss, R.M. and F. Grundy (1945), *Report on Luton*, Luton: The Leagrave Press.

Titmuss, R.M. and F. Le Gros Clark (1939), *Our Food Problem*, London: Pelican Books.

Titmuss, R.M. and Kathleen Titmuss (1942), *Parents Revolt*, London: Secker and Warburg.

Tocqueville, A. de (1835; 1840), *Democracy in America*, 2 vols, trans. H. Reeve, New York: Alfred A. Knopf, 1948.

Tönnies, F. (1887), *Community and Civil Society*, trans. J. Harris and M. Hollis, Cambridge: Cambridge University Press, 2001.

Turner, B.S. (1986), *Citizenship and Capitalism: The Debate over Reformism*, London: Allen and Unwin.

Viner, J. (1928), 'Adam Smith and laissez-faire', in J.M. Clark *et al.* (eds), *Adam Smith, 1776–1926*, New York: Augustus M. Kelley, 1961.

Webb, B. (1948), *Our Partnership*, ed. B. Drake and M.I. Cole, Cambridge: Cambridge University Press, 1975.

Weber, M. (1904–5), *The Protestant Ethic and the Spirit of Capitalism*, trans. T. Parsons, London: George Allen and Unwin, 1930.

Weber, M. (1918), 'Politics as a vocation'; reprinted in H.H. Gerth and C.W. Mills (eds) (1948), *From Max Weber: Essays in Sociology*, London: Routledge and Kegan Paul.

Weber, M. (1922a), 'Bureaucracy'; reprinted in H.H. Gerth and C.W. Mills (eds) (1948), *From Max Weber: Essays in Sociology*, London: Routledge and Kegan Paul.

Weber, M. (1922b), 'The sociology of charismatic authority'; reprinted in H.H. Gerth and C.W. Mills (eds) (1948), *From Max Weber: Essays in Sociology*, London: Routledge and Kegan Paul.

Weber, M. (1922c), 'Structures of power'; reprinted in H.H. Gerth and C.W. Mills (eds) (1948), *From Max Weber: Essays in Sociology*, London: Routledge and Kegan Paul.

Weber, M. (1922d), 'Class, status, party'; reprinted in H.H. Gerth and C.W. Mills (eds) (1948), *From Max Weber: Essays in Sociology*, London: Routledge and Kegan Paul.

Woodhouse, A.S.P. (ed.) (1938), *Puritanism and Liberty, Being the Army Debates (1647–9) from the Clarke Manuscripts, with Supplementary Documents*, London: Dent.

Wright, D. McCord (1951), 'Schumpeter's political philosophy', *Review of Economics and Statistics*, **33**, 152–7.

Index

absenteeism, Swedish 201–2
absolute deprivation 222, 247
absolute power 35–6, 92
achievement, educational 251
active citizenship, democracy as 28
administrators
  preconditions for politics 81
  social rights 220–23
affluence
  and altruism 149, 230
  democracy and exchange 10
  political power 191
  versus welfare 199–200
agency dimension, political choice
  63
agenda
  capitalism and democracy 107–8
  precondition for politics 78–80
  socialism and democracy 113–16
  socialism and social rights 214–15
agreement, democracy as 28, 31, 42
alcohol, taxation on 321
allocative efficiency, market mechanism
  230–31, 297–8
altruism
  and affluence 149, 230
  as counterproductive 56
  welfare decisions 239
  welfare and democracy 126–8
American Constitution 92–3
American democracy 23
anarchists, modern libertarian 306
Arblaster, A. 43
aristocracy *see* elective aristocracy;
  landed aristocracy; ruling elite
Aristotle 2, 5, 6, 7, 11–12, 27, 28–30, 33,
  77, 176–7, 189–90
art, collapse of the old order 19
aspirations, liberal democracy 110
association 178
Athenian *polis* 26–7
authoritarian power 256–7

authoritarian states, and economic
  outcomes 323
authoritarianism 110
autonomy, individual 30

bad laws, justice and the repeal of
  309–10
balance, social 146–50
Barbalet, J.M. 173, 209, 216, 220
Bay of Pigs invasion (1961) 145–6
beauty, transcending interest in 149–50
Becker, G.S. 114
beliefs
  democratic 87–8
  religious 179–80
Bell, D. 82
belonging, citizenship as 173, 176–7
benefits, equal rights 216
Bentham, J. 47
Beveridge Report (1942) 170, 275
bias, political markets 57–60
birth and breeding
  supply of bureaucrats 82
  supply of politicians 75
birth control 271
Birth, Poverty and Wealth 272–3
birth rate, declining 271–2
Bismarck, O. von 102, 198, 235
blood, gift relationship 279–80
Bosanquet, B. 36–41
Bottomore, T. 189, 206, 218
bourgeois socialism 113
bourgeoisie 76, 101, 102, 105, 107
bribes, private administration of justice
  307
British socialism 156–71, 292–3
British Welfare State
  as an accident 199
  war as cause of 274
Buchanan, J.M. 306
budgets, social rights limited by 220
bureaucracies, public and private 138